Tudor and Stuart Women Writers

WOMEN OF LETTERS

Sandra M. Gilbert and Susan Gubar,
General Editors

TUDOR AND STUART WOMEN WRITERS

Louise Schleiner

With Verse Translations from Latin
by Connie McQuillen,
from Greek by Lynn E. Roller

Indiana University Press

Bloomington and Indianapolis

The paper used in this publication meets the minimum
requirements of American National Standard for Information
Sciences—Permanence of Paper for Printed
Library Materials, ANSI Z39.48-1984.

Manufactured in the United States of America

Library of Congress Cataloging-in-Publication Data

Schleiner, Louise.
Tudor and Stuart women writers / by Louise Schleiner ; with
translations from Latin by Connie McQuillen, from Greek by Lynn E. Roller.
p.   cm.—(Women of letters)
Includes bibliographical references and index.
ISBN 0-253-35098-0 (cloth).—ISBN 0-253-20886-6 (pbk.)
1. English literature—Women authors—History and criticism.
2. English literature—Early modern, 1500–1700—History and
criticism. 3. Women and literature—Great Britain—History—16th
century. 4. Women and literature—Great Britain—History—17th
century. I. Title. II. Series: Women of letters (Bloomington, Ind.)
PR113.S35   1994
820.9'9287'09031—dc20
93-44997

1 2 3 4 5 99 98 97 96 95 94

To Winfried and our daughters—
Anne Marie, Christa, and Emily—
for all they have given up for my work

Contents

FOREWORD

"On the Field of Letters"

> Then Lady Reason . . . said, "Get up, daughter! Without waiting any longer, let us go to the Field of Letters. There the City of Ladies will be founded on a flat and fertile plain, where all fruits and freshwater rivers are found and where the earth abounds in all good things. Take the pick of your understanding and dig and clear out a great ditch wherever you see the marks of my ruler, and I will help you carry away the earth on my own shoulders."
>
> I immediately stood up to obey her commands and . . . I felt stronger and lighter than before. She went ahead, and I followed behind, and after we had arrived at this field I began to excavate and dig, following her marks with the pick of cross-examination.

So WROTE CHRISTINE de Pizan at the beginning of the fifteenth century in *The Book of the City of Ladies*, the first feminist utopia. She was imagining a "strongly constructed and well founded" community which would be inhabited by "ladies of fame and women worthy of praise," and one of her speakers prophesied, "as a true sybil, that this City . . . will never be destroyed, nor will it ever fall, but will remain prosperous forever, regardless of all its jealous enemies. Although it will be stormed by numerous assaults, it will never be taken or conquered."

Founded on the "Field of Letters," the female literary tradition *is*, at least metaphorically speaking, the City of which Christine dreamed. Yet despite the optimism of this Renaissance woman's vision, most of its walls and towers disappeared from view for centuries. Even when its individual inhabitants gained recognition as "ladies of fame and women worthy of praise," the avenues they strolled and the cafes where they conversed were largely forgotten. Louise Labé, Aphra Behn, Jane Austen, Charlotte Bronte, George Eliot, Emily Dickinson, Gertrude Stein, Virginia Woolf—all these figures were duly recorded in literary histories, but their membership in a "strongly constructed and well founded" community—a *female* literary community—went, until recently, unremarked. Only in the last two decades, in fact, have feminist critics established thematic and stylistic links between women from very different places and periods. Moreover, only in recent years have scholars begun "to excavate and dig" in a general effort to recover the lives and works of forgotten or neglected "women worthy of praise." Mary Wroth, Mary Astell, Charlotte Smith, Kate Chopin, Charlotte Perkins Gilman, Mary Elizabeth Coleridge, H. D., Zora Neale Hurston—all these figures had been relegated to the margins of literary history despite the fact that they too deserved places on the "fertile plain" where Christine's utopia was founded.

Our "Women of Letters" series is designed to introduce general as well as academic readers to the historical situations and aesthetic achievements of many of the citizens of Christine's City. The national, chronological, racial, ethnic, economic, and social circumstances of these women vary widely: the contours of the female literary community are complex, its highways and byways labyrinthine and often unfamiliar. Thus each volume in this series will pay close attention to what is in effect a single neighborhood. At the same time, precisely because the subject matter is complex, no volume in the series is intended as an encyclopedic guide to women writers in a particular place or period. Rather, each book will have a distinctive argument of its own, framed independently by its author; we should stress that we have not provided blueprints or even construction codes to the surveyors of our City, all of whom have used their own methodologies and developed their own critical perspectives. We do, however, expect that every volume will explore the individual situations of literary women in their specific cultural contexts.

Finally, we should emphasize that we see this series as part of an ongoing project in which a range of feminist critics, scholars, essayists, novelists, and poets have increasingly participated in recent years, one that seeks to understand the strictures and structures that may have affected (or will affect) the lives and works of, in Christine's words, "ladies from the past as well as from the present and future." Such a project can by its nature come to no definitive conclusion, offer no single last word, because the City of Ladies, along with our vision of the Field of Letters, is growing and changing all the time. Furthermore, the heightened awareness on the part of current feminist theorists that such a City has always existed, and that it is ever evolving, has itself transformed our general sense of history, putting in question received modes of periodization, traditional genre hierarchies, and what once seemed to be universal evaluative criteria. Yet, diverse as may be the solutions posed by different thinkers to theoretical problems presented by contemporary literary study, we hope that in their various ways the volumes in this series will confirm Christine's faith that the City she helped found might be a "refuge" as well as a "defense and guard" against enemies and that it would be "so resplendent that you may see yourselves mirrored in it."

Composed c. 1405, Christine's utopia was little published and seldom translated for more than five centuries, a fact that gives special urgency to the admonitions with which she concluded her text. Indeed, her advice should still be taken to heart by those who study the field of women's letters: " . . . my dear ladies," Christine counseled, "do not misuse this new inheritance" but instead "increase and multiply our City." And as she herself knew, such a resettlement of the old grounds can best be accomplished by following "the marks" of Reason with "the pick of cross-examination."

Sandra M. Gilbert and Susan Gubar

Acknowledgments

THANKS ARE OWED to Washington State University for a sabbatical during 1990 that allowed me time for much of the research represented here, and also to the MS and rare book libraries at the following institutions, whose collections I was fortunate to be able to use and quote: Cambridge University Library (referred to in citations as C.U.L.), the British Library (B.L.), the Herzog August Bibliothek of Wolfenbüttel, the Henry E. Huntington Library, the Bancroft Library of the University of California, Berkeley, and the Folger Shakespeare Library—with special thanks to Laetitia Yeandle of the last. My linguist colleague Lynn Gordon did selected corroborative applications of the topic-focus distinction, to help with my analysis of the *Basilicon Doron* text. Of other colleagues at Washington State for whose partial readings, help, or suggestions I am grateful, I want to mention especially Rhonda Blair, Diane Gillespie, Nicolas Kiessling, Stanton Linden, J. M. Massi, and Carol Siegel, and of scholars elsewhere, Sandra Gilbert, Christopher Grose, Susan Gubar, Elizabeth Hageman, Margaret Hannay, Katherine Keller, Alan Nelson, Julian Roberts, Florence Sandler, Gerald Schiffhorst, and especially my husband Winfried Schleiner for pleasant hours of help with initial reading of the neo-Latin texts in Cambridge. Donald Foster sent me his transcription of the poem by the Countess of Arundel (previously unknown to me), along with genealogical information about the Southwell family. And Donald Cheney passed along the discovery (by Susan Bassnett) of Elizabeth Weston's birth record.

I thank the English Department of the University of California, Davis, for the courtesies of visiting faculty status and computer time during recent summers, and Valerie Tumins of that university for translating materials on Elizabeth Weston from Czech. Finally, the verse translators, Connie McQuillen and Lynn Roller, deserve much credit for good-naturedly tolerating my persistent badgerings and suggestions toward closer approximation of iambic meter in their renderings—only for friendship could such "professional service" be done.

Introduction

CERTAIN ISSUES LATELY important to feminist theory can appear in a new light if they are studied in the context of women's writings from early modern periods. One would probably not get far in such an effort by simply setting the rallying cries of *écriture féminine*, nor a program for identifying foremother traditions either, on facing pages across from Isabella Whitney's evocations of London or Lady Elizabeth Russell's Greek and Latin funerary verse.[1] Only try to imagine even the French love poet Louise Labé or the morally rebellious Lady Mary (Sidney) Wroth touching pages with the verbal-labial ecstasies of Hélène Cixous or Luce Irigaray, and one may wonder what points of contact can be found. Yet they can be—indeed they are already being found. And such studies are profitable not only to feminists and scholars of early periods but also more generally to theorists of language and culture. In earlier decades there was a natural inclination among literary feminists—most of whom began as specialists of modern period literatures—to theorize as if the world had begun in 1800 and as if all Euro-American women across these two centuries ought to have felt female just as "we" (Euro-American educated women of the late twentieth century) do—even though no definition of that feeling can be agreed on. Nowadays little feminist work is blind-sided about cultural diversity (indeed, the current trend, as in Helena Michie's *Sororophobia*, is to stress direct conflicts between different women's modes of gendering, depending on factors including race, class, ethnicity, age, and sexual preference); but a longer historical perspective is also needed—diachronic as well as synchronic diversity.

Feminist theory, for its part, can be fertile for new approaches to study of early modern periods and their women's writing, as for me Mary Jacobus's *Reading Woman* has been. Let me circle down to her book from a broader view. Issues in feminism are often debated within the general oppositional frame of empiricism versus constructionism (or representationalism): the one is the view that "the feminine" can be usefully defined and put to work in investigations, if not panculturally and ahistorically, then at least within culturally located and interrelated materials, perhaps within linear traditions of women writers drawing on earlier ones; the other is that of deconstructionist feminists, who variously pursue "the feminine" as something not definable but evocable, as an "alternative libidinal economy" of discourse (Jacobus 109), to be evoked performatively in various modes of glossolalic theoretical musement. Jacobus's book mediates between these two views (though it does not reconcile them)—pursuing some of the goals of each within a single project. In place of a linear writing tradition from foremother to granddaughter, she traces a slaloming zigzag with gaps, and lapses into maleness, crisscrossing the terrain necessary to feminism's current critical engagement with the psychoanalytic tradition of Freud-Lacan-Kristeva. In her book the halves of each of the following pairs are thus, in a hitching chronological succession, brought mutually to "read" each other: Mary Wollstonecraft's *Vindication of the Rights of Women* and Charlotte Perkins Gilman's "Yellow Wallpaper," Charlotte Brontë's *Villette* and Josef Breuer's "Frln. Anna O.," George Eliot's "Lifted Veil" and Freud's *Studies in Hysteria*, Eliot's *Mill on the Floss* and Irigaray's *This Sex Which Is Not One*, Freud's *Hysteria* and Julia Kristeva's *Abjection: The Powers of Horror*. Positing that it will no longer suffice simply to "privilege indeterminacy" (290), she shows how someone with continuing allegiance to deconstruction can yet find ways of culturally contextualizing women's writings in relation to those of other women (and men).[2]

Her discursive slalom ends with a description of her book as a new kind of "feminist move": "a putting in play (a reading) of the structures which produce and reproduce meaning, whether sexual or textual" (Jacobus 288). In her particular version of this move, such reading from the position of femininity occurs when "femininity itself comes to be a figure for this meaning that is a difference—both sexual and textual—rather than a content." It occurs when feminists are "(re)reading textual correspondences" by installing themselves, qua feminist critic, as a "figure" for breaking, interruption, rupture, "holding open a gap" in "the seamless continuum of masculinist critical and theoretical reading," and from there exposing the "correspondences which are always near misses (Mss.)" (Jacobus 288).

Trying the new move in another arena and by procedures different from those of Jacobus, I have sought to put into play several interrelated readings of "the structures that produced and reproduced meaning," both gendered and textual, in early modern England. I have sought ways of pursuing this goal that could incorporate more sociopolitical concreteness than has so far been done in studies focusing on psychoanalysis and epistemology. Although one might indeed "look in vain for a specifically feminine linguistic practice in *The Mill on the Floss*" (Jacobus 78), we will have no trouble studying a specifically female "reading formation" (cf. Tony Bennett, and Michel Foucault on discursive formations) in the practice of both gentry and servant waiting women's reading aloud to their aristocratic ladies—and vice versa—thereby triggering in each other urges to write. And when I take up Kristeva, whom Jacobus summarizes at length, it will be to apply her (albeit psychoanalytically grounded) concepts of intertextuality or transpositioning and of the ideologeme, in order to help explain how various kinds of libidinally invested writing, utterance, and other cultural production comprised a social text for early modern Englishwomen, in their own positions within it. For example, in studying King James's court, I will explore how certain women could improvise usages of male-enunciated ideologemes—i.e., units of (or Deleuzean "desiring machines" for producing) cultural meaning. From a different angle, the marginal but speakable position of women within ideologically distinct religious activist groups will be analyzed with the help of part of Jürgen Habermas's theory of ideological group dynamics.

My recurrent thematic question is how Tudor and Stuart women came to write anything for public or semipublic circulation when they faced so many kinds of obstacles to doing so.³ The terms in which we can find answers with explanatory power vary, depending on which women we consider. But the various analytical models I have tried out here are roughly congruent with each other. They fall within the spheres of recent studies of textuality, gendered writing- and reading-processes, and the interpenetrations of texts, writer- and reader-empowerment, politics, and local cultural patterning; that is, they use concepts from text linguistics, discourse pragmatics, linguistically based psychoanalytic theory, and linguistically informed neo-Marxism, retooled for gender study.⁴ I also include certain formalist kinds of observations necessary for, say, describing the musico-poetic experimentation within a coterie group that helped define its political identity (cf. chapter 3 on the Countess of Pembroke). In short, I have resolved to be eclectic in trying out my own version of that "move" Jacobus recommends, of putting into play readings of the structures— we might better say systems—that enabled production and reproduction of meaning, both gendered and textual, in early modern England.

At present in the study of early modern women writers, scholars are faced with two kinds of tasks at once, which in earlier scholarship have usually been separated. One is to find, verify, and provisionally edit texts; the other is to integrate the newly considered texts into the ongoing, intermingling streams of existent commentary on a period, as well as those on feminist and other theoretical issues. Ordinarily in scholarship on male writers, these tasks of unearthing and of integrative commentary have been done by two distinct sets of people: the one by habitués of the record offices and manuscript rooms, well versed in paleography, quirkish cataloguing and reference systems, and tangles of Latin legal abbreviations, but oblivious to literary-theoretical developments; and the other by exegetes who, except for occasional forays into rare book rooms or widely available microfilms, mostly sit at keyboards working out up-to-date interpretations and retheorizings of the much-studied texts already available. This division of labor has an obvious advantage in that the one sort of scholar can carry on with the aim of "getting things right" with texts, while the other can ruminate along under the assumption—cutting across several stripes of current scholarship and theorizing—that there is no such thing as "getting things right" with texts (the very idea being repugnantly phallic for many). For better and for worse, people working on early modern women's writings presently need to be something of both kinds of scholar at once. As I worked in England on materials for this book, there seemed to be a stimulating clash of perspectives in a day of searching manuscripts or rare books in the morning, reading Gérard Genette and Habermas in the afternoon, and hearing a lecture by Lisa Jardine, Germaine Greer, or Muriel Bradbrook in the evening.

Facing a cataloguing system where, to find even the published women's works, I had to know the names of their male editors, I found myself amidst the underpinnings of current British patriarchy, some more worm-eaten than others. (Only under "Gary Waller" could one find the Countess of Pembroke's original poems, not under Sidney, Herbert, nor Pembroke; or one had to know of A. C. Dunstan to get Elizabeth Cary's *Mariam*.) Down among the cheerful many-centuried genealogies of county families, where men would even give up their father's name to get their mother's father's land, and among the voluminous Catholic Record Society volumes, where women's histories are told for reasons that modern women may not want to hear about—in such chilly regions where the lights clunk off every six minutes, one gets ideas about how to see women and their constructions of their gender identity in the various interacting networks of sociopolitical and intimate experience of their own times.

These recollections are offered to help explain why readers may find in these pages a disconcerting mixture of modes of discussion and analysis, even though I have as much as possible kept archival details to the footnotes or published them separately. For me it has been part of gaining a sense of who various women were to try tracking them through systems of regulation and record-keeping that left their lives only faintly traced, their voices barely audible—or in some cases only a recitation of prescribed verbal forms. In the records for the parish of Waterbeach near Cambridge are dozens of certifications that penitential decrees of diocesan courts have been fulfilled. Item: on the morning of February 20, 1595, and again on February 22 and March 1, one Kathryn Mayne of Waterbeach came to the church and conducted herself as follows (C.U.L. Add MS 6605.254):

> The saied Penitent [Mayne] shall vppon Sunday being the xx daie of Feb. next clothed in a white sheete downe to the grownd and hauing a white wand in her hand resort vnto the parish church porche of Waterbeach aforesaid and there shall stande from the second peale to morninge praire vntill the reading of the second lesson desiring the people that passe by her into the chyrche to praie to god for her and to forgiue her at wch time the minister there shall come down to the penitent and fetch her into the chyrche with the psalme of miserere in Englishe and place her in the middill alley there aparte from all other people where she shall penitently kneele vntill the readinge of the

ten commandments at wch time the minister there shall come to this penitent and cause her to say and confesse as followeth viz.

Good people I acknowledge and confesse that I haue offended almightie god and by my euill example you all for that I have broken his diuine lawes and commandments in committinge the most shamefull & abhominable sinn of adultrie or fornicacion for wch I am most hartily sory and I aske god and you all most hartily forgiueness for the same promising by godes help neuer to offend hereafter in the like againe.

And at the end of this confession the first daie the minister to read the homily against Adulterie or fornication and the third daie to read the homily of repentance the penitent standinge by all the while and in like manner and forme in euery pointe and condicion as aboue is prescribed she shall do two other sundaies or holydaies next ensuing after the first. And of the penitent doinge hereof vppon all the saied three seuerall sundaies or holydaies shee shall vnder the handes of the minister and churchwardens there personallie certifie togeather with these privately . . .

The minister and two churchwardens have signed (one of the latter with an "x"), in certification that Kathryn Mayne carried out her penance on the three days prescribed. Presumably, whenever a widow or unmarried girl turned up pregnant, the above scene occurred, or threatened to occur. If women could be forbidden to speak in public, they might also, by direct inversion of the meaning of female public speech, be ordered to do so, for shame.

The records show men at times also doing such penances, for sins like "entertaining evil company at my house in time of divine service" (doubtless bargained down from a more colorful charge), or working for wages on St. John's day rather than attending church—but they repented under a shorter form, at least in these documents, and without the melodrama of the white sheet and the individual pleas at the church door. Married couples had to repent together their fornication, if the first baby turned up too soon. (Did Shakespeare and Ann Hathaway risk or endure such an appearance?) The penitents in the Waterbeach records appear to be all common householders or villagers—we may suppose that gentry would usually have known how to avoid these sentences.

To us it sounds almost unspeakably cruel. Was it so perceived by penitents of the time and their families? At best it must have been with crushed spirit that a woman stood alone draped in white begging each parishioner at the church door for forgiveness, then knelt for long minutes in the middle aisle in the gaze of all eyes while the ten commandments and a sermon were read at her, then repeated aloud a confession. But the practice would have made churchgoing serve, among others, a function akin to soap opera viewing, and with a participatory edge, since the pool of actors and audience was the same. Who could know what would next be confessed, perhaps by someone from the neighboring pew? Or when might it be one's own turn? Perhaps few would have favored abolishing such an entertaining business, even knowing that they themselves might at some point be on show.

How must women have thought of themselves—and of the possibility of claiming any public textual space for a written voice—when aside from street vendor women hawking wares, the above kind of instance represented the only public female voice they knew? Very few could have managed to hear the queen utter anything publicly, though sometimes she did; even she had male criers for all proclamations. School teachers were all male, public orators, town criers, ministers in church, and actors on the stage, even those playing the women's parts! What must this universal absence of any but humiliated or déclassé public female voices have meant to the women we will study here?

How did they find or carve out situations where they could at least speak to a small group or claim a textual space intended for some more-than-private audience? What tasks of self-imaging did they face—out of what social materials did they build or find a support system for their self-imaging, in order to be able to speak? I found, in studying the several women here treated, that the answer varies depending on the circumstances, social-class status, personal relationships, and religious identity within which a woman lived. And thus not just one but a number of kinds of sociosemiotic and historical modes of study are needed as we pursue the question of how they managed to write—and collaterally, with what awarenesses we may best learn to read them. One English pattern I discern—perhaps a surprising one—is that the farther off an aristocratic woman was from Queen Elizabeth's court (not necessarily physically, but emotionally), the better might be her chance of forging for herself a basis for a written voice. For men of the time, the opposite was true. As has been thoroughly studied (see, e.g., Louis Adrian Montrose), men's usual mode of defining what I will call a gendered enunciative subject position and a voice— able to speak with the force of libidinally invested selfhood—was to devise some deft and effectual relation of address to the queen and her court and from there to shape and claim a personalized version of the queen's image, at the same time as—and against which—they shaped and maintained their own self-image. Women were closed out of that possibility. A sociolinguistic way of showing just how effectually they were closed out has been presented in my forthcoming study *Cultural Semiotics, Spenser, and the Captive Woman*, and, as was mentioned above, another instance of the same kind of analysis will be presented here in chapters 5 and 6 (which work closely in tandem), in terms of a concept of an ideologeme with a definedly male enunciative position. The effort here will be to place women's writing and activism among and within the productions of the men with whom they daily interacted at the Jacobean court. My organizational assumption about the theoretical concepts at work in this study has been that readers may prefer to learn about them as we go along considering women's writings and lives, rather than to read an extended theoretical presentation here at the start. A brief epilogue pulls together the theoretical concepts and makes some of their connections explicit.

Sometimes I have cited rather longer stretches of the texts being considered than is customary in literary analysis (often whole poems), because many of the treated women's writings are still not widely accessible—some not at all except in manuscript or rare book. I have also included as Appendix 2 some further writings by the women treated, beyond those interspersed in my text. This appendix makes no claim to be a critical edition. Its purpose is to encourage wider familiarity with these women, a process out of which incorporation of some of their writings into literary-historical canons may come—and eventually careful editions of those that prove most appealing. In line with this purpose, I have often cited verse in modern spelling and punctuation, to encourage reading by nonspecialists (assuming that anyone wanting to see the original text can look it up in EETS microfilms or in published editions). But exception is made for material from unedited manuscripts or otherwise obscure sources, where I have generally given original spelling and punctuation.

Tudor and Stuart Women Writers

1

Women's Household Circles as a Gendered Reading Formation

Whitney, Tyler, and Lanyer

IN TUDOR AND Stuart England, did women's relations with each other have a bearing on their motivations and abilities to write? Did they find value in other women's writing and speaking? Did their own variantly gendered self-concepts play into their work as writers, constrained as it was by various forms of male dominance? Did they at times develop sheltered female spaces, into which husbands, masters, lords, or vicars would hesitate to intrude?—(as my stepfather used to say that he would rather take a beating than have to put his hand in a woman's purse).[1] As in the work of scholars such as Teresa de Lauretis and Ann Rosalind Jones,[2] such considerations are here based on the idea of systems of domination as involving negotiation between the dominant and the dominated, rather than as static chains of command. Such a perspective will allow us to test some limits of Catherine Belsey's thesis that early modern Englishwomen had no "space from which to speak" (149). And with Margaret Ezell, we can look for ways to study their writing that do not stay within diachronic models of tradition and "progress," though these can still be included at times.

Feminist study of nineteenth- and twentieth-century Anglophone writing, at the prompting of Virginia Woolf, has worked to identify such diachronic traditions—foremothers touching off and influencing writer-daughters across generations (Showalter *Literature*). The approach is useful in study of certain Tudor and Stuart women, primarily those of the Sidney family (cf. Hannay "Aunt"), although Aemilia (Bassani) Lanyer may also have been inspired by the example of Mary (Sidney) Herbert, Countess of Pembroke.[3] Mary Ellen Lamb[4] has described the Sidney family milieu as influencing both the countess's niece Lady Mary (Sidney) Wroth and also another unidentified woman, by whom three engaging lyrics survive in a manuscript associated with the Sidneys (*Gender* 199–209).[5] Incidentally, for the lyric that, according to Lamb, has undecipherable words in its opening line, I would suggest that it be read as follows because of its evident relation to "Zefiro torno" musical settings (deriving from the composer Luca Marenzio):

> The breath all [Zephyr's blowing ho]ldeth forth
> Comforts the flowers which the blasts did kill,
> And Phoebus' beams beat back the chilling north
> Whose nature's riefs the earth with storms did fill.
> Now Philomela sweetly doth bewail
> That falsehood could on true love so prevail.

The succeeding two stanzas, in a kind of time-lapse picture effect and with smooth yet original phrasing, pursue sequential images of the unfolding season gathering strength, from "drowsy dark" to longer days, from buds to blossoms to "knotted fruit." The gathering power of springing life is registered in each stanza's revision of the Philomela refrain: from "bewailing," the bird goes to singing that "true love lasts sweet," and finally that "Philomela loud and sweetly cries, / Who bides in love lives still and never dies." Here indeed one may sense the influence of the lutenist countess of Psalm metaphrases.

But aside from the Sidney-Pembroke circle (see chapters 3, 5, and 6 below), dominant as it was in court factions and political networks across three generations, there is so far little evidence that Englishwomen knew of other women's published or circulated writings. Queen Elizabeth, when she wanted her intellect and writing celebrated, chose to be seen as quasi-male, *supra sexum foemineum*, her force of mind deriving from her male "body politic" rather than her female "body natural" (cf. Axton). When women did appeal to female precedent, they looked not to writers but to traditional chaste and patriarchally approved figures: Deborah, Lucrece, Pilate's unnamed perceptive wife. I have not yet seen any Englishwoman citing Christine de Pisan's *Cité des Dames*, though an English translation of it by Brian Anslay had been published in 1521. And even Lady Wroth's lengthy, in several ways feminist, topical romance *Urania* (see chapter 6) draws not on any prior woman romancer—one might think of Marie de France—but primarily on her uncle's *Arcadia*, along with Ariosto and other popular continental writers.

Englishwomen's favorite writings and modes of discourse to echo, tease into their texts, or handle revisionistically are the Bible, devotional commentaries on it, Ovid (the *Metamorphoses, Heroides,* and *Amores* in translation), Virgil's *Aeneid* (mainly the Dido episode in translation), vernacular histories coalescing material from late classical writers such as Diodorus Siculus (see chapter 7 on Elizabeth [Tanfield] Cary, Lady Falkland), and Senecan or other translated moral aphorisms (see chapter 5 on "News" for one effect of such reading of sententiae). As one would expect, given the meagerness of usual female education even among aristocrats, much of their reading material was thus indirectly known, coming through, besides translated compendia, the rhetoric and commonplace books of moralistically censored excerpts from famous authors, organized by themes or "places": one such source also widely used by men was Richard Rainolde's *Foundacion of Rhetorike* (1563, an adaptation of Aphthonius's *Progymnastikon*). And there was, as already mentioned for Wroth, that other kind of material that we know women read avidly—the copies were often read to pieces[6]—namely romances such as the *Mirrour of Knighthood* and the *Amadis de Gaul,* apparently sometimes spot translated aloud from Spanish or French by waiting women. But few Englishwomen, in their own writing, dared an identifiable reference to such romances. The exception that we know of, besides the *Urania,* is a translation of Diego Ortuñez de Calahorra's *Mirrour of Knighthood,* Book I, by Margaret Tyler, a waiting woman to the Duchess of Norfolk.

In *Thinking through the Body* (1988), Jane Gallop has meditated on the relationship between seventeenth-century ladies and their waiting women, as portrayed in three paintings by Vermeer. Picking up from an essay by Annie Leclerc also citing one of these Vermeers, she, like Leclerc, sees in the depictions of a writing lady and attendant woman an image of a relationship in her own life. For Leclerc and Gallop, the lady and the woman poised to carry her letters portray their own ties with "the women who clean our houses, care for our children, type our manuscripts"—i.e., of a bourgeoise writer or upper-echelon academic with those paid to serve her. Gallop and Leclerc explore the potential love between server and served, and one can suppose that in the early modern period such relationships were, as she says, sometimes lesbian.[7] Direct clues on that point will have to be left to other studies, I would think drawing on women's personal papers. In this chapter, and occasionally in later ones, we will study the relations of ladies and waiting women as mutual readers and writers. The duties of both women-in-waiting and household servant women involved not only housework, child care, meal planning, shopping, and message posting, but also reading aloud to their ladies. Thus circles of women encompassing two or three social classes lived in daily association, reading and often making music together. Therein lies a gynocritical tale (see Showalter "Poetics")—not a diachronic but a synchronic one. For this "reading formation" of women's mutual reading aloud—to take Tony Bennett's concept, of which more anon—both shaped and was shaped by their gendered self-imaging and, I suggest, created new possibilities for women as writers. In a circle where most of the hands were busy with embroidery, other needlework, or sewing, the waiting women (and sometimes serving men) would read on command to their aristocratic ladies and, in effect, to each other from the various kinds of material surveyed above. And sometimes the high lady herself would read:

> . . . here was Dalinea sitting under a cloth of estate of carnation velvet, curiously and richly set with stones, all over being embroidered with pearl of

silver and gold, the gold made in suns, the silver in stars. . . . But she, standing, appeared so much brighter, as if all that had been but to set forth her light. . . . Her ladies who attended her were a little distant from her in a fair compass window, where also stood a chair wherein it seemed she had been sitting. . . . In that chair lay a book. The ladies were all at work, so as it showed, she read while they wrought. (*Urania* Pt. 1, Salzman ed. 149)

That this practice might inspire various urges to write, up and down its encompassed social spectrum, should come as no surprise. To speak just of romance—one important component of its materials—the place of romance in that formation makes its constitution as a genre contrast markedly with that of romance in an Anglophone women's reading formation of our own time: i.e., in single-family houses or apartments, middle-class or working-class women—making a time alone for compensatory gratification in lives absorbed in nuclear family and routinized work—read formulaically overdetermined, very conventionally gendered fiction written by other unknown women who are supplementing similar lives with the small extra writing income thus gained (Radway and Rabine). By contrast, Renaissance women's reading, of romance and other texts, was largely companionate reading aloud of several kinds of vernacular materials, in some of which (especially the romances) the rigid gender concepts of their societies were at times suspended, even wildly so.[8]

Isabella Whitney—"Harvestless and Serviceless"

Let us take a closer view of such reading circles, and first from a woman lamenting her loss of one: Isabella Whitney's book *A Sweet Nosegay or Pleasant posye. Contayning a hundred and ten Phylosophicall flowers* (1573) includes numerous verse epistles asking help from relatives and friends, refers several times explicitly to a falling out with her lady of service (caused mainly, she claims, by the defamation of unnamed enemies),[9] and centers on a hundred Senecan moral sayings or sententiae, the "flowers" of her "nosegay," which she has coded through selection and ordering to present an indirect plea for restoration to her post (see n. 12). The loss of it has left her miserable, only now fully aware of its intellectual and material value. She begins by portraying herself at loose ends on an October day, longing to read but finding no pleasure in reading alone, and recalling most of the reading matter we have just reviewed:[10]

This harvest time I harvestless,
    and serviceless also,
And subject unto sickness, that
    abroad I could not go,
Had leisure good (though learning lacked)
    some study to apply,

To read such books, whereby I thought
   myself to edify.
Some time the Scriptures I perused,
   but wanting a divine
For to resolve me in such doubts
   as passed this head of mine
To understand, I layed them by
   and histories 'gan read. . . .
I straight waxed weary of those books,
   and many other more,
As Virgil, Ovid, Mantuan,
   which many wonders bore.
And to refresh my mased muse
   and chear my bruised brain,
And for to try if that my limbs
   had got their strength again,
I walked out; but suddenly
   a friend of mine me met
And said, if you regard your health,
   out of this lane you get,
And shift you to some better air
   for fear to be infect
With noisome smell and savors ill—
   I wish you that respect. . . .
And I went home, all sole alone,
   good Fortune was my guide,
And though she never hath denied
   To hoist me on her wheel,
Yet now she stood me in some stead,
   And made me pleasures feel:
For she to *Plat* his Plot me brought,
   where fragrant flowers abound

(A5v-A6)

Fortune's gift that turns Whitney's lassitude to hope is a new book of 883 translated Senecan sayings, Hugh Plat's *Floures of Philosophie* (1572), which gives her the idea for an elaborate, indirect, she will hope pleasing message to her offended lady, a way to get back her post: she will arrange and paraphrase into verse a selection of these flowers herself, organized for fending off the "plague" of slander that has robbed her of the lady's favor. (A common notion was that the plague was spread by foul odors and that an herbal or floral nosegay offered protection.) Adapting each prose aphorism into two fourteeners, she picks them to emphasize the joys of parted friends' reunions and the integrity of the person who pays no heed to slander."¹¹ She also, as noted, adds verse letters to many relatives and friends, so cast as to show the lady that she now has a most entirely dutiful concept of "service": in the letter admonishing her two younger sisters to perfect industry and submissiveness in serving their ladies, she advises that "flyting [quarreling] is a foe / Experience hath me taught." The hundred aphorism-flowers are followed by a verse letter to her brother Geoffrey Whitney (the emblematist), portraying the "aucthor" herself bringing a copy of her verbal nosegay to the former Lady, a gift that

> I do for present bear
> Unto a vertuous Lady, which
> till death I honor will:
> The loss I had of service hers,
> I languish for it still.
>
> (C6ᵥ)

Such was the plan with which Dame Fortune (a dubious muse) kissed Whitney on an October day as she tottered, weak from illness, in a smelly London lane—or so she portrays herself. Her prefatory poem to the reader points out that those who wish can gather the ensuing flowers in a meaningful order, and she hopes to have chosen a good one.

> And such as will with order get,
>   may gather whilst they list . . .
> And now I have a nosegay got
>   that would be passing rare
> If that to sort the same aright
>   were 'lotted to my share.
>
> (A7)

This points explicitly to the coded level of meaning in the appropriated flowers (see n. 12), in case her primary intended readership of lady and women might miss it. She asks that if the readers (i.e., especially her lady) are too displeased to receive these flowers, they might "refer them to some friend of thine, / till thou their vertue see," or might read further in Plat's own book, in case some of the unselected sayings might speak more effectively.

Maintaining the metaphor of Plat's book and her own as a flower garden, she continues:

> In any wise, be chary that
>   thou lettest in no Swine,
> No dog to scrape, nor beast that doth
>   to ravin still incline.

> For though he [Plat] make no spare of them
>   to such as have good skill
> To slip, to shear, or get in time,
>   and not his branches kill,
> Yet bars he out such greedy gulls
>   as come with spite to tote,
> And without skill both herb and flower
>   pluck rashly by the root.

The lady is enjoined to show the book only to those who have the gentility to appreciate its flowers—by implication *not* to the spiteful swine who have slandered the author. This and several other hints in the book's verse letters suggest that the enemies—who along with Whitney's own sharp-tongued moments of "flyting" have cost her the lamented post—were fellow serving women or men of the lady's own entourage. One can easily imagine that rivalries for the high lady's affection and approval might arise.

The rest of what we can gather about Whitney's life from such indications in her poems is that she was born probably sometime in the late 1540s and raised in the Smithfield district of London, was jilted by a fiancé in the mid-1560s (see her *Copy of a Letter . . . to her vnconstant Louer* [1567?]), was in the early seventies gentlewoman-in-waiting to a lady in "the country" near London,[12] lost her post through someone's ill reports and her own overbold tongue, and was still writing poems in the mid-seventies, since she is in all likelihood the woman whose elegy on the death of a William Griffith, and possibly other poems, appeared in the *Gorgeous Gallery* miscellany of 1578.[13] Beilin (90) lists the names of her brothers and sisters, and the *Feminist Companion* proposes (on the basis of Geoffrey Whitney's will mentioning a "Sister Eldershae") that she later married someone named Eldershae and had children. Whitney was a gentlewoman, but her way of life was little different from that of literate merchants' daughters who might serve a high-ranking lady.[14]

A Copy of a Letter had already shown her command of light irony, spoken from a moral high ground easily claimed, as she berated her former betrothed for faithlessness—possibly her dowry fell short of his hopes, through the financial duress of a country squire's family with four daughters. The *Nosegay* shows her becoming a more versatile poet, building in combinations of irony and warm sympathy with both her imagined subjects and her projected readers. A number of the verse epistles are in pairs: i.e., a letter and its reply from the addressee. In one case a third piece, Whitney's response to the response, is added: having written to her friend Thomas Berry, who from his own introductory epistle would seem to be the book's main promoter, she got "An answer to comfort her, by shewing his haps to be harder," then wrote the following epistle. Gently commiserating with him, she at the same time pours out her own malaise: people who claimed to be friends have betrayed her (stanza 3), leaving her trapped and helpless like a hunted animal (stanza 4).

"A Replye to the same" [to Thomas Berry's verse letter]

The bitter force of *Fortune's* frowardness
    is painted out by B. his changed hue;
Report bewrays that tyrant's doubleness,
    which I by trial prove (alas) too true.
    Constrained I am on thy mishaps to rue
As oft as I consider thine estate,
Which differs far from that thou wast of late.

Where be thy wonted lively looks become?
    or what mischance hath dimmed thy beauty so?
There is no God that deals such doubtful doom,
    no *Jupiter* hath brought thee down so low:
    thy hapless fate hath wrought thy overthrow.
For as *Saturnus* 'reaves the *Berry's* joy,
So Fortune strives to further thine annoy.

O Fortune false, O thrice unsteady joys,
    why doth not man mistrust thy subtle shows?
Whose profers prove in time to be but toys.
    Is this the fruit that from your blossom grows?
    then may you rightly be compared with those
Whose painted speech professeth friendship still,
But time bewrays the meaning to be ill.

For time that shows what erst I could not see
    hath brought about that I suspected least,
Complaining still on our simplicity,
    who headlong run as doth the careless beast
    till hunters' snares have laid his limbs to rest.
For when we least mistrust a dread deceit,
Then are we snared, with unsuspected bait,

As lately unto thee it did befall,
    whose hap enforceth me to rue thy chance.
For thou that flourished erst at beauty's stall
    hath felt the force of froward *Fortune's* lance,
    compelled to furnish out misfortune's dance;
See here the surety that belongeth aye
To mortal joys whereon the world doth stay.

But live in hope that better hap may light,
   for after storms Sir *Phoebus'* force is seen,
So when *Saturnus* hath declared his might,
   and *Winter* stints to turn the world to teen,
   then pleasant *Ver* shall clothe the ground in green
And lusty *May* shall labor to restore
The things that *Winter's* spite had spoiled before.

Then shall the *Berry* cleave her wonted hue,
   and eke my B. that long hath tasted pain—
When Fortune doth her former grace renew,
   they hoisted be to happy state again—
Delighting oft among his friends and kin,
To tell what danger erst his life was in.

Which happy sight of mortal creatures who
   shall more rejoice than I, thy friend, to see?
And while Dame Fortune yielded not thereto,
   but doth proceed to prove her spite on thee,
   yet shalt thou not so ill beloved be
But that thy Fame forever flourish shall,
If IS. her pen may promise ought at all.

             (D4ᵥ-D5ᵥ)

Finishing on the classical note of the poet's promise to the addressee of an immortality of fame, she comforts her friend with cyclical imagery of a springtime renewal that fortune's turning wheel will bring. The conventional deuteronomic theology of seeing in misfortune a punishing divine hand she rejects, with casual scorn ("There is no God that deals such doubtful doom"). The poem's attitude seems akin to conventional Protestant neostoicism (cf. the Countess of Pembroke's later Mornay translation), but there is no brave talk about the strength of isolated integrity and power of mind. In trouble one should take comfort from the friends who have remained faithful and should avoid seeing divine intervention in mere chance. Here we note in passing that her circle of primary intended readers obviously included men as well as women, a point whose articulation, as part of the reading formation we are studying, will be taken up later.

Perhaps Whitney's most enjoyable poem, the last and longest, is her mock testament, "The Aucthour . . . fayneth as she would die and maketh her Wyll . . . with Legacies of such . . . riches which she moste aboundantly hath left behind her: and maketh London sole executor."[15] In her prologue, claiming to give up on her effort to regain a position, she nevertheless hints that she might meddle ("mell") with the world again, if she could find encouragement.

The time is come I must depart
  from thee, ah famous City;
I never yet to rue my smart
  did find that thou hadst pity.
Wherefore small cause there is that I
  should grieve from thee to go.
But many Women foolishly,
  like me and other moe,
Do such a fixed fancy set
  on those which least deserve
That long it is ere wit we get
  away from them to swerve.
But time with pity oft will tell
  to those that will her try
Whether it best be more to mell,
  or utterly defy. . . .
Yet am I in no angry mood,
  but will, or e'er I go,
In perfect love and charity
  my Testament here write.

She continues in the whimsical, satiric tone that will prevail.[16]

I whole in body and in mind,
  but very weak in purse
Do make and write my Testament
  for fear it will be worse.

The poem follows a catalogue format that evokes images of Whitney taking farewell strolls through London, fixing it all in memory, and claiming to "leave" to the city everything it already has.

I first of all to London leave,
  because I there was bred,
Brave buildings rare, of churches store,
  and Paul's to the head.
Between the same fair streets there be
  and people goodly store . . .
First for their food I butchers leave
  that every day shall kill,
By Thames you shall have brewers store
  and bakers at your will.
And such as orders do observe
  and eat fish thrice a week, . . .

Watling Street and Canwick Street
   I full of woolen leave . . .
And those which are of calling such
   that costlier they require
I mercers leave with silk so rich
   as any could desire . . .
And plate to furnish cupboards with,
   full brave there shall you find,
With pearl of silver and of gold
   to satisfy your mind,
With hoods, bungraces, hats or caps
   such store are in that street
As if on t'on side you should miss
   the t'other serves you fit . . .
For purse or knives, for combs or glass,
   or any needful knack
I by the stocks have left a boy
   will ask you what you lack.

(E2v-E3)

Her sense of a writer's imaginative ownership of the whole lively city—where in fact she owns nothing—is the poem's vivid effect. It is as if she has a right to hold it together through sympathetic vision and affection, like a whimsical motherly version of Jesus looking out over Jerusalem (Matt. 23:37), wryly lamenting its miseries and loving its human richness. Not only the upscale shoppers and their many goods but wage-women at work under matron supervisors, and all the underbelly of city life—from tavern rowdies and male prostitutes to bankrupts, prisoners, and the insane—are encompassed in her scanning vision:

Some roisterers still must bide in thee
   and such as cut it out,
That with the guiltless quarrel will
   to let their blood about.
For them I cunning surgeons leave,
   some plasters to apply,
That ruffians may not still be hanged
   nor quiet persons die . . .
At Stilliard store of wines there be
   your dulled minds to glad,
And handsome men that must not wed
   except they leave their trade.
They oft shall seek for proper girls,
   and some perhaps shall find

(That need compels or lucre lures
    to satisfy their mind.[)]]
And near the same I houses leave
    for people to repair
To bathe themselves so to prevent
    infection of the air . . .
I will to prisons portions leave,
    what though but very small,
Yet that they may remember me
    occasion be it shall. . . .
And at those sessions some shall 'scape
    with burning near the thumb . . .
And such whose deeds deserveth death,
    and twelve have found the same,
They shall be drawn by Holborne hill
    to come to further shame.
Well, yet to such I leave a nag
    shall soon their sorrows cease,
For he shall either break their necks
    or gallop from the press. . . .

                (E5v-E7)

And Bedlem must not be forgot,
    for that was oft my walk,
I people there too many leave
    that out of tune do talk.
At Bridewell there shall beadles be
    and matrons that shall still
See chalk well chopped and spinning plied
    and turning of the mill.

                (E7)

Self-reflexive comments as well as details from her own life are included.
Having willed to the Fleet prison "some Papist old / to underprop his roof /
And to the poor within the same / a box for their behoof," she suddenly imagines an audience chuckling at her account, and waggishly shakes a finger at
them, pretending that it is all to be taken *very* seriously, for who would jest in
the hour of death while making a will?

What makes you standers-by to smile,
    and laugh so in your sleeve?
I think it is because that I
    to Ludgate nothing give.

I am not now in case to lie,
  here is no place of jest;
I did reserve that for my self
  if I my health possest,
And ever came in credit so
  a debtor for to be . . .
Yet 'cause I feel myself so weak
  that none me credit dare,
I here revoke, and do it leave
  some *Bankrupts* to his share.
To all the bookbinders by Paul's
  because I like their art,
They every week shall money have
  when they from books depart.
Amongst them all my printer must
  have somewhat to his share;
I will my friends these books to buy
  of him, with other ware. . . .
To Smithfield I must something leave,
  my parents there did dwell,
So careless for to be of it,
  none would account it well.
Wherefore it thrice a week shall have
  of horse and neat good store,
And in his 'spital, blind and lame,
  To dwell forevermore.

(E8v-F1)

Of Smithfield, where she was raised, she remembers the "spital" (hospital) and the horsebutchers. Punning on "credit"—people will not seriously credit her writing, just as they never credited her enough even to let her become a debtor and thus a bankrupt—she laughs at herself through her imagined full-sleeved city readers, both male and female, and "wills" them, her friends, to her printer as clientele. The passage directly indicates the sense of implied readership natural to the reading formation of women with their lady, where men would sometimes also be present, but in positions of genteel submissiveness to the lady, whose servants they would be or whose patronage they would be seeking.

This last point illustrates what Catharine Stimpson, drawing upon anthropologist Peggy Sanday, hypothesizes, "that women achieve economic and political power or authority when they have economic autonomy and when men are dependent upon their activities" (156). I would gradualize this and say "to the extent that women control money, and to the extent that men are dependent on their activities." Possibly it was in part through that subordinated male presence, in this particular reading formation, that they achieved the beginnings of a sense of competence and empowerment for public writing or other public cultural production.

Drawing toward her conclusion, Whitney ironically declines to leave anything to cover her own funeral costs, but notes that the hard-hearted city will have good reason to "cover" them (and her) anyway:

> Now London have I (for thy sake)
> 　　within thee and without
> As comes into my memory
> 　　dispersed round about . . .
> And though I nothing named have
> 　　to bury me withal
> Consider that above the ground
> 　　annoyance be I shall,
> And let me have a shrouding sheet
> 　　to cover me from shame . . .
> I make thee sole executor because
> I loved thee best.
>
> 　　　　　　　　　(F1ᵥ)

The *coup de grace* follows soon, where we see that this whole parodic "will and testament" has been an ingenious exhortation; like the rest of her *Nosegay* book, it aimed at, as primary readers, the lady of lost service and those who might have influence with her.

> To all that ask what end I made
> 　　and how I went away
> Thou answer mayst: "Like those which here
> 　　no longer tarry may."
> And unto all that wish me well,
> 　　or rue that I am gone,
> Do me commend and bid them cease
> 　　my absence for to moan,
> And tell them further, if they would
> 　　my presence still have had,
> They should have sought to mend my luck,
> 　　which ever was too bad.
>
> 　　　　　　　　　(F2)

There is still time to prevent this sad "death" if her lady will relent.

Reading Formations, and Subject Positioning
from Gendered Discourses

Let us now take a closer look at Tony Bennett's concept of reading formations, before we see what further we can learn in other sources about ladies and
their women as readers and writers. He defines such a formation as "a set of
discursive and intertextual determinations that organize and animate the practice of reading, connecting texts and readers in specific relations to one another
by constituting readers as reading subjects of particular types and texts as ob-
jects-to-be-read in particular ways" (Bennett, "Texts" 7). This definition includes kinds of text-reader relationships that do not assume the defined readers
actually to be sitting somewhere together: they need only be an identifiable set
of implied and (in potential instances) actual readers. Thus the one we are
looking at represents something of a materialist's "ideal" of reading formations,
whereby the readers actually sat together, reading aloud and listening.

Most of the texts women read, as noted above, were not exclusively tagged
as women's reading nor so considered; they were a selected part of the general
literate, nonscholarly textual culture of minimally educated bourgeois and mon-
eyed readers of the time; however, when women read them in this way, they
were received as something rather different from what they might be in a soli-
tary man's reading, or even in family after-supper readings. As Bennett goes on
to explain in a Kristevan formulation (see Kristeva, *Desire in Language* [29],
on "social text"), his reading-formation concept is a way "to think of context
as a set of discursive and intertextual determinations, operating on material and
institutional supports, that bear in upon a text, not just externally, from the
outside in, but internally, shaping it, in the historically concrete form in which
it is available as a text-to-be-read, from the inside out" (8). One illustration of
this point is that the formation we are considering found explicit embodiment
or thematization within some of the most appropriate texts for being received
into it, namely sixteenth-century romances: for example, Sidney in his *Old Arcadia*, thinking of his countess sister and her circle of women who made his
Wilton audience, has his narrator address them at times as "Dear ladies," and
even shows a whimsically parodic version of his conceived narrator (himself)
and audience in scenes such as that where Pamela has Prince Musidorus, in the
position of a supposed shepherd-servant, narrate his own life story to her while
the serving woman Mopsa listens or dozes; there we have the formation humorously depicted.

These points relate to a series of useful questions that Stimpson formulated
(85–87), which we can take up here as a way of sharpening our application of
Bennett's "reading formation" concept to the particular gendered instance being considered. The first two we have already been thinking about: in a given

context Stimpson asks, What is the degree of devaluation of women as "producers of public culture" brought on by pervasive insistence that women's work is only "eros and reproduction"?—I would add, household affairs. Here the devaluation degree is nearly total. And second, What responses have women made to that devaluation? One, I suggest, is the development of the reading formation we are examining, part of which is a personalization of the political within a private system of discursive exchange, to be seen in narrative form below in Margaret Tyler's rendition of the *Mirrour of Knighthood*, whereby all texts are read as if they were personal letters. Stimpson goes on to recommend considering, if one would study the gendering of a text (here we take a whole reading formation rather than just a text), what notions of gender differentiation—what interlocking senses of maleness and femaleness—are represented. And further, is something "written for women, for what kind of women, and with what intent toward them"? I will adapt this to say, "Is something *received as* having been written for women," that is, received into the reading formation as already on some level gender-coded. And lastly she asks, what "sense of community" with women does the writer of any text establish, through "projection of a shared society or of shared experiences" (Stimpson 87)?

"Shared society" and "shared experiences" can be rendered more incisive analytical concepts if replaced by something linguistic that can work within their sphere, namely the discourse-psychologist Wendy Hollway's concept of gendered discourses, i.e., discourses that operate to effect and maintain gender identification in the persons using them, by offering gender-tagged subject and object positions. In present day Britain and for talking about heterosexual relationships, Hollway (228–52) identifies three such "discourses . . . that make available positions for subjects to take up": the "male sexual drive discourse," the "have-hold discourse," and the "permissive discourse." Each is a set of terms, phrases, and typical assertions presupposing, and thereby offering, gender-tagged subject and object positions. The first assumes that men have an ineluctable "need to fuck," to pursue and penetrate, come whatever may; women inevitably occupy the metasyntactic object position in this mode of discourse. In the have-and-hold discourse (involving statements about commitment, closeness, etc.), a sociosemiotic counterpoise to the first kind, the subject position is female tagged, the object male—so that when men speak it they cast themselves as effeminate. In the permissive discourse, which assumes the rightness for everyone of casual sex with changing partners, the subject position is gender-neutral, but the large degree of overlap in other features between it and the male-drive discourse, Hollway notes, makes it sometimes function as a kind of trap for women adopting it.

In Tudor and Stuart England, at this analytical level we can also identify at least three operative modes of discourse about heterosexual relations, which supplied gendered utterance subject and object positions. First there is a superior-female-chastity discourse, whereby a woman, cast as an unsexed or nonde-sirous being, either can occupy an object position for male subjects defining otherness or can take up a subject position by presenting herself as either in-different or superior to sexual desire.[17] Next we can recognize the extramari-tal-seduction discourse, that of, e.g., Wyattesque and popularized Petrarchan sonnets, pastoral flirtation dialogues, and some other conventional, variously contextualized lingos (which in the late Renaissance appropriated also popular neo-Platonism as a flirtation code). Its subject position is male, while the object position is doubly gendered by a construct of overheard utterance: behind the clearly implied female enunciatee at the textual or utterance surface stands a male secondary enunciatee (e.g., Petrarchan sonnets are typically addressed, in social fact of circulation, to an overhearing male audience [see Enterline]). A third mode may be called demonized-female-object discourse: a male subject defames or denounces anarchic aggressor-females such as witches, Amazons, shrews, adulteresses—or women writers who have transgressed prescribed sub-ject boundaries. Here again the subject position is male and the object position doubly gendered, but this time behind the implied male enunciatee at the ut-terance surface stands a secondary female one (who should get the message of rage). Men angry or disappointed with some woman can flip into such misogy-nist discourse at the snap of a finger, as does the initially dewy-eyed lover Post-humous Leonatus in Shakespeare's *Cymbeline*, making plans with his male friends to kill his supposedly unfaithful wife. It will be seen that these gendered discourse modes offer women only one unproblematic subject position, the su-perior chastity one that Whitney took up in her first book, the *Copy of a Letter*, denouncing her fickle fiancé. That one also supplies the base point of textually female voice (whether a man or a woman was the writer) in polemic treatises proposing to defend women from their detractors, such as Jane Anger's (see Woodbridge), and in Emilia Lanyer's verse, to be studied shortly. Lamb ("Women Readers" 215) describes what I would call, in the interactive processes of gendered reading and writing, a correlate to this female subject position in the sphere of the implied reader, namely in writings on female education, the good woman whose "reading of selected authors" signifies chastity.

What were some of the permutations when these modes of discourse were taken into the reading formation we are here considering? Of those one could expect from the scheme just described, some may have occurred that we have no record of, since so few women's writings have survived. But a quite telling one will be illustrated below in Tyler's romance translation, in a speech of the waiting woman Fidelia: she frames this speech to her lady, front and back, with superior-female-chastity discourse, urging rejection of the knight Rosicleer as a socially unsuited lover, but stuffs the middle of it with a parodic or inverted version of demonized-object discourse. It works this way: a female character, having claimed a subject position through the female-chastity discourse, draws as it were on the approbation of the assumed female audience to slide from there into a subject position in one of the other two discourse modes, yet while still speaking as a woman.

Margaret Tyler's Translation: The Reading Formation Thematized, Rapists Contained, and a Subject Position Co-opted

A scene like those from the *Arcadia* noted above—thematizing a reading formation into which the text is tagged as directed—occurs in the waiting woman Margaret Tyler's translated romance *The Mirrour of Knighthood*, Book I (1578, Spanish original by Diego Ortuñez de Calahorra); as noted above, it suggests that women in this practice read and heard histories, romances, Bible readings, and moral sententiae in somewhat the same way as they did personal letters addressed to them.[18] It is thus no surprise that much of the verse waiting women wrote was verse letters, as with Whitney, above, and Lanyer, to come.

In the *Mirrour* scene I am referring to, the British Princess Olivia with her circle of attendant waiting women (including her bosom friend and trusted woman Fidelia) and ladies (including two resident princess-guests), being together in her sitting-room, are startled and hurry to the windows to gaze upon the arriving corpse of a fearsome rapist-giant, which Princess Olivia's admirer Rosicleer has sent as a "message" to her, having killed him for her honor. The textual correlate of that grisly corporeal message is a personal letter that Rosicleer wrote and has smuggled into the jewel coffer he rescued from the giant's clutches. The other two princesses, likewise having received in the coffer letters from their knight-admirers (Rosicleer's companions in errantry), take them into a side chamber to read them aloud to each other for shared enjoyment, while Princess Olivia, too excited to read the letter from Rosicleer by herself, saves it until bedtime so as to have her favorite woman Fidelia read it out to her (109–12v)—only from Fidelia's lips does she want to hear it. Such a habit of reading would naturally incline women to see the texts accessible to them as interlarded with codes incorporating various levels of reference to their own personal situations and desires. Deprived almost totally of any chance to produce public writing or other public culture, women created, I suggest, a kind of hidden version of such cultural circulation within the confines of private circles, reproducing the political within the personal and vice versa. The fantasy rapist-giant cast at the princess's feet by her admirer knight has the content of male power controlled by other men at women's behest—a kind of converse of Spenser's chaste Lady Britomart's conquest of the Amazon Radigund (a usurper-woman ruling over captive men), which returns men to their supposed proper dominance (*Faerie Queene* V—see Benson chaps. 9 and 10).

To pursue these issues further, let us consider a little more of this *Mirrour of Knighthood*, whose translator tells in her prefatory epistles of having served in the household of Margaret Audley Howard, Duchess of Norfolk, in the early 1560s and indicates that she was originally commanded to do the translation she is now publishing (on her life see Schleiner "Margaret Tyler"). Here we see a mode of Renaissance romance in several ways explicitly attuned to the female readership we are considering, written by savvy men working through their commercially profitable "sense of community" with it. Stock medieval romance motifs of male sexual power, for example, are here set in various new frames of fantasized female control, as in the following scene from chapter 45 of the *Mirror*. Three young princes are in quest of the missing hero Rosicleer.

> . . . they tooke their horse and riding throughe a beaten pathe at the side of a pleasaunt woode they heard a noyse, wherat being moued they tourned backe to see what it might be. Out of the thickest of the woode they sawe a wylde Boare driuing so fast as possibly it might, and in the pursuite thereof, a young gentlewoman vppon a mightye courser and a Boare speare in hir right hande, hir hunters weede was all of greene veluet, hir tresses hanging downe in colour lyke the golde of Araby in hir left hand a wande of golde and two rich Pearles hanging at hyr eares. She came spurring hir horse in such wise and with such courage to ouertake the Boare that she much delyghted them, and at suche time as the Boare crossed the way betweene them and hir she strake the Boare on the flancke, that hyr speare appeared at the other side of the Boare. The game was gotte, and the Lady not taking heede of the other knights perhappes shaddowed by the trees retourned with softe paces to hir company, but the knights ouertooke hir and as I may say abashed at that whiche they had seene, at hir graces and beautie, they only gased one vppon the other not once making offer to salute hir, wherat the Lady more bolde then the men as it were to awake them out of their dreames tooke and winded a faire horne which honge at hir necke so loude and shryll that all the forrest and valleyes rang thereof, and when she had thus done she came to the three Princes in hir seming the proprest knights that euer she set eye on, whom she friendly welcomed on this wise. God saue you gentle knights and sende you the comforte of your loues. (ff. 150–51)

The sentences roll fluidly along, with prepositional phrases often made parallel to participial and absolute constructions—a syntax allowing for exuberant accumulations of visual details, loosely linked. The rhetorical effect is of leisurely simplicity, but it is a syntax capable of ironic subtleties: e.g., the knights here are actually abashed, not as is stated by the so proper trait of "beauty" suddenly and with light irony attributed to the lady after her easy kill of the boar, but at her astonishing strength and skill in a manly deed. She goes on to order her own knights into test combats with the visitors for the possession of her ladies' affections; as the visitors win all the jousts and thus all the ladies, the whole episode becomes a highly colored gratification for both the female and the déclassé male readers/listeners in the women's reading formation, who in their personal experience have very little of such freedom or power. That is, the knights out of whose perspective the episode is revealed (the centered-consciousness male perspective of the narrator is close to theirs) conquer some ladies' hearts by conquering their attendant knights; yet they do so in the process of gratifying a powerful but most beautiful and decorated lady who rules the fictive scene and rules those knights, defining the whole action. Probably the Duchess of Norfolk and her circle greatly enjoyed such episodes.

Or again, the earlier conventional romance identity test of young Rosicleer (the hero being searched for by his friends in the above scene) is a challenge to draw out from its sheath a sword accessible only to the right man: his success at this test is framed and valorized both by his defeat of the above-mentioned rapist giant formerly in possession of the sheathed sword (who in turn, as thief of the sword, is standing in for two further rapist giants besieging the enchantress who made it), and by the gaze of the Princess Olivia over him, who after the fight is given the power to reward or not to reward him, and to decide on his prize (93–96v). Thus such romances had internal coding directly fitting them for reception into the reading formation we are studying, where a high-ranking lady controlled the activities, and her women found themselves on an unaccustomed footing, approaching equality, with the men courting their lady's patronage.

How might other forms of reading be received and made to signify inside this reading formation, forms that did not have such direct coding? In a further passage from this same section of the *Mirrour*, we recognize in the waiting woman Fidelia's admonition against love the very same kinds of moralistic reading of extracted *sententiae* or wise sayings, summarized histories, and rhetorically arranged *topoi* that we noted in Isabella Whitney. (See also chapter 5 on *sententiae* in women's uses of literacy.) Hearing that the beloved Rosicleer is supposedly not of sufficiently high social rank to court her, Princess Olivia laments in private to Fidelia the unfairness of the standard. In response the waiting woman, referring for authority to the "histories" they have read together, launches into a conventional "counselor" speech obviously constructed by stringing together all the examples from some moralized rhetoric book; she runs through a string of instances from the "place" or *topos* of "high merit in the low born," from the biblical Jephtah and the worthy Socrates down to Cicero and the Gothic Bamba. But as noted above in my discussion of superior-chastity discourse, Fidelia inconsistently declares before and after this string that the princess must nevertheless renounce Rosicleer because, in modern times, "God hath given us over to a wrong judgment in matters of high estate, rather to prefer wealth than Vertue, and sith you are now fallen unto that time, wherein this error . . . is strengthened by the consent of men, I would counsel you to yield unto the time and . . . forsake him then" (117)!

Bending all her "reading" to reinforce the princess's real wish, to love Rosicleer, Fidelia yet officially frames her consent with a declaration for the "honorable" course sure to please the princess's father. As suggested above, she thus effectuates a slippage from mode to mode of gendered discourse, whereby the Princess Olivia in fantasy can claim a quasi-male subject position that lets her deploy for her own desirous utterance the moral force of male reading (i.e., reading material that is per se male-tagged in its enunciative position although not explicitly part of the gendered discourses listed above). This can be accomplished because Fidelia is speaking within the reading formation, as waiting woman to her lady.

The Spanish author of this romance was out to appeal to ladies and gentlewomen by writing idealized possible situations of female power and gratification directly into his treatment of male adventures, and clearly his fiction worked quite as well for Englishwomen as for Spanish women. Indeed we are here probably studying an international reading formation, one that obtained in circles of aristocratic ladies and their waiting women quite as much on the continent as in England, and that continued little changed for over a century.[19] The particular vernacular histories, rhetoric books, devotional works, and romances chosen for reading would be updated as the decades passed, but the kinds of reading remained the same. In Castiglione's famous *Courtier* (trans. Sir Thomas Hoby—see chapter 2 on his wife Elizabeth), with its Duchess Elisabetta in charge of elegant conversations and readings by a select household circle of women and visiting courtiers, we have an idealized and male-appropriated portrayal of the formation. At the other end of the mimetic scale, we have in the Overburian "characters" of c. 1613 a misogynist satiric version of this reading formation, in a portrayal of a chambermaid (probably not by Sir Thomas Overbury himself, but by an associate). She is a frivolous, chattering and ducking, sexually loose woman, incapable of whole sentences, who in between dabbings of makeup onto the lady is busily reading aloud to her—what but exactly the *Mirrour of Knighthood*:[20]

> She is her mistress's she-secretary, and keeps the box of her teeth, her hair, and her painting very private. . . . If she lie at her master's bed's feet, she is quit of the green sickness forever. . . . She reads Greene's works over and over, but is so carried away with the Mirror of Knighthood she is many times resolved to run out of herself, and become a lady-errant. If she catch a clap, she divides it so equally between the master and the serving-man as if she had cut out the getting of it by a thread. . . . her mind, her body, and clothes are parcels loosely packed together, and for want of good utterance, she perpetually laughs out her meaning. Her mistress and she help to make away time, to the idlest purpose that can be either for love or money. In brief, these chambermaids are like lotteries: you may draw twenty ere one worth anything. (Witherspoon; Warnke 200)

Was this what it had been like when Margaret Tyler and others read aloud to the Duchess of Norfolk, perhaps at the duke's main residence of Kenning-hall, which boasted the first known bathroom in England, with copper tubs for warm soaking and mythological murals around the walls? (cf. Neville Williams). Probably not. Tyler's preface to the reader—an extensive, witty defense of women's right to "pen" stories and translations—shows her a strong-minded, articulate woman, bearing scant resemblance to Overbury's chamber-maid[21] (on Tyler's preface see Krontiris). Overbury's parody of the reading formation flattens it out socially, demoting all the declaiming readers to the lowest rank among a lady's staff, that of chambermaid. But while the term "chamber-maid" could be loosely used to refer to a gentlewoman in waiting (the usage basis of Overbury's strategy), chambermaids in the strict sense—those who actually cleaned the rooms—were rarely literate. Of literate staff in a great house we recognize, besides the upper-echelon waiting women of gentry rank, also middle-level servants, who in a large entourage such as that of the Duke and Duchess of Norfolk would have been the wives of comparable literate men-servants: lawyers, document scribes, secretaries, and overseers. Such, I believe, was Margaret Tyler, possibly the wife of one John Tyler who in the same years of her service did tenant land records for the duke.[22] The middle-level literate servants capable of spot-translating from foreign reading would presumably have come either from merchant families in international trade (daughters who were bookkeepers, such as Elizabeth Lucar of London, were taught Spanish)[23] or from the staffs of diplomats who had lived abroad, picking up a language conversationally.

A usefully detailed record of the women's reading circles is seen in *The Diary of Lady Anne Clifford*. Although Lamb's recent discussion of Anne Clif-ford argues well that she eventually developed reading habits according with a male self-concept,[24] it is important to see that she spent her adolescence and early adulthood clearly within the standard patterns of the aristocratic women's reading circle, only stretching its borders in certain selected texts. Complete with a list from the 1610s of the household staff serving "my lord" (Richard Sackville, Earl of Dorset), "my lady" (herself), and "the child" (Margaret, later Countess of Thanet), her diary records month by month who was reading to her out of what book. Her two women of gentry rank, Kate Burton and Moll Neville, who in Sackville livery accompanied her to church and on other out-ings, were called on to read primarily from the Bible, Sidney's *Arcadia*, and the works of Spenser,[25] while lower-ranking serving women would apparently suf-fice at times to read from the Bible or devotional works: there is record of a Kate Buchin doing so (if this is not a misreading for Kate Burton—I have not seen the manuscript) and years later of one Anne Turner.[26] When something considered "learned" was to be read to "my lady" and her women, such as a treatise on Turkish government or Montaigne's *Essays*, a manservant, such as one Rivers, or Wat Conniston, got the task (see n. 20). It is a mark of special commemoration of her mother, the Countess of Cumberland, when Lady Anne herself takes up and reads from "My Lady's Book of Praise," i.e., a manuscript commonplace book of religious writings that her mother had collected.

Emilia Lanyer, Lady Anne Clifford, and the Countess of Cumberland at Cookham Dean

In Emilia Lanyer's *Salve Deus Rex Judaeorum* (1611)—in the long central title poem (see Appendix 2 for excerpts) and the several poems surrounding it—we have a full-scale celebration of the women's reading circle and especially of a loving relationship of a waiting woman to her lady within it. That relationship, I suggest, enabled Lanyer to write feelingly, at the center of "Salve Deus," her revision of Christian typology, where she casts Adam's guilt as primary and Eve as the truer forerunner of Christ. Lanyer's poems indicate that she served the Countess of Cumberland and her daughter only briefly during a particular summer, perhaps for a few weeks, but that was enough for an attachment to form that inspired this former mistress of Lord Chamberlain Hunsdon.[27] A likely year would have been 1607, when George Clifford, Earl of Cumberland, had just died,[28] willing his lands to his brother in contravention of a writ of Edward II (which had stipulated that certain of them should go to the heirs in the direct Clifford line, male or female). The countess that year took her only surviving child, the seventeen-year-old Lady Anne, on an extended tour of "her" lands, which till then she had never seen (Williamson) and which she would not control for many years yet. They went both to inspect the properties and to gather documents for the legal battle (Williamson 77–78). This situation is indirectly evoked in Lanyer's poems (see Lewalski *Writing* 216, 225). Cookham, a royal manor between London and Oxford in the use of Lady Cumberland's brother Lord William Russell (*Writing* 396 n. 21), would have been a suitable starting-out point; the depicted time is early summer.

Emilia Lanyer, daughter of one Italian musician of Queen Elizabeth's court and wife of another, must have been employed among temporary staff at Cookham Dean: in her concluding poem "The Description of Cooke-ham," she portrays herself waiting there for the ladies' party to arrive and still being there after they have left (137, 140–41). Musical ability may well have been one of her qualifications, since she says that she "did always bear a part" in the ladies' "recreations" and portrays the countess often singing Psalms (139). The "Cookham" poem centers her nostalgic reminiscences on a favorite tree under which the ladies often rested in their walks through the estate's park and reports that "many a learned book was read and scanned" there (141).

The spirituality of Margaret Russell Clifford, Countess of Cumberland, daughter of Francis Russell (the staunchly Protestant Earl of Bedford), clearly made a strong impression on Lanyer. Her earlier life—as Lord Chamberlain Henry Hunsdon's mistress and mother of an illegitimate son, then as a fortune-seeking client of Simon Foreman—had evidently been worldly enough, whether or not she was Shakespeare's "dark lady" (see n. 21). The whole lengthy "Salve Deus Rex Judaeorum" poem (the second part of its title taken from the sign Pilate is said to have posted on Jesus' cross) is a personal and political tribute to the countess, offering her a version of the Christ that Lanyer celebrates as Lord of the high lady's sensibility. One stanza indicates that the countess experienced visions of Christ as a kind, elderly shepherd (Rowse ed. 121—see end of Appendix 2). An earlier one portrays her, on a memorable moonlit evening, telling Lanyer to write of "that delightful place" Cookham (79, or see below). The Cookham poem that Lanyer does eventually write (following the "Salve Deus" and concluding the whole book—see Greer for excerpts, or Rowse or Woods eds.) culminates in a description of the countess kissing the favorite oak tree farewell and Lanyer herself thereupon also kissing it to gather up the Lady's kiss, too fine for insentient wood. The portrayals of her affection and admiration for the countess in these two poems ring much more true than does the conventional patronage adulation of the other ladies whom Lanyer's book addresses in its several dedicatory poems, and the countess may have encouraged Lanyer in a newfound religious intensity.

Taking the conventional paratextual metaphor for her book as a "mirror" to be held up to high-ranking readers and to reflect their own virtues, Lanyer in her opening verse epistles to several high ladies builds in multiple versions of the formation to be seen there, which is just what we are studying, a lady's circle busy with readings, music, and devotions. That is, she begins with a poem to Queen Anne, wife of James I, inviting her to "Look in this Mirror of a worthy Mind, / Where some of your fair Virtues will appear" (Lanyer, Rowse ed. 42), then next has a poem "To all virtuous Ladies in general," followed by single patronage poems to each of a circle of highest ladies of the queen's court (Susan, Countess of Kent—whom Lanyer served in youth—Lucy, Countess of Bedford, Lady Arbella Stuart, etc.). These ladies are portrayed waiting upon the queen and "looking" into the "mirror" of Lanyer's book—i.e., listening to it read aloud.

> Each blessed Lady that in Virtue spends
> Your precious time to beautify your souls,
> Come wait on her whom winged Fame attends, . . .
>   Let this fair Queen not unattended be
>   When in my Glass she deigns herself to see.
>   ("To all virtuous Ladies" 1st stanza, 48)

Obviously these poems to the high-ranking ladies, some of whom Lanyer did not know, are appeals for money or a job, though to what extent they succeeded we do not know (probably not much). But they are also part of her deliberate design. As pieces exhibiting the standard traits of paratextual patronage verse (particular epideictic stances, meters and metaphors conventional for the genre, etc.), they are yet using that genre revisionistically. For Lanyer, when she comes lastly to praise the lady her whole book is really celebrating, subtly decenters and recenters her initial arrangement of the alleged intended readership of Queen Anne with surrounding ladies (including the Countess of Cumberland): that is, the long central title poem—the account of Christ's passion with epideictic addresses to the countess framing it before, after and in the margins—*is* the patronage poem to that beloved lady whom she served at Cookham Dean. Thus, in the row of poems inscribed to the different high ladies, the countess gets at first only a brief prose epistle, but then at the end of the row this vastly longer poem, followed by the concluding Cookham country estate poem. That "mirror" which the queen and high ladies all surround and gaze into thereby becomes a textualized Margaret Russell herself, who is "from the Court to the Country retired, / Leaving the world, before the world leaves thee" (84). The paratextual being a sphere where women had come to be granted a voice (speaking from the subject position of superior-chastity discourse), Lanyer makes a whole text of ostensible paratexts and thus enables the long central one, in default of any other textual center, to take the position of centered text.

This strategy is at the same time a political decentering and recentering. In the exaltation of the Countess of Cumberland (as supreme virtuous addressee who has drawn herself away from court to countryside), we can recognize a political dimension of Lanyer's writing project, i.e., to support the countess's and her daughter's campaign, just beginning, for the contested lands. The center of the book's portrayed world of women revising Eve (analyzed by Lewalski, Beilin, and others) is by Lanyer's design shrewdly shifted: from the queen's court at Somerset House to the countess's idyllic greensward at Cookham. There too we find a female circle—in this case of the lady, her daughter (Anne Clifford), and waiting women hearing readings and singing Psalms. The "Salve Deus Rex Judaeorum," after a stanza picturing in heaven the now departed Queen Elizabeth (to whom the countess herself had been primary lady-in-waiting), declares itself—as a portrait of Christ—to be Margaret Russell's poem and a tribute to her as center of a proper, virtuous court. Queen Anne's court, by contrast, where potentates of different factions were already lobbying against the Clifford ladies' land claim, thus becomes a counterimage, admonished to reform itself.

> To thee great Countess now I will apply
> My Pen to write thy never dying fame,
> That when to Heaven thy blessed Soul shall fly

These lines on earth record thy reverend name:
And to this task I mean my Muse to tie,
Though wanting skill I shall but purchase blame.
　　Pardon, dear Lady, want of woman's wit
　　To pen thy praise, when few can equal it.

And pardon, Madam, though I do not write
Those praiseful lines of that delightful place,
As you commanded me in that fair night
When shining *Phoebe* gave so great a grace,
Presenting *Paradise* to your sweet sight,
Unfolding all the beauty of her face
　　With pleasant groves, hills, walks and stately trees,
　　Which pleasures with retired minds agrees.

　　　　　　　　　　(Lanyer Rowse ed. 79)

In these opening stanzas of the "Salve Deus" poem, we learn that Lanyer took no occasion to revise her manuscript: at this point in it, the speaker does not know whether she will manage to finish her planned design by writing the concluding Cookham poem, i.e., the part of the book actually suggested to her by the countess. Thus the text stands at the diegetic level of declared first draft: an implied speaker is talking who cannot with confidence foresee the end of her text. When Lanyer did finish, she must have hustled her manuscript off to the printer with ink still wet, hoping for speedy material as well as spiritual returns. She entirely lacked an editor, or even any chance for self-editing, and what we need for enjoying her prolix "Salve Deus Rex Judaeorum," which I think has potentially within it a more moving and vibrant poem than the "Cookham" one, is an excerpt version. I have suggested one in Appendix 2, but perhaps as discussion of the poem continues, someone will work out a better extract.

In the "Cookham" poem Lanyer celebrates her affection and admiration for the countess directly, through reminiscences of their time together. When male poets of the age wanted to write thus directly to and about a dearly loved person, they typically moved into Latin (see, e.g., Spenser's and Harvey's affectionate letters to each other, or Milton's ode to Charles Diodati, the "Epitaphium Damonis"). Although Elizabeth Cooke had been able to move into Latin to write of her love for Thomas Hoby, that particular textual recourse for needed minimal distancing (of writer from textualized implied speaker and addressee) was by Lanyer's time unavailable to women, and it seems that the Cookham poem suffers from a kind of emotive overexposure, for instance in its excessive use of prosopopoeias of kindly Nature (what would later be dubbed "pathetic fallacy"). In the "Salve Deus," by contrast, Lanyer is able to focus a strong measure of erotic and indirectly political intensity on her self-defined task of portraying an image of Christ in selected biblical language and imagery—not just any version of Christ, but the one she perceives in the mind and emotive life of her beloved countess, Lady Margaret. Thus through working revisionistically out of biblical language (including Psalms and Canticles), bouncing her feelings back through and from the language of the devotional Bible readings and commentary that she heard daily in the reading circle around the countess, she attains a mode of indirection for turning love celebration into poetry.

After a bow to the deceased Queen Elizabeth, noted above, her poem moves into an invocation segment that suggests the beauty of God through vivid images from the Psalms (cf. Psalm 104): He rides upon the wings of the winds, "decked with light, as with a garment fair," and even that garment of the beautiful heavens is to him a mere "vesture," that eventually shall wear out and "depart, as when a scroll is rolled"; the poet ends this section with an evocation of the Lord himself, unveiled: "He is exceeding glorious to behold, / Ancient of Times, so fair, and yet so old."

There follows an apology to the countess of several stanzas, where Lanyer's strategy of indirection comes to the textual surface:

> Pardon, good Madam, though I have digressed
> From what I do intend to write of thee,
> To set his glory forth whom thou lov'st best, . . .
> [Thy] high deserts invites my lowly Muse
> To write of Him, and pardon crave of thee, . . .
> [What] to thy holy Love may pleasing be:
> His Death and Passion I desire to write,
> And thee to read, the blessed Soul's delight.

She next laments the feared inadequacy of her muse, comparing it with Icarus and Phaeton, mythic aspiring boys who soared too high for their powers—such images of boyish aspiration seem accessible to her as a woman—then replaces them with a female role model of lowliness but goodness who received Christ's commendation: the generous widow who gave her last pence.

> But yet the Weaker thou [my Muse] dost seem to be
> In Sex or Sense, the more his Glory shines,
> That doth infuse such powerful Grace in thee
> To show thy Love in these few humble Lines;
> The Widow's Mite with this may well agree,
> Her little All more worth than golden mines.

This substitution of weak but immensely loving female valuation for powerful but corrupt male valuation (the latter imaged chiefly through the figures of Adam and Pilate) supplies the defining perspective for the deft account of

Christ's passion and death that follows. Men torture and kill him; women offer consolation and lament. Pilate is hard and unfeeling, his insightful wife ignored. The narrative builds to an asserted revision of traditional Adam-Christ typology that Lanyer draws from "defense of woman" treatises: it is Eve, loving, uncomprehending victim of Satan's wiles, who best prefigures the loving and suffering Lord; Adam with his greater intelligence and strength knowingly succumbed to evil.

Moving then to a devotional admiration of Christ, the poem presents his dying body, as in so many paintings of the time, by eroticizing it through imagery from the Canticles. Lanyer thus comes to the end of her biblical rendition, after which she will move to direct description of the countess's spirituality and its expression in good works.

> This with the eye of faith thou mayst behold,   TO MY LADY OF
> Dear Spouse of Christ, and more than I can write . . .   CUMBERLAND
> This is the Bridegroom that appears so fair,
> So sweet, so lovely in his Spouse's sight,
> That unto Snow we may his face compare,
> His cheeks like scarlet and his eyes so bright
> As purest Doves that in the rivers are
> Washed with milk, to give the more delight;
>   His head is likened to the finest gold,
>   His curled locks so beauteous to behold,
>
> Black as a Raven in her blackest hue,
> His lips like scarlet threads, yet much more sweet
> Than is the sweetest honey dropping dew,
> Or honeycombs where all the Bees do meet;
> Yea, he is constant and his words are true,
> His cheeks are beds of spices, flowers sweet,
>   His lips like Lillies, dropping down pure myrrh,
>   Whose love before all worlds we do prefer.
>
> Ah! give me leave, good Lady, now to leave   TO MY LADY
> This task of Beauty which I took in hand;   OF CUMBERLAND
> I cannot wade so deep, I may deceive
> Myself before I can attain the land;
> Therefore, good Madam, in your heart I leave
> His perfect picture, where it still shall stand,
>   Deeply engraved in that holy shrine,
>   Environed with Love and Thoughts divine.

Using the doubled marginal tag to stress the human addressee of this devotional intensity, the poet at the end of this verbal picture draws back, seemingly surprised at the force of her own words. She ends with an assertion that she was destined from birth to write this celebration of the countess and with an appeal to her assumed audience of Queen Anne's ladies to recognize the superior virtue and generosity of this "Great Lady of my heart" and "Arctic Star," who has now withdrawn from court to country. The political dimension of the poem's import is that no one else could so well deserve and manage vast inherited lands as she.

Conclusion

In sum, we saw in Isabella Whitney's verse a waiting woman grieving for her loss of the reading formation of a women's household reading circle (and in the process illustrating much of its typical material), calling to the lost lady to restore her post. She thus created a whimsical, unusually down-to-earth writing perspective from which to pen a record of a self-aware but impoverished gentry-woman's life, and her affection for the city of London. As we took the concept of the reading formation further, through questions about gendered texts posed by Stimpson and through Hollway's idea of gendered subject/object positions offered by particular modes of discourse about sex, we studied several passages from the waiting woman Margaret Tyler's translation of *The Mirrour of Knighthood*; there we saw how the genre of Renaissance prose romance, par excellence, could build in or thematize the "intertextual determinations" fitting it specifically to the gendered terms within the women's reading formation, with its included serving men. And then, in the "Salve Deus Rex Judaeorum" poem of Emilia Lanyer, we saw how a relationship of waiting woman to lady-of-service could empower a woman to write a poem revising Christian male typology about guilty Eve, through celebrating a beloved lady who had encouraged her writing.[29]

In conclusion, I suggest that within this reading formation, the female-tagged subject enunciative position that waiting women could take up, when they "claimed the floor" for utterance or writing, was one initially and primarily within the superior-female-chastity discourse, a female subject position from which they could address themselves upward (in terms of social class) to the lady of service, by moving across the gender-neutral primary enunciatee implied by the group, with its included déclassé male participants, as surface syntactic object in Hollway's terms.[30] By contrast, when the great lady herself might find a voice supported by this reading formation, it appears that the direction of address would rather be outward—to an implied, politically construed male enunciatee beyond the bounds of the reading circle; so we will see in chapter 3, on the Countess of Pembroke and her writings.

2

Activist Entries into Writing

Lady Elizabeth Hoby/Russell and the Other Cooke Sisters

AS IN THE collection *Silent but for the Word* (1985), modern study of Tudor and Stuart women's writings focused at first on texts concerning household affairs and religion (topics on which women could sometimes write with male approval) and showed that on religion they mostly did translations. But some of those who began with translation went on to other kinds of writing as well. How shall we tune in more closely to the written voices of these women? How did they come to make for themselves such textual spaces? They were working at first in the sphere that Gérard Genette has taxonomized as the "paratextual" (prefaces, dedicatory poems, patronage epistles, and at one of its borders, translations—see chart in chapter 3). There they sometimes managed intimations of things that they in particular wanted to say, and a few of them even moved on from such paratextual margins and borders to claim other kinds of textual space—for example the "speaking stones" of tombs, out at another margin or bourn, from beyond which no traveler returns. Not "marble nor the gilded monuments" of nobles would do for Shakespeare's poems, but for Elizabeth (Cooke), Lady Hoby/Lady Russell, they were the only semipublic space she could get. Here I want to try out another approach to the question, pursued in the preceding study of a women's reading formation, of how women came to write anything for public or semipublic circulation, when they were afforded so little chance to do so.

First, I think with Alan Sinfield that we have to "take [their religion] seriously" (vii)—as Sinfield does the Calvinism of Spenser and Sidney. And for the women who went on to write other things as well as religious translations, study of these translations will be part of learning to catch their voices. I assume that for studying a preface one should look at what it is prefacing, for a dedicatory poem that which it dedicates. I also propose to take as potential corpus (though not all of it will be treated) the complete known writings of each woman studied, including verse in Latin and, more rarely, in Greek. That certain Tudor women wrote at times in the learned languages had, I believe, a different motive from the usual one of men in doing so (reaching a scholarly, including an international, audience): it was partial protection against male opprobrium to remove one's writings from the ken of the less educated, though it was no sure safeguard. As for religious translations, to understand why certain women wrote them in that age, we must do more than note that men gave them permission because confessional conflicts were intense and leaders were glad of their help. Factional conflicts in other times and places have also been intense but, we may assume, have not necessarily resulted in giving marginalized people a new voice. We should consider how these conflicts did so and how the women's socializing, writing, and activism made a part of the religio-political processes of their time.

It was not that, as in some cultural contexts, religion was considered women's business—far from it. To begin with two obvious reasons, women wrote about religion because such debates were a place where they could find deeply engaging talk and writing in which they could sometimes (we will shortly consider at what sort of times) be taken seriously as participants, albeit only paratextual or marginal ones. And of course from the male perspective, they were permitted to do so in part because the Reformation had set before everyone a fearsome choice of churches that was held to determine one's eternal fate: some men came to see, then, that it was scarcely fair to forbid women to talk over and even write about that choice. As was noted by an editor of Susanna Hopton (a seventeenth-century religious writer who had converted to Catholicism, then back again to Anglicanism), women as well as men should give careful consideration to "a matter of that vast consequence" and should not "take up, nor change their religion upon trust, but make a thorough search into the principles of both churches" (Ballard 391).

Habermas's "Consensual Discourse," the Inner Dynamics of Ideological Groups, and Women's Paratextuality

Beyond these obvious points, women's entryway into writing through religion can be illuminated if we consider it in the light of Jürgen Habermas's concept of consensual discourse,[1] i.e., the characteristic talking and writing on group-pertinent topics done among people who share a group identity that matters for their personal identities (Habermas 2–6, 106–16). Such context-specific talk and writing can also be called a discursive formation in Foucault's sense (*Archaeology* 31–40); but Habermas offers ways to probe inside the workings of such a formation. Over time, the ideological center of such a group often becomes contested, Habermas notes: that is, a circle of people communicating within the address mode of "we/you-and-I"—in these cases within a religio-political cause—may at some point start to disagree about issues they consider definitive for their group identity. Scholarly and aristocratic Protestant activists of the late 1560s and 1570s, for example, were fighting out just where the consensual center of English institutionalized reform would be. (Analogously, in the late 1610s and early 1620s, Catholics and doctrinal Anglo-Catholics were fighting something out within a "we/you-and-I" identity, namely of people desirous of partial reunion between the Anglican and Roman churches; in London they centered in the Arminian frequenters of Durham House—see chapter 7).

I propose that such scenes of intraconsensual conflict proved to be one kind of stimulus to women to write, even in the face of all strictures. In the earlier case, we find the four Cooke sisters at work, the wives and sisters-in-law of no less than Lord Treasurer Burghley and Sir Nicholas Bacon, the chief judiciary officer—the two most powerful officials in the realm; the sisters were strung out toward the reformist end of the spectrum from those two compromising potentates. The women's efforts to press for further Protestant reform through writing were eventually silenced, but even then their commitment continued as quiet activism; as Habermas would say, they shifted from consensual communicative action within the still intact group to strategic action (adversarial activism against opponents one no longer tries to persuade of anything—Habermas 117, 209) in what they considered the continuing and correct ideological direction, after the group consensus collapsed. Habermas distinguishes strategic from communicative action as follows: "In communicative action a basis of mutually recognized validity claims is presupposed; this is not the case in strategic action. In the communicative attitude it is possible to reach a direct understanding oriented to validity claims; in the strategic attitude, by contrast, only an indirect understanding via determinative indicators is possible" (209).[2] (Analogously, in the mid-1620s, when the consensus of the Durham house group and their Catholic associates collapsed, with the entrenchment of the Arminians into the court faction of Laud, Cousen, and Buckingham, Lady Falkland would fall out on the side of popery and carry on with strategic action.)

That is, Habermas proposes that when consensual discourse has continued for a time, enabling some conflicts to be resolved, a point may come when the consensus starts to break down. Then opposing subgroups move into what he calls "discourse" (proper), that is, argumentation attempting to reach some new, mutually acceptable base definitions from which to rebuild consensus (3–4, 209, on "action" versus "discourse"). A flurry of back-and-forth polemical documents, publicized or circulated, typically signals this stage of things—for example, the debate in the early 1570s between conservative-prelatical clerics and parliamentarians, on the one hand, and the reformist "admonishers" of Parliament John Feild and Thomas Wilcox, on the other. If that effort fails, the "we/you-and-I" identity collapses (though it may continue a while in quasi-consensual discourse), some of the people one formerly identified with become "they"—the opponents or enemies—and the former group members turn to strategic action against each other.

Exactly in the latter part of a stretch of time when that sequence is occurring, I suggest,[3] a sense of urgency or desperation may allow previously silent people within the group to conceive of a new, albeit marginal way to write, through which they can contribute paratextually to the efforts in progress to reestablish consensus. This idea arises naturally from Habermas's analysis, because at the point where consensual speech action starts to break down and "discourse" (in his semiadversarial sense) to begin, fissures can open that allow something important to become newly visible: namely, the otherwise concealed inner boundaries of the system of domination till then operative within the consensual group. This would presumably include categories of gender, race, class, economic status, or age. Habermas's concepts involve tracking diachronically down the life of a consensual group and suggest that at a certain stage of its existence, such winning of some attention by the previously silenced becomes more probable. At such a time, group members who had previously been silent, as to writing, may find a paratextual voice, then later move on to "saying" textually something more. This, I suggest, was a pathway women found into writing through religious activism.

While I find Habermas's concepts especially applicable to the inner dynamics of groups, this analysis could perhaps also be seen in Pierre Bourdieu's terms of "symbolic capital," of which he says that some people have so much that they "effortlessly command attention," while others are "not in a position to speak (e.g. women) or must win their audience" (650). Bourdieu notes that dominated people consent to their position because of the workings of "euphemization" (regular casting of statements into terms acceptable to the anticipated audience's viewpoint) within a shared discourse, which makes the relations of power "misrecognizable" by concealing "the violence they objectively contain and thus by transforming them into symbolic power, capable of producing real effects without any apparent expenditure of energy" (*Language* 170). Bourdieu also mentions, although with reference to a different kind of context, that there may be changes in the "labour of symbolic production . . . in crisis situations, when the meaning of the world is no longer clear" (*Language* 236). Such was the socioideological context in which the Cooke sisters found themselves as marginalized female participants in the reformist activism of the 1570s.

What I have so far been noting takes its historical cues from Hugh Trevor-Roper's observation that the Anglican church was in the 1570s and 1580s defining its border against the puritan or reformist end of the spectrum of positions, while in the 1620s and 1630s it was doing the same toward that of Roman Catholicism (69). The outcome in the first case found its definitive statement in Richard Hooker's *Laws of Ecclesiastical Polity* (Pt. I, 1593), in the second in

William Chillingworth's *Religion of a Protestant* (1638), in combination with his godfather William Laud's liturgical orders. In this chapter we will study the Cooke sisters, especially in their relation to the reformist cleric Edward Dering, whose notorious sermon before the queen in 1570 had sparked off the "admonishers" and their debate in Parliament. Some of the sisters' other verse and prose that has survived will also be considered.

The Cooke Sisters' Translations and Verse: Ochino Sermons and Sylva's *Giardino Cosmografico*

The Cooke sisters had early on participated a bit in defining the character of English aristocratic Protestantism, as it took shape during the crucial mid-century decade, that of the Somerset protectorate government of the boy king Edward VI (1548–1553), to whom their father was a reader. (Sir Anthony Cooke and other avid Protestants went into exile in Strasbourg during the Catholic Mary Tudor's succeeding reign, 1553–1558.) Cooke, through his position at court and his devotion to his daughters' education, made marriages for the two eldest that put the family at the center of the ideological processes we have in view. After noting something of its life in that earlier time, we will consider a set of politically motivated verses by the sisters (1572); and we can then see why, after that last joint written reformist effort, they were obliged to turn to semicovert activism in a continuing engagement, and why the sister who has left us the most poems took tombs as her venue.

The story of Sir Anthony Cooke and his "female university" at Gidea Hall has been told often enough, in accounts usually stressing the humanist father as educator of women (see Barns, Rowse, Lamb "Cooke Sisters," and McIntosh). It may be that Mildred, Ánne, Elizabeth, and Katherine formed such an intense lifelong commitment to their father and his reformist ideology because he was a privately educated man (apparently never having attended a university), going through a self-chosen program of readings in Greek and Latin authors side by side with his children (McIntosh 240). The experience of learning along with an admired father who was also excited about intellectual discoveries goes far to explain the bonds and interests of these four women. Central to their studies were the Greek fathers of the church, with their devotional warmth and their emphasis on doctrines stressed by Protestants, such as justification by faith.

Of those studies, a translation from Greek survives by the eldest daughter, Mildred, later Lady Burghley, from a St. Basil sermon on Deuteronomy 15 (B. L. MS Royal 17B. XVIII). Of other pieces from the sisters' youthful activism we have Elizabeth's translation from Latin of Bishop John Ponet's (or Poynet's) *Diallacticon . . . de . . . substantia corporis et sanguinis Christi in Eucharistia,* that is, *A Way of Reconciliation . . . touching . . . the body and blood of Christ in the Sacrament* (1605), written decades earlier but published in her old age as a parting shot dedicated to her youngest daughter.[4] And there is Anne Cooke's translation (c. 1550) from Italian of nineteen sermons by Bernardino Ochino, who before turning Protestant had been a preacher of the Capuchin order, with the pope as his booking agent, drawing overflow crowds through all Italy.

Escaping to England, he found his audience reduced to his fellow expatriates of the Italian "foreigners' " church and certain English Protestants who knew or wanted to learn Italian. Among them was the enchanted Anne Cooke, whose dedication of her sermon renditions to her mother conveys a sense of how striking Ochino must have been for her. He is "the sanctified Barnardine," from whose "happy spirit . . . the excellent fruit" of his sermons proceeds. A contemporary account portrays him as tall and winning, with arresting voice and full hair and beard, in the pulpit seeming powerful and vigorous even after fasting (Church 56–57). Violating the decorum of female public silence (though in the first printings anonymously), Anne published her translations[5] of a set of sermons focusing on predestination and the joys of the elect in their sense of enfolding divine love. As Lady Bacon she would later be better known as translator (then from Latin) of the standard work in defense of the English church's secession from Rome, namely Bishop John Jewel's *Apologia Ecclesiae Anglicanae* (1562).

In the 1550s and 1560s the sisters moved in a circle of excited, internationally oriented Protestants who as yet had experienced little conflict among themselves, and they found the absorption in their cause highly energizing: Elizabeth Cooke was reading such treatises as the Ponet one she later published; Ponet himself had recently translated Ochino (namely, the satirical Latin *Tragedie or Dialog*, translated 1549, ridiculing the pope and cardinals through dramatic scenes where, among others, the devil speaks); and Anne Cooke, as noted, was translating Ochino. The sisters probably did more that has not survived. As a sample of their work of that period, let us look at a few passages from the Ochino sermons.

The following, treating the sermon's title question, "Whether it be necessary to saluacion to believe that we are elect or not," illustrates the style and working of this rendering. It presents several traditional doctrines—divine providence, beneficence, and omnipotence—in such a way as to turn them into a support system and ratification of a particular style of individual subjectivity. In a moment we can see how that functioning permeates also the larger rhetorical structure of an argument running through the nineteen sermons that Anne Cooke selected, perhaps marshalled by her arrangement.

> It is impossible, that one that doth not beleue to be elected shoulde beleue as he ought to do any of the artycles necessarye to saluacion. And to proue that this is true, if thou beleuest not that thou art one of the elect, thou

beleuest not in god, in the maner that thou art bound, bycause that it suf-
fyseth not to haue a certeine dead opinion that God is, but thou must effec-
tuouslye beleue that he is thy God, that he loueth the, that he is propiciatory
to the, that he is continually beneficial to the, that he hath most special cure
of the and causeth euery thinge to serue the to saluacion, and therefore that
thu arte electe. Yea whoso beleueth not that he is electe, doeth not fele in
spirite, the benefyte of Christe. Therefore being without Christ, he is without
god, and knoweth him not as Paul wryteth. Then how is it possible that thou
mayst beleue perfectli that he is thy father if thou do not beleue that thou
art his sone, and therefore his heire and saued. Thou canst also neuer earnestly
beleue that God is omnipotente, if thou vnderstande not, that continually he
vseth his omnipotency towards the, in doyinge the good, which when to the
spirit thou didst proue, thou shouldst of force beleue thyself to be his heyre,
if thou beleue not thou art electe, how canste thou beleue that God hathe
created the heauens, and the earth, and that he susteineth and gouerneth all
to thy behofe hauing of the most singular cure? It is nedeful, that with liuely
fayth, embrasing al the world for thy owne, thou perceiue effectuallye the
goodnes of God, in euerye creature. And when that is, thou shalt be inforced
to beleue, that thou arte the sonne of God. (*Certayne Sermons of . . . Master
Barnardine Ochine,* J-Jverso)

Proper religious belief per se is the topic here: mere opinions about God
are not engaged beliefs and thus not "effectuous" for procuring the "benefit
of Christ," the sense of union with God that allows one to "embrace all the
world" for one's own. Such benefit is accessible only to those who see themselves as individually chosen by God with no respect whatever to their merits—
chosen from out of the fearsome void of the real possibility of *not* being chosen
(and thus some people are not chosen, the doctrine being that of "double predestination"). The key terms above are the second person pronouns, either pos-
sessive or receiving attribution—*thy* God, beneficial to *thee,* *thou* art his son,
doing *thee* good, all to *thy* behoove, embracing all the world for *thine* own—
along with the regularly interspersed intensifier adverbs: effectuously, continually, perfectly, earnestly, effectually. These two features jack up the appeal of the
elect identity held out to the reader to a very high level of intensity. If one
allows oneself to enter the offered, elevated sense of election, that will mean
that one is indeed among the elect, who alone are able to feel it!

The reader is being offered the kind of group identity, at once abstract and
concrete, that can sustain and make an essential part of individual identity.
There I think we must find the explanation, difficult for us viewing the case
from our time of universalizing religious thought in the West, of how educated
people of good will such as the Cooke sisters could not only believe but want
to believe in a God of double predestination (to be persuaded that something
is simply true and thus must be credited is one thing, but to revel in one's own

fortunate elite status may seem another). We need not feel superior. We have our own senses of elite identities to which "I and certain other of the right-minded few—or we/you-and-I" belong, while most of humanity are left outside to gnash their teeth. For any circle by virtue of having an "in" side also defines an outside. (Perhaps the great challenge of applied social science will be to find ways of helping people participate in such empowering group identities while yet minimizing the destructive effects of their inevitable anathematizing.) The predestinationist contentedly consigning most of humanity to eternal damnation by arbitrary decree of a just and loving God was different from the rest of us in historical detail, not in the general dynamics of social processes. I have just illustrated the point in setting myself (and you, reader) in a class of "educated people of good will" who would not believe in any such doctrine as double predestination.

In similar fashion the sermon passage above throws out a net to catch its readers, beckoning them into the company of the elect so paradoxically defined as that which one cannot choose but can only be overcome by. For humanistically educated women like the Cooke sisters, the power of this appeal must have been enormous. Where else in their experience had they ever been offered so much respect for their capacities as to be beckoned into the company of yoke-fellows in the Lord's work of gathering together and sustaining his beloved Elect?

Further, the appeal to the reader to see himself or herself as that redeemed, effectuous "thou" is only one of Ochino's two basic sender-receiver strategies. The other is its natural alternative within the oppositional terms of enunciatee-definition here, to assume a damned reader: a cynic raising question after question against the sacred doctrine, thereby demonstrating incapacity to understand it and a sure identity among the reprobate. Note an example from the sermon "Whether it be good or euell to beleue that we are elect."

> If also thou wouldest say in beleuinge to be elect thou shouldest peraduenture be begyled, therefore it is euell. I wold yet answer, that I would soner geue faithe to the holy gost whiche testifieth in the hartes of the electe, that thei are the sonnes of God (as Paule wryteth) then to the that woldest put me in doubt of it. The electe do heare inwardlye in their hartes a spirituall voyce, quycke and diuyne, whiche biddeth them not doubte, and that they are sure of theire saluacion, and that God loueth them, and hathe taken them for his chyldren. . . . If thou woldest sai it might be, not the spirite of God but their imagynacyons, I saye, that what so euer it is they knowe better then thou, for that (as Paule saythe) none knoweth what is in man but the spyryte of man, that is wythin hym. (Sermon no. 15, H7-H7verso)

One can picture Ochino rising tall in the pulpit and taking on a face of mixed sadness and intimidation: the questioning "thou" reader is belligerently accused of competing with the Holy Spirit, causing needless painful doubt, and pre-sumptuously claiming better knowledge of the inside of people's subjectivity than they have themselves. Within the progression of addresses to this second, questioning "thou," several such exclusionary ploys push the questioner out step by step from the celebrated feeling-state of the elect and into an identity every way repudiated.

The sermons on predestination, making up just over half the set of twenty-five (and most of the nineteen translated by Anne Cooke),[6] oscillate back and forth between addressing the hypothetically saved implied reader—installed within the address relationship of "we (thou and I)," as Habermas defines it[7]—and the hypothetically damned reader challenging the doctrine. Whether the ordering of the sermons is Ochino's or Anne Cooke's, it does seem deliberately based on this oscillation pattern. The rhetorical effect for the actual reader (as opposed to the two implied readers) must have been one of being shunted back and forth over the void between damnation and salvation and being urged to leap across.

The reader who responds positively, then, must do so with full and active assent, becoming a self-canceled self leaping into a new identity based on the feeling-state of exhilaration at being enfolded among the elect, where this ex-hilaration becomes the only fundamental value, the only key to self-conceptu-alizing. The elect must have cast away entirely their own past sense of merit, conceding that the new redeemed self is utterly a matter of God's choice and doing, for if their salvation "in the least iote depended vpon them," they would be damned. To put off the old Adam and to put on Christ in this way is "as if a poore man were sodenly made an Emperoure . . . [he] chaungeth thoughtes, effectes, desyres and wyll, chaungeth frenshipes, practises, words, worckes and life." And further, in the same concluding sermon (15: "Of the effectes wrought by the spirite of God when it entred into the soule"):

> These such for that they walke accordying to the vocacion of god, haue hon-our of euery enterprise that they take in hand, they cannot be letted or re-sisted, no more then God. Yea it is force that euery one feare theym, as Herode feared Saint John Baptyste. . . . They are daylye more firme and stablyshed . . . althoughe their mind be conuersaunt in heauen, neuertheles descendying by Christian pytye, to fele the miseryes of theyr brethren, they laboure also to drawe them to Christ, and moue them to haue the spirite.

The dubious logic of trying to "move other people to have the Spirit" if their chance of doing so has been predecided for them from all eternity shows that the predestinationist's doctrine is a determinant not for discriminations in particular choices and behavior, but sheerly for identity formation and the valu-ations dependent upon it.[8] For the answer to this objection was that one might perhaps be called to be the instrument of a certain elect person's coming to salvation and thus, always hoping the best, should try to be so in every case. The doctrine would sustain a sense of God as choosing one for intimacy as a person chooses another person for such, it being not thinkable after all to choose everyone in that way.

Lady Bacon and her sisters remained of this Calvinist viewpoint throughout their adult lives, and it needs to be kept firmly in mind when we study them. It did not result in the emotional fluctuations familiar in modern evangelical Protestantism (periodic devastation of the self-concept and reconversion); rather it seems to have supplied them with a steady sense of validation that was fundamental to their practice as writers and activists, as if they thought indeed that they should "not be resisted, no more than God." It was not the working-class predestinationism of later "dissenters" like the tinker-preacher John Bunyan; it was rather an aristocratic identity that in some measure counteracted the silencing import of their identity as women. For them, rereading such texts as these Ochino sermons after one had already long considered oneself elect would be a reinforcing of that identity formation through momentarily, in an act of imagination, looking again down into the void one had left behind and feeling a renewed intensity through communion with those who might be doing so for the first time.

The Cooke sisters and their male coactivists in the battles of religious ideology were eventually silenced, as the party of ongoing radical reform lost its campaign to reduce prelatical and royal power in the English church and to replace traditional with iconoclastic liturgy. (It was, incidentally, very much the same effort in which Spenser's *Shepheardes Calender* in 1579 took part, even though he saw Mildred's husband Burghley as one of the chief enemies—by then the sisters had lost their contest with the queen to keep Burghley toward the reformist end of the spectrum.) Lady Bacon, after 1576 a widow with a fairly free hand, became noted for illegal sheltering of delicensed preachers, whose offenses typically were that they refused to wear clerical robes when saying service, continued taking part in forbidden prayer and Bible study meetings called "prophesyings," and preached improvised sermons of their own rather than reading out the prescribed homilies. By then she had, in Habermas's terms, moved from communicative to strategic action only.

In 1572 the Cooke sisters had worked together on a set of verses addressing that moment of late intraconsensual conflict that I have described above. It was an effort to help the celebrated preacher Edward Dering, who, as noted, had insulted the queen in a sermon of 1570, preached in her presence; he had urged that she was being sinfully complacent in tolerating an ill-educated clergy and mercenary leadership in her national church. Dering was a powerful polemicist and up to that point had taken a centrist position, for the sake of unity urging the more radical clergy to conformity in what he agreed to consider superficial matters, like the wearing of vestments. But his loss of preaching license and related experiences in the two years after the notorious sermon pushed him into a more radical position. He was moving across—and thereby helping to set the location of—what would become the reformist border of the late Elizabethan church. From 1570 to 1572, efforts were made to regain for him a modicum of royal toleration. One such was a treatise in Italian (the queen's best modern foreign language), channeled through its dedicatee, her greatest favorite the Earl of Leicester, who was supporting Dering: it was a compendium of received scientific thinking called the *Giardino cosmografico coltivato*, by a Doctor Bartholo Sylva of Turin, who there shows himself to have been an exile seeking favor at court, and a Protestant convert—so it would seem from the prefatory materials' presentation of him.[9] Dering's Greek verses in the MS say that he himself has "opened up this dense springing thicket," i.e., of Sylva's cosmographic garden treatise, suggesting that he helped prepare the 'garden' treatise for court presentation and also converted this "Silva" (wood) to Protestantism.[10] Besides Dering's verses, the treatise was adorned with other dedicatory pieces in Greek, Latin, and several more languages by, among others, the four Cooke sisters and Dering's wife, the former Anne Locke, a close friend of John Knox who herself had published translations of Calvin's sermons and a sequence of sonnets in English, perhaps by Knox, though some scholars argue they are her own.[11]

The manuscript (C.U.L.Ii.5.37) has strikingly well executed color illustrations, for example of Chaos with swirling, interweaving storm shapes in various colors shading into each other, and of two new world cities, Peruvian Cuzco and Aztec Temistitan, the latter shown spread around its pale lakeful of islands, with fiery volcanos lining the southern shore. On geography it is up to date: the straits of Magellan and the discoveries of Menendez's 1566 voyage are included; it notes the French colonies in Canada and Florida, the Spanish ones around the Carribbean and South America up to the bay of Baja California, and the island of Japan bounding the Pacific Ocean. A color diagram shows the global lines of latitude and longitude. Yet around this up-to-date earth, in another chart in gold ink and elegant, subdued colors, glitters an armillary sphere of the Ptolemaic universe with all eleven "heavens," out to the primum mobile, the habitation of God and the most elevated angels. Chapters on what we would call chemistry and biology taxonomize the things of the sublunary world, consisting of earth, air, fire, and water, and many poems or excerpts of verse on natural philosophy (i.e., science) by Petrarch, Alciato, Ariosto, and others are included. A full-color picture of the dark and handsome, trim-bearded Dr. Bartholo Sylva, age thirty, adorns the flyleaf. Matters of religious controversy are not broached. The whole production was calculated to please the queen. She loved things Italian in general and handsome, learned young Italian men in particular (points that Sylva hints at in praising her in his preface to the reader). The book was to be an intellectual and visual treat for Leicester and the queen.

The dedicatory materials include a whole page of verses in Greek by Dering, Lady Burghley, and Lady Hoby: the Burghley name under Dering's would bespeak the queen's ever-faithful secretary, just then busy arranging to have the Duke of Norfolk executed for trying to overthrow her,[12] and the Hoby name was to remind her of the widow's former husband Sir Thomas, who had translated Castiglione's *Courtier* and died in Paris at his post as ambassador, being then honored for his service by a letter to the widow from the queen herself. The whole production was to stress without explicit statement that Dering and the reformist party supporting him are learned, cultivated, internationally respected, and loyal to the queen—not to be ignored. Ochino's sermon image about the godly elect as possessors of all the thinkable world has here taken elegant visual and textual form.

Lady Hoby's poem, like most of the others playing on the name Sylva as a "wood," is as follows. This and the other translations from Greek are by Lynn Roller.

Τὶς πόθεν ἦ ἀνερῶν ὁ χαρακτηρίσας ὁ Σύλβας
    τοῦδε πέδον κήπου τοῦ σάφα οἶδε φίλε
'Αλλ' εὕρημ' αὐτοῦ καὶ καλῶν αἵρεσις ἄνθων
    τιμία τὴν πρώτην ὦσχην ἐμοιγὲ δοκεῖ
῎Εινεκ' εὐαρμόσου καὶ εὐωδέως ἔινεκα κήπου
    προσφόρα τ' ἥρωι τοῦ προσένεικε δόσις.

{Who, from where among men, has designated for Sylva
    The place of this garden, which he clearly knows, O friend?
In any case his discovery and choice of lovely flowers
    Seem to me honorable things, the first shoot
Through the fragrant, harmonious garden a boon
    To the hero, of things his gift has brought forth.}

There may be a pun on *haeresis*, choice, playing on the Catholic term "heresy" for Protestantism: a choice and a "heresy" of intellectual flowers are here. The Earl of Leicester as dedicatee is presumably the noble hero to whom this "garden" is offering these first fruits of Sylva's intellectual efforts. The locale of the garden here intended is that of the redeemed, Edenic nature, newly growing in the woodsy author Sylva; since this metaphoric point is made in a number of the dedicatory poems, he seems to have been a fairly recent Protestant convert.[13] Most tellingly, Dering's case as a suppliant for renewed tolerance from the queen is plugged since, with this poem of Lady Hoby's appearing right under his own, the rhetorical question (*who* designated for Sylva the way to grace?) hints at Dering as the powerful preacher who converted him. (See n. 9 for Dering's own poem here, making the same case that he could convert a man such as Sylva, but has not yet recovered royal favor.)

Having earlier looked at Lady Bacon's translation of Ochino on predestination, let us consider as another sample of the *Giardino*'s dedicatory pieces the one that is in all probability her contribution, although the name above it has been carefully erased (the only such erasure here), leaving the initials "A. B." with the right number of spaces for Anna Baconia. Her husband, Sir Nicholas Bacon, as Lord Keeper of the Great Seal was the judiciary officer chiefly responsible for prosecuting Dering in the Star Chamber when he was, the next year after the manuscript's completion, permanently deprived of his preaching license (Collinson *Mirror* 21); thus the name Anne Bacon was presumably ordered erased, though the other three sisters give their full names in Latin form.

As do Lady Hoby's Greek verses, Lady Bacon's Latin hexameters play on the name "sylva," the forest, to suggest Bartholo Sylva's putting on of a new godly self in religious conversion through the image of his nature's being transformed from a wild, thorny, wood into a cultivated, neo-Edenic garden, textually set forth in this "garden" of his book. This is one meaning of her opening line, that the book reveals its nature in its title; she also means that the "garden" is stocked with rich intellectual fruits ("helps," as scholars called them) that one will delight to have at hand, ready for plucking—i.e., for looking up when queries arise. This and the subsequent translations from Latin are by Connie McQuillen.[14]

> Se titulo prodit liber hic, quantasque recondat,
> Ipse suo fidens nomine monstrat, opes.
> Promittit mundum, promittit sidera, sed quem
> Ad se non rapient nomina tanta virum?
> Nec coelum tenebris, nec mundus sentibus horret.
> Scilicet artificem sentit uterque manum.
> SYLVA prius, sed nunc est hortus amoenior, ut tu,
> Quisquis es, in mediis ex patiere rosis.

>> {By the title this book declares itself, its wealth of aids
>> Stored up it shows, on its own name relying.
>> It offers the world, offers the stars, but what man
>> Will not such names themselves enrapture?
>> Heaven does not shudder at darkness, nor earth at thorns.
>> For each perceives the crafting hand.
>> What first was a SYLVAN wood is a more amenable garden, so
>> Whoever you are, you may stroll off your path into roses.}

These verses by the mother of Sir Francis Bacon make a suggestive, compact meditation on the experience of perusing the scientific treatise. The power of artifice is seen as selection and cultivation from out of a universe of darkness and thorns. The orderliness of the "crafting hand" is reflected in the ideationally chiasmic symmetry of the phrases (ll. 3 and 5) *promittit mundum, promittit sidera . . . nec coelum, nec mundus,* i.e., a chiasmic pattern of "world-stars-heaven-world." And the metaphor of the human compared to the divine craft of making, soon to get notable expression in Sidney's *Apology for Poetry*, is here *in nuce*: Sylva's crafting of his book is seen as analogous to and emergent from the divine crafting of a redeemed "garden" nature within himself.

Ann Rosalind Jones (8) notes that Renaissance women, in order to write, sometimes created an authorial persona for themselves by dramatizing themselves as respected members of some intellectual group; here we see Anne Bacon thus dramatizing and identifying with her intended readers (invited to walk in the roses), in the person of one among them, the pious appreciators of a treatise on science, who can admire and take part in the worldview of the group of educated, highly placed Protestants supporting Dering and Sylva.

The two oldest Cooke sisters, Ladies Burghley and Bacon, as wives of such prominent officials, seem to have been even more constrained in their efforts to write than were their younger sisters: like the Greek verses for Sylva's treatise, every piece of writing that has survived of Lady Burghley's (or of which mention has survived—e.g., a dedication letter with a Bible she is said to have donated to Cambridge University—see Barns; McIntosh) was either in Greek or was a translation from Greek, truly a medium for the few, in which scandal was unlikely to be caused; and as mentioned, we here in all probability see Lady Bacon being forced to erase her name. (She was no less committed to the cause for all that: she allowed her Ochino sermons to be reissued about this time, even though Ochino by 1570 was no name to conjure by.)[15]

The most militant of the sisters may have been the youngest, Katherine, wife of the Cornish diplomat Sir Henry Killigrew: her warm affection for Edward Dering, indicated in his surviving letters to her,[16] suggests that she may have been the initiator of this Sylva treatise's presentation as an effort to help Dering. Such relationships as hers with Dering, like the earlier one of Anne Locke (later Dering) with John Knox (see Collinson "Women"), show us further dimensions of the energies and dynamics of these circles of people as ideological groups: an intelligent and committed woman could find an affectionate relationship with someone other than her husband, all in the godly cause.

Following the "A. B." verses is a longer piece by Katherine, likewise in Latin and celebrating Sylva's religious transformation into a lovely garden nature, but going into more naturalistic detail. Her verses urge support for the author (and behind him the preacher) through a clever mode of address: the implied reader is made to represent at once the author Sylva and the reader enjoying Sylva's treatise: as *you* seek the nature of the world, as you explore the stars, may you find a safe haven here, etc. That is, the details apply equally to Sylva as a refugee seeking favor and to the reader as a mental pilgrim seeking knowledge; the device works to make the desired patrons identify with the learned Italian doctor and the Dering cause that his treatise serves.

Cathelina Chilligrea in D. B. Sylua

Qui cupis assiduos coeli cognoscere cursus,
    Et quas observent astra superba vices.
Qui vaga scrutaris sinuosi climata mundi,
    Quam varios habeat patria quaeque situs.
Siste gradum, tutos intret tua cymbula portus,
    In nostro properum littore siste gradum.
Huc, citus huc properes, simul hoc versatur in horto
    Quicquid habet mundus sidera quicquid habent.
At modo SYLVA fuit spinosis ob sita dumis,
    Crevit in inculta sentis acutus humo,
Iam pellunt hirtos argentea lilia sentes.
    Dumorum subeunt alba ligustra locum.
Iam cedit violae siluestris spina intenti,
    Praestat odoratas terra reculta rosas.
Quae modo montanis concessit pascua bobus,
    Coecaque carnivoris praestitit antra feris,
Serta Palatini producit laurea Phoebi,
    Et Parnassiacis terra rigatur aquis.
Ergo frondiferae sit gratia plurima SYLVAE,
    Nam parit auricomas SYLVA reculta rosas.

[Katherine Killegrew on D. B. Sylva

You who wish to know the heavens' eternal course,
    And the vagaries that lofty stars observe
You who track the shifting climates of sinuous earth,
    How diversely each country holds its quarters;
Stay your step, let your skiff come into harbors
    On our shore, stay your hastening step.
Hither, hasten here, in this garden dwells together
    Whatever belongs to the world or to the stars.
The SYLVAN WOOD was lately full of sharp briars,
    The prickly thorn controlled the untilled earth,
Now silver lilies push away rough thorns.
    The white privet takes the bramble's place
The thorn now yields the violet to an eager woodland,
    The renewed land presents its fragrant roses.
The pastures it lately left to mountain cattle
    And dark caves it kept for carnivorous beasts,
Produce the laurel garlands of Palatine Phoebus,
    And land watered by Parnassian streams.

So let there be many thanks to the leaf-bearing SYLVA
For the WOOD recultivated bears gold-petaled roses.]

Other Verse by Katherine and Elizabeth

Besides that one from the cosmographic garden, we can take as a further sample from Katherine Killigrew's pen a little occasion poem to Lady Burghley that she wrote at some point when she wanted influence applied to prevent her husband's being sent abroad on a mission—perhaps a time of approaching childbirth.[17] Like Elizabeth's first husband Hoby, Killigrew was a diplomat, veteran of Marian exile travels, and an influential county gentleman who supported reformist causes and ministers.[18] The following occasion poem from Katherine to Mildred must date from between November 1565, when Katherine married, and late 1570.[19] It was recorded and admired by Sir John Harington in notes to his translation of Ariosto's *Orlando Furioso* (313–14); it also appears in the commonplace book of one W. Kytton (C. U. L. MS Ff.5.14, fol. 107), who seems to have been a reformist cleric[20] and perhaps knew Mrs. Killigrew.

Si mihi quem cupio cures Mildreda remitti
Tu bona, tu melior, tu mihi sola soror:
Sin male cessando retines, vel trans mare mittis,
Tu mala, tu peior, tu mihi nulla soror.
Is si Cornubiam, tibi pax sit et omnia laeta,
Sin mare, Ciciliae nuncio bella. vale.

Kytton did the translations below as he copied the verses into his book, taking two versions in poulter's measure rhymes to get the sense of the compressed lines. Written within a few years or perhaps months of the original, his renditions may serve as our translation here.

If Myldred thowe procure, my Joyes retorne to be,
Thow shalt be good and better to, a sister dere to me
But tryflynge yf he staye, or passe the seas he shall,
thow shalt be yll, and wors then yll no sister then at all,
To Cornwall yf he come, in peace then shalt thow dwell
but yf to Sea, to Cycyll then, I warre proclaym, farewell

[Another way]

If Myldrede thowe retorne, my Joye to me ageyne,
Thowe shalt be good, and better to, my onelye syster then,
but yf thow hym deteyne, and to the sea assygne,
thowe shalt be yll, and more then yll, no sister then of myne
To Cornwall yf he come, great pleysure shall ensue,
but yf to sea, to Cycyll then I warre proclayme, Adewe

The fun of the Latin original is in its phrasal symmetry (*tu bona* balanced against *tu mala*, etc.) and in its whimsical mock seriousness ("I proclaim war against the Cecils"), playing off a sisterly intimacy against the tone of public weightiness that such compressed Latin verse usually has. The one sister is playfully reminding the other of their youthful days at Latin grammar, when they had to recite "good, better, best" and "bad, worse, worst"; she varies the mock exercise by revising the chain to "good, better, and only" sister, counterbalanced by "bad, worse, and no" sister. Here we seem to catch a personal note of Katherine's temperament; she was reputed the best-natured of the sisters. She wrote her own epitaph[21] and died young, and her sister Elizabeth, too, wrote some elegiac verses, also on her tomb (Ballard 204–205—see Appendix 2).

It is Elizabeth, writer of the Greek verses above, who by becoming a specialist of the graveside has left us, along with quite a few letters,[22] a considerable body of verse, including some in English. The disappointment of having both husbands die young and on the verge of notable career success, in the second case advancement to the peerage, led her to channel her writing urges into memorials for them and other family members. In that vein she is perhaps most remembered for the still surviving Hoby tombs at Bisham (see Rowse's vivid account and a photograph in Wilson, and for the texts my Appendix 2 below, taken from Ashmole 2:464–71): there her statue kneels in a viscountess coronet, signifying her status as wife of the first Russell heir of the Earl of Bedford; before her lies a wrapped infant figure for Francis, the Russell son she lost, behind her the three youthfully dead daughters, the two Hoby ones having died a week apart aged nine and seven (perhaps of something like polio, since their younger brother grew up undersized and deformed); then outside the canopy are her three surviving children, Edward Hoby and the brother just mentioned, Thomas Posthumous Hoby (Sir Thomas had left her pregnant when he died in Paris), and Anne Russell Herbert.

As we recall her commemorations of her first marriage, we should note that for the Hobys and Cookes, Castiglione's neo-Platonic *Courtier*, of which Hoby's translation became so influential, was very much a part of their internationalist Protestant worldview. The Sylva treatise illustrations visualize its neo-Platonic ideal of the loving soul rising level by level from contemplation of earthly beauties to contemplation of God. Reformational historians point out that Ficino had gone from study of Plato and Christian neo-Platonists to analysis of the Pauline letters, on which he gave lectures that influenced Colet and Lefevre, and through them Erasmus and Luther (Church 2). Thus Castiglione's duke and duchess presiding over the idealized courtly sociability and hospitality of the household where those marvellous conversations about love occur must have been in the back of Lady Russell's mind when, in the mortuary verse for her husbands, she portrayed them at the communion of the elect in heaven. The combination of neo-Platonism and Protestant theology often noted in Spenser and Sidney was already in place for them in the thinking of such people as the Hobys, for whom Italy meant not so much the pope's country as a land of much-admired oppressed Protestants like their friends Ochino and Sylva. (Tedeschi [7] notes that the Italian Protestant church in London was attended by more English people than Italians, and partly for the purpose of learning Italian.)

As a fuller example of Lady Russell's verse let us consider what is in effect an elegiac cycle of poems from the Westminster Abbey tomb she ordered erected for Lord Russell. I make this choice in order to clarify what lies behind the eighteenth-century English translation of some of these verses, by Richard Bentley the Younger, printed in the modern anthology *The Paradise of Women* as if it were a poem originally in English by Lady Elizabeth Russell.[23] Other funerary verse of Lady Russell's has been recorded, besides that at Bisham and on Katherine Killigrew's tomb as noted above, that from the Cooke tomb at Romford[24] and from a neighbor's tomb near Bisham (Ashmole 2:491). Incidentally, Lady Russell had written more verse for both the Hoby and Russell tombs than she was allowed to include: she has a line to that effect in both sets (see below). This is one of the instances where we see the little textual space women thought they had won being trimmed (see also on Elizabeth Weston, below). It was unusual to have extensive verses carved on tombs, even of the wealthy and prominent; most simply give the decedent's titles, vital statistics, coat of arms, and perhaps a pious saying. The stone-carvers' patience may have been tried.

The best text of the Russell cycle is in *Reges, Reginae, Nobiles, et Alii in Ecclesia Collegiata B. Petri Westmonasterii sepulti* (1606, 44–46). In working out the following text, the translators and I have also consulted the other two surviving sources.[25] The Calvinist tenet noted above about faith as source of the only permanent elements in the saved person's identity is evident in the first poem here.

[Tomb of Lord John Russell, Westminster Abbey]

> 'Εις θάνατον φιλτάτου καὶ λαμπρωτάτου αὐτῆς ἀνδρὸς Κυρίου Ρυσσελλίου τὸ παρὰ τῆς 'Ελιζαβήτης Ρυσσελλίας γράφεν ἐπιτάφιον.

{On the death of her most beloved
and most illustrious husband Lord Russell,
the epitaph written by Elizabeth Russell.}

Mens mea crudeli laniatur saucia morsu,
Cum subit oblatae mortis imago tuae.

Vere novo haeres Comitis tu floris ad instar,
Usque cadens miseras, meque measque facis.
Quippe decor[,] vultus, linguae, moresque probati,
Tum doctrina perit, sed viget alma fides.

{My wounded mind is torn by death's pitiless feeding
When the figure of your death, now solemnized, approaches.
Indeed so lately heir of an earl, like a flower always,
In falling you leave both me and mine wretched.
Truly elegance, looks, language, and just character
Perish, then teachings too; but nurturing faith grows green.}

Carmina aerumnosae matris in superstites filias.
{ *Verses of the devastated mother on her surviving daughters*}

Νῦν ψυχῆς γλυκυτερπνὸν ἐμῆς οἴκου τε φάεινον
    πάτριδος ἤδε πόθον τῇδε· κέκευθε κόνις
φεῦ μὴν οἱ ξυραὶ χήρη κοῦραι τε θύγατρες
    τερπωλὴν ζωῆς αἷς περιεῖλε θανὼν
εὐσεβίης ἕνεκα πλὴν ὄλβου σεμνὸς ἐπαυρεῖ
    οὐρανίου μετόχους συγγενέας καλεῶν.

{Now dust has covered the sweet delight of my soul
And house, and shining longing of this fatherland.
Alas for the shorn ones, the widow and maidens his daughters,
For he in dying took from them life's delight.
Through his piety, the blessed man partakes of joy,
Calling the dwellers in heaven his spirit-kindred.}

Eiusdem in eundem Latine.[26]

Plangite nunc natae, nunc flebile fundite carmen,
    Occidit heu vestrae gloria sola domus.
Mors rapit immitis florentem stemmate claro,
    Praesignem literis, tum pietate patrem.
Haeredi Comitis quin vos succrescite, tali
    Ortu qui nituit sed bonitate magis.

{*By the same on the same in Latin*

Weep now, daughters, now chant out a mourning poem,
    Alas he has died, the only glory of our home.
Bitter death has ravished that flower in bright nobility,
    Distinguished in letters as in piety, your father.

Heirs of an earl, grow up indeed—from such a springing
Start you have thrived—but grow mainly in goodness.}

Carmina aerumnosae matris Dominae Elizabethae Russ in obitum filii.

En solamen avi, patris pergrata voluptas,
Ipsa medulla mihi, tristia fata tulit:
O utinam mater jacuissem lumine cassa
Solvissetque prior justa suprema mihi!
Conqueror ac frustra, statuit quia numen id ipsum,
Orba ut terrenis sola superna petam.
IN ALTO REQUIES.

{*Verses of the devastated mother Lady Elizabeth Russell on the death of her son*

O comfort of a grandfather, a father's happiest desire,
The very marrow of me, sad fate has taken you:
O that I, the mother, lay dead, the light denied me,
And he had first fulfilled my final rites!
I weep but in vain, for divine will itself has decreed that
Alone, bereft of earthly things, I seek the spheres above.
REST ON HIGH}

*In obitum honoratissimi viri Domini Johannis Russelli, soceri
sui charissimi Ed. Hobii Militis Epicedion.*

Mors (Russelle) tibi somno suffudit ocellos,
Mens tamen in coelis nescia mortis agit.
Qui vitam sanctam meliori fine peregit,
Vivit, & evicta morte superstes erit.
Quis, qualis, quantus fueris tua stemmata monstrant,
Integra vita docet, morsque dolenda probat:
Sat sit privigno, posuisse haec carmina pauca;
Tu sibi mente parens, filius ille tibi.

{*An Epicedion by Ed. Hoby, Knight, on the death of the most
honorable man Lord John Russell, his most dear step-father*

Death, Russell, has covered your beloved eyes in sleep,
But your mind, not knowing death, has gone to heaven.
Whoever has lived a holy life with still better end
Lives, and when death is vanquished will survive.
Who you were, what sort, and how much, your heraldry shows,
Your unstained life teaches, and your woeful death proves.

> May it suffice for a step-son to have offered these few verses,
>   You in spirit a father to him, he a son to you.}

Right noble twise by vertue and by birth,
Of heauen lou'd, and honour'd on the earth;
His Countries hope, his kindreds chiefe delight,
My husband deare more than this worlds light
Death hath me reft: but I from death will take
His memory to whom this tombe I make.
Iohn was his name, (ah, was) wretch must I say
Lord Russell once, now my tear-thirstie clay.

Quod licuit feci, vellem mihi plura licere.

> {I have done what was allowed, I wish more were allowed me.}

The lost husband's worth is elevated through the perspectives of several valuating respondents surrounding his death: countrymen, kindred, above all "heaven" (of his place among the godly elect she has no doubt), and intermittently throughout, the grieving wife herself. From the macabre opening image of the corpse at the funeral, looking already partly eaten away by death—imagined as an animalistic feeder preying upon it—to the concluding pentameter couplets in English, portraying the poet dropping her small useless tears into the long dryness of the tomb (his "tear-thirsty clay"), the cycle manages to create some striking effects. And in case we might wonder whether Lawrence Stone (98) was right about the "low affect" parent-child relationship of aristocrats in those times, i.e., that mothers became inured to all the many deaths of their children, this poem on little Francis Russell (as even more the Bisham one on the two Hoby girls—see Appendix 2) gives us some data.

Mortuary verse is of course quite limited in the range of material that will be found decorous—Lady Russell cannot show the deceased as he lived and breathed, in his daily quirks and ways. All must be spoken in that solemnly respectful tone of the time after a recent death. Within those limits it seems to me that she succeeded in marking out these deaths from many others. The German traveler Paul Hentzner in 1598 was struck by the first two pieces (in Latin and in Greek) and copied them out as a single macaronic poem—the one beginning with death's pitiless feeding and the other ending with the blessed man's compensatory communion in heaven.

After Lady Russell had managed to get up this monument with its verses to "the surviving daughters," young Elizabeth Russell, not a month after her sister's grand court wedding to Henry Herbert, heir to the Earl of Worcester, died bizarrely of bleeding from a needle prick. Lady Russell then went back to add that other monument, described above, to the tombs at Bisham; there all her recalcitrant children, living and dead, Hoby and Russell, are brought together kneeling, in an image embodying her high ambitions: that she and they should be exalted on earth and in their deaths blessed in the Lord. (Her eldest son, whose "epicedion" we have just seen, she had matched up with a daughter of Henry Carey, Lord Hunsdon, the queen's cousin; and her Russell daughters, like their aunts the countesses of Warwick and Cumberland, had been ladies in waiting to the queen.) She was an ambitious woman. She tried to keep a hand in the affairs of the church through her powerful brother-in-law Burghley and his son Robert Cecil, who eventually took over his father's secretaryship: she sought to influence appointments of bishops and other clergy (see Wilson). She wanted to help create a worthy family and a worthy national church.

Rowse and Wilson portray her as an overly aggressive, crotchety old woman while conceding also her intelligence and habit of often proving right. I see her as a frustrated poet, who tried to shape her family into the poetry for which she could find so little public space. She should be remembered not only as Robert Cecil's bothersome old doctrinaire aunt but as the young woman of elegant, oval face and penetrating eyes in Holbein's Edwardian sketch of her, translating Ponet, later perhaps reading Castiglione with Thomas Hoby,[27] and eventually commemorating her husbands and children in effective verse in three languages. The patronage project of Sylva and Dering had given her a rare chance at a paratextual space for showing off her Greek. But the tombs became her metier.

In the Cooke sisters' surviving writings we can trace the progression that I earlier suggested and theorized through the concepts of Habermas, a progression that humanistically educated women with writing ability sometimes went through, as activists within ideological circles: they began with the most subordinately paratextual mode of writing, namely translations of polemical works, then some of them, possibly, moved to a more individualized sort of paratext offering a chance for the writer to express something of her own thinking, such as prefaces and dedicatory verse; of those who proceeded thus far, a few might manage to move on to some other kind of textual space affording still more opportunity to speak with one's own voice, as Lady Russell did in her mortuary elegies. If those scholars are right who argue that Anne Locke herself wrote the sonnets she published along with her Calvin sermon translations (see n. 11), she would be another example of a woman moving to that third stage, finding a voice through religious activism and its writing.

3

Authorial Identity for a Second-Generation Protestant Aristocrat

The Countess of Pembroke

M ARY SIDNEY HERBERT, Countess of Pembroke, used her resources to work for the international reformist cause, as the Cooke sisters had, and like them turned to writing efforts aimed both within and beyond the circle of her ideological fellow travelers—as Habermas would say, to both communicative and strategic action (see chapter 2). And since her husband did not hold any very sensitive political office and tolerated her activities, keeping to property affairs, she enjoyed more scope than the Cooke sisters had. But her generation's major reformist effort would not be for further liturgical and structural change within the English state church (the 1570s had seen the end of that, with the failure of the "admonishers" and then the close shave of the queen's proposed Catholic marriage). Rather, they would primarily push for maximum support of French and Dutch Calvinism. After the battlefield death abroad of her much-loved brother Sir Philip Sidney, she found her own interconnected ways to do that: by cultivating his image as a martyr through editing and publishing his writings, by interacting intellectually with certain writers, musicians, and clerics, and by continuing in her own household her brother's experiments with verse translation, prosody, and Psalms, as well as the explorations of pastoral, in which she had been an intimate partner of his original writing of the *Arcadia* (done mostly "in your presence," his dedication says). While commentators have lately downplayed the countess's patronage,[1] these interlinked processes, including some measure of patronage, enabled her to develop herself as a writer through carrying on much of her brother's political identity.

At the center of these processes was her life amidst the readings and singing of her local circle of waiting women, male employees (chaplain and doctor), and occasionally present protégés—those "nymphs and swains of Pembrokiana" portrayed by her most devoted poet Abraham Fraunce in his *Ivychurch* part 3. Thus we see again that nurturing ground of writing studied and theorized through Tony Bennett's concept in chapter 1, the "reading formation" of a lady and her mostly female entourage. Now we look at an instance of the upper end of that formation's social spectrum: in this case the great lady rather than a waiting woman found written public voice.

Extensive work has already been done on the countess by Waller, Hannay, Brennan, Lamb, and others. Here I want to focus on psychodynamic and group-centered aspects of her development as a translator and writer finding in her own carefully formed reading circle a base for addressing a broader audience to urge commitment to international Protestantism. She had largely to create this circle for herself, as locus for an authorial identity.[2] As was mentioned in chapter 2, Ann Rosalind Jones has observed that a Renaissance woman could sometimes "construct a public self through group identification" by dramatizing "her participation in a prestigious literary circle" (8), but Jones gives no examples of Englishwomen in this category. The countess did construe her literary identity through interaction with a reading circle, but not an independently existent one; not being able to expect acceptance as a writer at court (partly for sociosemiotic reasons I have treated elsewhere),[3] she relied on her own Wilton circle, extended by experiences at her London residence and extended textually by manuscripts sent (often dedicated) to her, as well as by the circulating of her own manuscripts. Thus she became the "Pembrokiana" and "Lady Regent" of Fraunce's pastorals, the (reascribed)[4] "Delia" of Samuel Daniel's sonnets (Daniel's original Delia was presumably someone else if not a fiction proper),[5] the Phyllis of Thomas Watson's posthumous *Amintae Gaudia* (1592), the Phyllis of some of Nicholas Breton's lute-song lyrics as well as the "Princesse"-patroness of his account of Wilton in *Wits Trenchmour* (*Works* II: 18–19), and the Urania and Clorinda of Spenser (who addressed her presumably from afar, continuing her Urania image from the *Arcadia*). Through these efforts and her own, her circle (or set of concentric circles) took on a certain character and continued the Sidneyan Protestant piety and "areopagite" experiments and debates concerning classical meters, music, and versifying.

As mentioned, Fraunce portrays her reading circle in pastoral form. The attendant ladies appear as Fulvia, Philovevia, Amaryllis, Licoris, Cassiopoea, Dieromena, and Sylvia, plus two others more particularized: Aresia "of a severe and maydenlike disposition," and "good old Daphne . . . odd in conceit," who tells a satirical tale of Cambridge pedants. Fraunce's list of nine suggests that the countess kept a large entourage of women (though some of these may be relatives present for the occasion being described), and that in his mind certain of them were distinctive in personality and preferences. In a portrayal implying that the countess actually commemorated her brother's death anniversary each year with lamentational "passtimes," they meet in the park of her small Ivychurch estate near Wilton to tell stories and read out poems. Each woman strives to speak well, because "Soe much wrought in her hart sweete sight of *Pembrokiana*, / Soe much did she desyre to be praysd of *Pembrokiana*" (sig.

E$_{IV}$). Fraunce is no doubt presenting himself in "Elpinus," supplying learned commentary on the ladies' Ovidian tales. The other swains presumably refer to writers who have praised the countess, perhaps even some who never visited Wilton (i.e., the scene may be idealized, as is Spenser's "Colin Clouts Come Home Again," which includes people who were not actually there at the portrayed meeting). As in Fraunce's earlier writings for the countess, the sources of his terms are Tasso's pastoral play the *Aminta*, where a poet-lover seemingly loses his beloved shepherdess Silvia to death (though she eventually turns out to be alive and they are united), and the work that became for Elizabethans its cross-cultural extension, Thomas Watson's neo-Latin eclogues paraphrased by Fraunce into English hexameters as the *Lamentations of Amyntas for his Phillis* (1587).

Of the probably depicted swains besides Fraunce himself, Breton was a prolix writer whose best talent was with lyrics for music (see Fellowes and below). And there would be Daniel, who credited the countess with giving him the idea at Wilton to publish his "Delia" sonnets as a book (1592).[6] In the early 1590s there seems to have been a rivalry for her favor, of Fraunce against Breton and Daniel: Watson depicts Fraunce before the countess as "Corydon" debating against one "Faustulus."[7] The two sides continued the Dicus and Lalus positions of Sidney's Arcadian debate over neoclassical quantitative meters versus native stress-based "rhyming." (Daniel's *Defense of Rhyme* would later [Fraunce then being dead][8] give the *quietus* to this quantitative project, which had hung on, I believe, partly because of its relation to musical developments.)[9] But Fraunce in the late 1580s and early 1590s kept turning out his quasi-hexameters and asclepiads, such as we find represented in the countess's Psalms 122 and 123 (Rathmell ed.), while Breton and Daniel were challenging her with varieties of verse in the rhyming tradition, in her Psalms far more amply represented (see Freer *Music*). A fourth literary man, resident at Wilton, was Hugh Sanford, tutor of her son William and her assistant in editing the *Arcadia*.[10] Thus the countess's waiting women, perhaps a female relative or two, her doctor and chaplain, along with Fraunce, Breton, Daniel, and Sanford are roughly the circle that we should imagine in the *Ivychurch*.

Further, the influential pastoralist, sonneteer, and song translator Thomas Watson was by the early nineties physically at the edge of the group, though, as noted, already important to it through his eclogues. Watson could easily have visited the countess in London; just before he died he was trying to work his way into her patronage through dedicating to her the new eclogues of his *Amintae Gaudia* (Joys of Amyntas), where he depicts himself as a more skilled rival to her other protégés.[11] Perhaps his Catholic background, including studies at Douai and association with the Earl of Oxford (see Eccles and chapter 4), made her wary of dealings with him.

Abraham Fraunce was a lawyer in the court of the Marches of Wales under

the Earl of Pembroke's patronage (Hannay *Phoenix* 106–12). A devoted attendant whose studies had been funded by Philip Sidney, he had been first to find
favor with the countess after Sidney's death in 1586; his dedication to her of
the first edition of *Lamentations of Amyntas* (further editions also dedicated to
her) had presented it as his own intense lamenting for Sidney, and she seems to
have taken it as a personally offered poetic world of grief, where her sorrow
too could find words and music. Implications of this point will be considered
below.

The countess and her associates followed the same technical strategies of
pursuing poetry as had her brother and other courtiers of their generation:
"Englishing" selected Italian and French writers read neo-Platonically, especially Petrarch, and at the same time experimenting with prosody and with
figures of rhetoric.[12] Although she did at least one original poem early in her
efforts (either an early draft of "The Lay of Clorinda," if that is hers [see n.
29], or some other, lost elegy, presumably on her brother),[13] she afterward ex-
perimented through translation and other paratextual writing before eventually
producing more sophisticated, strictly original poems in English, of which at
least three have survived (see Waller ed.).

Levels of Translation: A Charting of Its Kinds

The Countess of Pembroke's verse Psalms should also be considered original poems. In order to make the distinctions needed for description of her
development through translation, I draw now on the field of discourse pragmatics. Gérard Genette has taxonomized the sphere of the "paratextual"
(*Seuils*), classifying into interrelated categories everything from titles to author-
ial-fictive prefaces, to footnotes, to physically nonattached "epitexts" (like
author interviews), describing all such paratexts as variously serving the function of a vestibule ("seuil"), a sphere of negotiation existing between a text
and the social realm of its potential reception, where the author and allied
parties try to fashion a desired pertinent readership. (See also chapters 2 and 7
on the paratextual.) Genette ends by noting that he has excluded translations,
though they have "an undeniable paratextual pertinence," because he wanted
to define the outer border of paratext—that between it and the world of textual
reception—conservatively, and not end up saying that "everything is paratext."[14]

For the purpose of studying what people in Renaissance England did with
translation, I want to take up where Genette left off and propose a graduated
scale of levels of translation, running from most to least directly paratextual,
i.e., most to least directly contingent upon and correlatable with the source
text. We can then better study the Countess of Pembroke's writings with reference to some of the cues she gave and took within her circle of Fraunce,

Breton, Daniel, and others. We can gain a sense of how, as she moved from level to level of translation, she developed her abilities.

Translation Modes from Most to Least Directly Paratextual
(Particular texts can represent gradations between these.)

1. An interlinear world gloss, with no effort at target-language syntax (e.g., Old English glosses within Latin texts)

2. A translation sticking as closely as possible to the source text, in correlated lexical acceptations, grammar, and syntax, even at the price of stiffness and stylistic oddity, though achieving minimal target-language correctness (e.g., a language exam rendition, where the point is to show one's competence in the source language)

3. A translation closely imitative of the source text in lexicon, grammar, and syntax, except that within small-scale grammatical units it occasionally sacrifices word-for-word correlation in favor of naturalness of idiom in the target language

4. A clause-by-clause translation closely reproducing the source text's lexicon and usually its grammar and syntax, but with the translator taking liberties, as these might seem to give a more effective result: e.g., to eliminate word or phrase doublings, and/or to continue metaphoric or other rhetorical figures of the source text into succeeding sentences; or to alter sentence grammar so as to replicate source-text structures such as parallelism

5. A sentence-by-sentence paraphrase often departing from the source text in grammar and syntax and sometimes showing only loose lexical correlation with it, representing the translator's interpretation of the gist of each sentence, in whatever phrasing seems appealing and suitable within the target language (e.g., the exclusively licensed English translations of Thomas Mann's novels)

6. A paraphrase taking paragraphs or other large units as the correlation base unit (e.g., for verse, a whole stanza), not reproducing smaller source-text units of clause or sentence but rendering the general sense of the larger unit, at comparable length (e.g., some of Wyatt's translations of passages from Petrarch's Rime)

7. A. A commentative, expansive paraphrase, including new illustrative material by the translator (e.g., the eighteen-line translation "sonnets" of Thomas Watson's Hekatompathia, 1582, or many of the Countess of Pembroke's psalms)—Svensson and Brennan refer to such a work as a "metaphrase" of its source

or,

B. A condensed version representing, in the translator's view, the central gist of the source text, omitting material considered redundant or supplementary

8. An original text ("original" in the concept underlying its selectivity) consisting mostly of selected translated passages at one or more of the above levels 4–7 (e.g., Spenser's "November" and "December" eclogues of The Shepheardes Calender, *largely paraphrased from the French of Clement Marot)*

9. An original text incorporating occasional passages of allusive, paraphrastic translation (scarcely any "original" Renaissance literary text would fail to fit this category, which is really one kind of intertextual [or in some cases by Genette's terms, hypertextual][15] imitation)

So far I have omitted a range that should be shown, so to speak, as *a shifted set running beside each level from 5 through 8, wherein rhythmic sound in the target language becomes a determinant.* At level 7, for instance, these shifted possibilities would include the following: a paraphrastic rendition determined as much by auditory considerations—e.g., music to which the new text will be sung, and/or a meter and rhyme scheme—as by attempted correlation with the source text (e.g., to take an extreme case, Watson's *Italian Madrigals Englished,* rendered "not to the sense of the ditty but after the affection of the note"). And finally, as *a second shifted set of possibilities that again should run alongside numbers 5–8 of this chart, those constrained by the determinant of mediator texts:* for translators may work there (but not at levels 1–4) primarily or exclusively through intermediate translations, while having little or no knowledge of the source language.[16]

The Countess of Pembroke, for example, did her psalms entirely from intermediate texts and commentaries, we must assume, without knowing Hebrew. And she did them with further determinants of rhythmic sound: rhyme, meter, and probably often particular music planned to be sung with a text. In other words, her psalms are only very distantly related to the Hebrew originals, being at level 7 in both "shifted" ranges just defined—at the outer edge of what can be called translation, indeed closer to mediated hypertextual imitation. Just as no one has balked at enjoying Wyatt's or Spenser's more closely translated pieces as poems in their own right (representing levels 6 and 7 on the above chart), there should be no objection to studying the countess's verse psalms as such (at level 7 twice shifted); they are not translations in the same sense as are her other translated works.

As for the relationship between paratextuality and other forms of transtextuality (cf. nn. 13 and 14), we may note about the above chart that between numbers 7 and 8, with no precise dividing line possible, we move from the sphere of the paratextual (translation being one of its borders) to those of the hypertextual and intertextual, in possible relations between source text and new text. Of course, translation in its various modes was the general training ground for Renaissance writers, because they were having to develop new traditions of literary prosody and stylistics in the vernacular languages, which had undergone such sweeping changes of inflectional patterns and sound that most of their medieval verse conventions had become unusable.

The Countess of Pembroke's Translations: One Woman's Track through the Paratextual

Of the countess's surviving translations, the earliest represents level 4 above, being a close but eminently readable prose rendering of an eloquent Christian-stoic treatise on death by her brother's Huguenot friend Philippe du Mornay-Plessis (French seems to have been her best language, and this treatise well expresses the Francophile Calvinist piety of her household, reflected also in Breton's devotional books). Her verse translations of Robert Garnier's play *Marc Antoine* and of Petrarch's "Trionfo della Morte" represent an intermediate station, somewhere between numbers 4 and 5, in the shifted range influenced by rhythmic constraints. Eventually, after learning from these efforts, she would be able to write sophisticated poems. But we want to do more here than mark the parabola of her experiments.

Diane Bornstein has well analyzed the stylistic features and translation practices represented in the Mornay piece, pointing out that the countess retained the syntactic parallelisms of its French sentences, sometimes adopting a different English clause structure to do so; that she reduced doublets and deleted emphasizer adverbs to gain conciseness; and that she sometimes continued effective metaphors into succeeding phrases. Bornstein compares the translation with a contemporaneous one of the same treatise, by Edward Aggas (which I would place on the above chart as a rather defective attempt between levels 2 and 3); she notes that the countess is both more accurate than Aggas and "more successful in capturing the style of the original" (131). In short, at a time when English syntax was still rather unsettled, "the Countess translated Mornay's sophisticated French prose into a smooth, idiomatic English that fully reflected its rhetorical ornaments" and "even improved the original by making it more concise, more specific, and more metaphorical" (134).

In view of the countess's later occasional passages of difficult syntax and strained elisions, it is important to recognize, from the early translations, that she was fully capable of unproblematic edited syntax, so that we do not take those features of her later writing as basic incompetence. It seems that they were sometimes deliberate structures, part of an effort to convey intellectual complexities; I believe they also reflect, in the countess's ever-greater challenges of prosody and rhetorical word-patterning, occasional resort to colloquial locutions that are not part of our own standard English (thus hard for us to follow), as will be shown below. By contrast with that later mode, consider as illustrative of the countess's usually smooth, effective blank verse in her translated play of *Antonie* the passage beginning Cleopatra's speech after she has learned of Antony's accusation that she deliberately betrayed him in fleeing from a sea battle.[17]

> That I haue thee betrayed, dear *Antony*,
> My life, my soul, my sun? I had such thought?
> That I haue thee betrayed, my Lord, my King?
> That I would break my vowed faith to thee?
> Leave thee? deceive thee? yield thee to the rage
> Of mighty foe? I euer had that heart?. . .
> Rather fierce *Tigers* feed them on my flesh:
> Rather, o rather let our *Nilus* send,
> To swallow me quick, some weeping *Crocodile*.
>
>   (*Antonie*, ls. 387–98)

In the Countess's translation of Petrarch's "Triumph of Death," however, we begin to encounter the labored syntax and sometimes confusing elisions of words and syllables that make some passages of her psalms and other poems ponderous for readers of our own time. While, as Gary Waller notes (*Triumph* 13–18), in certain passages her rendition is vigorous and effective, in others she has resorted to such strains, in following the meter of terza rima, that one can scarcely find clear grammar or sense.[18] Consider a passage describing Lady Laura and her virtuous female companions as figures of chastity returning from their victory over Cupid and first encountering the figure of Death (the "Triumph of Chastity" has been the previous poem of Petrarch's set, ending where this "Triumph of Death" takes up). Note, incidentally, that this group of paragons of chastity is in effect another thematization (cf. chapter 1) of the women's-group formation of readings, speeches, and devotions: one attraction of this Petrarch poem for the countess may have been its portrayal of a world of imagined female agency, where both paragon and demon are female.

The first two lines offer no syntactic problem, but what of the rest?

> Their speeches holy were, and happy those
>   who so are born to be with them enrolled.
> Clear stars they send, which did a Sun unclose,
>   who hiding none yet all did beautify
>   with Coronets decked with violet and rose;
> And as gained honor filled with jollity
>   Each gentle heart, so made they merry cheer,
>   when lo, an ensign sad I might descry,

Black, and in black a woman did appear,
    Fury with her, such as I scarcely know
    If like at Phlegra with the Giants were.
        (*Triumph* ed. Waller, ls. 23–33)

What does it mean that the ladies "send clear stars" (their eyes?), which stars
"unclose a sun," who "beautifies all with coronets"? The countess has not quite
made sense here, though neo-Platonically the sun must somehow be Laura,
with her shining light gracing the others, whose starry eye-beams intertwine
with her light. Second, the use of "gained" before "honor" as an adjective (the
honor they gained) is a possible construction but sounds more Italianate than
native. And third, where the countess would like to say "in black a woman did
appear, / A fury with her, such as I scarcely know / If the like at Phlegra with
the Giants were," she is so set on having ten syllables per line that she omits
the needed articles "a" (before "fury") and "the" (before "like"), leaving us
doubtful at first whether we should think of a personification (*a* snaky-haired
fury) or of an abstract "furiousness." In such passages the effect is of jotted-
note shorthand, or sometimes of confusion.

    By contrast, a fourth instance here of unusual syntax strains the language
to good effect: "an ensign sad I might descry, / Black, and in black a woman
did appear." The first "black" is not only postpositional but rather distant from
the noun it modifies, "ensign"; yet no confusion results since there is nothing
else for it to modify. And the unusual syntactic rhythm, doubling the black
ensign and the black garment of the woman, makes for a quite effective introduction of the poem's dread protagonist—a female figure of Death. In other
words, I believe the countess sometimes deliberately stretched syntax and that
such structures can be a positive feature of her personal style. One needs to
look closely to see if there is a way to read them aloud that makes them clear
and interesting.

Fraunce, Breton, and Daniel as Her Fellow Learners

    Now let us look more closely at the writers who influenced her and she
them, and thereby consider how she found a politically different way of evolving an authorial identity from that of male writers. For Elizabethan men other
than commercial dramatists, as has been often studied, the usual path was to
operate either as courtiers or functionaries, finding some relationship to the
court's power structures and thereby some way of one's own to address the
queen and her attendants, thereby to construe a feasible, ideologically shaped
image of the queen and, correlatively, an empowered self-image of the writer
controlling it. That whole set of patterns, I have elsewhere argued, can be studied in culturally semiotic terms, as a milieu for diverse usages of units of cul-

tural meaning that can be called ideologemes, and I identified a pervasive ideologeme at Elizabeth's court as that of the "captive woman."[19] This male path into writing or artisanship was not open to women.

The countess created a kind of alternative court of her entourage and protégés, a social and physical space of piety drawing from and playing into the activities and energies of the Essex faction, a household where things could come rather closer to comprising a neo-Platonic garden of the spirit than they could for the queen because the tasks of administration there were limited: the countess and her circle could devote major energies to music, writing, and religion (though doubtless things did not always go idyllically—cf. n. 6). They could affect and learn from each other's efforts.

As recounted above, within a year after her brother's death Fraunce provided the symbolic groundwork of this situation by dedicating to her the work that put him squarely in her favor for years: his rendition of Watson's Latin *Amyntas*. Despite its lumbering sound, it has many passages of lyric intensity; and its strong popularity is shown by its going through five editions in less than a decade, as well as by many laudatory references to it, even from the vituperative Thomas Nashe.[20] This work of pastoral grieving, I believe, provided her with a way at once to mourn for her brother and to begin thinking of herself as a writer. We cannot doubt its high favor with her; Fraunce even added, as part of its fourth edition (namely the *Ivychurch* Parts I and II of 1591), a translative adaptation of Tasso's play *Aminta*, from which the characters of Amintas and his lost beloved had come, where he added a section incorporating Pembrokiana herself and her shepherds and nymphs into the play. (I.e., this adaptation of Tasso's play is Part I of *The Countesse of Pembrokes Yuychurch*—of which Part II is the fourth edition of the eleven translated *Amyntas* eclogues from Watson's neo-Latin, plus a new original one by Fraunce, number 11, directly celebrating the countess's literary milieu.) The Watson/Fraunce Englished eclogues are laments of a lover grieving for the recently dead shepherdess whom he wanted to marry. Among its strategies for acting out grief is reminiscence of the lovers' happy time of mutually expressed passionate admiration for each other (represented in the last scenes of Tasso's play), contrasted with depiction of the "present" time of Amyntas's grieving. As Eccles notes (168), in the late 1580s and early 1590s the countess showed herself especially fond of poems about the dying Amyntas and his beloved Phyllis.

They were, I suggest, characters developed by Fraunce into a love-pair centering her own world of grieving and celebrating imagination by serving as gender-inverted figures for herself and her brother. In the Amyntas motif the countess could see herself grieving for her brother of affectionate memory. She is the image of the dying Philip (*morientis imago Philippi*), invited to continue the literary-magical realm of Amyntas's grievings. In the vein of that grief for "Phillis" she could do her own work of grieving for Philip. While presumably neither she nor other poets made such an equation explicit, they often press its button, as in Fraunce's dedication to the *Ivychurch* Part III:

Nympha Charis Chariton, morientis imago Philippi,
Accipe spirantem post funera rursus Amintam:
Accipe nobilium dulcissima dogmata vatum,
Delicias, Musas, mysteria; denique, quicquid
Graecia docta dedit, vel regia Roma reliquit,
Quod fructum flori, quod miscuit vtile dulci.

   [Dear beloved nymph, image of the dying Philip,
   Accept Amintas, breathing again after the funerals:
   Accept the most sweet teachings of the noble poets,
   Their delicacies, muses, mysteries; in short, whatever
   Learned Greece provides or royal Rome bequeaths,
   What fruit each joins with the flower, what profit with sweetness.]

The gender-inversion of Phyllis for Philip works because the beloved woman in this pastoral fiction is also an inventor and singer of verses, who had intertwined her own songs with those of her lover. At the same time as it let the countess step into a passionate fictive world beyond death centering on a couple she could feel to be herself and her brother, it let her step into a rare female subject position that could textualize her own social and intellectual position among surrounding admirers. Thus in readings aloud done by Fraunce and her women, she was given a writerly self-image as poet/lover/lamentor of the lost Philip—a major part of the self-image she needed for empowerment as a writer. The following passage concluding "The Second Lamentation" of *Amyntas* will illustrate these points. Fraunce's metaphrasis becomes especially wordy here, as the Latin rhetorical figures, expressing mutuality through syntactic balance and devices of word repetition, send him into a veritable fit of anaphora and *reduplicatio*; but we can afterward look at a few of the Watson lines that he is translating and see how such passages on reunion with the lost beloved in the Elysian fields were important to the countess. She would soon represent her brother similarly in her elegy "To the Angel Spirit of Sir Philip Sidney," drafted by 1592 (see below).

   But let death, let death, come speedily give me my passport,
   So that I find fair fields, fair seats, fair groves by my dying,
   And in fields, in seats, in groves faire Phillis abiding.
   There shall Phillis again, in courtesy strive with Amintas.
   There with Phillis again, in courtesy strive shall Amintas,
   There shall Phillis again make garlands gay for Amintas,
   There for Phillis again, gay garlands make shall Amintas,
   There shall Phillis again be repeating songs with Amintas,

Which songs Phillis afore had made and sung with Amintas.
    But what, alas, did I mean, to the whistling winds to be mourning?
As though mourning could restore what destiny taketh.
    Then to his house, full sad, when night approached, he returned.

Fraunce's six lines beginning "There with Phillis again" translate five Latin ones that arrange their symmetries more tightly. The last four are

Florea serta tuo capiti mea dextera texet,
Florea serta meo capiti tua dextera texet,
Amboque sub viridi myrto repetemus amores,
Quos olim parili versu cantavimus ambo.

> [Flower garlands for your head my hand weaves,
> Flower garlands for my head your hand weaves,
> And both together under the green myrtle we repeat our loves,
> Which in times past in equal-paced verses we have both sung.]

Fraunce has duplicated the simple repetition structure of the first two lines but not the more complex chiasmic structure of the other two, which places *ambo* ("both") at the beginning of the first line and the end of the second. The countess delighted in such constructions, whether inventing them herself or replicating them in translation. Her ear for patterned repetitions of sound, especially as they could elaborate complex ideas, was so keen that modern readers often have trouble following her combinations.

Nicholas Breton's lyric vein favored less intricate wit and simpler syntactic structures, though certainly he loved the repetitive musical "figures of sound." He was a prolific writer of devotional verse, much of it dedicated to the countess, sometimes even put into the mouth of her persona under titles like *The Countess of Pembroke's Passion*. Incidentally, he began that "Passion" with a pastiche intermingling lines of his own with several from Thomas Watson, presumably meant either as a plug for a still-living Watson or as a tribute to him after his death. (We do not know just when Breton wrote it.)[21]

Looking for a common denominator among the poets she patronized, we find that it is neither devotional writing nor neoclassical metrics (though those are prominent), but music—an interest in how verse may achieve musical effects. This point must be kept in view as one studies her characteristic styles in her psalms and other poems. For although her own most individual voice would become something different, set off as it were against song-mode verse[22] by contrast, she wrote song verse well when she wanted to, and some of the best Elizabethan lyrics came from writers of her broader circle (cf. Freer *Music*): some of Watson's *Italian Madrigals Englished* and lyrics by Breton and Daniel. Further, it is noteworthy that musical settings of two of her psalms survive (numbers 51 and 130, in B. L. Add. MS 15117), and probably others were done. Since the countess herself played the lute often enough to need her strings replaced several times (Hannay, *Phoenix* 115), and since Thomas Morley in dedicating to her his *Canzonets* for five and six voices (1593) asked that she promote them through her singing, we can assume that actual music was important in her psalm experiments. Some of them would be direct contrafacta texts, that is, written to fit preexisting tunes. In sum, powerful song verse emerged from her circle and appeared in some of her own psalms. One might suppose that quantitative verse such as the Fraunce hexameters above would be difficult to set, thus of little interest to composers. But in fact the driving musical-humanist motive behind such verse was the claim that correlating it with rhythmically suitable music would revive the fabled ancient affective powers of music over people's spirits, and composers were willing enough to try it. What they usually heeded was the unintended, musically interesting stress patterns of mixed doublets and triplets, rather than the largely inaudible system of supposed long-and-short syllables. But through the process they devised interesting new rhythmic lines and in turn influenced subsequent lyric poetry.[23]

An example of Breton's contribution to the countess's musical experiences of verse is one of his well-known song lyrics, the mysteriously suggestive "Fair in a morn, O fairest morn," appearing with lute accompaniment in Morley's *Airs* (1600). (The song is fairly common on recordings now.) Given the linkage of both Breton and Morley with the countess, and the common use of "Phillis" (here in a Latin inflected form, "Phylida") as one of her pastoral names among poets addressing her, I think that in this much-admired song we should imagine her most established poet-admirer Fraunce as "Corydon" (both Watson—see above—and Spenser refer to him under that name);[24] Fraunce is shown paying a devotee's tribute of admiration for her pious mourning, in the context of his own grief for her brother. Breton had explicitly represented the countess in very similar phrasing in his devotional poem "The Countesse of Penbrookes love" (1592—Grosart ed. 1b:21ff.), which begins "Faire in a plot of earthly paradise, / Upon a hill, the Muses made a Maze: / In midst whereof within a Phoenix eies, / There sits a grace, that hath the world at gase." That "Countess's Love" poem goes on to present her in her hilltop seat of Wilton, full of all graces, reviewing all the loveliest things the world has to offer her and rejecting them for love of God, which Breton (as elsewhere) images as sunlight on a radiant face. The Breton/Morley song refers to just this context.

> Fair in a morn, O fairest morn, was ever morn so fair?
> When as the sun, but not the same that shineth in the air,
> But of the earth, no earthly sun, and yet no earthly creature,
> There shone a face, was never face that carried such a feature.

And on a hill, O fairest hill, was never hill so blessed,
There stood a man, was never man for no man so distressed.
This man had hap, O happy man, no man so happed as he,
For none had hap to see the hap that he had happed to see.

And as he beheld, this man beheld, he saw so fair a face,
The which would daunt the fairest here and stain the bravest grace.
Pity, he cried, and Pity came, and pitied for his pain,
That dying would not let him die, but gave him life again.

For joy whereof he made such mirth that all the world did ring,
And Pan with all his nymphs came forth to hear the shepherds sing,
But such a song sung never was, nor ne'er will be again,
Of Phillida, the shepherds' Queen, and Corydon, the swain.

(Fellowes ed. 629–30)

In this riddling song, which weaves a fabric of echoing phrasal repetitions around details of the barest simplicity, Breton is at his best in verbal music, setting a standard the countess would answer to in some of her song-mode psalms. In a fair morn there shone an earthly sun that was nevertheless not "of the earth," appearing to a grieving man alone on a hill; it was the sunlike face of a lovely shepherdess who showed pity to the fear-stricken Corydon, indeed the face of Phyllis, queen of shepherds. We also note the very similar names and theme in Breton's "Pastorell of Phillis and Coridon" (Grosart ed. 1d:12), from the *Arbor of Amorous Devises* (1594), where Phillis, the shepherds' queen, sits on a golden chair atop her hill, giving light and life, and seemingly in reference to the countess's translation of Petrarch (which opens with Chastity's victory over Cupid) is said to have blinded Cupid and spited Venus.

While the above song's meter seems at first to be fourteeners, commonest of "bald rhyming" meters, it instead shows a distinct rhythmic pattern registering as a recurrent departure from that initially evident meter, namely that in every stanza, each fourteener line but the last begins with the choriambic foot common in openings of French chansons of the time, ʹxxʹ, rather than ˣʹxˣ. This figure would have sounded normal to the ears of the countess and her poetic circle, not only through French songs but through the adapted hexameters and asclepiads of Sidney, Fraunce, and other quantitative experimenters: the hexameters always end the lines with a pattern that, heard accentually, is ʹxxʹx, while the asclepiadic lines begin with just this figure, opening three of every four lines here. Morley follows the verse rhythm with great precision and keeps the harmonic interest in the lute part subordinate (as in continental monody); he avoids tedium through variable melodic pacing on the last line of the shapely tune he devised, repeated with each stanza. It would not be farfetched, though only speculative, to suppose that Breton and Morley wrote this song together to send to the countess.

Another brief song lyric of Breton's will illustrate one of her favorite "figures of sound" in her psalms and elsewhere, antimetabole. Here he weaves a tissue of word music around antimetabole, as he did around the figure of ploce (single-word repetitions in phrasal variation) in the "Phyllis" song just noted.

> Lovely kind, and kindly loving,
> Such a mind were worth the moving:
> Truly fair, and fairly true,
> Where are all these but in you?
>
> Wisely kind, and kindly wise,
> Blessed life, where such love lies.
> Wise, and kind, and fair, and true,
> Lovely live all these in you.
>
> (Breton *Melancholike Humours* 42, 1600)

Breton's talent was rather like that of Theodore Roethke in our own time, for making striking lyrics out of the simplest words through inventive phrasal rhythms made of figures of word repetition. (Here we see an emphasis on the admired lady's "mind" and "wisdom" characteristic of poets' modes of address to the countess.)

The countess herself, when she used this figure of antimetabole in verse, more typically did so for a different purpose from Breton's. For example, in her 1599 presentation poem to the queen accompanying her psalms, she calls King David God's "loved choice," while Queen Elizabeth is His "chosen love"; but in her poem, far from being primarily a textured piece of word music, this "figure of sound" becomes one of a series of subtly varied and foregrounded logical oppositions—e.g., that "all applaud" David while "none reprove" the queen—challenging the queen to firmer commitment in the Protestant cause (see chapter 6 of my forthcoming *Cultural Semiotics*).

As for Daniel, we cannot determine just when his literary relationship with the countess began, but two points show that it was no later than 1591, possibly sooner. First, his *Delia* sonnets (1592) are an expanded version of a group of poems published by Nashe without authorization in 1591 (along with some of Sidney's *Astrophil*). Comparing the fuller set in the 1592 edition with those of 1591, we see that Daniel has added, before what had been the introductory sonnet (now number 2 "Goe wailing Verse, the Infants of my loue"), a new number 1 keyed to the poems' identity as now dedicated to the countess (see n. 4), namely, "Vnto the boundlesse Ocean of thy beautie." The unauthorized Nashe book, then, seems to have set Daniel and the countess to joint literary endeavors on the editing of his sonnets and her brother's, though the two were probably acquainted earlier (see n. 5). In 1591 Daniel had just returned from Italy, where he had met the famous pastoralist Guarini, author of *Il Pastor Fido* (Spriet 46ff.); perhaps he and the countess had much to talk about. Secondly, among Daniel's papers his later publisher found and printed (mistakenly as his) a 1592 draft of one of the countess's presentation poems written to accompany her psalms, namely, "To the Angell spirit of the most excellent Sir Philip Sidney." Thus she must have given or sent Daniel this copy as she was preparing the psalms for presentation to the queen—for she had a draft of them done by 1593.[25]

Svensson (38–49) has demonstrated yet another close link between Daniel's sonnets and the countess's writings. The *Delia* sonnet number 1 features in its first two quatrains the same two metaphors of tribute and of self-evaluation that she herself uses in the poem just mentioned, "To the Angell Spirit." They are, first, of the writer's relationship to an inspirer of creativity (Daniel's to the countess, hers to her brother) as a river running to its ocean, and second, of the writer doing an account-book audit of debts to that inspiring person:

> Unto the boundless Ocean of thy beauty
> Runs this poor River, charged with streams of zeal:
> Returning thee the tribute of my duty,
> Which here my love, my youth, my plaints reveal.
> Here I unclasp the Book of my charged soul,
> Where I have cast th'accounts of all my care:
> Here have I summed my sighs, here I enroll
> How they were spent for thee; . . .

The comparable passage in the countess's early draft, from Daniel's papers, is as follows (speaking of her book of psalms):

> But since it hath no other scope to go,
> Nor other purpose but to honor thee [Sidney],
> That thine may shine, where all the graces be;
> And that my thoughts (like smallest streames that flow
> Pay to their sea their tributary fee)
> Do strive, yet have no means to quit nor free,
> That mighty debt of infinites I owe
> To thy great worth, which time to times enroll,
> Wonder of men[,] . . .
> O when from this account, this cast-up Sum,
> This reckning made the Audit of my woe,
> Some time of ease my swelling passions know,
> How work my thoughts, my sense is stricken dumb,

That would thee more than words could ever show,
Which all fall short.

The countess links the two metaphors logically by saying that her thoughts
of her brother, like rivers pressing to pay tribute to the sea, long to pay off her
immense debt to him; Daniel simply poses the two metaphors in succession,
without a conceptual linkage. Whichever poem came first,[26] it does appear, from
the close parallel and from Daniel's having a copy of the countess's poem, that
the two were reading each other's work.

Svensson goes on to compare Daniel's and the countess's uses of the image
of "river tribute to the ocean" to that of the sonnet recorded on the Ditchley
portrait of Queen Elizabeth by Marcus Gheeraerts the Younger, probably of
September 1592, where the queen stands on the north of a map of England
with rivers and coasts highlighted. While the sonnet has been mutilated, we
can see that it reads the painting through this metaphor: the rivers of England
flowing to their seas and being drawn up again through underground springs
(according to contemporary geology) are paying tribute to their princess by
flowing to her.

To make the point clearer, let me offer a conjectural text of the Ditchley
sonnet, based on the fragments of missing letters and a likely rhyme scheme (a
sestet of dbcbee):

> The prince of light. The Sonn[e] by whom thing[s liue]
> Of heauen the glorye, and [of] earthe the [grace]
> Hath no such glorye as [thee] grace to g[eue]
> Where Correspondencie May haue no plac[e].
> Thunder the y[m]age of that [po]wer deu[ine]
> Which all to nothing with a worde c[an smite]
> Is to the earthe, when it doth ayre r[efine]
> Of power the Scepter, not of [wrath the might.]
> This yle of such both grace [and] power [the site]
> The boundles ocean [humb]lye [doth em]brace
> P[eerless] p[rincess vnder] the[arth a]ll-[thine]
> Riuers of thanckes retourne for Springes [of grace]
>   Riuers of thanckes still to that oc[ean flow]
>   Where grace is grace above, power po[wer below.]
>   (ascribed to Sir Henry Lee—nonbracketed text from Svensson's
>   reproduction of the painting)

Whether or not my conjectural readings are correct, it is clear that here, as in
the similar continental metaphors traced by Svensson, the boundless ocean is
an image of awesome power, to which, as also to the queen at the upper end
of the cycle, rivers and their "tributaries" pay tribute. In this case, the queen
is made to preside mythically over the island's life-giving flow and return of

waters, so that they pay tribute to her "power" in falling to the sea, but to her "grace" in rising to replenish their headwaters ("Grace is grace above, power power below").

Whether Daniel and the countess knew the Ditchley portrait before they used the metaphor, whether the painting drew upon them, or whether it was just in the air in 1591, their combined uses of it in effect pose an alternative England, with the rivers flowing between the celebrated sibling pair, the countess and her enshrined brother, as figureheads of the Protestant cause: she is the headwaters, he the ocean of England's link to the larger international Reformed church. The political positioning, then, of the countess and her circle as a kind of ideologically invested alternative court is registered in the dual, co-opted usages of this regal metaphor. When in 1599 the countess revised her poem "To the Angell spirit," along with one addressed to the queen herself, for inclusion in the presentation copy of the versified Psalms, this metaphor of the countess's own passions as rivers paying tribute to her brother of oceanic memory remained prominent. We will return to that revised form of the "Angel" poem shortly.

Style and Voice in Her Psalms

As well as in her lower-level translations discussed above, completed while she and Fraunce, Breton, and Daniel sometimes exchanged ideas and manuscripts, we can also study her style and development in her metaphrastic psalms; there—at least in the opening stanza of each poem, where she devises the stanza shape to be followed—she is relatively free from prosodic and semantic constraints. Casting each psalm verse into a unit ranging from two (shorter or longer) lines to a whole stanza, and interpretively expanding the sense along the lines of Beza's and Calvin's commentaries, she has created versions that we (like Rathmell in his "Introduction") can well call poems in their own right. My chart above has given a fairly precise account of their large degree of textual independence from their sources: greater than that of, say, Wyatt's renditions of passages from Petrarch, as great as Spenser's "November" and "December" eclogues are from Clement Marot.

In the psalms I want to look first at a poem that deserves study not only at the level of the versification features we have been considering but also in terms of the broader issue of how the countess came to consider her writing important enough to commit regular amounts of time to it. Obviously, part of the reason, as is often noted, was her wish to round off and publish her brother's work. But perhaps other women also had strong motives to write, who yet did not find a fruitful context, as the countess did. She was in a quite unusual position for cultivating an enabling self-image, evolved through the admiration of other active writers who would seriously ascribe to her, woman though she was, some measure of the combined talent, piety, and politico-symbolic importance that her brother had held. In other words, she found an enabling authorial identity as "sister unto Astrophil" by partially assuming the male one of her brother, by making it live through transferring the devotion of the poets he had patronized into devotion to her, and by bringing their tributes to auditory life in the reading voices of her women and menservants.

Her brother, in dying after completing Psalm 43, had stopped at an interesting point if we assume that she began with the next succeeding ones; the second of these was that extravagantly glorious royal wedding psalm of poetic self-awareness, *Eructavit cor meum*, Psalm 45, which she renders as follows.

> My heart indites an argument of worth,
>   The praise of him that doth the Scepter sway:
> My tongue the pen to paint his praises forth,
>   Shall write as swift as swiftest writer may.
>   Then to the king these are the words I say:
> Fairer art thou than sons of mortal race:
>   Because high God hath blessed thee for aye,
> Thy lips, as springs, do flow with speaking grace.
>
>   (Rathmell ed., spelling modernized)

The psalmist here identifies with the king through ascribing to him eloquent lips that, like the poet's pen, will "flow with speaking grace"; thus by an implied exchange the poet appropriates to his own writing the king's beauty and power and commits his eloquence to the king's service. Here the countess found a miniature study in the attainment of writerly voice and political identity, which she would have interpreted typologically as addressed to Christ and his bride the Church. The lesson continues:

> [Of] the fragrant riches of Sabean grove
> Myrrh, Aloes, Cassia, all thy robes do smell:
>   When thou from ivory Palace dost remove
>   Thy breathing odors all thy train excell.
> Daughters of kings among thy courtly band,
>   By honoring thee of thee do honor hold:
> On thy right side thy dearest Queen doth stand
>   Richly arrayed in cloth of Ophir gold.
> This Queen that can a king her father call,
>   Doth only she in upper garment shine?
> Nay underclothes, and what she weareth all,
>   Gold is the stuff, the fashion Art divine;

The psalm then calls upon the bride-queen to submit herself fully to the king in his beauty and power, forget her parents, plan for his children, and accept the poet's written tributes to her beauty (even to her golden underwear) as supplying an adequate identity. The psalmist, like the attendant ladies who "hold honor" by honoring the king, has himself stepped into this female identity of the bride; by speaking of even her undergarments, he presents himself as inside the female perspective. He thus vividly portrays and modifies the perspective she has and (by his urging) ought to have, on her new life as submissive queen, swathed and adorned in harem luxury.

> Brought to the king in robe embroidered fine,
> Her maids of honor shall on her attend
>   With such, to whom more favor shall assign
> In nearer place their happy days to spend.
> Brought shall they be with mirth and marriage joy
>   And enter so the palace of the king:
> Then let no grief thy mind, O Queen, annoy,
>   Nor parents left thy sad remembrance sting.
>   In stead of parents, children thou shalt bring
> Of partadg'd earth the kings and lords to be:
>   Myself thy name in lasting verse will sing.
> The world shall make no end of thanks to thee.

What may the countess have thought of this psalm, in traditional typology showing David as proto-messiah and in Protestant politics considered to portray him as model reformist king? Perhaps at first it made an enticing and comfortable female writerly identity for her, lyricizing the most extravagant traditional attributes of patriarchal womanhood in a form assimilable to Christian devotion—a pampered beauty, a powerful husband's devotion to that beauty, vicarious status through one's male children, typologically a slot as bride of Christ, the Church universal—all through a male psalmist-poet's ability to find glory in that identity. As the psalmist could assume a female voice and identity, why should she not do the converse and assume the mantle of her brother's calling?

For observing how the countess developed her own poetic style and most characteristic voice in her psalms, let us compare some excerpts from her admirer Fraunce's Psalm 73 with the analogous passages of hers. While it would not be worthwhile here to review Fraunce's rules for quantitative scansion, taken from Drant and Sidney,[27] we can see, in a line like the second hexameter below, both the frequent feminine or falling endings and the combinations of doublets and triplets to which this verse accustomed the English ear (common in Italian songs and madrigals such as Sidney and Watson adapted).

> God, th'eternal God, no doubt, is good to the godly,
> Giving grace to the pure, and mercy to Israel holy:
> And yet, alas, my feet, my faint feet 'gan to be sliding,

And I was almost gone, and fall'n to a dangerous error.
For my soul did grudge, my heart consumed in anger,
And mine eyes disdaing'd [sic], when I saw that such men abounded
With wealth, health, and joy, whose minds with mischief abounded. . . .
Which makes them with pride, with scornful pride be chained,
And with blood-thirsting disdain as a robe to be cov'red.
Their fare is delicate, their flesh is daintily pampered,
Their eyes with fatness start out. . . .
Tush, say they, can God, from the highest heav'ns to the lowest
Earth, vouchsafe, think you, those Princelike eyes to be bowing?
'Tis but a vain conceit of fools, to be fondly referring
Euery jesting trick and trifling toy to the Thund'rer.

Rathmell and others have noted that the countess gives the Psalms an Elizabethan voice; certainly Fraunce does so here as well, though a quite different
Elizabethan voice from the ones in the countess's psalms. A characteristically
neoclassical effect is created with God as Jove the Thunderer, looking
down with winking "princelike" eyes on human foibles; thereby the powerful evildoers are cast as shallow abusers of humanist learning, along with
their other faults. Perhaps not much more can be claimed for merits in Fraunce's
rendition.

By comparison consider the lyric voice, largely in rhetorically heightened
speech rhythms, of the countess's Psalm 73. Here we will go beyond the point
where we stopped in Fraunce's version, to show how her iambic verse with a
high incidence of monosyllables, unlike Fraunce's lumbering lines, creates an
effective self-dramatizing of the anguished psalmist in his wavering thoughts—
now denouncing the godless oppressors, now questioning God's justice, repeating the alternation, noting the social danger in expressing his doubts before
the people, and finally coming to the view that evil will somehow be punished.
Notice too that while Fraunce gave no visually clear presentation of the metaphors of pride as a ponderous neck chain on a fat grandee and of cruel scorn
for the poor as a rich robe, the countess combines these details—just the sort
she likes to sharpen up—with the glittering eyes surrounded by fat, to create a
full-dress metaphoric picture of the wicked oppressor, evocative of some Holbein painting.

It is most true that God to Israel,
    I mean to men of undefiled hearts,
    Is only good, and nought but good imparts.
Most true, I see, allbe almost I fell
    From right conceit into a crooked mind,
    And from this truth with straying steps declin'd.

For lo, my boiling breast did chafe and swell
  When first I saw the wicked proudly stand,
  Prevailing still in all they took in hand.
And sure no sickness dwelleth where they dwell. . . .

Therefore with pride, as with a gorgeous chain,
  Their swelling necks encompassed they bear;
  All clothed in wrong, as if a robe it were:
So fat become, that fatness doth constrain
  Their eyes to swell: . . .
And thus they reasons frame: how can it be
  That God doth understand? that he doth know,
  Who sits in heav'n, how earthly matters go? . . .

Nay ev'n within myself, my self did say:
  In vain my hart I purge, my hands in vain
  In cleanness washed I keep from filthy stain,
Since thus afflictions scourge me ev'ry day:
  Since never a day from early East is sent,
  But brings my pain, my check, my chastisement . . .

Until at length nigh weary of the chase,
  Unto thy house I did my steps direct:
  There, lo, I learned what end did these expect,
And what but that in high but slippery place
  Thou didst them set: whence, when they least of all
  To fall did fear, they fell with headlong fall.
For how are they in less than moment's space
  With ruin overthrown? with frightful fear
  Consumed so clean as if they never were?
Right as a dream, which waking doth deface. . . .

But as for me, nought better in my eyes
Than cleave to God, my hopes in him to place,
To sing his works while breath shall give me space.

Her lyric style here is strongly reminiscent of some of the *Astrophil* sonnets,
such as #5, "It is most true that eyes are formed to serve / The inward light."
But she probably had not found it easy to work into her brother's modes of
lyric, and we may assume she had done so slowly, as the distinctive voice we
begin to hear at this point in the psalms is not so evident in the earlier ones.

One must speak not of "a voice" but of a set of voices that she learned to
use—some more song-like, some more in the mode of rhetorically heightened
speech. When she did want to write in the rhythmically variable, short-lined
song mode of poets like Breton, Watson, or Daniel in their song veins, she

could do so, a good example being her Psalm 130, of which (as noted earlier) a setting for voice and lute survives:

> From depth of grief
>   Where drowned I lie,
> Lord for relief
>   To thee I cry:
> My earnest, vehement, crying, praying,
> Grant quick, attentive, hearing, weighing.

In this short sample we see all three features that the quantitative experiments had taught song poets to use, even in stress-based meters: the choriambic variation on "Lord for relief," the triplet among doublets in "vehement," and the interspersal of feminine or falling endings with masculine ones—here on "praying-weighing."

Another song meter she could use well, one that her brother had introduced in contrafacta poems for Spanish and Italian tunes, was that of the seven-syllable modified trochaic line (cf. Sidney *Poems*, Ringler ed. 427)—the meter of, for example, his Astrophil song "O dear life when shall it be." She puts it to work very fittingly for the brief Psalm #93 *Dominus regnavit*, it being exactly suited to the pounding concentration of monosyllables that she works it into.

> Clothed in state and girt with might,
>   Monarch-like Jehovah reigns,
> He who Earth's foundation pight,
>   Pight at first and yet sustains,
>   He whose stable throne disdains
> Motion's shock, and age's flight. . . .
>
> Rivers, yea, though Rivers roar,
>   Roaring though sea-billows rise,
> Vex the deep and break the shore:
>   Stronger art thou, Lord of skies.

But besides such uses of song, she became equally good at her own vein of speaking voice lyric, apt for a poetic self-dramatization such as we saw in her Psalm 73. It will be this vein that she taps in two of the three original poems for the presentation manuscript of her psalms for the queen, as we will consider shortly. In lyric mode it represents a vein prominent in the mid-portion of her psalm renditions, such as that of Psalm 55, *Exaudi, deus*, with its meditative voice and syntactic periods extended across several metrical lines, in this case developing a little allegory of personified oppressions and mischief. God's enemies can "walk the cittie walles both night and day," and

Oppressions, tumults, guiles of ev'ry kind
Are burgesses, and dwell the middle near;
About their streets his masking robes doth wear
    Mischief, clothed in deceit, with treason lined,
Where only he, he only bears the sway.
But not my foe with me this prank did play,
For then I would have born with patient cheer
    An unkind part from whom I know unkind; . . .

But this to thee, to thee impute I may,
    My fellow, my companion, held most dear,
My soul, my other self, my inward friend:
Whom unto me, me unto whom did bind
    Exchanged secrets, who together were
God's temple wont to visit, there to pray. . . .

Who but such catives would have undermined,
Nay overthrown, from whom but kindness mere
    They never found? who would such trust betray?
    What buttered wordes! yet war their hearts bewray;
Their speech more sharp than sharpest sword or spear
Yet softer flows than balm from wounded rind.

We hear a meditative account of a speaker's memories and emotions upon being betrayed by a close friend, cast in alternately rhyming pentameter lines that do not impose any severe constraints of stanzaic shape or intricate rhyme pattern. (The countess came to rely on this flexible meter for long psalms.) It is characteristic, though, that even in this meditative speaking voice with colloquial exclamations like "What buttered words!" she would also intermingle the kind of rhetorical figure more usual for song or declamatory modes of verse, the antimetabole "Whom unto me, me unto whom . . . " The effect of the whole is to give us the voice of a forceful speaker, a powerful aristocrat confident of listeners' attention, who now and then pauses to intermingle a piece of self-aware word play when it will make an apposite point—as here the reciprocity of the two former soul-mate selves.

The "Angel Spirit"

Since, as noted, I have elsewhere discussed in some detail the other two paratextual poems in the presentation manuscript of her Psalms, let me here focus on "To the Angell spirit of the most excellent Sir Philip Sidney" (Waller ed. 92–95). As we find especially when we compare its 1592 and 1599 drafts, it is in several passages pushed to syntactic obscurity by an effort to pack into it the greatest possible depth and intensity—as if the countess knew this would be the rare chance to write a few poems spoken in her own persona, and overloaded them with meanings. The features of elliptical syntax and strained metrical elisions of syllables, which we noted above in her "Triumph of Death," reappear with a vengeance: even some clauses that had been grammatically clear in the 1592 version lose their coherence in 1599, as the countess seems deliberately to strive for an unending flow, with closure deferred for ever longer stretches. For example, what in 1592 had been "Nor can we reach, in thought, / What on that goodly peece, time would haue wrought" becomes in 1599 "nor in the reach of thought, / howe on that passing peece time would have wrought," removing the only finite verb ("can reach") in a lengthy series of clauses that now never reach syntactic closure.[28]

Such alteration is not the only difference between the two versions: by 1599 the countess has completely cut two stanzas of the 1592 draft that portray how her own grieving process had found a home in the Watson-Fraunce fictionalized pastoral rites of Amyntas's grieving for Phyllis at Ivychurch. In those earlier stanzas, after exclaiming at the pain of newly remembered grief ("Ah memory, what needs this new arrist?"), she qualifies the thought of pain, to meditate on the sweetness of a new participation in poetry that grief has brought her:

> Yet blessed griefe, that sweetnes can impart
> Since thou art blest. Wrongly do I complaine;
> What euer weights my heauy thoughts sustaine
> Deere feeles my soule for thee. I know my part,
> Nor be my weaknes to thy rites a staine;
> Rites to aright, life bloud would not refraine:
> Assist me then, . . . thy losse hath layd to vtter wast
> The wracke of time, vntimely all defac't,
> Remayning as the tombe of life disceast:
> Where, in my heart the highest roome thou hast;
> There, truly there, thy earthly being is plac't:
> Triumph of death, in life how more than blest.

In 1592 she had seen herself as burdened container of her ingenious brother's unfinished works—the challenge of giving them some form that would let them make a public mark had weighed heavily upon her, while poetic indulgence in grief taught her to write.

But in 1599 she cuts out this reflection that there can be a sweetness in grief through the creativity it brings; for the new version a different metaphor has come to her for envisaging a public and lasting form of her brother's works, and she presents it in three new stanzas, replacing the two she has cut. It is of a great architect-builder's "goodly buildings," not completed, but far enough finished that, with a little rounding off and functionalizing by caretakers, the lines of their unique genius, "beyond compare above all praise," can be made evident to "all mens eies."

Because of its syntax, this dedicatory poem for her manuscript of psalms, for all its inherent interest, is going to be difficult for modern readers to appreciate. Yet it and its companion piece deserve our extra efforts. For they are no mere *pro forma* tributes: into them the countess has poured years of effort to say what her brother's life meant. Here I would like to offer a particular text of the poem as a kind of footnote, or aid to reading. It will modernize spelling, use the syntactically indicative resources of our own punctuation, and supply elided elements in square brackets. Of course, as noted, sometimes the countess's flow of clauses across points of closure is deliberate, an example of synchysis, such as the line "Wonder of men, sole born perfections kind," which in the long flow of nonclosive punctuation refers both backward to "my thoughts pay the debt I owe to thy great worth, exceeding Nature's store, / Wonder of men . . . " and forward to " . . . Wonder of men, Phoenix thou wert, so rare [was] thy fairest mind." A reading through of this modernized text may send us back better armed to the original, able at least to feel where the long periodic sentences overlap.

Notice how, especially in the poem's second half, she deliberately enjambs sentences across each stanza's end, as if to allow no full stop until the flow of her thought ceases. (Note too that "deign" in stanza 2 is used as a transitive verb, with no "to do" phrase required to follow—i.e., "deign his own" equals "accept his own.")

To the Angel Spirit of the Most Excellent Sir Philip Sidney

> To thee, pure spirit, to thee alone's addressed
>   This coupled work, by double interest thine:
>   First raised by thy bless'd hand, and what is mine
> Inspired by thee, thy secret power impressed.
>   So dared my Muse with thine itself combine,
>   as mortal stuff with that which is divine;
> Thy lightning beams give luster to the rest,
>
> That heaven's King may deign his own (transformed—
>   In substance no, but superficial 'tire
>   By thee put on to praise, not to aspire
> To, those high Tones so in themselves adorned,
>   Which Angels sing in their celestial Choir,
>   And all of tongues, with soul and voice admire
> These sacred Hymns thy Kingly Prophet formed).

Oh, had that soul which honor brought to rest
    Too soon not left, and reft the world of all
    What man could show which we perfection call,
This half-maimed piece had sorted with the best.
    Deep wounds enlarged, long festered in their gall,
    Fresh bleeding smart; not eye but heart tears fall.
Ah memory, what needs this new arrest?

Yet here behold (oh wert thou to behold!)
    This finished now [that] thy matchless Muse begun,
    The rest but pieced, as left by thee undone.
Pardon, O bless'd soul, presumption too too bold:
    If love and zeal such error ill become,
    'Tis zealous love, Love which hath never done,
Nor can enough in world of words unfold.

And sith it hath no further scope to go
    Nor other purpose but to honor thee
    (Thee in thy works, where all the Graces be),
As little streams with all their all do flow
    To their great sea, due tribute's grateful fee,
    So press my thoughts, my burdened thoughts, in me
To pay the debt of infinites I owe

To thy great worth, exceeding Nature's store;
    Wonder of men, sole born perfection's kind,
    Phoenix thou wert, so rare [was] thy fairest mind,
Heavenly adorned, [that] Earth justly might adore,
    Where truthful praise in highest glory shined:
    For there alone was praise to truth confined—
And where but there?—to live for evermore.

Oh, when to this Account, this cast up Sum,
    This Reckoning made, this Audit of my woe,
    I call my thoughts, whence so strange passions flow,
How works my heart—my senses stricken dumb—
    That would thee more than ever heart could show,
    And all['s] too short; who knew thee best doth know
There lives no wit that may thy praise become.

Truth I invoke (who scorn elsewhere to move,
    Or [that] here in ought my blood should partialize),
    Truth, sacred Truth, Thee sole, to solemnize
Those precious rites well known [that] best minds approve—
    And who but doth ([that] hath wisdom's open eyes,
    Not owlly blind the fairest light still flies)
Confirm no less? At least, 'tis sealed above,

Where thou art fixed among thy fellow lights.
　My day put out, my life in darkness cast,
　Thy Angel's soul with highest Angels placed
There blessed sings (enjoying heav'n delights)
　Thy Maker's praise, as far from earthy taste
　As here [are] thy works, so worthily embraced
By all of worth, where never Envy bites.

As [would] goodly buildings to some glorious end—
　Cut off by fate before the Graces had
　Each wondrous part in all their beauties clad,
Yet [with] so much done as Art could not amend—
　So thy rare works, to which no wit can add,
　In all men's eyes which are not blindly mad,
Beyond compare above all praise extend,

Immortal Monuments of thy fair fame,
　Though not complete; nor [is it] in the reach of thought
　How on that passing piece time would have wrought,
Had Heav'n so spared the life of life to frame
　The rest. But ah, such loss! Hath this world ought
　Can equal it? Or which like grievance brought?
Yet there will live thy ever praised name,

To which these dearest offerings of my heart,
　Dissolved to Ink while pens' impressions move
　The bleeding veins of never dying love,
I render here: these wounding lines of smart,
　Sad Characters indeed of simple love,
　Not Art nor skill, which abler wits do prove;
Of my full soul receive the meanest part,

Receive these Hymns, these obsequies receive;
　If any mark of thy sweet sprite appear,
　Well are they born, no title else shall bear.
I can no more: Dear Soul, I take my leave.
　Sorrow still strives, would mount thy highest sphere,
　Presuming so just cause might meet thee there—
Oh happy change, could I so take my leave!

The main expressive effort here is not, as in many laments for Sidney, to portray intense grief, the joys of heaven, and pity for his early death and unfulfilled talents—though these points are included—but to act out the countess's emotional process of trying to become, out of love for her brother, the writer and patron who could step into his harness and carry on. Her presentation of the process begins with a bold image of her own Muse mating with her brother's, "So dared my Muse with thine itself combine," the first of a set of such metaphors suggesting a giving or dissolving of self into tribute to the beloved one, such as would bring on creation of inspired words. The next is a zeal to do endlessly what can never be done enough as response to his honor and his inspiration of her, namely to "unfold Love" into a "world of words." The formulation evokes a memorable scene of the *Arcadia*, where Pyrocles on the banks of the river Ladon adores Philoclea bathing and composes an ecstatic song of her beauties and virtues, after which the narrator describes his own composing of words as "desire cut out in endless folds." We recall that Sidney had declared the *Arcadia* to have been written only for his sister, and mostly in her presence.

The third such metaphor of writerly giving or dissolving of the self into tribute to the loved brother is the one studied above in connection with Daniel's first Delia sonnet, the Ditchley portrait of the queen, and the countess's 1592 draft of this "angel" poem: "as little streams with all their all do flow / To their great sea, . . . So press my thoughts . . . To pay the debt of infinites I owe / To thy great worth." Such a flow of streams of honoring, from herself to him, was the writing of these psalms now finished. And finally, the penultimate stanza reinvokes the wound of stanza 3, opened and "fresh bleeding" (along with flowing "heart's tears"), and draws heart's blood for transmutation into flowing ink: "these dearest offerings of my heart, / Dissolved to Ink while pens' impressions move / The bleeding veins of never dying love, / I render here . . . Sad Characters indeed of simple love"—as if she had tapped into a vein and let red ink flow till the psalms were done.

These four effectively interrelated metaphors—of the mating brother and sister Muses, of endless unfolding of love into words, of love rivers flowing to a boundless sea, and of heart's blood poured out as the ink of devoted writing—express the fullest possible engagement of the countess with her brother and his life's work. As speaker of this poem she seems out to justify, or to supply a grounding for, the highly unusual case of a woman's devotion to such a love and such a calling as writer; for in the 1599 text of the poem she adds a whole stanza of appeal to "sacred Truth," called upon to "solemnize" the rites of this dedication of her psalms, as if an obligation courageously to declare the "true" basis of her years of labor were upon her. And the final stanza repeats the word of appeal, "receive," three times, amounting to a kind of incantation ritual concluding her rites of dedication. She ends her self-imaging, then, in the guise of a priestess lifting up the sacrificial offering (of poems), as in the communion service, for that angel-addressee in heaven to take to the divine throne, asking that it be received.

Within the frame of these four related metaphors the poem has further images to offer, as she reflects on the writer she has become. There is, as noted, the concept of Philip Sidney's works as strikingly designed buildings, now finished enough for functioning and preservation through the countess's editing and additions. And secondly, stanza 2 explains what sort of translation the two of them, in this "coupled work," have tried to do in daring to render a book of divinely inspired scripture in their own experimental modes of verse. They have only meant in their work "to admire these sacred Hymns," not claiming to have replicated them, just as they only hope "to praise, not to aspire to" the angels' songs of heaven, in trying to imitate those. It is a modest concept of both translation and imitation: one does not claim to reproduce the source text but only to offer something that can stand in praise and admiration of it. The notion also clearly expresses a paratextual dimension of translation, as charted above in Genette's terms.

In this poem, as also in its companion piece and in many of the psalms, we hear a distinctive speaking voice of the countess as a poet, different from any of her brother's typical poetic voices, although she learned many techniques from him: high-toned and aristocratic, though also earthy; intelligent and fond of carefully worked out rhetorical figures, especially figures of sound interwoven with logical figures of opposition; always ready to descend into convoluted syntax or elision, for the sake of a telling phrase or metrically fitting line.

To sum up the observations here of how the Countess of Pembroke, uniquely among Elizabethan women, developed the sustained authorial identity that allowed her to speak with this voice, she did so through interacting with a fairly consistent circle of committedly Protestant writers and other contemporaries. And she had essential advantages that no other woman of her time and place possessed in such measure: first, a situation of adequate wealth and standing to allow her to make her own reading circle of admiring associates— integrated with a usual aristocratic lady's reading group of gentlewoman and menservants; a male protégé supplying a supportive imaginary world of poetic grieving (Fraunce); and two other, better poets (Daniel and Breton) sometimes in attendance. Second and crucially, she could with these associates' help draw upon a past mutual love experience with a brother of great literary accomplishment; she was able to nurture his memory and channel his ideology into her own identity and development as a writer. Out of these advantages, her greatest achievement, so far as we know, was her metaphrastic psalms; otherwise we have only a few original poems, most of which fell officially within the sphere of the paratextual, framing her brother's work.[29]

4

Catholic Squirearchy and Women's Writing

The Countesses of Oxford and Arundel and Elizabeth Weston

IN THE FIRST two decades of Elizabeth I's reign, the struggle of English
Protestants to control the throne, after the setback of the Roman Catholic
Mary Tudor's reign, was by no means secure in outcome. It was contested by
forces centering economically and symbolically in landed families of pre-Tudor
lineage, whom the clever Elizabeth gradually learned to control. I have called
their ideological self-concept squirearchical (see n. 5), although literally a squire
was a country gentleman farm-owner of relatively low aristocratic standing;
however wealthy and entrepreneurial some of them might be, the paradigmatic
center of their ideological self-imaging was the feudal notion of an independent, divinely ordained lord of the castle—defender of a long-defined, stable
agricultural unit of land with its people.[1] Through the 1560s the queen was
casting about for a workable balance of forces that would let her manage the
mix of ideological groupings she faced in that era of uncertain Reformation
and emergent capitalism, even secretly discussing returning England to the Roman church, in exchange for a declaration of legitimacy for herself. Just as the
Pope tired of that game and finally excommunicated her (1570), absolving
Catholic subjects of loyalty to her, the Catholic rival claimant for the throne,
Henry VII's great-granddaughter Mary Stuart, Queen of Scots, had become a
prisoner of Elizabeth (1568–1569), fleeing Scotland under an accusation of conspiring her husband Darnley's murder. These factors in Elizabeth's particular
Protestant identity, thus by 1571 politically determined, must be recalled as we
consider what importance a Catholic identity had for Englishwomen as potential writers, an identity different from that of Catholics on the continent. The
Elizabethan social text (to take Kristeva's concept of the combined processes
and productions of all the interactive meaning systems at play in a given milieu)[2] had to read differently for them from the way it read for Protestant
women inclined to translate, polemicize, or versify.

Out of this unprecedented situation from 1569–1587—that of a putatively
murderous but legitimate female monarch (female rule itself being a contested

concept) stewing in captivity under an illegitimate, excommunicated female monarch busy evolving her own state church—out of that multi-layered dyad of the two queens grew a particular sociosemiotic complex of meaning systems within which, I suggest, certain new possibilities for gender construction emerged. And of course, the ways in which either women or men found themselves gendered made a distinct factor in their self-concepts as writers. What men generally did about it, Elizabeth herself actively cooperating, has been abundantly studied in accounts of the Petrarchizing of Elizabethan political discourses,[3] which defined themselves by taking the queen as sociopolitical enunciatee: within that discursive formation she posed as a regally silent, surrounded object of adoration, either nodding or frowning to show either favor or withholding of favor. In such a set of meaning systems, the imprisoned Mary Stuart was forced to be Elizabeth's opposite on this grid of garrulity-silence too, as on so many others: she babbled incessant and unheeded epistolary pleas for help to all and sundry. (Her only perhaps satisfying outlet for aggression through meaning-making was the emblematics of the embroidery needle, in which medium she portrayed her hope of Elizabeth's demise in such images as a pruning of the Tudor tree, and the thistles worked into a gown sent to Elizabeth as a gift.)[4] Thus the garrulity-silence opposition (strongly emphasized by conduct books on women's behavior, and see below on *Euphues*), like so much else in England, attached itself sociolinguistically to the dyad of the two queens. (I have elsewhere argued for the existence of an Elizabethan ideologeme, growing in part out of this opposition of queens, namely that of the captive [independent, repelled, tolerated] woman.[5])

Part of the impact such a factor had on gender imaging arose from its broader epistemological edge. It created new possibilities for doubt, repressed fear, and zealotry about the rightness of one's own religious and gender perspectives, since to each confessional group, "our" queen was the bright and good one, the other being the dark and evil usurper; that is, holders of the two perspectives must have been uneasily aware that they shared exactly the same symbolic/oppositional terms, merely reversing their poles of valorization—as when the earth sometimes supposedly, and unaccountably, inverts its magnetic field, making north south. Something of the resultant blank-cipher quality of this gendered power imaging—and of gender imaging itself—must have entered people's subliminal awareness.

Once the 1569 Catholic uprising of the northern earls had occurred, a Catholic identity was ineluctably subversive. Yet Elizabeth understood the continuing appeal of old faith practices, especially among rural people, who liked to pin their personal identity to concepts of many-generationed name and merit and to patterns of domination based on continuity of estate ownership, even amid the radically changing economy of land enclosure, shop production of wool, and capital accumulation. They would typically see themselves as either "old-family" offspring or dependents of such in a quasi-feudal relation, whether they were town dwellers or actually tenant farmers. Queen Elizabeth pragmatically pretended, at certain levels of political functioning, that this identity was not subversive, that Catholics, keeping their religious identity, could yet be her loyal subjects. Some were. But the plots to free Mary Stuart—periodically forming around that magnetic pole of the unjustly imprisoned shadow queen and several times tending to their logical end phase of overthrowing Elizabeth—made her supposition notoriously difficult. She continued the balancing act of its pursuit through the 1570s, an effort culminating in her attempt of 1579 to marry a French Catholic royal scion, the Duke of Alençon and Anjou. That marriage would have shifted the balance distinctly against further Protestant reform and in favor of codified civil toleration of Catholics.[6] But after giving up on it by 1581 and finding still more plots fomenting around Mary Stuart, she at last ceased her effort at interconfessional balance, permitting the parliamentary Recusancy Act of 1580 to impose heavy fines and other penalties on practicing Catholics. By 1587 she would execute Mary Stuart, not without agonizing; for the idea that any crowned head might roll was anathema to her.

As noted, we are reviewing—and to some extent retheorizing—these well-known matters so as to consider the importance of English Catholic squirearchy in the lives of women as potential writers. As Catholicism became less and less tolerated (further Parliamentary acts tightened the screws until in 1592 Catholics could not even travel more than five miles from home), educated Catholic households became quite different from that pre-Reformational image of the beneficent, father-controlled haven portrayed by Erasmus, Vives, and More, where the intellect and spirituality of wives and daughters was to be fostered, though only for private uses. After the Act of 1580, since married women could not be fined because they were legal nonentities (who could own no property), a surprising inverted gender pattern developed among Catholic gentry.[7] Husbands submissively attended Anglican services and otherwise upheld public Protestant appearances to try to avoid recusancy fines, while wives at home sheltered priests, took part in conspiracies, held private masses, maintained secret travel networks, and sometimes gained a degree of initiative in religious affairs well beyond what most of their Protestant counterparts could exercise. They also were in a particular way less dependent on marriage for livelihood and for self-imaging, since there was potentially the respected alternative of entering a convent on the continent. Eventually these conditions would lead to so enterprising a Catholic activist for women's education as Mary Ward (Rowlands 169–74; Warnicke 198–99). Meanwhile, they must have thrown new side-lights on gender. Behind them sociolinguistically was always the symbolic unit of the imprisoned shadow queen: threatening or enticing, depending on one's viewpoint—a kind of darkling or glittering female terra incognita. She, even more than other Catholic women, was placed outside the moral control of male codes for women by her anomalous situation: from her viewpoint, as a rightful monarch so foully abused by false imprisonment and denial of any chance to answer the charges against her, anything that might free her was fair game. She eventually told Elizabeth so, in various letters.[8]

From 1571 to 1573, Elizabeth had fended off major threats to her emerging politico-religious center from opposite directions: she executed the Duke of Norfolk (1572) for having conspired to free and marry Mary Stuart (he had probably at first meant only to restore her to her Scottish throne but fell in with the more radical Ridolfi plot to overthrow Elizabeth); and in Parliament Elizabeth defeated the Puritan, antivestarian "admonishers" Feild and Wilcox, along with delicensing their militant fellow reformist preacher Edward Dering (see chapter 2). The man who managed both these feats for her was that shrewdest of centrist politicos, her chief secretary William Cecil, Lord Burghley, whose daughter Anne was married in December 1571—just at the height of these developments—to Edward de Vere, seventeenth Earl of Oxford and Norfolk's first cousin.

The Sonnets of Anne Cecil, Countess of Oxford, and a Poem of Anne Dacre, Countess of Arundel

The context just evoked is that of Anne (Cecil) Vere, Countess of Oxford, and the six poems attributed to her in John Soowthern's *Pandora* (1584, dedicated to her husband Oxford). Already a matter of some doubt, her authorship of these has been directly contested by Steven May, but I will offer a case in favor of it, while describing and analyzing the poems.

In returning to her husband's crypto-Catholic household in 1582 after several years when he had refused to live with her, Anne was entering a milieu and mindset quite different from that of her parents, Lord Burghley and Mildred Cooke Cecil; and it appears she did so eagerly, having very much wanted to marry Oxford in the first place (see Burghley's letters in Read, *Burghley*, especially 275). It is matter of speculation why Oxford had married her,[9] or why a few years later he repudiated her, claiming that she was adulterous (a claim vehemently disputed by both contemporaries and historians). According to Jenkins, he married her at Christmas 1571, in the belief that Burghley would pay his (Oxford's) large debts and would save Norfolk from execution.[10] When Burghley did neither, Oxford took revenge on him—and told one acquaintance that he was doing so—by leaving and defaming Anne for some five years after the birth of their first daughter in 1575 (claiming the child was not his).

During the first three years of that time he traveled on the continent, became a secret Catholic, and returned with a habit of Italianate dressing (parodied by Gabriel Harvey in *Speculum Tuscanismi*); a talented poet himself, Oxford then patronized writers of squirearchical and in some cases explicitly

Catholic leanings, some of whom, like him, had lived abroad. When he came to court in 1578, he took on, along with a large train of liveried dependents, a company of actors and the playwright/prose-writer John Lyly, whose new book *Euphues, the Anatomy of Wit* (1578) and its sequel *Euphues and his England* (1579) made such a hit that Euphuism became a conversational fad at court (Salzman *Elizabethan Prose* xv). No one was anyone who could not talk in hypotactic sentences, with diversely patterned syntactic parallelisms and chiasmas, generously interlarded with Ovidian allusions and metaphors citing quasi-scientific lore, in certain characteristic locutions. (The strength of the fad registers Oxford's period of greatest political impact, when he was the highest ranking supporter of the queen's desired French marriage.)[11] This Euphuism is the stylistic mode of the four sonnets and two quatrains that John Southern attributes to Lady Oxford (*Pandora*, 1584). They should be seen in the context of her return to her husband and participation in his identity and political engagement at court, even though his attempts to maintain standing and influence were already failing (largely because of the queen's rage over his having fathered a child on one of her maids of honor, Ann Vavasour).

Steven May argues that Southern wrote these poems himself because, May believes, they are in exactly the style of the other verse in *Pandora*.[12] He proposes that Southern was engaging in a particular kind of prosopopoeia, a rhetorical device of writing a speech or passage "such as" a given persona, real or imagined, might have spoken, and attributing it to the said personage, in this case as a kind of flattery. But I find that the poems Southern presents as his own are stylistically distinct from the Lady Oxford sonnets in several telling ways and thus that there is no ground for discounting his attribution of them to her. (In a case of such unambiguous attribution, the burden of proof must be on those who would deny it.)

The first reason for not accepting May's theory is a point with which it ill accords: a writer devising such a prosopopoeia would hardly claim that the honored personage has written a larger body of material, out of which he has made selections, two of these being excerpted quatrains cut from complete sonnets. Such a presentation would be pointless, indeed a detraction, if his aim were to publish some elegantly flattering imagined poems, spoken as in the persona of the high lady though not actually hers. Yet in fact, Southern printed as hers, besides four complete sonnets, the concluding four lines from each of two others, exactly so labeled: "OTHERS OF THE FOWRE LAST LYNES, OF OTHER THAT SHE MADE ALSO," and alongside the lines in each case "11, 12, 13, 14."

His high self-esteem, in being confident that he could choose and display the good bits from the lady's efforts, is of a piece with what the rest of *Pandora* shows of him. He was a Frenchman proposing to do for English versifying something akin to what Thomas Watson (another protégé of Oxford's and a former student at Douai—see chapter 3) had done two years before in his *He-*

katompathia, or Passionate Century of Love (1582, also dedicated to Oxford).[13] That is, Southern was seeking to import the techniques of Ronsard and the Pleiade—experiments in quantitative (i.e., non-stress-based) meters—just as Watson had imported the techniques and metaphorics of Petrarch and Serafino. Southern's experimental poems were thus Pindaric odes, Anacreontic lyrics, and even rhythmically odd, nonscanning sonnets. Along with the frequent gallicisms in Southern's verse—i.e., non-English syntax and phrasing, French forms of names ("Ulysse" for Ulysses, etc.), and neologisms based on French words—another fact unmistakably identifies him as a foreigner, namely his *impresa* printed both at the end of his dedicatory ode to Oxford and on the title page: above a woodcut of a poet crowned with laurel wreath stands "*Non careo patria, Me caret illa magis*" [I do not miss (or lack) my country, rather it misses me]. He was sure France was the worse for his absence.[14]

The second reason for attributing the six poems in question to the Countess of Oxford and not to Southern lies in the contrast of two sets of distinctive features: those few minor ones (possibly edited in by Southern) that they share with Southern's own poems in *Pandora*, and those more prominent ones that they do not share with his poems. The following paragraphs will make this case.

The sonnets ascribed to the countess do, as May says, have some features in common with the poems presented as Southern's own: "arhythmic meters, [certain] principles of rhyming [i.e., sometimes on final unstressed syllables], and abbreviated forms of certain proper nouns" (May 9–10). But these features do not add up to an indication that Southern wrote the poems himself (May 14). Rather, they support two feasible conclusions: first, that Southern either was her tutor (perhaps for French) or was otherwise one of the Earl's protégés whose verse experiments she partially imitated; and second, that he had a free hand to edit the verses he ascribes to her (as he shows by his excerpting he did have), pushing them a little further toward his own habits. On the score of Southern's French name forms, we do find a few in the Bulbecke sonnets (Lord Bulbecke being the name of the countess's lamented infant son), but in these instances she might well have written "Destinies," "Adonis," and "Pelides," which Southern in his keenness for his French-sounding, staccato lines could have edited to "Destins," "Adon," and "Pelid." The only one that might indicate more extensive gallicizing ("Promet" rhymed with "heat") will be considered shortly.

More prominent than these similarities are three features of the verse presented as Southern's own that we notably do not find in the sonnets ascribed to the countess: his gallicisms of phrasing and diction, his practice of hyphenating across line endings to get exact syllable counts in particular lines, and his failures with English syntax. Instead we see in the Bulbecke sonnets a poet fully in command of English syntax, and while experimenting with heavily accented Euphuist phrases and with the odd rhythms that resulted from adapting the abstract, nonaudible system of quantitative meters from Greek and Latin, yet never using hyphenation across line endings.[15] The first sonnet illustrates these points, with the penultimate line in the voice of Venus implying the construction 'As I was the mother of Cupid, even so I am the mother of it.'

> Had, with the morning, the gods left their wills undone,
>   They had not so soon 'herited such a soul;
> Or if the mouth time did not glutton up all,
>   Nor I nor the world were deprived of my son,
> Whose breast *Venus*, with a face doleful and mild,
>   Doth wash with golden tears, inveighing the skies.
> And when the water of the goddess' eyes
> Makes almost alive the marble of my child,
>   One bids her leave still her dolor so extreme,
>   Telling her it is not her young son *Papheme*;*   [Cupid]
> To which she makes answer with a voice inflamed
> (Feeling therewith her venom to be more bitter):
> As I was of Cupid, even so of it mother,
> And a woman's last child is the most beloved.

In a sophisticated and synchretic female appropriation of Ovidianism, the grieving speaker steps into the role of Venus grieving and enraged, coalescing several highly emotive moments of the goddess's portrayal in different poems of Ovid. That is, the rage echoes, among other places, portions of the *Metamorphoses* where Venus turns those who offend her into horned animals or into stone (e.g., *Metamorphoses* 10, ls. 220ff.). Further, the speaker's grief and intense longing that the boy's body might come alive draw on both the Pygmalion story (of the beloved stone statue made alive by Venus—cf. "makes almost alive the marble of my child"), and the *Amores* III, 9, where Ovid portrays Venus's angry grieving for her adored boy lover Adonis, in order to claim that she is grieving thus again for the subject of his elegy, Tibullus the love poet.[16]

Indeed, this famous poem of Ovid's ("Memnona si mater, mater ploravit Achillem") seems to have been pervasive in the countess's thoughts, as they emerge here in sonnet form. It begins with an invocation of goddess or demigoddess mothers lamenting their dead sons—Aurora for Memnon, Thetis for Achilles. Next the elegy itself is addressed and personified as a grieving mother, unbinding her long hair for the funeral rites; then the reminiscence of grieving Venus leads to a declaration about inexorable Death, who profanes all the hallowed people with her dark touch. Later in the poem, Venus weeping is evoked again ("Avertit vultus Erycis quae possidet arces; / sunt quoque qui lacrimas continuisse negant"), and Ovid ends on the urbane but intense note that if anything of a human being really survives among shades, Tibullus will be in

Elysium graceful and happy, among other great poets. These evocations of Venus as an angry and grieving mother—a powerful figure, herself shadowing a female image of death—become the focal images of the countess's sonnet.

The English female voice here expressing such "inflamed" bitterness is also enabled by the kind of portrayed female speech the countess would know in John Lyly's *Euphues* (see above), that most fiercely misogynist of Elizabethan prose fictions, which presents aggressive and verbally adept women only to vilify them. That is, we see in "Had with the morning" the typical Euphuist restrictive-appositional pairs ("the mouth time"), postpositional adjectives ("face doleful," "dolor so extreme"), and parallelisms incorporating ellipsis ("as I was of Cupid, even so of it mother"). Lucilla, the heroine of *Euphues* (like a whole line of her successors in its imitations of the 1580s and 1590s), is so assertive, talkative, self-centered, changeable, and rebellious against male authority that, as with the Scots' queen in captivity, almost anything seems morally possible for her; conventional male codes for women seem blanked out. I see this courtly tale-spinning and rhetoric-spinning of *Euphues* and some of its imitations— i.e., the repeated plot of a callow youth battered by treacherous women in particular and Dame Fortune in general as he tries to mature—as a squirearchical mode of fictionalizing, expressing male fears of, so to speak, woman out of hand inside a sphere deliberately screened from male public codes by the necessity of Catholic privacy (see above). In one referential layer, the woman-out-of-hand is Queen Elizabeth, running rampant over the old and right order of the land. Another layer would be the situation of Catholic gentlewomen as it was coming to be defined—slipping from male control both public and private through their legal nonstatus. In drawing, as it were perversely, upon Euphuism as a distinctive style and in claiming its male-constructed female voice, the speaker of Lady Oxford's sonnets sounds more like an aggressive Lucilla or Mamillia (cf. Robert Greene's gender-inverted *Euphues*-imitation of that name) than like the pious Protestant voices of her mother and aunts, the Cooke sisters (see chapter 2). In such a vein the countess can pour out her grief and anger. She would have especially needed to do so, for the lost boy was not just any mother's dead and bewept child; as the eighteenth Earl of Oxford he would have been just the achievement to heal her wounded name.

By contrast with the above poem, with its features (just noted) not found in Southern's own verses, let us observe Southern at work in the following passage; note especially what happens in the second half of it when he tries for complex English syntax. In this case he is not writing a sonnet but a lyric in a sort of quasi-dimeters, counting syllables per line so carefully that he hyphenates at times to get the right number, as noted above. "Warrior" here, as in Ronsard, refers to his addressed supposed lady (politically, also to Queen Elizabeth):

from "Elegia. 3. *To his Diana*"

> . . . if any golden words,
>   In well composed verse,
> Could lively show the picture
>   Of an amorous rage,
> Then should I without doubt amo-
>   lish a Tiger's courage,
> And move to pity, warrior, if
>   it were, the universe.
> But since words neither can prescribe
>   My amour nor my pain,
> Time shall itself witness how much
>   both are in me, certaine:
> And that of my passioned soul,
>   The Divine great loyalties,
> Do the sacredness of all o-
>   thers, I of the gods pass;
> And more than the silver maje-
>   sties of your Christall face,
> Underneath t'other *Phebes*, do
>   Excell all other *Beutaes*.

Aside from obvious gallicisms or errors—like the verb *amollir* (soften) pressed into English service as "amolish," the parenthetical qualifier phrase "if it were" (for something like "it might even be"), the word "prescribe" where he means "describe," *certaine* as an adverb (rhymed with "pain"), and "beau-*taies*" rhymed with "face"—besides all such, the still more obvious nonnative feature of the English here is the hopeless syntactic muddle of the last eight lines. Just what was the intended sense may be indeterminate, but probably something like this: "As the amour and pain of my passionate soul, great divine loyalties, surpass the sacredness of all other feelings, so I surpass the gods; and more than the silver majesties of your christall face excell those of the other *Phebes* [planetary nymphs],[17] do you excell all other beauties." He was attempting some such pair of comparison-parallels, with characteristic Euphuist ellipsis of words he thought readers could infer. But elliptical syntax in English was beyond Southern's competence. Nowhere in the six poems ascribed to the Countess of Oxford do we find these features.

Furthermore, we do not find in Southern the features imitative of *Euphues* (see above) and of Watson and Petrarch that the Bulbecke sonnets exhibit. Consider the countess's number 3, structured according to the principle of correlative verse, illustrated in Watson's *Hekatompathia* (e.g., no. 47, "In time the bull is brought to wear the yoke"). Such a poem has a list-and-relist organization, whereby certain items or themes (usually three) are set forth in the first line or two, then each of them treated in the poem's midsection, and finally reiterated again in the conclusion (cf. also Shakespeare's sonnets no. 77 and no. 91). She also here uses personifications typical of Petrarch and his imitators, i.e., of abstractions such as Death (e.g., Watson's *Hekatompathia* no. 54). We even recognize here explicitly Petrarch's "Amor, quando fioria mia spene" (part of which was famously set as a madrigal by Luca Marenzio: "Ahi dispietata morte, ahi crudel vita"), which laments the passing of Laura just at the height of the poet's love for her (see my *Living Lyre* 21–26). That is, the countess's line "Life doth keep me here against my will" (l. 4) directly translates Petrarch's "l'altra [i.e., la vita] mi tien quaggiu contra mia voglia." Thus the mother's love for her dead boy child is, intriguingly, infused with that of a male sonneteer for his newly dead lady.

> The heavens, death, and life have conjured my ill:
>> For death hath ta'en[18] away the breath of my son.
> The heavens receive and consent that he hath done,
>> And my life doth keep me here against my will.
> But if our life be caused with moisture and heat,
>> I care neither for the death, the life, nor skies:
>> For I'll sigh him warmth, and wet him with my eyes,
>> And thus I shall be thought a second *Promet'*.
>>> And as for life, let it do me all despite:
> For if it leave me, I shall go to my child,
>> And it in the heavens, there is all my delight.
> And if I live, my virtue is immortal,
> "So that the heavens, death, and life, when they do all
> Their force, by sorrowful virtue th'are beguiled."[19]

Line 2 (which actually reads "hath take"—see n. 17) and line 6 of this sonnet contain the only possible grammatical gallicisms that I find in the six Bulbecke poems, and as noted, these could easily have been edited in by Southern: one would suspect that the countess wrote "I care neither for death, nor life, nor the skies," but that Southern, for some quantitative scheme he fancied, wanted the hendecasyllabic line to be in a different pattern of officially short and long syllables (see n. 13). Or perhaps he was just thinking of *la mort* and *la vie*. This Frenchified line falls within the same quatrain containing the "Promet"-"heat" rhyme, so perhaps in this one passage we have an instance of larger-scale tampering by Southern.

To sum up the case for the Countess of Oxford's authorship of the six Bulbecke poems and against that of Southern, they contain nothing like the Southern poems' high level of gallicisms in diction, word form, and syntax (the few instances of these features could easily have been edited in), nor do they hyphenate words across line endings. The Bulbecke poems do show a versifier competently practicing a fashionable Euphuist style, fashionable imitation of Watson's sonneteering habits, and a female usage of Elizabethan Ovidianism— features not prominent or not present in the verse presented as Southern's own.

A few more points are worth observing here, as we get acquainted with these poems. The Bulbecke sonnet number 2 opens with the Ovidian image of the mythic Tityus, who for assaulting a goddess was condemned to have his liver eternally eaten by a vulture, then restored and eaten again (cf. Watson's *Hekatompathia* nos. 51, 62). The countess turns this to an image of herself as a vulture of grief endlessly gnawing her own heart.

> In doleful ways I spend the wealth of my time,
>   Feeding on my heart, that ever comes again,
> Since the ordinance of the Destins' hath been
>   To end, of the seasons of my years, the prime.
> With my son, my gold, my nightingale, and rose
>   Is gone: for 'twas in him and no other where.
> And well though mine eyes run down like fountains here,
>   The stone will not speak yet, that doth it enclose.
>   And Destins' and gods, you might rather have ta'en
>   My twenty years than the two days of my son.
> And of this world what shall I hope, since I know
> That in his respect it can yield me but moss.
> Or what should I consume any more in woe,
>   When Destins', gods, and worlds are all in my loss.

In good Euphuist fashion for glossing images of natural philosophy (i.e., science), a marginal note on the *Pandora* page explains the gold, nightingale, and rose as best of metals, sweetest of birds, and fairest of flowers.

In the final excerpted quatrain, as Moody has noted, the countess deftly applies the Ovidian story of Niobe turned to a water-covered rock formation, weeping for her dead children. By referring to Niobe as Amphion's wife rather than by her name, the countess evokes with pride the image of her own husband Oxford as poet-singer, having lost his heir; and at the same time with the rock image she expresses the numbness, inwardness, and loss of all sense of time in her grieving: for in this imagined stony self she can be both Niobe, the timeless weeping rock, and the sepulchre rock that will hold the child's body, as once she held him in her womb.

> Amphion's wife was turned to a rock. O
> How well I had been, had I had such adventure,
> For then I might again have been the sepulchre
> Of him that I bare in me, so long ago.

The Countess of Oxford herself was not, so far as anyone knows, a Catholic. But I suggest that these sonnets show her as a young woman of poetic ability who, once reunited with her husband, attuned herself whole-heartedly to his self-defined political and continentally artistic mannerist milieu and absorbed herself in it. Oxford was not of the stuff of martyrs; he had already backed out of his Catholicism, once its agenda had lost at court.[20] He would leave others of the Howard family and faction to carry on the cause. The last try his entourage would make for the cause of saving Mary Stuart was John Lyly's best play *Endymion* (1585–86), which while center-stage ecstatically idealizing Leicester's long and newly restored relationship to the queen, in a subplot quietly frees the captive Mary Stuart figure ("Cynthia's" duplicitous rival Tellus [Earth]) by marrying her off to a safely containing country nobleman— that "final solution" which the Catholic and crypto-Catholic faction had so long advocated. Burghley and the queen still did not heed the urging and would soon execute Mary (1587).

A woman who was part of the Howard family by marriage, namely Anne (Dacre) Howard, Countess of Arundel, has left us at least one poem, in the form of a verse prayer[21] that is (in its English part) either her composition or her redaction of a lyrical prayer by her husband's great-great-grandmother Eleanor Percy Stafford, Duchess of Buckingham (the final stanza seems to leave somewhat in doubt how much of the text she is attributing to the duchess). Herself from a northern family known for Catholic commitment, the Countess of Arundel had been in childhood the ward of the later executed Norfolk and was the wife of his eldest son Philip, who, unable to inherit his attaindered father's title, became Earl of Arundel in his mother's right. After living with his wife long enough to father another Earl (to become the Jacobean Arundel), Philip Howard spent the rest of his fairly short life in the Tower on a charge of treason, becoming revered as a Catholic martyr. Mary Stuart, from her own captivity, wrote to the Countess of Arundel (July 30, 1585) in consoling fashion, addressing her as "cousin"[22]—she would have become Philip Howard's stepmother, had the Norfolk marriage plan succeeded.

Unlike the Countess of Oxford, the Countess of Arundel was an avowed Catholic, and unlike Lady Oxford's fashionably experimental courtly sonnets, the prayer she signs is a devotional lyric in triplets with old-fashioned diction, created as commentary on a medieval kind of verse in rhyming Latin.[23] I thank Donald Foster for generously sending me a transcript of it, prepared for his extensive forthcoming anthology *Women's Works*, which will have the original text; here I have modernized the spelling and punctuation. The Latin verses, "compiled" and used by the Henrician Duchess of Buckingham as a prayer for herself, would be a liturgical or devotional piece, presumably either for Ascension Day or for one of the feasts of the Virgin Mary (Annunciation or Assumption), in this case taken as text for a woman facing her own death. In meditating on each of the rhyming phrases through a lyric in English (on the left), the Countess of Arundel at once remembers Eleanor, prays for her salvation, and reclaims the text for herself as well. This kind of intertextual response and incorporation reflects the sense of communion and ideological oneness among aristocratic Catholic families of the period. Anne Dacre Howard cannot have known Eleanor, so the choice of her soul and her copied out Latin poem as subjects for personal devotion is a matter of feeling an integral part of this long-persecuted family in which she had been raised and married, with one of its most prominent men having been executed in almost every sixteenth-century generation (starting with Eleanor's husband the Duke) for being enemies of the Tudors.

Oratio Eleanor Percy, Ducissa Buckingham

Good Virgin, and mother being
To Christ Jesus both God and king,
By thee blessed, yare* him conceiving—

Gabrielis nuncio
       * *(straightway)*

Good Virgin, of all humility
Showing to us thy Son's humanity
When he without pain born was of thee—

Cum pudoris lilio

Good flower of thy Lord and Son
Dying (without gift) for our redemption,
To thy great joy and our salvation—

Fulgit resurrectio

Good for Christ ascended is
With all triumph t'eternal bliss,
From whence he came first, Iwis*—

Motu fertur proprio
       * *(I know)*

Good sweet rose, for thy blessed ure*
Assumed thou wast with angel cure,
With joy evermore there to endure—

       * *(ways)*
In coeli palacio

Good Virgin and mother of grace,
Pray to thy Son for our tresspass,
That we may come to that heavenly place,

Secretorum contubernio

Whereas the fruit of thy womb truly
To our most comfort, most dear lady,
Shall still there reign everlastingly—

In prophetem gaudio

This prayer compiled of virtuous memory
By the right noble Duchess Buck'hammie,
Whose soul God pardon, late Eleanor Percy.

Verit[as] a titulo.

Say one pater noster and one Ave Marie and one credo for her soul and all Christen souls.

Jesus   Lady
                    Anne Arundel
Maria   Help

(B.L. MS Arundel 318. fol. 152)

The line "Dying (without gift) for our redemption" seems to mean that while usually someone "redeeming" something (e.g., a piece of foreclosed land) would receive a "gift" or recompense for doing so, Christ redeems mankind without receiving any payment. I would render the Latin poem as follows (emending the final line as Foster suggests from *verit atitulo*, which is metrically defective by one syllable and makes no sense, to *verit[as] a titulo*, though perhaps there could be other possibilities): "Through Gabriel's message / With the lily of chastity / The resurrection shines forth, / He is borne up by his own motion, / In the palace of heaven, / In the company of those hidden away / In the prophet for joy, / [He] the truth by his title" [i.e., as Son of God].

Each triplet stanza takes one of these phrases as its theme and is set in an appositional series of addresses to the Blessed Virgin, as bearer of the redeemer Christ. Each is also a piece of loving praise celebrating one of her adored traits, put into a rhythm of syntactic pattern repetition that enables the meditation to accumulate force as it continues: motherhood as blessing, humility without pain, flowering as resurrection, a holy life raised directly into heaven, motherhood as grace. There is a lightness in the motion of the brief lines that makes them emotionally "carry up" the reciter, as the prayer asks may be done. Its miniature celebrations build up to its version of the central request of Marian devotion, that the Blessed Virgin pray to her son for the sinner's salvation. The traditional idea is of course the sense that mothers sometimes have, as it were, credit with their sons when no one else may.

The poem's devotional linkage of the families of Dacre, Howard, Stafford, and Percy strikes the note of English Catholic identity of the late Elizabethan decades. For readers who might care to look further into this political context and its poetry, some striking verse of martyred Catholic youth, staring death in the face and intensely evoking what will be missed of life, can be found in the surviving writings of a young poet named Chiddiock Tichbourne, one of twelve executed for a part in the Babington plot of 1585, the last attempt to free the Queen of Scots. She herself, existing at one vortex of the symbol systems circling around the dyad of the two queens, out of her depths of frustrated longing through eighteen years of imprisonment, wrote some moving poems; the following stanzas are among several found in a Book of Hours she owned.

Qui iamais dauantage eust contraire le sort
  Si la vie mest moins utile que la mort

Et plustost que chager de mes maus laduenture
   Chacun change pour moi dhumeur et de nature. . . .

Un Coeur que loutrage martire
   Par un mepris ou dun refus
A le pouvoir de faire dire
   Je ne suis plus ce que ie fus. . . .

Pour recompense et pour salaire
   De mon amour et de ma foie
Rendez men ange tutelaire
   Autant comme ie vous en doye

                  (Arbuthnot ed., 167–68)

{Who else has had a lot so thwarted
   That life matters less than death?
And rather than take up my cursed cause,
   To me all men in humor and nature change. . . .

[Mine is][24] a heart that outrage torments
   Through falsifying, or denial
Of the power to speak out—
   I am no more what once I was. . . .

As recompense and as reward
   For my love and faith,
My guardian angel, grant me
   As much as I have given you.} [my translation]

"Westonia": A Catholic Poet in Exile

The poems and exile life of Elizabeth Jane Weston Leo (or Löwe, 1581–1612) let us observe what a Catholic Englishwoman's[25] writerly self-image might be if she lived amid a quite different social text from that of the Elizabethan repression of Roman Catholicism. In September 1583, the former Joan Cooper Weston and her new husband the alchemist Edward Kelley left England for the Continent, along with Kelley's partner in angelic seances, Dr. John Dee. It appears that her small children John and Elizabeth stayed behind, probably until December 1584; the boy (now called John Francis Weston) was registered in the Jesuit Clementine school in Prague in 1585.[26] Their father had been one John Weston "clark," buried at Chipping Norton near Oxford May 6, 1582.[27] According to the story that later spread in Bohemia—perhaps propagated by Kelley and his wife[28]—the father, a nobleman, had traveled to the Continent also but had died a few months after arriving (Kaplicky 107 and *Allgemeine deutsche Biographie* report this).[29] On the basis of various accretions of such misinformation, the lives of Edward Kelley and of Elizabeth "Westonia" the neo-Latin poet have been separately noted for centuries, but in 1928 the Czech scholar Karel Hrdina (see *Enchiridion* 5: 473) pointed out that Edward Kelley was Joan Cooper's second husband, and thus Weston's step-father. In Prague it appears that the couple held a second wedding,[30] perhaps to have their marriage recognized as Catholic (Kaplicky 118).[31] Kelley was knighted by the Emperor Rudolf in 1589,[32] and moved soon afterwards to the town of Jilov, where he had mining interests given him by his patron Peter Wok von Rosenberg (Kaplicky 125–26); there his stepdaughter Elizabeth learned reading, presumably in a petty school, from a master named Jan Sarsan Vodnansky (Kaplicky 165ff.).[33] According to Dee's diary, Joan Kelley went to England during this time, but she was back with Kelley in Prague by early 1591.[34] When Kelley was imprisoned in May 1591,[35] she and her mother moved to the town of Most (in German Brüx), where she continued her schooling with a certain immigrant, "Jan Hammon" or John Hammond, an Oxford man (Binns; Bassnett 4)[36], becoming a fluent neo-Latin versifier by age fourteen. In England at this date a girl— Protestant or Catholic—would have had little chance of receiving a grammar-school education (cf. Adamson; Cressy; Hull). But Elizabeth Weston was supposedly a gentleman's daughter, and perhaps in an exile community it seemed worthwhile to educate such a girl. By her midteens, though raised in English-speaking households, she spoke Italian, German, and Czech, as well as writing Latin habitually, even for letters to her brother.

As for neo-Latin verse, when her family was in dire financial straits, Weston began writing it in earnest, in one of the more marginal forms of public or semipublic writing, outside even the paratextual (see Genette *Seuils*) in its proximity to textual space for a public voice of one's own, but akin to it in conventions of address, format, theme, and metaphorics: a sort of public/personal writing, namely the verse patronage plea. It is akin to paratextual verse in that it mimics the look of a dedicatory poem accompanying a text or other gift offered to a patron but has nothing to offer beyond itself. Upon Kelley's loss of all property and death (possibly a suicide) in 1597 after an attempted escape from prison (*Enchiridion* 5:471), Elizabeth and her mother were stranded in debt, becoming even more desperate when her brother, then a student at Ingolstadt, also died three years later. Through the five years following Kelley's death she wrote, to powerful men at the emperor's court, sophisticated and polished neo-Latin poems. Coming so astonishingly from a charming girl who spoke several languages, these quite won the patrons over to her cause of trying to persuade the emperor to restore some income to her mother from Kelley's confiscated properties. These courtiers failed to persuade the emperor but meanwhile supported her. Astonished herself in turn at how such flattery could bring an income, she began to turn her poems into self-reflexive explorations of her odd dependent life and poetic medium, in some of them leaving the genre of patronage verse behind for other experiments. In 1603 she married a lawyer and agent of the Duke of Braunschweig-Wolfenbüttel at the imperial court, Johann Leo, or probably Löwe,[37] from Eisenach (see her poem to "Leo" in Appendix 2). She would have seven children and die in 1612, leaving three surviving daughters.

One of her patrons, the Silesian Georg Martin von Baldhoven, published a slender octavo of her poems, *Poemata . . . Studio ac opera* (Frankfurt-on-Oder, 1602), most of which she lightly revised for another edition, *Parthenicon* (Prague, n.d., probably 1607).[38] Though she had left England in infancy, she had been raised with a story of a proud family and thus had a sense of English identity to give substance to her longing to return home after Kelley died—so the Ovidian poem below indicates, as does other evidence. Kelley's death in disgrace would obviously have inclined her to revive her Weston identity, omit all explicit mention of Edward Kelley in her published poems, and speak there only in general terms of her family's dreadful misfortunes (his brother Thomas Kelley is, however, named as a relative in a letter printed in her book). When King James came to the English throne, she wrote him a grandiose Latin verse letter in the hope of patronage support for a return home. But he was uninterested; she got nothing better than a secretary's recommendation letter to the emperor and the demeaning experience of being told that her authorship of her own verses had been discounted at James's court.[39] Indeed, under King James, who disliked learned women, the nadir of support for humanist female education would be reached.

The following poem is one of a pair of birthday (actually "name day") pieces to Elizabeth's patron Jindrich Dominacek z Pisnic (or Heinrich von Pisnitz), town chancellor or mayor of Most as well as vice chancellor to the emperor, who gave her and her mother extended hospitality in his own household after Kelley's death. They were linked to this high-ranking official through the marriage of Thomas Kelley to von Pisnitz's niece, Ludmila Lazicka z Pisnic (Kaplicky 137), who would shortly leave for England along with Thomas and their two little sons.[40] The first of the two poems offers very conventional appropriate wishes, while the second, below, takes the theme of the poet's own name day and explores her frustration with the state of helpless dependency in which she lives.

Ad Eundem, De Die S. Elizabethae

Lux hodierna mihi fulsit, Patrone; quid ergo
    Hospitibus ponis fercula lauta meis?
Apposito solvis Baccho mea vincla; solutam
    Suscipis & mecum more parentis agis.
Jure tuo perago grates, tu munera promis
    Jure meo; imparibus daes, capioque modis.

O tibi natalis fausto tuus aethere currat
  Saepius, & faciat nos meminisse tui!
Sic pia sit conjunx longos in Nestoris annos
  Salva, diu valeant pignora cara tori.
His etiam, nostri memores quos nominis esse
  Convivas video, fata benigna precor.
Si res arcta sinat, proprio nunc aere pararem
  Pocula, magnificas instrueremque dapes.
Sed fortuna meam siquidem rapit invida sortem.
  Alterius vivo (quam patienter!) ope.
Hinc quia sum nodis aliorum libera, per te
  Vincta tibi meritis fio, patrone, tuis.

{To the Same [Henry of Pisnic], on St. Elizabeth's Day
[this and following translations by Connie McQuillen]

  Patron, the light of today has shone for me; why then
      Are you serving my guests these finest dishes?
  With wine set out, you dissolve my bonds; solvent
      And free you keep me, and as a parent, guide me.
  As *per* your right, I render thanks; you grant support as *per*
      My right; you give, and by unequal measures, I take.
  O may your birthday more often under propitious skies
      Come round, and may it make us mindful of you.
  May your faithful wife live well all the years of Nestor,
      Long may your bed's dear pledges grow in strength.
  And for our table companions too, our status in mind,
      For these at hand, I pray a kindly fate.
  If circumstance allowed, I'd now myself prepare the finest
      Gilded cups, and spread a festive banquet.
  But envious fortune, truly, despoils my share in life.
      By another's wealth I live—how patiently!
  Then since I am free from others' bonds through you,
      Patron, bound to you I become, through your merits.}

Kelley and his new family had enjoyed considerable wealth and noble status during a brief stretch of her childhood, but she steadily proclaims an aristo-cratic self-concept based rather on her supposed noble Weston identity. In this and many of the other poems we see the distress of the family's total deflation of fortune keenly explored from her viewpoint.

She turns the phrasal symmetry of her Augustan Latin mode to her own purposes, one being to cope with the asymmetry of the patronage relationships whereby her writing supports and will support herself and her mother until she might marry, about which possibility one poem expresses her attitudes (it is addressed to a bride, Lady Margarethe von Baldhoven—see Appendix 2). Of this syntactic symmetry and emotional asymmetry, lines 5–6 offer the most striking example: it is as if by creating a poem setting "my right" and "your right" in perfect, elaborated syntactic balance she could cancel out the imbalance of dependency that the rest of the poem laments. Unable to get the triple pun on *solutam* into one English word, Connie McQuillen has rendered it "solvent and free"; in two of the three senses of course it is ironic. Relaxed ("dissolved") by drink she literally is at the time, but as for being financially solvent, and free, she is as her last line ruefully says free from monetary and legal bondage only by having entered another and personal sort of bondage, to her patron. Often in reading Weston one wonders what the addressed men may have thought of this sort of thing, whether they did not take it ill. Perhaps some of them only put the poems in pretty drawers unread, while others found them fitting.

Another patronage poem with a note of personal perception is on the garden of the emperor's personal secretary, Johannes Barwitz, where Weston portrays herself walking with that crucial "contact man"; she is reflecting on how a place of lovely, fruitful plants, laid out as a site of recreation and recovery for a pressured official, can seem to exude such potency for making or breaking the appellants lucky enough to have an interview there. As for the poem's functioning in the task of winning patronage, the four-times-repeated word "*hic*," supplying an anaphoric rhythm to the first half of the poem, is a kind of stitch at regular intervals creating the binding she wants to make between "this" garden "here" as a defined place emanating calm recovery and companionship of friends, and the pleas of "widows" and "clients" such as herself, who come in hoping for a taste of its fruits of favor.

In Hortos Eiusdem [i.e., of Johannes Barwitz]

> Hortus oderatus hic est cultissimus herbis,
>   Barviti assidua cultus, & altus ope.
> Hic, quoties lassum te Caesaris aula remittit
>   A curis relevas pectora fessa tuis.
> Hic locus est fidis etiam concessus amicis;
>   Hic datur aspectu colloquioque frui.
> Hic audire preces viduarum, & vota clientum
>   Suscipere, innata pro bonitate, soles.
> Sic Domino servit decoratus floribus hortus:
>   Atque horti Dominus gaudet honore sui.
> Quid precer huic igitur? ne vel Zephyritida Cauri
>   Aut Euri rabies impetuosa fuget.
> Sed vireat variis ita fructibus, atque quotennis
>   Suppeditet Domino munera grata suo.

Quidve precer Domino? ne laedat livor in aula;
  Virtuti semper qui comes esse solet.

(*Parthenicon* I, A₈)

[On the Garden of the Same Man (i.e., Johannes Barwitz)

> Here is a fragrant garden, with plants well cultivated,
>   Tended and nourished by Barwitz' constant work.
> Here when Caesar's court returns you weary,
>   You lighten your exhausted breast of cares.
> This place indeed has been granted for faithful friends,
>   Here one is to enjoy the view and company.
> Here normally you hear the widows' prayers and receive
>   The pleas of clients, out of innate justice.
> Thus the garden adorned with flowers serves its lord
>   And the lord rejoices in his garden's honor.
> Then what shall I ask for it? that neither the northwest Zephyr
>   Nor the rage of fierce southwestern winds destroy;
> Rather may it flourish with its various fruits
>   And yearly supply its lord with pleasing gifts.
> Or what shall I ask for its lord? that he who is always virtue's
>   Companion, that he not suffer envy in the court.]

Folded into a set of four poems (the other three being quite conventional patronage pieces) to her publisher, von Baldhoven, one patron who undoubtedly did read them, is a quite personal one addressed to Ovid (Publius Ovidius Naso—called "Naso" in the Renaissance), whom Weston regards as a kindred spirit because he suffered exile, as she had, and lamented it in poems, and because one of these is addressed to a young woman poet, Perilla, portrayed as his former pupil (*Tristia* 3.7).[41] Weston steps into the role of this young woman, as it were, and replies—in a kind of plea for commiseration that represents another way (of those we have noted) that a woman could find and motivate a voice. She replies to her exiled poetic mentor and model of ancient Rome, revealing that she still considered herself English and would have liked to return home. The first line refers to the belief that Ovid was officially being punished for an offense given to Augustus Caesar by his *Art of Love*.

In 2 Ovidii. Trist.

Sors tua, Naso tuae precium artis, plurima mecum
  De proprio voluit participare malo:
Cujus in haec tandem creverunt agmina vires,
  Effundi solitas ut superent lacrymas.

Duco reluctantes extrema per omnia Musas:
 Nec mihi, qua pergo, quave recedo, via est.
Perpetuine igitur luctus iniere Calendae,
 Exiit auspiciis ultima meta meis!
Torqueor, & miseri quaerens solamina casus,
 Tristibus inficior, Naso, misella tuis.
Ultima enim primi repetens documenta libelli,
 Eventus video fati utriusque pares.
Dum mea me in similem rapuerunt tempora sortem,
 Quamvis dissimiles causa det ipsa modos,
Qui te Sarmaticas mensis projecit in oras,
 Prima idem fati visus origo mei.
Missus in exilium freta per diversa luisti
 Supplicio culpam tu graviore tuam:
Exsul ego heic dudum peregrinae supplico terrae,
 Quae mala dat quovis horridiora freto.
Te piger hospitio profugum rigor excipit Ursae,
 Qua jacet extremo terra subacta gelu:
Arctophylax nostro non multum a vertice distat:
 Longaque Phoebum atris nubibus addit hyems:
Una tibi Nerei movet inclementia bilem,
 Quam tamen amplexu vel Thetis una levat.
In me perpetuos armat fera turba furores.
 Ah dolor! in me aditus impetus omnis habet!
Scribenti, cartam feriunt tibi gurgit[es] undae:
 Et mea, sed lacrymis, scripta rigata madent.
Propria tu destes incommoda: me omnia solam,
 Qua vix ingenuae sunt toleranda, gravant.
Tu patriam, incolumes patriae sed linquis amicos:
 Mi pater & patrii hoc interiere lares.
Sauromatae infestant crebris tibi cuncta rapinis:
 Et mihi, quae non dat, gens furibunda rapit!
Noxia fecisti tu lumina: & artis honorem
 Laesisti: poenas carmen, & error habet:
Pro pietate mihi crudelis reddita merces:
 Culpa etenim tanti nulla probata mali.
Jamque tui tecum poterat querimonia luctus
 Fortia Magnanimi frangere corda viri.
Quem non & tenerae moveant lamenta puellae,
 Damnaque barbaricis vix superanda Getis?
Ergo tuo liceat mea fata dolere dolore!
 Ah melior quanto sors tua sorte mea est!

 (*Parthenicon* I, C$_{5v}$)

{On Ovid's *Tristia*, II

Your lot, your exile Naso, price of your *Art*,
  Offers me ways to see my own misfortune,
The effects of which have grown to these forced marches
  That overpower tears so often wept.
I lead reluctant Muses through all extremes;
  Nor can I go forward nor return.
The months of endless sadness have begun,
  For my hopes the point of return has passed by.
I am tortured, and seeking comfort for my misery
  I find solace, Naso, in your *Tristia*.
Re-reading the final lesson of your first book,
  I see we share the same events of fate.
For my furies have thrust me into similar straits
  Although for me the cause is different.
The month that saw you out to Sarmatian shores
  Was the same that saw my fate take hold.
Sent into exile through diverse seas, you paid for
  Your offense with a deeper humiliation.
An exile here, I am brought low in a foreign land
  That gives me hardship worse than any sea.
The dull harshness of the Bear-sign receives you, an exile,
  In a land that lies subdued by bitter cold. [*Tristia* 3.4.47]
The Guardian of the Bear is not far above my head,
  And lengthy winter adds dark clouds to the sun.
For you one storm of Nereus stirs your indignation,
  Which Thetis, though, brightens with one embrace.
For me a fierce throng provokes unending fury.
  Ah Sadness! Every attack has access to me.
For you, writing, the sea dampens your book with waves;
  My letters are also wet, but with tears.
You lament your inconveniences; I all alone am burdened
  By everything scarcely to be endured by a gentlewoman.
You leave behind your homeland and your friends, yet unharmed;
  I have lost, with these, both my father and his home.
For you, the Sarmatians attack with repeated plundering;
  For me, a furious nation takes what it does not give.
You have made your eyes guilty, and dishonored
  Your art: a poem and an error bring punishment.
I've been paid a cruel reward in answer to my piety.
  And truly no offense deserves this luck.

Could your complaint of sadness then move
  The heart of a great-minded man?
Who would not be moved by a girl's laments,
  And losses that the fierce Geta could scarcely endure?
So let me grieve for my fate through your grief.
  Oh how much better your lot than mine.}

Perhaps the most notable general effect in the above poem is her boldness in claiming for herself a status comparable to Ovid's as exile poet. In taking his identity as part of her own through imagining herself to be his female pupil (as noted), she revalues her losses and sorrows, shedding modern tears onto an ancient poetic seascape. Ironically, if she had been able to stay in England or return there, she would almost certainly have been just as "insolvent" and never able to publish poems. Elizabeth Weston was one of the rare women who found, in the two published editions of her poems, a way to move into a public textual space where a voice of her own could take center stage. Exchanges of verse letters and other circulation of her verse had gained her a high reputation as neo-Latin poet at the emperor's court, behind only the long-time imperial poet Paul Melissus Schede.[42] She achieved this status through a humanist grammar-school education and the pluck to improvise out of it a unique poetic voice and identity, as a girlish, supplicating, yet self-examining and ostensibly aristocratic prodigy.

A few times she leaves the patronage mode behind and creates simply a poem about something she has observed and thought. In the following one, the convention of reference to things Christian under classical terms makes Wenceslas Square into "the forum" and the cathedral into a temple of the gods. It is a forceful account of an actual flood, sweeping with heavy and swirling lines to the final quietly breathed prayer that the waters might subside.

De inundatione Pragae. ex continuis pluviis exorta

Evocat iratos Coeli inclementia ventos
  Imbreque continua nubila mista madent
Molda tumet multum vehemens pluvialibus undis
  Prorumpens ripis impetuosa suis.
Largaque per latos diffundit flumine campos,
  Et rapidus siccos proluit amnis agros.
Spumosus, verrit per praeceps omnia gurges:
  Et misere, insanis cuncta feruntur aquis.
Hinc seges, hinc fructus distracti fluctibus undant:
  Inde vir, inde thorus, foeminaque inde natat.
Cerne, trabes, pinus, & tecta natantia, cerne;
  Volvuntur rapidis prodigiosa vadis.

Septa procelloso late stant gurgite mersa:
　　Sic alto pereunt omnia mersa mari!
Cymba forum sulcat; piscis delubra Deorum
　　Contemerat; refugis fluctibus ara madet.
Astant adtonitae, sed veste liquente catervae,
　　Inve[ti]tisque dolent cuncta perire malis.
Talis erat facies furibundum cernere Moldam;
　　Et similes undae Deucalionis erant.
Tu qui monstra freti rabidosve dormare furores,
　　Jhova potes, nutu tot mala merge tuo.

(*Parthenicon* II, C$_{IV}$)

{Of the Flood of Prague, risen from continuous rains.

The inclemency of heaven calls forth angry winds,
　　And continuous gathered clouds are drenched with rain.
The violent Moldau swells with rain-soaked waves,
　　Breaking its bank impetuously.
It flows in great flood through the wide expanses,
　　The rapid river, as it inundates dry fields.
Headlong the foaming whirlpool sweeps all that is before it:
　　Desperately all are carried by the maddened waters.
Here grain, here wasted fruit are flooded by the waves;
　　There a man, there a bed, and a woman swim.
Look, timber, pine, and swimming roof tops, look;
　　Unnatural things are swirled in the rapid flood.
Far and wide stand walls submerged in tempestuous eddies,
　　So everything submerged is destroyed by the deep.
A small boat ploughs the forum; fish defile the holy
　　Places; an altar is soaked by receding waves.
A crowd, their clothing drenched, stand and watch astonished
　　And grieve for all destroyed by unrestrained evils.
Thus it was to see the face of furious Moldau,
　　Its waters seemed like those of Deucalion's flood.
Oh you who quiet the monsters of the sea and raging storms,
　　Jehovah, with your nod, submerge so many evils.}

Weston's Catholic identity, shown by the statement in the Ovid-in-exile poem that she is being punished for her piety—it would have been a sticking point in her difficulties with returning to England—is also clear in a set of religious poems included in her book, mostly epigrams and Ignatian meditations on biblical topics or liturgical feast days. The nature of this Catholic identity, which did not deter her from exchanging cordial Latin verse letters with

Protestant humanists, becomes understandable when we recall the extensive record in John Dee's diaries of his and Kelley's taking Catholic sacraments and
having theological discussions with Catholics, as well as Dee's utopian scheme,
important in his and Kelley's angelic seances, for an ecumenical movement to
heal the rift of Christendom. Dee in his travels could pass as Catholic but immediately reassume his Protestant identity on returning to England. Indeed,
Dee and Kelley at a couple of points during their partnership had had to flee
from agents of the Inquisition—they had various dealings with the ecumenical
equivocator and sometime priest Francesco Pucci, eventually executed in Italy
(see Firpo). Ecumenism could be a dangerous business in that age; one was
often mistrusted and attacked from both sides. Elizabeth Weston does not display such a chameleonic quality as Dee, rather a clear Catholic view in her religious poems (e.g., rejecting Protestant views on predestination in a poem [see
Appendix 2] celebrating the Feast of the Holy Name of Jesus—a new and ag-
gressively counter-Reformational feast day). But we can see that her Catholicism, like Kelley's, permitted cordial dealings with Protestants and the sense of
an intellectual identity transcending confessional lines, even while her devotional poems seem sincere and sometimes intense. An example would be the
one in Appendix 2 beginning *Quid mea mendosae laceratis pectora curae?* and
ending with the couplet "Dissolvi cupio vitae meliores amore: / Nam bene velle
sat est, & potuisse mori" [I long to be dissolved in love of a better life: / For
it is enough to wish and be able to die].

It is striking how much more open-ended and internationalist could be the
attitude of an English Catholic woman poet in exile, given a humanist education and the task of fending for herself intellectually, than that of Catholics as
an oppressed subculture in England, such as the inevitably martyr-focused circles linked to Mary Stuart, discussed above. The crucial importance of a writer's
immediately surrounding "social text" is in this point clearly evident. Even
though in her *Parthenicon* book Weston's public space was, surprisingly to her,
encroached on by certain poems by men (see n. 38), she had found a poetic
voice that she wished and managed to have circulated and preserved. It was a
perhaps unique humanist female voice, emerging from the modicum of learning, social positioning, and international Catholic religious identity that she
managed to claim: through Augustan word-craft she portrayed herself as an
inwardly noble though robbed and banished Christian lady, which she could do
by continuing her alchemist stepfather's golden though constrictive patronage
with such wealthy courtiers as Heinrich von Pisnitz and Peter Wok von Rosenberg, at the court of Rudolf II.

5

Parlor Games and Male Self-Imaging as Government

Jonson, Bulstrode, and Ladies Southwell and Wroth

Who would not be thy subject, James, to obey
A prince that rules by example more than sway?
Whose manners draw, more than thy powers constrain.

–Ben Jonson, from Epigram #35

W E NEXT CONSIDER a group of associated women at Queen Anne's court who were part of the third Protestant aristocratic generation in England (the Cooke sisters illustrating the first, the Countess of Pembroke the second); and we will do so in connection with the cultural-semiotic concept of the ideologeme, my use of it to be explained shortly. Reference to it continues in chapter 6, which should be read in tandem with this one. Some court women by whom writings other than strictly personal documents have survived are Lucy (Harington) Russell, Countess of Bedford (a poem of whose will be discussed in chapter 6); her kinswoman Cecily Bulstrode; Lady Anne (Harris) Southwell, wife of Sir Thomas Southwell of Spixworth, Norfolk (later settlers in Ireland);[1] and Lady Mary (Sidney) Wroth, author of the two-part prose romance with many poems (including the "Pamphilia to Amphilanthus" sonnets, lately much studied), namely the *Countess of Montgomery's Urania*, Part I, published 1621, Part II in manuscript[2] (see chapter 6), and also of a pastoral play to be discussed here, *Love's Victory*. In the period of 1605–1609, these four women were associated in different ways with Queen Anne's court, at her residences of Hampton Court and Somerset (or Denmark) House. They socialized and politicked in the midst of affairs that had great impact on King James and his reign.

The first three of them, at least, were associated with a coterie group including Sir Thomas Overbury, and some prose inventions by two of them, Bulstrode and Southwell, have survived in a book containing Overbury's poem "The Wife" and thus entitled *Sir Thomas Overbury his Wife* (1611, the "Newes" inventions first included 1614). These recorded "inventions" came from various rounds of the parlor games "Newes" and "Edicts." Once we have studied them, we will also consider Anne Southwell's extensive body of surviving poems from her later years in Ireland, in witty voices akin to that of the inventions in the *Wife*. Because of scandal the *Wife* sold well and was several times expanded from 1614–1616, for Overbury had in 1613 been murdered by Frances Howard Carr, Countess of Somerset, divorced Countess of Essex.

Who were the four ladies above and what had been their associations? As Barbara Lewalski has discussed ("Bedford," *Writing*), Lucy, Countess of Bedford, was a special favorite of the queen: she took the part of Splendor in the *Masque of Blackness* (1605) and its sequel the *Masque of Beauty* (1608). The satiric dimension of Jonson's *Epicoene* seems to imply, whether accurately who knows, that she too played "Newes" (see below). Her kinswoman Mrs. Bulstrode, attacked by Jonson as the court "pucelle," or whore, was lady-in-waiting to the queen and had a chamber that he in the same notorious epigram, *Underwood* number 49,[3] called the "pit" for the playing of "Newes." Lady Mary Wroth's particular place in Queen Anne's establishment is not known, but like the Countess of Bedford she socialized there, later appears to portray herself as having done "service in ordinary" (*Urania*, Pt. I, iv, 476), and danced among the chosen few in *Blackness* and *Beauty*.[4] Whether she ever socialized particularly with the "News" circle we do not know, but certainly she was well acquainted with Bulstrode's associates the Countess of Bedford and Ben Jonson. In another episode of her *Urania* (I. ii. 424, the story of Lindamira),[5] she portrays her court years, which coincided with those of the "News" players, as a time of devoted service to her mistress the queen, spoiled by a false rumor that got her sent home to her husband. Her developing affair with her cousin William Herbert, Earl of Pembroke (later to bring two children), and already gossiped of by 1610, I believe (see below on *Beauty* and n. 4), caused the queen to dismiss her—her romance hints, because of jealousy arising from the queen's own attraction to Pembroke (see Lewalski *Writing* 266, 284). As for Anne Southwell (b. Cornworthy, Devon, 1574, d. 1636),[6] who was much less prominent than the others, she and her husband must have courted favor through the early years of the reign, with Thomas eventually being knighted in 1615 (see n. 1) and receiving land in Ireland (Klene); they then lived at Poulnalong Castle, County Cork. Verse letters in her commonplace book (Folger V.b. 198, 1626) show her acquainted with prominent people in Ireland, including the Governor Henry Cary, Lord Falkland (see chapter 7), the Earl and Countess of Londonderry, and the Bishop of Limerick. To the Earl of Somerset, even in his disgrace, Lady Southwell later wrote a sympathy poem upon the death of his wife [fol. 23rect]; thus out of the London associations she, like several others of this group, seems to have kept a sympathy for him and his murderer-countess rather than for his murdered former manager Overbury, despite the fact that Overbury had been intimate with the "Newes" players.[7]

Socializing among Queen Anne's ladies involved regular playing of parlor games, some of which, like "News," called for impromptu verbal invention that obliquely incorporated gossip and political intrigue in the form of strings of witty sayings, drawing on the women's reading-circle experience of Senecan and other wise sayings or *sententiae* (see chapter 1), also well known to men from their schooling. Such games could involve an alternation of witty misogynist thrust and feminist or antimisogynist counterthrust, at which Lady Southwell seems to have been especially skilled. A few circumstances of the game-playing at the queen's court are condescendingly recounted by the humanistically educated Lady Arbella Stuart, the king's cousin, who wrote to her uncle that it often lasted from 10:00 P.M. till 2:00 or 3:00 A.M. and that the queen herself played "I pray my Lord give me a course in your park," "One penny follow me," and "Fire" (E. C. Williams 102). In this context Lady Wroth's play *Love's Victory* can best be appreciated; each of its first four acts is constructed upon a round of one such parlor game.

More than fun and games was involved in these structured pastimes, for through them moved information, innuendos, reputations, and the makings of useful or possibly harmful ties among courtiers (Peck *Patronage* 68–74). The "News" inventions recorded in the *Wife* were thus more actively political writing than women are usually thought to have done in that age. The Countess of Bedford, as her letters and records show, wielded much ongoing influence. John Donne, another participant in "Newes" with an invention in the *Wife*, spent the first nine years of James's reign actively courting her for civil preferment.[8] Doubtless, not everyone was clever enough to play such games as, in particular, "Newes" and "Edicts"—opting out of a too challenging game becomes, in *Love's Victory*, a failure showing someone unworthy of loves and friendships with the brighter characters.

Recalling the structure of Queen Anne's household will explain how a relative unknown like Anne Southwell could end up being loosely connected with important people. Edward Somerset, Earl of Worcester, in a letter of about 1605 describing his wife's quest for place and the competitiveness of the high ladies (as if "Envy hath tied an invisible snake about most of their necks"), says there are three ranks: the highest, those of "the bed-chamber," includes only the Countesses of Bedford and Hartford (on the latter see Foster "Falsehood"), though Lady Arbella Stuart and his wife Lady Worcester are hoping for places there; the second rank, of "the drawing-chamber," now includes the Countesses of Derby, Suffolk, and Nottingham [Elizabeth Southwell's stepmother], Ladies Rich, Walsingham, and [Elizabeth] Southwell, and Mrs. Susan de Vere; the third, "all the rest," are of the "private chamber," and are generally "shut out, for many times the doors are locked" (cited in Ashdown 81–82). Minor ladies like Cecily Bulstrode would be of this last, outer layer, where their chambers functioned, among other ways, as waiting rooms for people courting favor by seeking appointments with influential secretaries. Higher-ranking ladies would seldom be found there, but if on some occasion the Countess of Bedford did, for kindness to a kinswoman and love of wit, deign to come and play a round of "Newes" with Cecily, that would have supplied the material for such a dé-classé hinted portrayal as Jonson's in the satirical *Epicoene*. He can vent some spleen at the queen's establishment by pretending that its ladies high and low are absorbed in petty pastimes. Someone like Anne Southwell evidently had plenty of time in Cecily's room to cool her heels and hone her parlor-game skills with other favor-seekers such as Overbury, Donne, Thomas Roe, the diplomat, and the other players identified by Savage ("Introduction"), a notably Protestant circle of people patronized by both Pembroke and the Countess of Bedford.

We will here consider the writing of women in the contexts of courtly game-playing, royal ideology in the first Jacobean decade, and the libidinalized conceptual tracks that this ideology laid down to be followed by writers and other producers of public culture. *Love's Victory*, written some years later and closely associated with the *Urania*, was I think retrospective, depicting court socializing in the first Jacobean decade and, in its ideological import, offering an answer to the dismissal of Wroth from court. To study the relevant contexts for the women's writings, I will draw upon a text-linguistic analysis of King James's treatise on government, the *Basilicon Doron*,[9] as basis for identifying a particular ideologeme or Deleuzean sociopolitical "desiring machine" to be examined, as well as upon sample masquing usages of this ideologeme by Ben Jonson. (For description of the two main court factions as variant users of it, see chapter 6.) In such a framework we can understand what certain women did—including Queen Anne herself in directing Jonson to write *Blackness* and *Beauty*—about construing a position from which to "speak" when they tried to work with an ideological system that was definedly male in its subject positions.

An obvious assumption here is that women's writing should be studied in the context of the politics, ideology, and male creativity with which it interacted—thus I take seriously my discussions of writings by Jonson and Donne, as well as those by women.[10] And in terms of the history of women as writers, the study of ideologemes lets us begin to grasp the greatest masculinist obstacle that early modern women faced as would-be participants in public culture: it was not only bigotry, lack of education, lack of self-confidence, and lack of resources, but something sociolinguistically encoded in usages of their societies that operated to prevent them from having a voice (on related issues see Lamb *Gender* "Introduction").

Jonson's *Epicoene* and the Women Players of "News"

Jonson's play *Epicoene or the Silent Woman* (1609) is full of the same misogynist witticisms found in the "News" inventions; it lampoons a man so foolish as to wish for a silent wife, thereby satirizing women's supposed garrulity.[11] Indeed, one could regard the play metaleptically as one long dramatized "News" invention. I propose that it glances at, perhaps among others, the participants in this "News"-playing circle who socialized with Mrs. Bulstrode. Jonson satirizes the women in the play as a "colledge" of domineering court ladies who "live [away] from their husbands" (I.i.73ff.) with their "she-friends" (II.ii.102)—as did the Countess of Bedford and Lady Wroth—and patronize various ranks of men described as "wits," "braveries" (minor gentlemen), and "sermoneers" (Anglican divines), while spending their time meddling in other people's affairs "with most masculine, or rather *hermaphroditicall* authoritie" (I.i.79–80). When they show their learning (one knows some Latin and Greek), they are like "parrots" mimicking men. The skills they command are "writing letters, corrupting servants, taming spies" (II.i.102). While Jonson did not include any blatant references to particular women, the mention of the Prince of Moldavia (V.i.24–25) alludes to a rumor about an engagement of Arbella Stuart to that claimant to Moldavia, one Stephano Janiculo (Lewalski *Writing* 83), and there are also distinct hints at the Bedford circle. The play's beleaguered new husband Morose, whose wife the women plan to take off to their "colledge," complains that his wife is being turned into a "Penthesilea" (III.iv.57); the Countess of Bedford had just that winter played the Amazon Penthesilea (Herford et al. 10:495) in the *Masque of Queens*, which Jonson himself had written, performed February 8, 1609.[12] Furthermore, in the play Lady Haughty's woman Mavis is said to have a face not to be admired even "by candle-light" (i.e., a flattering light—V.ii.38), just as Jonson's epigram on Bulstrode says that her face could not please even by candlelight. And the name "Mavis" could glance at the Countess of Bedford's best friend Jane Meutys, Lady Wallingford.

The play's joke is that the "silent woman" turns out to be a boy in drag—an "epicoene" or ungendered being (hired by Morose's nephew to trick Morose into bequeathing his goods to the said nephew); when this boy immediately fits right in with the "collegiate" women, we realize that the satire of their supposed mannishness runs through every level of the play's construction and performance—the actors playing them are of course boys. It targets the same qualities that Jonson scorned in the "pucelle" epigram when he ridiculed Cecily Bulstrode as a writer and wit for working herself into an "epicoene" fury of inspiration through having "tribade" (i.e., Lesbian) relations with her muse and for daring to "censure poets"—such as himself. That the play was not well received and made trouble for him is clear.[13]

Jonson himself would seem to have played "News" and related games: besides the Bulstrode epigram lines about the game, he also has the *Epicoene* collegiates plan a round of it. He knew most of the players well (see chapter 6 on others of them) and sent them complimentary verses;[14] in his political inclinations and dependencies he was at one with them, that is, with the loose Pembrokean faction they were part of, even though he could also dash out tributes to people of the other, the Howard party, such as the Earl of Suffolk (Epigram no. 67). His falling out with Mrs. Bulstrode should be seen as an internecine matter, that did not result in his disaffiliating himself from the Pembrokes and Sidneys (though perhaps for a while after it he spent more time in the country). They continued treating him generously, the Earl of Pembroke giving him a yearly book-buying allowance of twenty pounds (*Conversations* 259–60); Lady Elizabeth Manners, Countess of Rutland (Philip Sidney's daughter), more than once entertained him at her own table (*Conversations* 301ff.), as did Lady Wroth, Robert Sidney's daughter and Pembroke's cousin. A possible view would be that in the flap that sent Wroth home to the country (see n. 35), Jonson for the moment sided with her immediate circle and against the courtiers around the Countess of Bedford.

In what way had Cecily and perhaps others enraged him? She criticized something in his writings, but I suggest that another development had also stung him, namely the "News" writers' reaction to an event that he himself later recounted to Drummond of Hawthornden, which was connected with the Countess of Rutland's habit of entertaining him. After noting that "Overbury was first his friend, then turned his mortal enemy," he told Drummond:

> Sir Th Overbury was in love with her [the Countess of Rutland], and caused Ben to read his "Wife" to her, which he, with an excellent grace, did, and praised the author. the morn thereafter he discorded with Overbury, who would have him to intend a suit tht was unlawful. The lines my lady kept in remembrance, "He comes too near, who comes to be denied." (*Conversations* 135, 173ff.)

Overbury was hoisted on his own petard, and Jonson, I believe, got such a red face from the "News" ladies' witticizing (see below) about this episode of his being sent as pandar and failing that he was sparked to the revenge of *Epicoene*. He agreed with the king in disapproving of witty, independent, politically active women who talked to each other as if they were men (see n. 8). Even while he was flattering the Countess of Bedford (Epigram #76) for having "a learned and a manly soul" and being able to "control the shears / Of destiny and spin her own free hours," he was satirizing the collegiates in *Epicoene* for wanting to be masculine state-women (II.iii.123) and "spin their own days." Whether or not this suggestion about the Rutland incident as particular cause of Jonson's rage is correct, *Epicoene* has many thematic links with "News" and its circle of players; thus the play fills in our picture of the game and the woman-dominated context of Cic'ly's "pit," in which it was played.

Mrs. Bulstrode's and Lady Southwell's Inventions, and Lady Southwell's Later Writings

We now look at some of the conceited aphorizing and *ripostes* that comprised "News." Recalling the women's reading formation presented in chapter 1, we can recognize that the importance within it of translated Senecan and other neoclassical sententiae or moral aphorisms, along with the kind of female exercise of paraphrasing them illustrated in Isabella Whitney's *Sweet Nosegay* and in the aphorisms of Elizabeth Weston (Appendix 2), gave ladies and waiting women a natural practice ground for the impromptu stringing out of witty sayings required by the game of "News." The Countess of Cumberland, between singing Psalms and sewing with her women and her daughter Anne Clifford, would frequently have pulled down her book of Seneca, shown on the shelf behind her in the Appleby Castle Triptych (Lamb, "Agency" 361, 363). A natural way of reading this material aloud would be to pause after each saying while the hearers mentally tested out its pith and applicability and called to mind analogues and related proverbs, enjoying and showing off their memory by decanting a few and perhaps even inventing variants on them.

In "News," the initial player, it seems, would choose or be assigned a theme, such as "the sea," "the court," or "the dinner table," on which to string out a set of clever sayings cast as "News from" the assigned place, incorporating imagery referring to it and taking the form of "that" clauses. The game must have been played with pen in hand, participants writing out each invention, then reading it aloud, since Jonson's epigram (noted above) speaks of Mrs. Bulstrode "writing" her news. After the initial player had read out a string of items, an opponent of the other "side" would propose antithetical responses to them, comprising an "answer." Let us take first a sample from the entry by Bulstrode entitled "Newes of my morning Worke"; its theme is a court lady's dilemmas.

> That the Diuell is the perfectest Courtier. That innocency was first cozen to man, now guiltinesse hath the neerest alliance. That sleepe is deaths Leger Embassadour. That time can neuer be spent: we passe by it and can not returne. That none can bee sure of more time then an instant. . . . That euery ones memory is diuided into two parts: the part loosing all is the Sea, the keeping part is Land. That honesty in the Court liues in persecution, like protestants in Spaine. That predestination and constancy are alike vncertaine to be iudged of. . . . That vertues fauour is better then a Kings fauorite. That being sicke begins a suit to God, being well, possesseth it. That helth is the Coach which carries to Heauen, sicknesse the post-horse. That worldly de-

lights to one in extreame sickenesse, is like a high candle to a blinde man. That abscence doth sharpen loue, presence strengthens it; that the one brings fuell, the other blowes it till it burnes cleere. . . . That constancy of women, and loue in men, is alike rare. That Art is trueths Iugler. That falshood playes a larger part in the world then trueth. That blind zeale and lame knowledge are alike apt to ill. . . . That womens fortunes aspire but by others powers. That a man with a female wit is the worst *Hermaphrodite*. . . . That the worst part of ignorance, is making good and ill seeme alike. That all this is newes onely to fooles.

Here we see why Jonson says that "News" "can at once . . . make state, religion, bawdry, all a theme" ("Court Pucelle" 11–12). It is an associative spinning out of witticisms that allows things political, theological, and sexual to be intermingled through a pattering flow of amusing invention, which could intermittently refer to something specific, but without being dangerously direct. The above line that "a man with a female wit is the worst *Hermaphrodite*" sounds like a reply to the jab in *Epicoene* about the collegiates' "most masculine, or rather *hermaphroditicall* authoritie." "Vertues favour is better than a Kings favourite" would inevitably glance at Overbury's management of his friend, King James's rising favorite Robert Carr (later Somerset). Perhaps the most striking image here is that of memory as a world of land and sea, the accessible portions being the land—this could likewise have political reference, to the convenience of selective memory, especially in context with the "honesty in the court" saying that follows it.

In terms of modern generic categories, we might read such an "invention" as a sort of satirical prose poem, consisting of sharp, associatively linked, sexually and politically invested musings on a theme. To sample an invention that has an "answer" within the recorded instances, we turn to the one by Overbury and its answer by "A. S.," i.e., in all probability Anne Southwell.

from "Newes from Court" by Sir T. Over.

It is thought heere that there are as great miseries beyond happinesse, as a this side it, as *being in love*. . . . [that] to be saued alwaies is the best plot: and vertue alwaies cleeres her way as shee goes. *Vice* is euer behind-hand with it selfe. That *wit* and a *woman* are two fraile things, and both the frailer by concurring. That the meanes of begetting a man, hath more increast mankind then the end. . . . That all Women for the bodily part are but the same meaning put in diuers wordes. That the difference in the sense is their vnderstanding. . . . That affectation is the more ridiculous part of folly then ignorance. That the matter of greatnesse is comparison. That God made one world of

Substances, Man hath made another of *Art* and *Opinion*. That Money is nothing but a thing which *Art* hath turned vppe *trumpe*.

from the "Answere to the Court Newes"

That *Happinesse* and *Miserie* are *Antipodes*. That *Goodnesse* is not *Felicitie*, but
the rode thither. That Mans strength is but a vicissitude of falling and rising.
That onely to refraine ill, is to be ill still. That the plot of Saluation was laid
before the plot of *Paradise*. That enioying is the preparatiue to condemning.
. . . That the soules of Women and Louers, are wrapt in the portmanque of
their senses. That imagination is the end of man. That wit is the webbe, and
wisedome the woofe of the cloth; so that womens soules were neuer made
vp. That envie knowes what it will not confesse. That *Goodnesse* is like the Art
Prospectiue: one point Center, begetting infinite rayes. That Man, Woman,
and the Diuell, are the three degrees of comparison. That this Newes holds
number, but not weight, by which couple all things receiue forme.

Here we see that respondents had some flexibility in ordering their ripostes: A. S.
sticks only roughly to Overbury's order. To his claim that the happiness of
attained love includes misery, she replies that happiness and misery are contradictory opposites (thus he must be wrong); to the claim that virtue clears its
own way while operating, she responds that virtue is not necessarily co-occurent
with happiness, but is the road to it; to the statement that wit and women, both
frail, are even frailer when concurrent (i.e., when a woman is being witty), she
only states archly that "enjoying is the preparative to condemning," i.e., some
witty woman he once enjoyed must have jilted him or grown stale for him, and
he is now condemning her for no better reason. And to his claim that every
woman's body is another instance of a single cipher existing for men to create
meaning with, she replies mysteriously that wit and wisdom are warp and woof
of the cloth [of meaning], and thus women's souls [whatever their bodies might
mean] "were never made up"—i.e., were never woven into a piece of cloth.

When played thus side against side, as the collegiates in *Epicoene* planned
that Mavis and their new friend the boy-wife would be a "side" (III.vi.54–57),
the "News" game seems to have required that one jot down and rattle out a
response to the opponent's news as quickly as possible. Indeed, whether it was
ever played any other way than side against side we do not know: only two of
the surviving pieces in the *Wife* have "answers," but that may mean only that
other answers were not thought memorable enough to print. From the gendered nature of the surviving instances, it would seem that the game was often
played as the men against the women. (Incidentally, the relevance of this sort
of game-playing as a practice ground for Donne's famous conceited witticizing
should hardly need remarking.)

But the female players of "News" operated within very constrained expressive possibilities. They had no such resources as the queen had in her masques—as we will find shortly—to make a culturally energized female statement by ingenious infiltration of an ideologeme that was so formed as to exclude women as subject-speakers. The "News" players were more in the position of Maggie in Tennessee Williams's *Cat on a Hot Tin Roof*, dancing a nervous verbal patter in an effort to get slept with, metaphorically speaking:[15] to become able to take an agentive part in the energized, politically libidinalized writing integral to court life. Their inventions, in relation to the ideologeme I will identify shortly, are more a kind of commentary on it than a usage of it: in satirizing male foibles, these pieces work as ironic, low-keyed feminist or protofeminist sniper-shots at the Jacobean ideologizing that defines women as soulless.

We can see such an import in Lady Southwell's round of another game closely related to "News," namely "Edicts." The latter required, from the same player in a given turn, an alternation of critiques of male and female behavior, which took the form of laws being laid down, rather than of observations being reported. Otherwise "Edicts" was like "News," involving the same themes and the same vein of ironic, generalizing yet allusive commentary on courtiers' behavior.

from "Certaine Edicts from a Parliament in *Eutopia*;
Written by the Lady Southwell"

Inprimis, Hee that hath no other worth to commend him then a good Suite of Apparell, shall not dare to woe a Lady in his owne behalfe, but shall be allowed to carry the Hierogliphike of his friends affection.

Just such witticisms as this, I believe, set Jonson's teeth on edge after his participation as go-between in Overbury's effort to proposition the Countess of Rutland.

A succeeding related edict on clothes, this time for ladies, was the following:

Item, that no Lady, which modestly keeps her house for want of good clothes to visit her Gossips, shall professe contempt of the worlds vanity, vnlesse she see no hope of the tides returning.

Here we see that in "Edicts" one wanted to end with a "but" or "unless" clause expressing a qualification to the preceding claim—but a somehow surprising or pointedly ironic qualification. This condition is usually though not quite always met; some edicts instead build their irony into the initial statement:

Item, no Lady that silently simpereth for want of wit, shall be called modest.

What happened to the ideal of "chaste, silent, and obedient" here? (see Hull).

The successor to the one about the silent simperer is equally barbed, and the amusing equivalence that the two together set up—between falsely praised female silence and tongue-tied male sexual aggression—represents a parody of the claim that "Silence in woman is like speech in man," a madrigal in *Epicoene*.

> *Item*, no fellow that begins to argue with a woman, & wants wit to encounter her, shal think he hath redeemd his credit by putting her to silence with some lasciuious discourse, vnlesse hee were [wear] white for *William* and greene for *Summer*. [William Summer was Henry VIII's famous fool—thus a name for a fool.]

Another item in this set of edicts seems very much to refer to Overbury's attempted propositioning of the Countess of Rutland (noted above), lampooning certain verbal backing and hoeing that Overbury would have done afterward.

> *Item*, He that hath reported a Lady to be vertuous, for the which he professeth to loue her, yet vnder hand commenceth a base suit, and is disdained; shall not on this blow which his owne vice hath giuen him, out of policy raile suddenly on her, for fear he be noted for a vicious foole: but to his friend in priuate he may say that his iudgement was blinded by her cunning disguise, & that he finds her wauering in goodnesse, and in time he shall openly professe to raile on her; but with such a modesty forsooth, as if he were loth to bring his iudgement into question; nor would he doe it, but that hee preferres truth euen out of his owne reach.

Jonson did not like to be on the receiving end of any such stuff; he only liked to dish it out. If this is not about the episode he reports concerning himself, Overbury, and the Countess of Rutland, it is about something so similar that the elucidation value of his story is equally great. The elongated string of twists and digs this edict gives the rejected suitor must have been extremely entertaining to the women, infuriating to the men involved.

The Lady Anne Southwell of the commonplace book (Folger V.b. 198) being edited by Jean Klene is, I believe, the same person as the author of these "Edicts" and items of "News," though the later manuscript material is mostly in verse, including verse letters, and mostly in a serious moralistic vein (again, see nn. 1, 6). Lady Anne Southwell's manuscript letter to Lady Ridgeway in defense of poetry (evidently answering one where her friend had favored prose) shows the same style of terse, thrusting assertions, preoccupation with number and measure, and preference for oppositional categories in which to cast the ideas set forth. For example, she argues that metrical ordering of words creates an elegant balance of opposites, just as God's creation of the world, including Lady Ridgeway herself, was a case of balancing opposites:

> Therefore, (Noble & wittye Ladye:) giue mee your hand, I will leade you vpp the streame of all mankind. Your great great grandfather had a father, & soe

the last, or rather the first father, was God; whose ˜euer enough to be admired creation, was poetically confined to 4. generall ͜enusses, Earth, Ayre, water & fire: The effectes which giue life vnto his verse, were, Hott, Cold, Moist & Drye, which produce Choller, melanchollye, Bloud & Flegme: By these iust proportions, all thinges are propagated. Now being [in your own body] thus poetically composed; How can you bee at unitye with your self, & at oddes with your owne composition[?] (Cavanaugh's transcript)

Lady Southwell addresses Lady Ridgeway at the opening of the letter as "my worthy Muse": if the ladies of the "News" group commonly addressed their women friends thus, there may have been more than light wit in Jonson's quip that Bulstrode had "tribade" relations with her muse—this would have been a stinging barb.

The letters and poems are recorded, mostly in Italic hands, in a bound volume that began life as an accounts book in the family of Capt. Henry Sibthorpe, Anne Southwell's second husband, who as it seems by his tribute in the last pages of the MS thought her verses worth preserving. The poem that Jean Klene cites from the manuscript would seem a very natural production of the "News" writer from days at court, now an Irish settler but still with the witty gentlewoman self-image that she gained in her courtier days, and perhaps with an admiring and unthreatened second husband for moral support:

> All maried men desire to have good wifes:
> but few give good example by thir lives
> They are owr head they wodd have us thir heles.
> this makes the good wife kick the good man reles.
> When god brought Eve to Adam for a bride
> the text says she was taene from out mans side
> A simbole of that side, whose sacred bloud.
> flowed for his spowse, the Churches savinge good.
> This is a misterie, perhaps too deepe.
> for blockish Adam that was falen a sleepe.
>
> (Klene 6)[16]

This amusing piece is in the same genre of satiric epigram as pieces by Jonson, Donne, and others, a verse mode of teasing social exchange. The pious-sounding lines of the poem's midsection lull readers and set them up for the kick of the final line. For of course, Pauline doctrine had made the wife the whole body, the husband its head; subordinating a wife to the position of heel alone, humorously alliterating with "head," accuses men (in the person of "blockish Adam") of having perverted the scriptural teaching into tyranny.

Every time Adam and Eve come up in the poems of this manuscript, Adam takes his licks, in tones ranging from whimsically condescending to markedly bitter. An instance of the former is the opening passage of a lengthy and polished poem (addressed to Bernard Adams, Bishop of Limerick) on faculty psychology, meditating on the ruination of memory, will, and understanding wrought by Adam's fall.

> Adam first preist, first prophet and first Kinge
> greate Lord of euery vegetable thinge
> true Image of his God whose awfull brow
> made euery creature wth obedience bow.
> A heauen on earth a litle world of wonder
> Ah, where's the power can bringe this Monarch vnder.
> And doth hee still theise rich endowments hold?
> more worth then mynes of purest pearle and gould
> Noe, hee is falne turn'd meere Antipodes
> and more then subalterne to each of theise
> Yet not soe falne as to his endlesse harmes
> but slipt from Justice ire, to mercyes armes . . .
>
>   (Folger V.b.198, fol. 18)

Adam here seems a naive boy, king of the vegetables, to be indulged and pitied, unable to imitate his Father God as he should, clinging to the embrace of a nurturing, sympathizing "mercy."

Anger and sorrow in a life with an ill-tempered, abusive husband (possibly the experience of Southwell's first marriage, though this is only speculation) are satirically expressed in the madrigalian lyric "Nature, Mistriss off affection" (see Appendix 2). Adam looks bad there too, by association with the foolish husband who fails to realize that in maltreating and alienating his wife, he harms himself as well: he is compared to a bald man who has ripped off his own hair.

> Eue to Adam, was his Croune
> and can baldness be renowne [?]
> thus thou pullst thy owne state down
>   O meere maddness
>
>   (Folger V.b. 198, fol. 11)

But far the greatest portion of her manuscript is taken up by a different sort of verse, namely by a long moralizing poem treating the ten commandments one by one, in a vein of sharp commentary on sinners' deeds approaching that of verse satire. Some of its pages appear to be out of order, and parts of it are perhaps missing; we will have to await Klene's edition of the manuscript to get a more concrete impression of it. To the extent that Southwell's poems are retrospective, retaining something of the libidinal-ideological loading described in my discussion of "News" and further below, I would suggest that they too, like the "News" inventions, work as a kind of metacritical commentary on—rather than a usage of—James's masculinist ideologeme.

To get acquainted with one more strain in Lady Southwell's manuscript, let us sample a two-page poem addressed to her friend Cassandra McWilliam Ridgeway, by this time Countess of Londonderry, a fanciful mock elegy lamenting the countess's supposed "death," which the poet pretends to assume because she has not heard from her for a long time (see Appendix 2 for the whole poem). The speaker imagines her friend traversing the heavenly spheres and poses questions for the ascending spirit—some whimsical, some more scientifically motivated—about the planets and stars, their natures and motions, and other speculative matters.

> Yet in thy passage, fayre soule, let me know
> what things thou saws't in riseinge from below?
> Whether that Cynthia regent of the flood
> wthin hir Orbe admitt of mortall brood?
> Whether the 12 Signes serue the Sun for state?
> Or elce confine him to the Zodiaque!
> And force him retrograde to bee the nurse
> (whoe circularly glides his oblique course)
> Of ALMA MATER, or vnfreeze the wombe
> of madam Tellus? wch elce proues a tombe,
> whether the starrs be Knobbs uppon the spheres?
> Or shredds compos'd of Phoebus goulden hayres?
> Or whether th'Ayre be as a cloudy siue?
> the starrs be holes through wch the good soules driue?
> whether that Saturne that the 6 out topps
> sitt euer eatinge of the bratts of Opps?
> Whose iealousye is like a sea of Gall
> vnto his owne proues periodicall?

Questions of whether certain forces drive or are driven by the planetary motions intermingle with playfully handled astrological lore in a quite original combination. The speaker goes on to muse about the foolishness of certain speculations she has read on heavenly things.

> Fayne would I know from some that haue beene there?
> what state or shape coelestiall bodyes beare?
> For man to heauen, hath throwne a waxen ball,
> In wch hee thinks h'hath gott, true formes of all,
> And, from the forge howse, of his fantasie,
> hee creates new, and spins out destinye.
> And thus theise prowd wormes, wrapt in lothsome rags,
> shutt heauens Idea upp, in letherne baggs.

> Now since in heauen are many Ladyes more,
> that blinde deuotion busyely implore,
> Good Lady, freind, or rather louely Dame,
> if yow, be gone from out this clayie frame,
> tell what yow know . . .

In the conclusion Lady Southwell moves from scientific or cosmological to moral issues that she must have enjoyed discussing with her friend, ending with an inverse comparison between the prophet Elijah being taken up into heaven and Adam, in baby bird form, tumbling down from the Edenic nest of his original bliss:

> But as the prophett, at his M^{rs} [Master's] feete,
> when hee ascended, up the Welkin fleete
> Watcht, for his cloake, soe euery bird, & beast,
> When princely Adam, tumbled from the nest,
> catcht, from his knoweinge soule, some qualitie,
> and humbly kept it, to reedifye,
> theyr quondam Kinge, and now, man goes to schoole,
> to euery pismire, that proclaymes him foole,
> But stay my wanderinge thoughts, alas where made I?
> In speakeinge to a dead, a sencelesse Lady.
> Yow Incke, and paper, be hir passeinge bell,
> The Sexton to hir knell, be Anne Southwell.

(Fol. 19$_v$ ff.—see Appendix 2)

In Lady Southwell we have a female "metaphysical" poet and direct associate of John Donne, who should have been receiving study along with Donne, Herbert, Carew, and company. (Unless the manuscript has been for some reason inaccessible, it seems a clear case of modernist chauvinistic canonicity that her poetry has been entirely ignored.) Like Donne, after the mid-1610s she seems to have turned mainly to religious versifying. Like George Herbert, she intermingles madrigal and lute song influence with the inventing of lively and "strained" conceits. For example, taking the traditional trope of the ridge in the chin of Helen of Troy, a blemish triggering erotic excitement, as a *cos amoris* or whetstone of love (cf. the opening passage of Lyly's *Euphues*), she writes a song lyric on divine love as the whetstone to all love: the love of all love, *amoris amor*, becomes the stone of love, *cos amoris*, on which she can pun with the Pauline idea of Christ as the cornerstone of the church triumphant in heavenly love. She weaves around this conceit a hymn structure in mixed meters similar to some of those Herbert was devising at about the same time or a little later: two eight-line stanzas in fourteeners are followed by a concluding stanza in rhymed pentameters, perhaps meant to be spoken after the first two were sung to a repeated tune (see Appendix 2 for the complete poem).

The more my soule doth shrinke from loue, ye more loue doth inflame her
   and when I seeke to find the cause, t'is Cos: amoris amor
I sett my reason Centenall, that passions may not shame her
   who tells me they like shadows pass, for *omnia vincit amor*
If with Angellick winges from hence, shee fly can mortalls blame her
   since from heauens lampe comes all her light, for *Cos: amoris amor*
Then let her mount with faith, hope, loue, where sine nor death can lame her
   where all afflictions end theire rage, for *omnia vincit amor.*

The following quasi-sonnet portrays Lady Southwell's own muse deferring to that of an admired friend who is said to be inspiring her poetry and who also is a writer—no name is given. Possibly the person is again the Countess of Londonderry, whom she called her own "Muse" in the letter cited above (the elegies to her—mock and serious—appear two folios later).

Fayne would I dye whilst thy braue muse doth liue
   Quaintest of all the Heliconian traine
Rays'd by thy arte-full quill, that liues doth giue
   Unto the Dullest things, thy fyery straine
Adds Immortalitye, maugre priuation
   And by thy power brings forth a new Creation.
Unhappy they that poesye professe
   Rayseinge their thoughts by any starr but thyne
Nor lett them thinke coelestiall powers will blesse
   Loose ballads or Hyperbolizeinge Ryme
Curst bee those sulphrous channells that make stincke
   Each christall dropp y^t in theyr cranyes sincke
In throne thy phoenix in Hi Jehouahs brest
   Since shee aproues hir selfe bird of that nest
Soe shall she liue immaculate and blest.

                  (Fol. 17)

The "King's Book" and the Ideologeme of the Propagated Male Self-Image

We next briefly examine the particular approach I have tried out here for contextualizing the political activism and writing of the women introduced above, a procedure for identifying a prevalent ideologeme of the first Jacobean decade, that is, a unit of sociopolitical meaning that English writers and other producers of artifacts in those years very commonly worked with, a "unit" that, however, should not be seen as a static linguistic pattern but rather as a Deleuzean "machine" for desiring-production, just as Fredric Jameson uses the ideologeme concept in *The Political Unconscious*. My concept, going beyond what Jameson proposed, is that the internal working of such a desiring machine can be analyzed through viewing it as charted by A.-J. Greimas's "base narrative program" formula. Greimas's formula represents—as one of my doctoral student colleagues Swift Dickison put the matter—a kind of "grab-ology": it says that an enunciating subject takes control of a secondary subject that has been conjoined with a value-invested object, thereby disjoining the latter from the S_2 and claiming it. And again, I propose that this formula, in its construct of interactive double subjectivity, can be said to chart the innards of a Deleuzean sociopolitical desiring machine or ideologeme, as understood by Jameson: for Deleuze and Guattari define their "desiring machines" as each consisting of two parts (psychoanalytically "partial objects") that create a flow of desire intermittently generated by one and interrupted by the other, and vice versa. (Readers interested in more text-linguistic detail on the Greimasian concept itself, which I have here appropriated for ideological analysis, are referred to Appendix 1 and to Greimas's *Semiotics and Language* dictionary.)

I have identified the particular ideologeme at issue here through a Greimasian text-linguistic analysis of the *Basilicon Doron* (1598—literally the King's Gift), a manual on kingship officially written for James's son Prince Henry but expressing his own viewpoint as he planned for ruling England. The book was republished in an English-spelling edition in 1603 for the occasion of the king's coronation; it sold in the thousands of copies and was often called simply "the King's book," though James had written other things too. People were naturally eager to learn how the new ruler presented himself. Such a text is therefore a good place to look for identifying the kind of ideologeme that Jameson, innovating from Kristeva and from Deleuze and Guattari, has proposed.[17] I assume that for identifying an ideologeme, rather than closing one's eyes tight, musing on the age as a whole, and spinning something out, it will be better to seek the identification through a potentially repeatable linguistic analysis of a text known to have been widely influential at the beginning of the period to be studied. My own modified usage of Jameson's concept involves no affirmation of the neo-Marxist view that study of economically defined class conflict is the ultimate critical operation (though I do here study an economically based factional and class identity, as site for a particular pattern of usage of the ideologeme—see next chapter); and further, I assume that ideologemes typically, perhaps necessarily, include the gender classeme, maleness-femaleness. As will be seen, that category functions in various ways in the play of meanings across the grids of iconographic and narratological possibilities that an ideologeme sets up.[18] In other words, my use of the term is somewhere between Kristeva's and Jameson's: ideologically less engaged than his, sociopolitically more concrete and specifiable than hers.

The ideologeme here is a unit of sociopolitical meaning through which producers of culture create (or are produced as creators of) libidinally energized artifacts, since through it they place their productions into the cultural-semiotic force lines of certain current workings of political power.[19] What kinds of forms its usages may take will become clear as we proceed; in general, a given ideologeme has the potential to take either visual-emblematic or narrative forms, in accord with its dual functioning on both sociosemantic and metasyntactic levels. Furthermore, as Don Wayne (7) proposed in a version of "historical semiotics" almost a decade ago, part of the complexity of a "great poem"—i.e., a cultural production that proves rich in its potential to generate interpretations—"is the result, at least in part, of a project that simultaneously asserts an ideology and places it in question" (20). Thus, tapping into or being propelled by a libidinal unit such as an ideologeme necessarily involves incorporation of dialectical or revisionist viewpoints on and within its ideological materials; this point is articulated here through the mapping of narratives onto the semiotic square, a pattern of interlocking contrary and contradictory oppositions. (For brief further comment on the ideologeme concept, see the Epilogue.)

The particular ideologeme I am describing here can be called governance through male self-imaging as self-propagation. It is explicit in the Jonsonian lines quoted as epigraph at the beginning of this chapter, hinted at in Waller's comment on the "cultural unconscious" quoted as epigraph to the present chapter's concluding section, and indirectly ciphered in a sentence of Overbury's "News" cited above, "That God made one world of *Substances*, Man hath made another of *Art* and *Opinion*" (which parallels the code that as the king reflects God, "man" reflects the king). Shakespeare, as chief playwright of the newly renamed "King's Men," was quick to take it up: he explicitly dramatized it in the second year of the new reign as *Measure for Measure* (1604). There a ruler sets in place a deputy who is to "be as ourself" in "Vienna," then steps behind the arras to watch and manipulate until the deputy becomes (he hopes) a proper replica of his own desired self-image as a balanced ruler, both merciful and just. Of course, what shockingly and comically ensues is only barely to be contained within the scheme, and Shakespeare thus poses a carefully hedged questioning of James's concept, as usages of it sometimes do, though at his court the play cannot have been performed so satirically as it is today. It is no accident that interpreters have seen in the play's duke—with his concluding playlet meant to solve all the plot's problems—an image not only of King James but of Shakespeare himself, as a dramatist trying to stage life (this illustrates one way in which a writer could move a text into the ideologeme's force lines): theatrical staging of one's own empowered self-concept as a metaphoric version of the king's ideologeme.[20] Shakespeare could wryly portray the ruler (and behind the ruler himself) as a bungling dramatist, patching over the flaws in his schemes with pasteboard solutions—just as James himself, for all his ideology of self-staging, could not make his subjects stick to the parts he wrote for them. A few years after this Shakespearean instance, Ben Jonson would likewise write a notable play—perhaps his best—by parodically staging the ideologeme, this time reflecting an alarmingly decadent moment in James's reign,[21] namely *The Alchemist* (1611): Lovewit leaves his servant Jeremy "Face" in charge of his house long enough for uproarious scenes of chicanery to play out, then returns to stamp his image of authority and legitimacy on the butler and his illicit doings.

We now review, in general terms, the steps I followed in analyzing the *Basilicon Doron* to derive what A.-J. Greimas would call its "base narrative program." For I hypothesize that the king's book contributed much to establishing—and thus that its "narrative program" will articulate for us—this very prevalent new Jacobean ideologeme.[22] The "base narrative program," as a concept, is a sort of metasentence representing a distillation of a text's semantic and metasyntactic makeup: it is derived from comprehensive analysis of word occurrence patterns in the text in question. Thus it formulates the text's particular potential for supporting diverse interpretive readings—at least, such readings as come out of hermeneutic practices valuing linguistically historical exegesis and whole-text derivation of interpretation.[23] It must be stressed again that Greimas's concepts themselves are strictly text-linguistic—he does not extend them to consideration of culture or politics in any such concept as an ideologeme; I have done that by pursuing my analytical result further, through concepts from Kristeva and Jameson, both of whom are also closely related to Greimas on the semiotic side of their thinking. (Jameson draws on him explicitly, Kristeva uses terminology overlapping with his.)

The next two paragraphs may be for many readers an unfamiliar kind of material and may need rereading. But I think it important, for an understanding of my approach here as it explores ways of theorizing writing and culture, to know in general terms what text-linguistic application I have tried out. For a more detailed presentation of the steps below (which are intended to be repeatable and to give recognizably the same result for anyone competent at reading Jacobean English), readers specifically interested in text-linguistics or discourse analysis are referred to Appendix 1.

Step one) is to eliminate from the corpus—the data-base of passages to be considered—all paratexts (prefaces, etc.) and all personal designations of the enunciator and primary enunciatee of the whole text, in this case James Stuart and his son Prince Henry Frederick. Step two) is to divide the text into segments, by noting boundary markers that serve as signals of continuity or signals of transition; here this process identified six segments, comprising

1. Sonnet. The Argument (I, p. 5)
2. The First Booke (pp. 25–51)

3. The Second Booke, portion comprising pp. 53–71, down to "And that ye may the readier . . . govern your subjects"
4. The Second Booke, portion comprising pp. 71–103, down to "But it is not ynough to a good King . . . well to gouerne, . . . if he joyne not therewith his vertuous life in his owne person."
5. The Second Booke, portion comprising pp. 103–61.
6. The Third Booke.
   (Of these, I used segments 1–3 and 6, comprising about three-fifths of the whole text, as data base for the present analysis; Segments 4 and 5 I omitted because they began with—and throughout continued—marker terms indicating downshift to concrete illustration of the treatise's previous abstractions.)

Step three) is to identify a set of semantically indicative words from the data base, which here I chose to do by excerpting (and then alphabetizing, so that the occurrent instances of each word fell together) the "focal" words from all the sentences of the selected segments; focal words, as described by the standard linguistic grammar of English (Quirk and Greenbaum), are, according to the principle of end focus in the intonation patterns of English clauses, those words recognizable by prosodic prominence as carrying the highest degree of new information. They are opposed to the "topical" word or phrase, reiterating something already in reference and occurring first in each sentence or information unit—that which serves as its topic. Carrying out this step gave me a list of all the stressed or focal words from the data base, from which I could then select the most frequently occurring ones for further study. (Of course I took only the "open-class" words, i.e., those with semantic import other than the purely grammatical—neglecting conjunctions, articles, etc.) Step four) is called "structuration," whereby we formulate the recurrent "sememes" or semantic units found wholly, or in some word instances partially, within the indicator words that resulted from step three; these recurrent sememes—or units of recurring semantic content—must be formulated in a metalanguage that will not exactly correlate with, but will overlap with, the language of the text itself. Step five) uses these sememes—each of which represents, as it were, a boiling down of a batch of synonymous and partially synonymous words that were found most frequent in the above completed list—it sorts these sememes, as components, into a version of the single formulaic sentence that is concluded to be the "base narrative program" of the text as a whole.

For the *Basilicon Doron*, I found the base narrative program to be that a {male ruler} [effects domination of] {a male ruler-image} [disjoined from] {an object} [invested with the dual modal values of] {having-to-be} and {wanting-to-be} (ruled). Here, as perhaps in most extended texts with a high degree of discursive unity, the base narrative program exists in the words of the text not only in the above base-form—i.e, the words "ruler", "image", and "subject" are among the frequently occurring—but also in several metaphoric versions or "figurativizations," together making up what is called the figurative isotopy of the text. The following list of these make clearer what this base program is in the *Basilicon Doron* and how it structures the semantic and metasyntactic core of the text. (The symbol "∧" means "conjoined with," "U" means "disjoined from," "S" means subject, "O" means object, "$_v$" means a value, and "F" means function.) The whole formula is framed as a "function" to indicate that the concept is not an essentialist one, but that of an observable sociolinguistic operation.

Base Narrative Program: $F[S_1 \dashrightarrow S_2 \text{ U } O_v]$

male-ruler	effects domination of	ruler-image	U	"citizen" having-to-be/wanting-to-be [ruled]
S_1	$\longrightarrow$	S_2	U	O $\quad$ v

Some Major Figurativizations

God	begets	Christ	U	Christian having-to-be/wanting-to-be [ruled]
king	writes/stages	prince	U	people having-to-be/wanting-to-be
private-self	writes/stages	public-self	U	other having-to-be, etc.

A Negative Figurativization

tyrant	writes/stages	public-self	∧	other having-to-be, etc.

As an ideologeme, this represents King James's particular writerly program for governmental control: to the king in an accession day panegyric, Ben Jonson gave the motto *Solus rex et poeta non quotannis nascitur* (Herford et al. *Ungathered Verse*, "A Panegyre")—James considered himself a born writer as well as king and considered government a case of writing his own image into his subjects. As for the gender classeme, the ideologeme presupposes that femaleness cannot tag a meaning-generating nor even a meaning-recipient linguistic subject; i.e., the subject positions (S_1 and S_2) in the base program and its figurativizations are definedly male. Femaleness can only tag the O (Object) position. (An unfortunate confusion arises here between two meanings of the word "subject": in the linguistic sense as the agentive position of a clause, and in the political sense as a person of King James's realm—thus in the formula's *object* position above I used the not-quite-appropriate word "citizen" instead.)

While the above base-sentence represents the ideologeme of male self-image propagation on its narratological (or metasyntactic) side, we can begin to represent its semantic side—and also note the kind of linkage between the semantic and the syntactic envisioned in this text-linguistic model—by looking at a sample articulation of its S_2 position on the semiotic square:

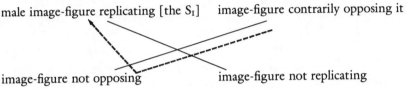

male image-figure replicating [the S_1]   image-figure contrarily opposing it

image-figure not opposing   image-figure not replicating

The plot of a fiction based on the ideologeme would commonly, for example, be represented by the above broken arrow, as a motion from contrarily opposing to replicating. Such was the masque of *Oberon, The Fairy Prince* contrived by Ben Jonson, Alfonso Ferrabosco, and Inigo Jones for the installation of Henry as Prince of Wales in 1610—a major event whereby King James's advisors hoped to increase the king's feeble popularity and thus persuade Parliament to subsidize the always-overdrawn royal treasury. The masque opens with a band of rustic, comical satyrs as antimasquers, longing for the invisible prince with his entourage to appear: as if they see the prince as an opponent to his royal sun-king father. When he does appear, the moveable platform on which he and the other noble dancers stand carries a moon image slowly traversing the space above them while the platform moves them gradually forward toward the focal point of the masque performance, the seated King James as the "Sun"; toward him the yet reflective "moon" of the fairy prince and his whole further moonlit entourage are approaching as they dance, and the musicians play and sing. Thus the king as shining sun reproduces in and appropriates from the prince (as shining moon) his own image, to which the rest of the court is through the dancing attached. The king is adored as "a god o're kings" who yet "stoupes / Neerest a man, when he doth gouerne men; / To teach them by the sweetnesse of his sway," and as "the sunne" who "Where he doth shine, quickens euery thing / Like a new nature: so that true to call / Him, by his title, is to say, Hee's all" (Herford et al. 7:353). The future of Prince Henry as the coming heavenly light of the kingdom is projected in the final song, where the "iealous Sunne" hurries to get his head above the ocean, "Lest, taken with the brightnesse of this night, / The world should wish it last, and neuer misse his [James's] light" (7:356).

Not surprisingly, masques sometimes followed the ideologeme pattern quite straightforwardly; as a genre, masque focused more on complexities of dance, music, costuming, and staging than on subtlety of text and plot. And Prince Henry fit the king's ideologeme perfectly—so well that James was sometimes jealous of him, since many people thought he would become a better king and "outshine" in too literally replicating—i.e., replacing—his "sun" father. (Nor was this an irrational fear—Scottish nobles had for their own purposes deposed James's mother to set him as an infant on the Scottish throne.) Yet the prince in 1598, when James had written the *Basilicon Doron* and used his little chip off the old block to generate ideology, had presumably not seemed so threatening.

While the plot just summarized represents a narrative usage of the ideologeme, an emblematic-pictorial (and politically telling) usage can be instanced in the retrospective account of a seventeenth-century ecclesiastical writer commenting on James's character:

> Consider the sweetness of this King's Nature, (for I ascribe it to that cause), that from the time he was 14 years old and no more, that is, when the Lord Aubigny came into Scotland out of France to visit him, even then he began, and with that Noble Personage, to clasp some-one *Gratioso* in the Embraces of his great Love, above all others, who was unto him as a *Parelius*; that is, when the Sun finds a Cloud so fit to be illustrated by his Beams, that it looks almost like another Sun. (Hacket I 227)

This is an apt image of King James's ongoing relations, always at once personal and either potentially or actively political, with his homoerotic favorites, one of them always succeeding the last in the chief position of favor. It was quite as much through his favorites as through his sons Henry and later Charles (whom he attached to Buckingham in his affections, as his letters show) that James saw himself as stamping his own self-image on his subjects, singly and collectively. It was the two greatest favorites Somerset and Buckingham, the former at first under the management of the shrewd Overbury (discussed above), who learned how to exploit the potential of their slot in James's ideological and erotic self-imaging.

Of course, women were deemed scarcely or not at all capable of holding the lofty image-impression from above: only if a woman had a "manly soul," as Jonson praised the Countess of Bedford for having—and as Donne would claim of Elizabeth Drury (see next chapter)—might she be capable of the impress—and then Jonson would lampoon her for it. Women, in this view, needed to be controlled generally by intimidation and propaganda rather than by efforts to instill in them the heliotropic and sun-like nature. It is no accident that the question whether women have souls at all runs through the masquing and game-playing of this reign. That James disliked learned women—probably the reason Stephen Lesieur presented Elizabeth Weston's neo-Latin poems to him as ghost-written, thinking they would make a better impression that way (see chapter 4)— ᴛt James's letters contain the coarsest misogynist jokes, or that he personally intervened in a judiciary action to award the Countess of Dorset's inherited lands to her cousin Henry Clifford—such things were not random events but symptoms of a thoroughgoing distaste for women. From 1607, when

he and Queen Anne began to live apart, he was able to surround himself entirely with men, and only such men as pleased him, spending his leisure time
in hunting and theological conversation.

The Twin Masques of Blackness and Beauty as Female "Speech"

Queen Anne of Denmark for her part took great pleasure in commissioning
and dancing in masques during Prince Henry's lifetime (after his death in 1612,
she would stage no more). Aside from the pleasure in glitter and spectacle that
historians generally credit her with, I will propose here that she had another
motive, namely a wish to use the king's ideologeme for a piece behind which
she projected the originating (as the commissioning and funding) voice. And
she resorted to quite intriguing tactics. She seems on various occasions to have
enjoyed skin blackness as a motif of entertainment. Her biographer Williams
mentions several instances of its use, of which the most titillating and (to us)
horrifying might have been the dance King James ordered performed for her
pleasure on the coach ride home from their winter wedding in Norway: "four
young Negroes danced naked in the snow in front of the royal carriage, but
the cold was so intense that they died a little later of pneumonia" (E. C. Williams 21). But in the masques of *Blackness* and *Beauty* she found a politically
nuanced use for this motif. In planning her first great double entertainment as
queen of England, she told Ben Jonson that she wanted to have herself and the
other dancers "*Black-mores* at first" (Herford et al. 7:169); from that instruction,
he says, he derived his invention. Her role in planning the masques may have
extended to other directives as well, perhaps on costumes and choreography,
since an Italian observer referred to her as "authoress of the whole" *Masque of
Beauty* (Herford et al. 10:457), though we cannot say just what that role was.
In the impressions created by a masque as performed, the poetic text played a
minor role, with dancing, music, costumes, and scenic machinery much more
important.

As Jonson worked out the text, the ladies would be daughters of the River
Niger, who having heard poets' accounts of female beauties of many lands, long
to have their unseemly black skins bleached. At the end of the first masque they
are instructed how to accomplish this and told to return next year to have the
British sun king complete the process. The sequel, *Beauty*, postponed until 1608
because of intervening wedding masques, carries out this plan, with the sun
king finishing the bleaching of the ladies with his temperate beams (this assumes as backdrop the myth of Phaeton, who as Jonson's notes explain had
caused the Ethiopians' blackness by driving the sun-chariot too low and scorch-
ing them; thus James as Phaeton's father Apollo could repair the damage).[24]
Art historians laud the wonders of this beginning of the collaboration between

Jonson and the designer-architect Inigo Jones, and D. J. Gordon (134–36) has identified the origins of practically every iconographic detail of the two masques in classical and Renaissance neo-Platonism. Jonson came up with his most striking neo-Platonic creation lyrics for the concluding songs of *Beauty*: the echo song "When *Love* at first, did mooue / From out of *Chaos*," and the famous riddle song that sends one's mind out into an infinite regress of origins for love, pondering the doctrine of *emanatio-raptio-remeatio* (the cycling emanation, rapture, and return of all love from the One, through created beings, and back to the One):

> So beautie on the waters stood
> When *loue* had seuer'd earth, from flood
> So when he parted air from fire,
> He did with concord all inspire!
> And then a motion he them taught
> That elder than himself was thought,
> Which thought was, yet, the child of earth,
> For Love is elder than his birth.

The ladies—their number having swelled since the *Masque of Blackness* from twelve to sixteen and several having been replaced—approach on a floating island in eight pairs, each pair bearing a hieroglyphic symbol of a virtue ascribed to the shining King James, to whom the whole spectacle is addressed. The Countess of Bedford as Splendor, for example, having been "drawn in a circle of clouds, her face, and body breaking through," steps off in a "robe of flame color naked brested, her bright hayre loose flowing." The formerly black ladies are to complete the last stage of their transformation by basking in the sunking's rays and reflecting his whiteness. When all sixteen have alighted, they do their first dance, ending in a diamond formation. The king was so delighted, Jonson reports, that he had them repeat this dance before they could go on (Herford et al. 7:192–94).

The penultimate song of the masque turns on the issue we have seen treated by Overbury and "A. S." in the "News," whether women's souls are somehow different from those of men, or if they even have souls. "A. S." had conceded only that "the souls of women and lovers are wrapped in the portmanque [carrying-bag] of their affections"—i.e., that their souls hover at the level of affectio rather than of ratio, the latter being a higher stage of return to union with the One, or God. This perhaps claimed enough soulfulness to suit women, leaving men the superiority of having greater "reason"—ironic because they often appeared to be deliberately backsliding in seeking that lesser state of the women and lovers. Jonson's handling of the topic in the penultimate song of *Beauty* resuscitates the doctrine of Anaxagoras that the soul is, in its essence, harmony.[25]

> Had those that dwell in error foule,
> And hold that women have no soul,
> But seen these move, they would have then
> Said women were the souls of men.
> 　　　So they do move each heart and eye
> 　　　With the world's soul, true harmony.

As Gossett notes [100], this graceful denunciation of those who say that women have no souls still does not exactly say that they do. It turns them into components of the soul-harmony of the cosmos, attached to particular men. After the ladies' dance following this song, "Januarius" declares that they have now, through this proper placing of their souls, completed the process of attaining beauty,

> 　　　. . . by impulsion of your destinies
> And his attractive beames, that lights these skies:
> Who (though with th'Ocean compass'd) neuer wets
> His hayre therein, nor weares a beame that sets.
> Long may his light adorne these happy rites.
> 　　　　　　　　(Herford et al. 7:389–92)

In directing Jonson to devise a masque plot that would have her and her ladies "black-mores at first" then turning white, the queen in 1605 had devised a remarkable way to write women into the king's ideologeme.[26] And Jonson, at once misogynist and fancier of women, was just the man to take the drift. Through the unself-conscious blatant racism of the age, he could contrive an exotic slot for them that they agreed to step into—under a disguise taking that affirming-submissive secondary subject position in the ideologeme. How stimulating Jonson found the process is evidenced by the fact that he was able, within it, to channel the full force of Renaissance neo-Platonism into some of his most powerful lyrics about love. It worked by defining a code equivalency between the unusable classeme of maleness-femaleness and that of whiteness-blackness—race for gender—and following a pattern on the valorized S_2 term (of the formula given earlier), into which the women step as blackamoors-to-be-whitened (read women-to-be-manned). They cannot become male but can become white, the racial sameness as it were screening their gender otherness. At the end of *Blackness* the first stage of their narrative motion around the possible terms was completed, at the end of *Beauty* the second.

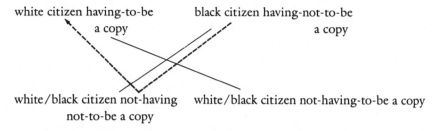

white citizen having-to-be
a copy

black citizen having-not-to-be
a copy

white/black citizen not-having
not-to-be a copy

white/black citizen not-having-to-be a copy

Jonson was ideologically attuned to the Pembroke party and, as in Prince Henry's *Oberon* masque diagramed above, tended to use the ideologeme in what was perhaps the typical pattern for people of that affiliation, namely in fictions that begin from a position of contrary otherness and bring an image-figure into conformity with its would-be model.

Lewalski refers to Queen Anne's measure of agency in her masques as "authorship" (*Writing* 37),[27] which in some sense is fair enough—I have called it female "speech" in the sense of a symbolic action operative, as female sponsored, at the sociolinguistic level of the ideologeme. But I would not go so far as to say, as Lewalski does, that the masques represent "a subversion of the trajectory of power" (37) or that their "effect was to subvert the representation of James as exclusive locus of power and virtue" in favor of the queen's power and virtue (29). Rather, I see these shrewdly devised narratological actions as a way for women to stake a claim, within operative sociosymbolic terms of the moment, for the limited measure of political agency that they as courtiers were just then managing to attain.

Queen Anne not only originated the masques' themes herself but also managed political balancing among the dancers, as among her regular attendant ladies. A privately practicing Catholic, she recognized the importance of both the Pembroke (the Protestant) and Howard (pro-Catholic) factions, and even of the "third-front" Cecilians, operatives of Secretary Robert Cecil, Lord Salisbury (on these see chapter 6). The French and Spanish ambassadors, favoring respectively the Pembrokeans' and the Howards' policies, vied for invitations to her masques, where they could not be asked together, and she dealt with the difficulties of the French ambassador's rage, while personally favoring the Spaniard (cf. Lewalski *Writing* 29ff.).

Among her ladies she cultivated a balance roughly reflecting the general balance of power James preferred, which somewhat favored the Howards and other old landed families in the first decade of the reign (Herford et al. 10:458). Besides her Scottish ladies, her four best friends of countess rank were the Countess of Bedford (a committed Protestant and political cohort of Pembroke, who along with Mary Wroth represented the Protestant Pembrokeans among the queen's ladies), Alethea Talbot Howard, wife of the Earl of Arundel and daughter of the Earl of Shrewsbury (both Catholic or Catholic-allied families—Alethea's husband being Suffolk's and Northampton's nephew), and the two sisters Elizabeth (Vere) Stanley, Countess of Derby, and Susan (Vere) Herbert, Countess of Montgomery—daughters of the Earl of Oxford, another old family allied with and related to the Howards;[28] these last two were also nieces of Salisbury.

Susan Vere Herbert was a swing person in these terms, an instance of one of the king's efforts to confuse and eliminate the factions by intermarrying them: she was Oxford's daughter but married to Pembroke's brother Philip (one of the king's early handsome favorites), in which marriage she had the chance to become Mary Wroth's best friend and dedicatee of the *Urania*. The king himself had presided at the Vere-Herbert wedding. (His most spectacular failure in that line would of course be the marrying of Suffolk's daughter Frances to the young Earl of Essex.) Frances Howard's sister Elizabeth, Lady Knollys (later Lady Banbury), was also one of the queen's honored ladies, as was Lady Elizabeth Hatton, another of Salisbury's nieces. Thus the queen surrounded herself with some women associated with each faction including the Cecilians, but gave those of Howard associations a numerical edge. When she chose the cast for the *Masque of Beauty*, three of the *Blackness* masquers having died in the interim, she added the four daughters of Northampton's ally, the Catholic Edward Somerset, Earl of Worcester.

It would seem that Cecily Bulstrode's chambers at Hampton Court were part of, so to speak, the Protestant wing of the queen's establishment, and practically all the "News" writers associated with her and appearing in the *Wife* were protégés of either the Earl of Pembroke, the Countess of Bedford, or both. While the Howards were in the ascendant in that first decade, the Pembrokeans suffered from scandal and a leadership vacuum: Essex was dead, Sir Walter Raleigh in disgrace, Essex's sister (the Stella of Philip Sidney's sonnets) living in open adultery, and then finally the Earl of Pembroke was having an affair with his cousin Wroth.

Love's Victory as Sexual Politics

> Predestination and constancy are alike uncertaine to be judged of
> —Cecily Bulstrode

Lady Mary Wroth's pastoral play has the political loading of a defense of the Pembroke-Sidney party as it had existed through the first decade of the reign, even though the play was written several years later; I propose that it is thus retrospective, though referring also to its own moment. To begin placing this pastoral piece in political perspective, let us first consider a pastoral play by Ben Jonson.[29] In his *Conversations* with Drummond (337–42) Jonson described a play of his called *The May Lord*, not now extant. The title indicates that it was conceived as in the same tradition with Sidney's pastoral pageant *The Lady of May* (performed before Queen Elizabeth in 1578 or 1579) and centered on the king as lord of a May festival. We can form a picture of its political frame of reference from Jonson's account. Overbury is represented there as one "Mogibell," he says, the Countess of Bedford as "Ethra," the Countess of Suffolk (later prosecuted by Bacon for graft along with her husband) as "an enchantress," usually an evil personage, and Jonson himself as the shepherd "Alken"; other people represented in the play, he adds, are Frances Howard, Countess of Somerset (the Suffolks' daughter), the Earl of Pembroke, the Countess of Rutland, and Lady Mary Wroth. Given this lineup of characters, the play would seem to have treated the Howard party's stealing of Somerset from the Pembrokeans, and perhaps also Frances Howard's 1613 murder of Overbury, depending on when it was written. It is clear that most of the "News" circle—especially Jonson—wound up with only contempt for their former friend the manipulative operator Overbury, murdered though he was (see above and n. 7); he was thus doubtless portrayed satirically in *The May Lord.*

While we cannot be specific about how the lost *May Lord* treated Overbury's rise and very likely his fall, it is notable that political conflict was there portrayed as the activity of women: Pembroke and Jonson himself, as playwright, are the only men in the cast. The Howard operative Lady Suffolk is lined up against two leading players of the other faction—Pembroke himself and the Countess of Bedford—as well as two further ladies of the Pembrokeans, Wroth and Rutland. The other details Jonson gives are that the play opens with Alken mending his broken pipe (i.e., Jonson reclaiming the stage after some loss of favor), and that it includes clowns "making mirth and foolish sport" (on pastoral drama as genre see Lewalski *Writing* chap. 9).

While Wroth's pastoral play does not portray any recognizable interaction between the court parties, I submit that it was no less political than Jonson's. It offers a moral justification of the Pembrokean leadership through a kind of love-religion based on the writer's own ideal of "constancy," acted out centrally through a fantasy revision of the sonnet love story of Philip Sidney and Penelope Devereux from *Astrophil and Stella.* Of the play's two chief lovers, Philisses is a version of Sidney's earlier pastoral self-designation Philisides and thus unmistakably alludes to Wroth's uncle Sidney, while Musella, the lady who has missed the chance to become betrothed to him and instead is to marry the blockhead "Rustic," stands for Penelope, the Stella of Sidney's sonnets, being forced to marry Lord Robert Rich.[30] "Musella" is constructed from Muse Stella—Astrophil's muse. Wroth bases her plot on the fact that there had been an early effort to betroth Philip to Penelope Devereux, which fell through probably because both families wanted more money out of matching their children (the play denounces letting "pelf" interfere with love). Wroth treats the episode as if the young people, having early fallen in love, then lost confidence in each other and, though still greatly in love, bowed to the pressure of Penelope's parents for her betrothal to Lord Rich. Wroth rolls back their story, as it were, to the point just before the cruel forced marriage is to occur and prevents it through a death pact of the lovers, which, in the final scene of their resurrection after seeming death, causes Rustic to renounce his claim and let them marry. Into that role of Musella about to be forced into misery Wroth infuses not only her uncle's and Penelope Devereux's supposed love suffering but her own, as having been forced to marry the blockish Sir Robert Wroth (Jonson agreed with her, telling Drummond that she was "unworthily married on a jealous husband" [*Conversations* 298–99]; and his verse letter to Robert Wroth, Forest #3, is a study in tongue-in-cheek compliment).

With the Philisses-Musella story Lady Wroth also interweaves, in Lissius and Simeana, the rumored midlife affair of Sidney's sister, dowager Countess of Pembroke, with Dr. Matthew Lister when both were living abroad at Spa (see Hannay *Phoenix*).[31] A further family echo, in the Forester-Sylvesta relationship, would seem to be the "Platonic" relationship of Philip Sidney's daughter Elizabeth, Countess of Rutland, with her reputedly impotent husband Roger Manners.[32] The play thus builds into one pastoral plot four love experiences, across two generations of the Sidney-Pembroke family: the love of Sidney and Penelope Devereux from the 1580s; that of Sidney's beloved sister the Countess of Pembroke (who had also been obliged to marry for policy), at last in the 1610s experiencing fulfilled love; that of Wroth herself as miserable wife, having been forced into an unhappy marriage lasting from 1604–1614; and that of Philip Sidney's daughter, reputedly faithful to her unconsummated marriage. About the first three of these four identifications Wroth does not leave any doubt, since, besides the Philisides allusion, she calls Philisides's sister's wooer "Lissius" (after Lister) and puns on both "Rich" and "Worth" (as Wroth was pronounced) in a speech portraying the insensitivity of Rustic,[33] just as her uncle had punned on the name "Rich" several times in *Astrophil*. In sum, looking back from the viewpoint of the late 1610s,[34] focusing on her uncle's star-crossed love for Essex's sister and on her aunt's little-known love abroad, and further portraying her own life indirectly (as we will see), Wroth treats constancy in love, despite all marital interference and failure, as a positive value.

Her experience at court, out of which came her desire to justify herself and her family, is allegorized in an episode early in Part I of the *Urania* romance, as is explained by both Roberts and Brennan:

Bersindor (a partial anagram for Robert Sidney), the 'second sonne to a famous Nobleman' (Robert was the second son of Sir Henry Sidney), was able to marry a 'great Heyre in little Brittany, of rich possessions' (Barbara Gamage was a rich Welsh heiress), thanks to the influence of his brother-in-law

(Robert's brother-in-law Henry, second Earl of Pembroke, had persuaded Barbara's guardian to ignore the blandishments of rival suitors). As Bersindor's history is recounted, we meet his lively and attractive eldest daughter, Lindamira (Lady Mary), who is much admired in court circles and is befriended by the Queen (Queen Anne). Unfortunately, malicious and unfounded gossip besmirches her reputation and, despite her impassioned protests of innocence, Lindamira loses the Queen's sympathy and regretfully withdraws from the court to live 'an unquiet life' with her jealous husband. (Brennan ed. *Victory* 5)

Since Wroth danced in the *Masque of Blackness*, in the text of which her name appears, and also in the sequel *Masque of Beauty*, in the printed text of which her name does not appear (I believe a discrete omission on Jonson's part), it is probable that 1610 was the year of the scandalous exit from court here recounted from her own viewpoint (see n. 4).

The life portrayed in Wroth's play is that of courtly socializing and game-playing among a circle of friends and acquaintances, as she had known it at court. As mentioned earlier, each of the first four acts is organized around a particular parlor game, chosen to suit the pastoral milieu. For act 1 the game first proposed is "tell a past love," whereby the effort will be to tell about one's love in generalizations and innuendos, allowing the auditors to enjoy detecting the references and the spin being put on them; but someone quickly vetoes this as potentially too revealing, and the first game instead becomes "let's each sing a song," with songs hinting at love complications to come. It is the characters incapable of serious love who most enjoy the "tell a love" game, for them a sort of voyeuristic exercise, and in act 3 they will get their round of it (i.e., "tell a love" is deferred until the plot is ready for the revelations it will bring). Indeed, voyeurism resonates throughout the play: almost every love encounter is observed or eavesdropped upon, while the lovers pretend or suppose they are alone. This reflects the nature of socializing among such a circle as that of the "News" players, where intertwined friendships and loves mutually fired each other on and competed.

Act 2's game is "draw a fortune"—one of the minor characters, Arcas, has prepared fortune slips attuned to the characters' love problems up to that point. For act 3 it is, as noted, "let's tell a love," and for act 4 it is "tell a riddle." (For similar riddling among the "collegiate" ladies see *Epicoene* V.ii.) By the time of this last game, some of the love confusions have been resolved, and the point is to show that the worthy characters have the intelligence to cast their own situations into riddle form, while the blockish Rustic refuses even to try riddling. Thus as Jonson did in his *May Lord*, Wroth has lightened the play with comedy, especially by having Rustic sing simple-minded songs, cut capers, and otherwise humorously show himself a lout.

We can get the characters better in mind through a couples chart. Remember that Simeana is Philisses's sister.

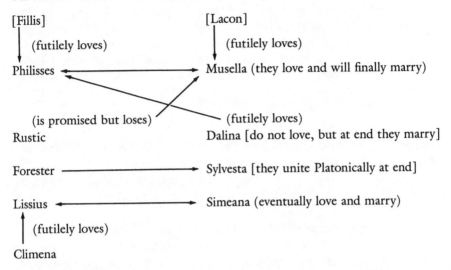

[Fillis]   [Lacon]

    (futilely loves)   (futilely loves)

Philisses ⟷ Musella (they love and will finally marry)

    (is promised but loses)   (futilely loves)

Rustic   Dalina [do not love, but at end they marry]

Forester ⟶ Sylvesta [they unite Platonically at end]

Lissius ⟷ Simeana (eventually love and marry)

    (futilely loves)

Climena

Arcas (gossips, loves no one, confuses and sometimes harms the others)

It is as if the admired people of Lady Wroth's paternal family, across two generations, have gathered and become part of a newsy, game-playing circle at Queen Anne's court.

     Act I opens with a scene evoking the powers of the youthfully dead Sidney as pastoral love poet, in a fitting song of Philisses, "You pleasant flowrie mead / Which I did once well love, / Your pathes noe more I'le tread." Then in a dialogue between him and Lissius, who is at first a scorner of love, Philisses's love pains for Musella are introduced. Once that initial scene has foreshadowed the two main loves, the more mysterious third relationship in the plot is introduced. In contrast to the other, explicitly name-tagged topical relationships, it flickers with double layers of reference. The person to present it first is its female half Sylvesta, who, through her later strong role in solving the love dilemma of the main couple, will be seen to echo not only Lady Rutland (who would immediately have come to mind for the audience as Platonic lover), but also Wroth herself, as writer revisiting and recasting the family stories. That is, Sylvesta presents herself as a devotee of Philisses (which would fit Sidney's daughter) but also an ex-nymph of Venus (which would *not* fit Lady Rutland but obviously evokes Wroth herself), who is now in love with chastity and writing, living as a nymph of Diana. In other words, I believe, Wroth is presenting herself—under the screen of her cousin Elizabeth Manners's aura of chaste constancy—as an upright widow who has left her Pembroke affair behind:

I, for one, who thus my habitts change,
Once sheapherdess, butt now in woods must rang;
And after the chast Goddess beare her bowe,
Though service once to Venus I did owe,
Whose servante then I was and of her band.
Butt farewell folly, I with Dian stand
Against love's changinge and blinde foulerie,
To hold with hapy and blest chastitie.
For love is idle, hapines ther's none
When freedome's lost and chastity is gon.

(I.121–28)

(In terms of the discourse theory in chapter 1 above, Wroth initially claims a female subject position by adopting "superior-chastity" discourse, though this observation is only a first point in the broader analysis here.) Sylvesta ends by denouncing love in terms that suggest Wroth's own past sorrows, and after a brief interim the Forester appears, lamenting his great and unrequited love for her, for the ears of the polite but skeptical Lissius:

Then know I lov'd, alas, and ever must,
Sylvesta faire, sole mistress of my joye,
Whose deere affections were in surest trust
Layd up in flames my hopes cleane to destroy.

(I. 213–16)

He explains that Sylvesta has not only scorned him and his affection but constantly pined for Philisses, who always scorned her, until at last she has made a vow never to let a lover even look upon her. And alas for the poor Forester, that was all he wanted! He says that he could even wish she had won Philisses or some other lover, for then he could at least enjoy gazing upon her:

Wowld itt cowld bee to any's gaine the most
Of glory, honor, fortune . . .
For then I might have her sometimes beheld,
But now am bar'd; for my love placed was
In truest kind, wherin I all excell'd
Nott seeking gaine, butt losing did surpas
Those that obtaine, for my thoughts did assend
Noe higher then to looke. That was my end.

(I. 255–64)

Lissius, astonished, gives a pragmatic reply to this avowal of Platonic heterosexual love, questioning the possibility of it.

What strange effects doth Phant'sy 'monge us prove,
Who still brings forth new images of love?
Butt this of all is strangest to affect
Only the sight, and nott the joyes respect.
Nor ends of whining love since sight wee gaine
With small adoe, the other with much paine, . . .
And sure if ever I showld chance to love,
The fruitfull ends of love I first wowld move.

The Forester replies courteously: "I wish you may obtaine your hart's desire, / And I butt sight who waste in chastest fire."

The name Sylvesta, combining "sylvan" and "vesta," implies a nymph devoted to chastity, as Lewalski notes ("Pastoral" 92–94), a stock figure of pastoral tragicomedy. Wroth in this character casts herself as having left her venerean ways behind, and even though someone is wooing her, being committed now to a chaste life and only the love of writing, in the form of her legendary uncle the poet-hero: writing has been her first and remains her greatest love. The ending of the play, which ties up as many marriages as possible, will bring Sylvesta and the Forester together with deliberate ambiguity: she declares that she now grants him her "chast love," and exits. To the other characters he responds:

My joys encrease, she grievs now for my paine.
Ah, happy proffer'd lyfe which this can gaine.
Now shall I goe contented to my grave,
Though noe more hapines I ever have.

(V. 519–24)

This can easily evoke the Rutlands, who died within a week of each other. But it also wraps up the functioning of the Sylvesta character as a slot for the play's enunciative position; "chaste love" is not necessarily a term for sexual abstinence here, since in the same scene Sylvesta has just enjoined the lovers Philisses and Musella, now at last about to marry, that they should "in chaste love still live, / And each to other true affections give." I believe that Wroth in Sylvesta and in the play as a whole was encouraging a wooer for her hand, with whom she saw herself just reaching the stage of chaste friendship. Thus it could well be that the play was written in connection with the negotiations in 1619 for a marriage of the widowed Lady Wroth to Henry de Vere, Earl of Oxford, younger half-brother of her close friend Susan, Countess of Montgomery, dedicatee of the *Urania*.[35] The play's probable performance milieu, indicated both by the text itself and by the derivation history of the two surviving manuscripts (see Roberts)—namely for a family social occasion at a country estate—would fit this purpose well. I have no evidence that it was actually thus performed (with Oxford present to recognize himself in the Forester and be duly urged on), but it might have been. We do not know how far those marriage negotiations went, only that they ultimately broke off.

To return to our review of the plot, after the scene between Sylvesta and the Forester, act 1 has most of the characters join Lissius for its singing game. The scene is strongly reminiscent of analogous, book-ending ones in Sidney's *Arcadia*, like them interspersing comical rustic songs with suave aristocratic lyrics, such as the shepherd Lacon's, "By a pleasant river's side." It evokes the intense lyric of desire by the River Ladon (note Lacon-Ladon), spoken by Pyrocles/Zelmane as he/she gazes on the beloved Philoclea bathing. With Musella as love object, Lacon here portrays himself as a sort of revised and pardoned Actaeon, having gazed not on Diana's bathing but on Venus's lovemaking, taking thence his own arousal.

> By a pleasant river's side
> Hart and hopes on pleasures tide,
> Might I see within a bowre,
> Prowdly drest with every flowre,
> Which the spring doth to uss lend,
> Venus, and her loving freind.
> I upon her beauty gaz'd,
> They mee seeing were amaz'd
> Till att last upstept a child,
> In his face nott actions mild.
> Fly away, sayd hee, for sight
> Shall both breed and kill delight.
> Fly away, and follow mee,
> I will lett thee beauties see.
> I obay'd him when hee stay'd
> Hard beside a heav'nly mayd,
> When hee threw a flaming dart,
> And unkindly strooke my hart.
>
> (I. 357–74)

Act 2 opens with the minor characters watching and then discussing an encounter between the Forester and Sylvesta, with her trying to flee as he begs her to stay; thus again that unusual "chaste" love is kept in our attention while the two other lover-pairs, during the course of acts 2 and 3, work through the hindrances temporarily keeping them apart. Rustic, in the "fortunes" game, gives his own primitive definition of love, a polar opposite to that highly idealized image of it held by the Forester: it is, he says, as "if I my bag or bottle

lost," I would naturally want to have it (II. 86). Other characters offer definitions ranging between the extremes of idealization and will to possess. (Lissius
at this moment humorously affects something like agreement with Rustic, and
thus is ripe to be hit hard by Cupid's arrow.) Philisses's definition, because of
who he is, carries great weight as an answer to Rustic's "lost bag" concept. Like
some prophetic forerunner of Deleuze and Guattari denouncing the phallocen-
tric "lack" concept of desire, he declares:

> Call you this love? Why love is noe such thing,
> Love is a paine which yett doth pleasure bring.
> A passion which alone in harts doe[s] move
> And they that feele nott this they cannot love.
> 'Twill make one merry, pleasant sad,
> Cry, weepe, sigh, fast, mourne nay sometimes stark mad.
> If they parseave scorne, hate, or els disdaine
> To wrap theyr woes in store for others' gaine.
> For that (butt Jealousie) is sure the wurst,
> And then be jealouse better bee accurst.
> But O, some bee, and wowld itt nott disclose
> They silent love, and loving feare . . .
> Be wyse, make love, and love[,] though not obtaine
> For to love truly is sufficient gaine.
>
> (II. 93–114)

Here we see that part of the mistrust keeping Philisses and Musella apart has
been his fear of being ridiculed by the lady, if his love is not fully reciprocated
(no idle fear among the witty women studied here).

Act 3 opens with a dialogue song of Sylvesta and Musella, both of whom
love Philisses but express contrasting views of him; Sylvesta, having given up
on attaining his love, wishes it to Musella, who still cannot overcome what she
sees as his mistrust of her. As for Lissius, who has at last fallen in love, we return
to him and his Simeana in a scene that would probably play very humorously.
Lissius is alone lamenting, eavesdropped upon by the rivals for him, Simeana
and Climena. He rhetorically asks pardon for his earlier scorn and ends by plead-
ing with open arms, "Take me a faithfull seruant now to thee," whereupon the
spying Climena jumps out and, no doubt grabbing him, answers "Deere Lissius,
my deere Lissius fly mee nott / Let nott both scorne, and absence be my lott."
Alarmed, he struggles to get away, saying that women must not woo, and when
he finally gets rid of her is ready to woo Simeana. Since Climena is described
as a foreigner, this episode probably refers to someone at Spa who made a play
for Lister just as he and the Countess of Pembroke began their relationship.
Act 3 ends with Cupid reporting his love-successes to Venus.

Is nott this pretty? Who doth free remaine
Of all this flock that waits nott in owr traine?

(III. 349–50)

In act 4 Philisses and Musella finally declare their love to each other, drawing allusively on the Song in *Astrophil* where Stella, for one of the very few
times in Sidney's sequence, speaks and tells Astrophil that indeed she loves him,
though she refuses to make love for the sake of his own reputation. In effect
Wroth as writer here steps into Stella's shoes at the point in *Astrophil* where
the lady had gained a voice. Musella states that even though fortune is keeping
them apart, they can remain emotionally true to each other:

Well then, I love you, and soe ever must,
Though time, and fortune should bee still unjust.
For wee may love, and both may constant prove
But nott enjoy, unles ordain'd above.

(IV. 97–100)

This ideal of an inward faithfulness, even if circumstances allow the lovers no
consummation and force them into loveless marriages, is evoked in other passages of the play, as in the Forester's initially unreturned affection for Sylvesta
(cf. above). In the play's mode of romance wish-fulfillment, Philisses and Musella will be luckier. Any reader who has grasped the intensity of desire that
Sidney wrote into *Astrophil and Stella* (whatever in particular was behind it
biographically) can also appreciate the fulfillment in Lady Wroth's fantasy revision of family history to give him and Penelope Devereux a lovers' marriage.

The other half of act 4 presents Musella as a loyal and effective friend,
intervening in a quarrel between Simeana and Lissius. This episode approaches
later sentimental novelistic treatments of love affairs and timely involvements
of friends. Simeana has accused Lissius of whispering with Climena, embracing
and continuing to flirt with her, although claiming now to love only Simeana;
Arcas saw their encounter and thus described it to her. Musella persuades her
that it was only civil of Lissius to have a little tête-à-tête with Climena, given
the latter's distress over his rejection of her:

Lord, how one may conjecture if one feare,
All things they doubt to bee the same they feare,
Though privatt must itt follow hee's untrue
Or that they whisper'd must bee kept from you.
Fy, leave thes follys, and beegin to think
You have your love brought to death's river brink . . .
Goe, ask him pardon.

(IV. 279–87)

Act 5 opens with an extended colloquy of Philisses and Musella, wherein he tries to content himself with the thought that even though she must marry Rustic, her "love in mee [will] still steddy rest, / And in that I sufficiently am blest" (V. 65–66). But neither of them can find that consolation enough, and soon they agree on an indirectly stated suicide plan (or double offering of each other as sacrifices), beginning with joint prayer in the Temple of Venus. Simeana, not understanding their intent, plans to go with them. While the other characters talk over the supposed wedding of Rustic and Musella, to occur that day, Sylvesta gets wind of danger. Just as Musella herself had saved the day for Lissius and Simeana, Sylvesta now does so for Philisses and Musella, taking away their daggers and persuading them instead to drink a supposed poison, actually a sleeping drug. Once they appear dead, she gets Musella's mother to give up her tyranny and Rustic to renounce his claim on Musella. After they awaken, the priests of Venus chant of their union: "Venus hath caus'd this wounder for her glory, / And the Triumph of love's victory." The betrothals of the other couples are announced, and the punishment of Arcas that Venus decrees, a kind of falsehood-mark of Cain on his face, along with gnawing conscience for life. Perhaps he alludes to some gossipy man who made trouble for Wroth.

It seems important in this woman's play that the tyrannical parent enforcing the bad marriage is the mother, not the father. Of course, behind the mother's obstinacy is a proviso of the father's will (V. 11–14), which doubtless would have financial consequences if disobeyed. But mother and daughter fight the climactic contest of wills, and a woman friend breaks the deadlock by writing them into a eucatastrophe. This friend, Sylvesta, indeed actorializes the operative mentality behind the play's action (the enunciative position, in Kristevan terms), cast also in the male figure of Cupid as king of love, as will now be analyzed. If my suggestion about the Oxford marriage negotiation is right, Sylvesta would at the same time be a voice of Susan Vere as best friend and other self of Wroth, trying to make a marriage between her friend and brother.

The five acts have been set within a frame of intermittent dialogue scenes between Venus and Cupid where, as in Italian pastoral drama, the love goddess and her son plan to make all the characters lovers, patterned after the goddess herself and honoring love: they decide, after putting the people through various sufferings, to have pity on most though not all (some are incapable of love, while some simply lose out). The denouement, when the main lovers Philisses and Musella "die" and revive, is set in this same temple where the two deities have after each act appeared and made comments. Thus the plot is neatly constructed, with its two diegetic layers of portrayed action converging in the end. Venus and her son, behaving in an arbitrary and demanding way, are of course a common feature of Renaissance pastoral poetry and drama. But in this play the faith that the characters come to have in them, and their rewarding of that faith, gives them a seriousness or validity quite different from the capriciousness usually ascribed to them in male pastoral. In *Love's Victory*, it is the human beings who are capricious and tyrannical, while the love deities, though they do demand reverence, are benign. This love-faith finds its manifesto in the chorus of Venus's priests ending act 2, which explicitly declares the play's seriousness about erotic relationships as base of value.

> Let your songs be still of loue
> Write no Satires which may prove
> Least offensive to his name.
> If you doe, you will butt frame
> Words against your selves, and lines
> Wher his good, and your ill shines.
> Like him who doth set a snare
> For a poore betrayed hare,
> And the thing he best doth love
> Lucklessly the snare doth prove.
> Love the King is of the mind,
> Please him, and he wilbe kind.
>
> (II. 311–22)

To see how Lady Wroth has achieved this version of pastoral drama, we need to reflect a moment on the standard Renaissance ways of presenting eroticism in terms of Venus and Cupid.[36] Love was seen most often as female, a goddess, having as a childish dimension her prankish son Cupid as the irrationality of love, whose displacement form the boy Adonis appears when Venus is to be imagined in process of lovemaking, thereby to trigger desire (we saw this functioning in Lacon's song of spying on the goddess and boy). Even when idealized in Christian neo-Platonism, the love force was seen as female, a goddess, whenever writers or artists wanted to figure it as a visualizable deity: her image was split into earthly Venus (sex) and heavenly Venus (love of the Beautiful and Good), as in Titian's famous painting of the two Venuses. A different and also ancient strategy of idealization is represented in Jonson's masque song "Beauty on the waters stood" (cf. above), which avoids using any pronoun, letting "Love" vibrate as both the Christian God himself and the neo-Platonic force of rapturous longing for return to the One—as indeed neo-Platonism and Hebraic traditions had early combined in just that way in the Johannine writings of the New Testament, where "God is love" (First John 4). Apart from that venerable neo-Platonic maneuver of masculinizing or ungendering the love force,[37] in most artistic expression the primary term for Love was female: Aphrodite or Venus, who could be given various thymic loadings, from capricious, ruinous whore goddess to kindly force of pleasure within marriage, to blessed force of unfulfilled Petrarchan longing channeled into creativity or spirituality.

But if Cupid appeared with her, he took over the traits of caprice and tyranny. McLaren (283–85; see also Donno ed.) traces some instances of this range of representational possibilities in pastoral works that Lady Wroth was probably familiar with.

As against the usual loving goddess/prankish son construct, Wroth here follows the lesser known Court of Love image, wherein the youthful god himself reigns over a scene of love devotees (see *Poems*, ed. Roberts 86); she thus reverses the usual loadings, making the queen of love more peevish and arbitrary than her son, who in carrying out her orders to subdue everyone shows himself inclined to be merciful in his arrangements. Furthermore, Wroth puts into the mouth of Venus herself a panegyric to Love as a male king, along with an injunction to the hearers to believe in his good will and submit to his dictates, as if she were delegating some of her authority to him, even though she continues to give him directives and will reclaim the stage at the end; she declares: "Love the King is of the mind."

In terms of the ideologeme we have been studying here, I believe this was part of Lady Wroth's maneuvering of her own gendered self-concept into the play's enunciative position, a position from which to write fruitfully—to write in a way that would energize the presentation. The play's Venus speaks sheerly as her love-force self in continued directives to make all the characters lovers; but it is Cupid—and his delegated female human agents—who must carry out this task, and do it beneficently, not capriciously or destructively. The human being who primarily steps into his slot and does the work of King Love is Sylvesta. Her position in the plot is as a second actorialization of King Cupid as kindly agent (in more precise Greimasian terms, of the actantial role he thematizes); it puts inside the discursive frame an image of Wroth herself writing the play, making the blessed revisions of love sorrows happen. In order to find intensity for her writing, in order to infuse it with the political and personal energies of her associates, friends, and family, as well as her own, she managed to tap into the ideologeme, with its male, S_1 subject position, that prevailed at the time of her own love disgrace, from which she is now performing a fantasy rehabilitation of herself and the people she cares about. Setting up a trajectory of King Love, as beneficent agent, reproducing himself in the female characters triggering and nurturing love enabled her to do so.

She thereby wrote a performable, potentially entertaining play that, if studied in its generic and sociopolitical contexts, offers an illuminating commentary on the often-raised issues of "decadence" and sexual politics at James's court. How did *women* see the position they were in, under pressure constantly to flirt and yet to avoid scandal, as part of the practice of courtiership as it functioned under King James? In the play, in Wroth's romance *Urania* (see chapter 6), in her poems, and in the writings of the "News" circle, I submit that we learn a good bit about how they saw their position. It involved many rounds of

Hobson's choices, perils of nonfunctional self-imaging, and risks of being denounced for just what one was pressured from all sides to do. To those challenges some of them brought a spirit of enterprise and imagination.

The Play's Male Enunciative Position

Att last upstept a child,. . . / Fly away, sayd hee, and follow mee, / I will lett thee
beauties see. / I obay'd him

Struggles for achievement, control, conquest, fame . . . are placed within and
provided with language by patterns of culturally produced discourses that name
and layer our unconscious.
Waller "Romance" 57.

To finish the account of Lady Wroth's framing of her dramatic fiction into the redefined control of Cupid as kindly King of Love, let us return more concretely to the semiotic analysis of the *Basilicon Doron*, in particular to its base narrative program, which was that a male ruler (S_1) takes control of a self-image (S_2) that has been disjoined from a ruled person or group (O) invested with the dual values of having-to-be and wanting-to-be [ruled] ($_v$). When we look at how particular writers evolved fictions along the force lines of such an ideologeme/desiring machine as is represented by that narrative program, we can identify the position from which a given text, as a discourse, has been spoken or enunciated. Either of the "subject" slots can also be, in Kristevan terminology, the enunciative position of a given text—above I argued that the queen's masques of *Blackness* and *Beauty* represented female speech appropriating the usually male S_2 position of the ideologeme.[38] My analysis here may be a more developed version of Waller's comment that "Wroth's writing is an act of self-assertion" though she is therein "caught up in discursive positions that she can occupy only at the cost of self-violation" ("Romance" 54).[39] I am here emphasizing, however, not violation or whatever psychic cost may have been involved for her, but the act of writing that she accomplished by her claiming of a male subject position.

Wroth's enunciative position for the play, considered as a discourse representing a usage or tracking of the royal self-imaging ideologeme, is that of Cupid as Love King of the mind, a kindly force to be trusted as the good characters' God. It perhaps arose for her out of the image of her cousin Elizabeth Rutland's marital chaste love; it became functional as the slot into which her own writerly self-image could step, through the hypostatized, always deferred chaste union of Sylvesta with the Platonic Forester, who exists to the very end as "male always in quest of female spiritual love" (somewhat as, in an analogous construct, the flighty Florimell in Spenser's *Faerie Queene* [like Ariosto's flighty Angelica of the *Orlando* before her] exists always in the state of fleeing a lover). In other words, from that "hermaphroditic" position of the hypostatized, nonconsummated combination of Forester and Sylvesta, Wroth could think herself into the image of Love as "King of the mind" and could herself, as writer, do the job of sparking imagined attractions and fueling relationships. Male Love thus "hermaphroditically" redefined is the enunciative position for this play, the slot for the S_1 considered as an actant or actantial role, with its chief "actors" being the busy Cupid, as redefined in the play, and Sylvesta as his primary human agent (i.e., in Greimasian terms a second actor for S_1). Love takes possession of "his" self-duplicating subjects, turned by the action of the play into love-triggering and love-enforcing beings themselves— i.e., Musella, Simeana, and predominantly Sylvesta herself—all of whom help friends to love satisfaction and thus become actors of the S_1 actant. This represents Lady Wroth's tapping into the ideologeme in metasyntactic terms: through writing Sylvesta-with-appended-Forester into the subject position of the plot—analogous to that of Shakespeare's Duke Vincentio or Jonson's Lovewit (see above)—she makes women the active agents within it, while the male characters become value-invested objects to be acquired by them, an exact inversion of usual patriarchal narrative construction.

Semantically, we can map this plot onto the semiotic square through the trajectory of the S_1 beginning on the contrary term at the upper right of the square, actorialized in Sylvesta; through this trajectory she assumes the necessary maleness to actorialize the enunciative position.

male figure replicating self in image	male/female figure being diametrically opposed by its image
(King Love has effected love, i.e., own image, in Phil. and Musella, Lissius and Simeana	(Love blocked by Arcas/mistrust, Phil.'s, Musella's, and Lissius's resistance to it)

female/male figure not being opposed by own image (Sylvesta-Forester removes love obstacles in Philisses/Musella, Musella those in Simeana)	[male figure not being replicated by own image]

In the play's particular usage of the ideologeme, then, we have an action of vicarious erotic satisfaction, achieved by Wroth's writing herself into the position of King of Love and thereby writing a set of imagined others into happiness. It brings to narrative embodiment the mode of gossipy, politicized, eavesdropping, and matchmaking social life of Queen Anne's court, as Wroth had known it, at the same time as it invents for her a way to step into the ideologeme's enunciative position and thus find a politically resonant voice. While her romance of *Urania*, when published, would bring her only trouble, perhaps this play found a positive resonance with a select sympathetic audience at a private country-house performance—at least it had the potential to do so.

If Donne in his "First Anniversary," as we will see in chapter 6, could devise a parodic inversion of the ideologeme, Lady Wroth could find a back door into it, by a similar strategy of reversing the tagging on a key term, namely that of the classeme of gender (on classematic oppositions see n. 18). But if we consider how seldom any woman with talent and inclination for writing would have been in a position to think her own writerly self-image into a functional position in such a way, we understand on a new level why women in early modern England wrote few other such original belletristic pieces as the *Urania* and *Love's Victory* (of plays there is only Elizabeth Cary's *Mariam*—see chapter 7). In Jacobean England, Lady Wroth was perhaps uniquely situated to do so, being able to draw on the political energies of her Sidney identity while remaining active in the on-going Sidney-Pembroke political faction and having also experienced at Queen Anne's court the expressive life and political activity of other intelligent, relatively independent women, such as those of the "News" circle. Like the lady "News" players, in order to write in a politically energized way she had been obliged to act, as Jonson's True-wit complained, "with most masculine, or rather *hermaphroditicall* authoritie."

6

Factional Identities and Writers' Energies

Wroth, the Countess of Bedford, and Donne

THE PRESENT CHAPTER is closely linked to the previous one, continuing study of the ideologeme of royal self-image propagation as rule in the first Jacobean decade, and how both male and female writers in the Pembroke circle worked in and out of—and were energized by—its functioning as a Deleuzean "desiring machine"; the two chapters should be read in tandem. Here we examine the Pembrokean factional identity (along with its major competitor) that was mentioned in the previous chapter; then, after considering how Lady Mary Wroth's *roman à clef* the *Urania* worked with some of its political materials, we go on to examine the Countess of Bedford's and Donne's elegies for Cecily Bulstrode, and finally a famous poem by Donne that I see as a parodic inverse usage—possibly even the death knell—of this ideologeme as a libidinally functional unit. An important reason to note such factional identities, though here we cannot pursue the point, is that the particular usage patterns of an ideologeme (which in itself can be operative for all interacting groups) vary according to the politics and economics of the faction with which a writer or artisan identifies; that factional identity serves as a way for the writer's own libidinal/creative energies to tap into and interact with the ones operative in the power structures surrounding the writing moment.

The Howards versus the Pembrokeans

Unlike Queen Elizabeth, who to some extent allowed factions to represent the competing ideologies and economic interests of her subjects and played them off against each other, King James tried to minimize factions (Prestwich 17) and have all his subjects live under his single fatherly rule, with lines of authority going down through no group powerful enough to challenge him. Another way of diagraming the ideologeme we have been studying may elaborate the point—this is an arrangement of some figurative isotopies of the base narrative program of *Basilicon Doron,* a few of which I listed earlier.

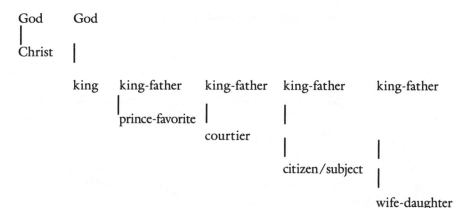

Here we understand in another way why women, in this ideological system, have so little soul.

The effect of the royal ideologizing on the workings of the factions was to make all but the most powerful people try to disguise their loyalties; this is one reason, though not the only one, why it is somewhat harder to recognize political allegiances in James's reign than in Elizabeth's. It is also important, as Peck stresses, not to see the factions as fixed, institutionalized parties nor even as unalterable groupings of particular people, but as probable alliances that would at times be dormant, then would coalesce again, somewhat revamped, at moments of crisis such as the death of Salisbury; as groupings of particular people, their ongoing existence was tenuous and depended on their leaders' negotiation of major shifts in the king's favoritism, as when Northampton, whose power had been based on alliance with Salisbury, managed after Salisbury's death to bring Somerset into alliance with him, although Overbury and the Pembrokeans had put Somerset in place. The practice of courtiers, writers, and other favor-seekers came to be scatter-shot flattering of high-ranking people of all persuasions. Jonson for one flattered everyone in graceful verse tributes, sometimes while lampooning the same people in his plays. Even the despised Cecily got a polite-sounding though ambivalent tip of his hat once she was dead (*Ungathered Verse* no. 9). His duplicity is portrayed as admirable in the figures of True-wit of *Epicoene* and Lovewit of *The Alchemist*; for example the former, having delivered a rabid misogynist tirade to the prospective husband Morose in an effort to prevent his marrying because True-wit thinks that such is the nephew and heir's wish, then instantaneously reverses himself upon learning that the nephew *does* want the uncle to marry (for a devious purpose); True-wit then claims that he has purposely tried to provoke the contrary reaction in the uncle and hasten the marriage, which indeed has luckily been the effect. But for all of such track-covering, if we look at the agendas and economic bases of the two most powerful factions that tended to reemerge at periods of transition or heightened tension, along with the writers' main social affiliations and sources of income, we can see where main loyalties fell.

Despite the king's effort to minimize faction, in practice through the first dozen years of his reign he showed greater favor to the group centering in the Howards: he felt obligated to them for what their relatives had suffered in the cause of his mother, the Catholic Mary Stuart[1] (see chapter 4), even though he himself was happy with the late Elizabethan combination of Calvinism and episcopacy, considering it to represent the true catholicity of the early church; and the Howards shared his desires for an end to wars of religion, a peace treaty with Spain (which they, not necessarily the king, wanted sealed by a Spanish marriage for Prince Henry), and greater civil toleration for English Catholics. Further, he quickly came to share their dislike of Parliament and the view that it should sit as little as possible, and that the crown should squeeze ever-larger revenues from its own holdings and perquisites.[2] The fact that no one of any party could restrain James's spending became a central issue of his reign. On that point our ideologeme throws a sidelight: since the king saw himself as divinely bountiful and self-reproducing in favored male subjects, he was unable to resist granting lofty sums and titles to men who pleased him (Peck "King" 36).

The leading men of the faction were Henry Howard, Earl of Northampton (a secret Catholic and brother of the Duke of Norfolk, who had died in Mary Stuart's cause), Norfolk's son Thomas Howard, Earl of Suffolk, later to be Lord Treasurer, along with his wife Katherine, also a major player in finance and politics, and their cousin the Armada hero of 1588 now in charge of the Navy, Charles Howard of Effingham, Earl of Nottingham (again, they should not be thought of as a lockstep group who always agreed with each other). They tended to be Catholics or Catholic sympathizers, allied with other landed families of pre-Tudor lineage, to whose members they often gave control of lucrative public offices, believing that such people could best manage these by holding an old-fashioned kind of loyalty from the clever merchants and financiers who kept things running. As to writers and intellectuals, their patronage went often to university men, neo-Latin writers, and especially experts on matters of lineage and heraldry like Sir Edmund Bolton, as well as to antiquarians like Sir Robert Cotton, the manuscript collector. The latter regularly wrote position papers for Northampton, emphasizing precedents drawn from pre-Tudor history (Peck *Northampton* 111–17).

James was drawn to antiquarianism because as a Stuart he needed someone to elaborate for him, out of conservative social materials, a substitute symbology for that of the Tudors. Northampton was a scholar himself and in the 1580s had cofounded the Society of Antiquarians. He was, and Suffolk later became by inherited position as his father had been, Chancellor of Cambridge University. Suffolk's main residence of Audley End near Cambridge was close enough to the royal hunting estate at Royston, where the king spent much of his time, for them to be in steady communication and for Cambridge students to come out and perform Latin plays, debates, and pageants. This milieu suggests the ambience of Howard ideological inclinations as contrasted with the city-centered, commercial and international orientation of the Pembrokeans. The Howards' academic base helped the homoerotic James at Royston to revel in a gratifying all-male sphere of sporting and sociosymbolic activity. I would hypothesize that an important writer who drew upon the energies of this royal ideological ambience and practice was Robert Burton, unmarried ascetic scholar, neo-Latin dramatist,[3] and writer of that vast and vigorous compendium of ancient and modern medical and psychoanalytic thinking, *The Anatomy of Melancholy* (even though Burton was at Oxford, not Cambridge—the other university did its best to please the king as well). It would be possible to trace Howardesque usages of the "self-imaging as rule" ideologeme, e.g., in academic drama and pageants. But since this faction was, as it settled in around James, obviously less permeable than the other to women's efforts to find an enunciatory niche for a public voice, that pursuit would take us away from women's writings.

By contrast, urban wits and literati of considerable doctrinal diversity found themselves drawn into the orbit of Pembroke/Sidney patronage (Jonson's entry into it coincided with his return to the Anglican church from twelve years of "popery"). This loosely Protestant faction opposing the Howards centered on William Herbert, Earl of Pembroke, and included in its upper ranks George Abbot, Archbishop of Canterbury; Henry, Earl of Southampton; Thomas Egerton, Lord Ellesmere (the Lord Chancellor); also by 1611 Sir Henry Neville, the parliamentarian and former ambassador to France; and Sir Ralph Winwood, another diplomat (Lee 242–45). While the Howards wanted a Spanish alliance, the Pembrokeans looked to France, where the former Huguenot Henri IV (to be assassinated in 1610) tolerated Protestants; they wanted continued clandestine support of the Dutch against Spain and certainly no Spanish marriage for Prince Henry. At home, while themselves also wary of Parliament for its growing puritan power, they wanted procedures of periodic negotiation between king and Parliament for subsidies to the royal treasury, and in 1610 they proposed to arrange this if he would give them authority.[4] (They planned to manage elections to get the right MPs seated, an activity the Howards also engaged in.)

When Jonson came to flatter the Pembrokes and Sidneys, he did so by describing them, whose grandfathers had been newcomers to wealth and titles, as if they were long-standing aristocracy. He appropriated an old ideological paradigm to a newly powerful class. In the famous ode to Robert Sidney's Penshurst, for example, he portrayed the estate as if it were an idyllic feudal demesne, surrounded by a loyal contented peasantry who would never wish its walls down, its lady Barbara Gammage a very Penelope of self-sufficient domestic competence (see Wayne for a related analysis). Robert Sidney's daughter Lady Wroth he celebrated as the reincarnation of a string of classical goddesses; and in dedicating *The Alchemist* to her in 1610, he extolled her extreme virtue, though without saying in what it consisted.[5]

While Secretary Salisbury lived, he stood in personal terms somewhat apart from the main factions (as his father Burghley had under Elizabeth), though in policy allied with the Howards; he appointed certain people answerable only to him and thus created a kind of third front of "Cecilians," though this would collapse when he died in 1612. Enforcing the king's views, he tilted the balance of power toward the Howards except on the point of greater civil toleration for Catholics: the notorious "Bye" plot of 1603 and gunpowder plot of 1607, failed Catholic coup attempts, had spoiled the chances for that. The king's following of lavishly patronized Scots, such as Lord James Hay (target of satire as Seralius in Wroth's *Urania* [Salzman ed. "References"]) made a kind of fourth faction, serving as it were to buffer the king's Scottish dialect and foreigner image against the English opprobrium of him on these points—they were politically unfocused but frequently denounced in Parliament for draining royal monies.

The Pembroke group were successors and many of them offspring of the militant internationalist Elizabethan Protestants and entrepreneurial investors earlier associated with the Earl of Leicester, then with Essex. Their hope for the future was in Prince Henry, who had indeed militant Protestant inclinations (see Strong); they, in alliance with the prince, are sometimes referred to as "the reversionary interest" (Prestwich 104). Their party was weaker than the Howards not only because the king inclined the other way but, among other reasons, because their leadership was scandal-ridden. (The Howards' turn for that would come later.) Southampton and Bedford, Lucy Harington Russell's husband, had been disgraced by their part in the Essex rebellion at the end of Elizabeth's reign (Essex himself had been executed); Sir Walter Raleigh remained in the Tower for some mysterious part he never confessed in the "Main" plot of the Brooke brothers[6] (oddly associated with the Catholic "Bye" plot), an attempt at temporary capture and coercion of the newly crowned King James; the greatest entrepreneur, Sir Francis Walsingham, had died a bankrupt; Pembroke himself, imprisoned in 1601 for getting a court lady, Mary Fitton, pregnant, was busy with his estates and eventually involved in an affair with his cousin Wroth—and then there was Lady Penelope Rich (Essex's sister and Sidney's "Stella," who as Essex stated at his trial had spurred him on to rebellion) and her years of open adultery with Charles Blount, Lord Mountjoy. In brief the party suffered from an image problem and a leadership vacuum. They could not carry much of the confidence and representation—as their Elizabethan predecessors had done—of London merchant interests, which now could find little political expression either at court or in the brief, frustrated Parliaments. The merchants had now mainly the financial brokers for the city of London, from which the crown borrowed heavily, as a means of influencing policy (cf. Bradbrook "Pageantry" 65).

To come back to the particular Pembrokean circle around the Countess of Bedford, some of them were or became Anglican clerics (the "sermoneers," in Jonson's term), notably John Donne and John Rudyard. There was also the latter's brother Sir Benjamin Rudyard, later appointed to a government post through Pembroke's influence (Prestwich 235). Of diplomats there was Sir Thomas Roe, later much praised for visiting the Great Moghul and India, inventing new procedures for diplomatic protocol in contacts with distant cultures, and setting the stage for the East India Company's success (Donne's biographer Bald [177] suggests that Thomas Roe was Mrs. Bulstrode's lover, and Strachan [12–14] fleshes out the theory). And there was Donne's friend the celebrated diplomat and committed Protestant Sir Henry Wotton, though he was often away, who as Savage well demonstrates almost certainly wrote the "News from abroad" in the *Wife* (cf. also Donne's verse epistle no. III to Wotton, "Here's no more newes, then vertue"). There was another traveling man, a merchant (one "W. S.") who wrote the "News from Sea," probably William Strachey, and another businessman John Coke (or Cook). And of course there was Sir Thomas Overbury, who would place Robert Carr at the pinnacle of power as James's first politically active favorite. (On Carr as depicted in Lady Falkland's *Edward II* see chapter 7, and on Ben Jonson's association with the group see chapter 5 on *Epicoene*.) They were, as we have seen, a London circle under the aegis of the Countess of Bedford, whose estate at Twickenham Donne portrays himself visiting, and presumably others of the circle did so as well. Cecily Bulstrode was buried at Twickenham in August 1609. We see the countess's high regard for her kinswoman Cecily in her elegy, to be discussed shortly.

In sum, the people of this following were generally connected with international trade and diplomacy and were internationally Protestant in outlook. Overbury used their Pembroke ties as he managed his longtime friend Carr's rise to favor with the king. His scheme was, when Cecil died (which foreboded by 1611), to persuade the king to appoint no replacement, but instead to act as his own chief executive, with Carr, by then Earl of Somerset, as his assistant to run the bureaucracy; since Somerset had very limited abilities, this would leave Overbury himself largely running things. (The scheme was to work perfectly except that once Somerset was in place, the Howards would capture him, partly through Suffolk's daughter Frances—perhaps Overbury made some deal with them.)[7]

The "News" circle should be seen, then, as allied with the Pembroke faction: Protestant but not puritan,[8] wanting to undermine the Howards' influence with the king, and seeing Parliament, with careful management, as the way to get a handle on his profligacy. Whether Queen Anne herself took part in the Bedford group's particular games and socializing we do not know. I have not seen any indication that she did; but they very much partook of her court's parlor-game habits and politically involved socializing. Donne was finding a new identity as a Protestant there, where the themes of witticizing were, as Jonson said in the Bulstrode epigram, "state, bawdry, and religion."

The Pembroke Faction and Amphilanthus

As Pembroke headed the faction just described, we may learn something further about it—from an inside angle, as it were—by reviewing scenes from Wroth's *Urania* that present a lively portrait of his character and habits in the persona of Amphilanthus; this review of a few of the vastly proliferated episodes of part 1 can also round out our picture of Mary Wroth's own emotional life, within the political scene of the early Jacobean years, and can offer a sense of what the *Urania* was like for Wroth's readers. Presumably some aspects of her (for a woman) highly unusual motivation for belletristic writing came from her closeness—emotional, physical, and political—to the head of the faction I have just been describing. She could speak from a position of political focus, if she could manage to devise an enunciative position gendered in such a way that she could think herself into it. In chapter 5 I argued that in *Love's Victory* she does so by making her authorial persona Sylvesta actorialize a male figure of Love as the dominant force of the mind, an actantial role generating the other characters' textualized love energies. But often in her lengthy *Urania* (which must have been written over several years), she was casting about for just such a position from which to speak. It seems that she was most successful when she exercised her dramatic abilities for scene-making and carefully polished dialogue between characters whose individual traits she was developing concretely through several or many episodes and whose real-life referents could be closely viewed from her political insider position. The point will be illustrated shortly, and it finds context in Weidemann's essay discussing the *Urania*'s "portrait of the female courtier as an actress" within a "vision of theatrical selfhood" (193).

Readers experienced in responding to the narrative and poetic registers required for enjoying Ariosto, the *Amadis de Gaul*, Sidney, or Spenser, with their modes of intermittent topical allusion and tapestry-like plot organization, will have to develop new reading strategies if they are to enjoy the *Urania*. Wroth apparently set out to write in the general mode of such works (see Quilligan "Wroth" on allusions to them); like them she weaves multiplex, thematically interlinked and prolific episodes around nodal points of highly colored symbolic-house episodes, such as the palace of Venus adventure depicted on her title page and occurring fairly early in Part I. But her impulse to allegorize and evaluate many shades of male-female relations in her own milieu and to idealize nothing but a constantly thwarted female will to "constancy" and psychic control in love relationships—these driving impulses of her writing push her romance, as it proceeds, outside the generic frame she began with. As Salzman notes, the *Urania* eventually (in the unpublished Part II, being edited by Roberts) works its way into something like a modern narrative of sentiment.

One comes to realize, as more and more of the romance's topicality comes clear in recent commentary (see especially Roberts), that Wroth was doing topical allegory in a way quite different from, say, Spenser's. While Spenser hints briefly, in a given episode, at particular people and events, then shifts into some other register of narrative so as to cover his tracks and partially defuse the reference, Wroth seems to treat her fictional people as steadily available, ongoing renditions of the actual persons who gave rise to them. Her storytelling runs along parallel to her life and its surrounding spheres, a kind of coded combination of reportage, gossip, and witty commentary, which must have been enjoyed episode by episode by its dedicatee the Countess of Montgomery and possibly other friends. Thus once Wroth was well along into her Part I, it would have begun to work as something similar to the continental *Merkur* publication of the same period, appearing a few times per year in Frankfurt and summing up recent news and gossip. The *Merkur* was read carefully by diplomats such as Henry Wotton and excerpted for letters home. Certainly the *Urania* had in its time a trenchant *roman à clef* effect of "traducing whom [the author] pleases," as one of her victims put it. Each year Wroth must have added a new batch of amusing depictions of developments around the court circles.

In feeling her way into this generic innovation, she seems in Part I not to have large-scale conceptual control of her vastly ballooning fiction. She had begun in a heroic romance genre only partially suitable to her motives, impulses, and sociolinguistic position as an aristocratic woman: impulses centering on the will to construe women characters exercising some measure of control over their own sexuality and marriages. And it would take some time to find the perspectival angle, in such a romance world, from which to exercise her best talents. The ladies in her fiction, like those in the life she knew, were frequently lost at sea, at a loss in their effort to imagine a society where they could find husbands and lovers to their liking, instead of being forced to live as pawns of male exchanges of wealth, trapped in marriages where often one's only options were emotionally deadening submission to an unsympathetic husband, or adultery, for which one would live under public opprobrium. The outlets for libidinal energy in effectuous political or professional activity were closed to most women. While a rare few like the builder Bess of Hardwick had found satisfaction in estate expansion and household management, and another few were successful courtiers like the Countess of Bedford, for most it was only in the

intensity of love affairs and/or in personal religious piety that they could look
for the registers of satisfaction that men could seek in several arenas. An attempted female voice, then, as generator and enunciator of romance or epic
romance—innately conservative genres because of their necessary relation to
some already functioning power apparatus—would probably be a voice at sea,
not able to exercise large-scale conceptual control over the many dimensions of
allegorical meaning simultaneously in motion in such a romance.

In the *Urania* there are, however, islands of sharply realized episodes that
I think modern readers can enjoy. These draw on Wroth's powers of rhetorically
sophisticated dialogue, sharpened in politically engaged courtly parlor games
such as were illustrated in chapter 5. Although in several episodes Wroth represents herself in various characters, such as Lisea, or Lindamira, daughter of
Bersindor (see Roberts ed. *Poems* and Brennan ed. "Introduction"), she portrays herself chiefly and recurrently as Pamphilia, the main heroine, whose voice
at times generates something close to a modern centered perspective—i.e., the
narrator's voice and Pamphilia's own can seem to speak from the same awareness. The Princess Pamphilia of Morea has been, by her childless uncle, designated heir to his kingdom—even though she has brothers who might have been
chosen—a patent allegory of her inheriting the writing ability of her famous
uncle Sir Philip Sidney.[9] The plot generated by this prospect and eventual occurrence—of her coming into her kingdom—supplies the central and self-ref-
erential strand in the romance's vast mix of narratives and presents at the level
of topical allegory just such a quest for a female writer's voice as we have been
studying in all the chapters here. The narrative issues of the quest are of traveling to her kingdom to take the throne and of gaining a suitable husband and
partner, these being the two entwined threads comprising that central plot
strand. At the center of the plot are the lover-pair of Pamphilia (combines
Pamela-Philoclea, the sister-heroines from Sidney's *Arcadia*, as well as suggesting the "all-loving" one) and her cousin Amphilanthus (the "lover of two")—
who are doubled by the mirroring lover-pair of her brother Parselius and Amphilanthus's sister Urania (the male party of which couple is also inconstant
like Amphilanthus). I suggest that Urania figures Susan Vere, Countess of
Montgomery, as dedicatee, title-supplier, and episodic chief audience of the
romance, just as "Urania" had figured the Countess of Pembroke in those roles
in Sidney's *New Arcadia*. Susan Vere was Pembroke's (Amphilanthus's) "sister"
through being married to his brother Philip.

If one could make an editorial selection—including material from the
manuscript Part II—of the primary episodes adumbrating the lives of these
four characters and their other siblings across two generations, a quite interesting family romance in a forward-looking seventeenth-century mode might
emerge, tracking loves and marriages through the cycles of interconnected individual lives. It would present an inversion of the *mis en abyme* techniques of

Renaissance male heroic romanciers, whereby refracted images of the writer himself are inserted into the borders of the fictional diegesis: Sidney as dying Phillisides, briefly singing his own song at the edge of his Arcadian lover-poets' circle, Spenser as a fragile Colin Clout piping on Mount Acidale, as if existing in only two dimensions of the fictional world, to be wiped out by a too-earthly gaze. In the *Urania* Wroth's image is instead, out of the psychic and sociosemiotic necessities I have been discussing, put not at the edge but at the dead center of her fiction, made the basis of an attempt to generate writerly energies of her own. Circling around the two interlocked central couples is a vast dance of royals, knights, and ladies from supposed regions of Greece, the Balkans, and northwards, crossing and recrossing each other's paths and recounting in-set tales that evaluate diverse male and female aristocratic behavior, under the guise of chivalric conventions of jousting, questing, flirting, and lovemaking.

Of all the knights, Amphilanthus (Pembroke), highly consistent in char-acter through many episodes, is at once the most gloriously lovable and the most fickle of the lot. At the end of *Urania* Book I, Pamphilia (Wroth) both takes the throne of her kingdom and learns at last that Amphilanthus privately reciprocates her love, though for the moment they do nothing about it: she is presenting herself and Pembroke as having been in love through several years but not physically involved.[10] This is the early period of her marriage and then time at court when, so she claims in her self-depiction in the Lindamira episode, the rumors about her were false. Later books will pursue the further trials of Wroth and Pembroke. But it is clear that Book I is presenting the view Wroth later wanted to promote of the years[11] leading up to her affair with Pembroke, thus overlapping with the time we have been studying in this and the previous chapter.[12] There are doubtless various refractions and measures of fiction and fantasy in the allusions to her social world; but the emergent lines in her portrait of Amphilanthus-Pembroke as a personality and political operative seem to catch him as he lived and breathed.

We first see Amphilanthus in an episode where, disguised in black, he res-cues from double rape (i.e., by two assailants) a lady who will become his first serious beloved, Antissia, Princess of Romania. She is later depicted as having close and recurrent contact with Pamphilia (the association continues into *Ura-nia* Part II), thus as someone Wroth was obliged to be with often in family associations—perhaps she stands for Pembroke's wife Mary Talbot, or one of his lady flames.[13] As Antissia after the rape attempt listens in renewed distress while the events are recounted to third parties, Amphilanthus notices her feel-ings and sympathizes with her, for his "heart was never but pitiful to fair ladies" (I. ii. Salzman ed. 48).[14] Few women, it seems, could resist Pembroke's com-bination of largesse of mind and purse, and warm, readily stirred sympathies. Some thirty pages later, when this courtship reappears, its blossoming is given the following nuanced account: as they journeyed, Antissia marked his loveliness, sweetness, bravery and strength. . . . This made her like, that made her love, and so she did (poor lady) to her lost liberty. He, the more he saw her respect to him, answered it with his to her. Kindness then betrayed them, she showing it, he (as a kind hearted prince to ladies) receiving it. By this time they were content to think they loved, and so to know those pains. He was not unexperienced, therefore soon saw remedy must be given, and cruelty he imagined it would be in him, who discerned he might by his art help her, if he refused that good to one so fair and so kindly loving. This made him in charity watch his opportunity, or at least not to lose any . . . (I. i. Salzman ed. 74–75)

His being "not unexperienced" in his loving "art" would refer to prior affairs (e.g., with Mary Fitton), but the import seems to be that this was the first involving strong emotional engagement for him. As the romance proceeds, it paints an ever-clearer picture of Pembroke as a man who had little will to resist any lady's blandishments, however intensely he might just have been involved with someone else. Even after having made a vividly portrayed love-hero's conventionally epic journey to an underworld of self-examination complete with articulate dwarves (I. i. Salzman ed. 161–68), where he meditated deeply on the nature of love and constancy and on his desire that Pamphilia (whom he now knows he loves) should reciprocate his feelings, he soon thereafter drifts into a casual flirtation with one Luceania, who seems to hint at Lucy Harington, Countess of Bedford.[15] If so, the episode portrays the countess making a move on Pembroke and him enjoying the flirtation. In the romance, at any rate, it comes to nothing more than his wearing her favor in a tourney, which Pamphilia just then arriving sees, and taxes him with unfaithfulness to Antissia:

> "Do you add to your inconstancy as fast as to your colours?"
> "None can be accused, dear lady," said he, "for their change, if it be but till they know the best, therefore little fault hath yet been in me. But now I know the best change shall no more know me."
> "Every change brings this thought," said she. (I. i. Salzman ed. 198)

How had he worked into this Luceania flirtation? By his usual habits of smooth talking, easy affection, and willingness to take political advantage of women's warm responses to him. Learning that a great lady was interested in knowing his name as he prepared for the tourney, "The prince was glad to hear this because he was now sure of acquaintance quickly there"; when her servant comes to ask his name, he gallantly replies "Can it be that any fair lady should so much honour me as to desire so worthless a thing as my name?" (194). Playing coy, he continues, "it is my ill fortune at this time that I am not able to satisfy her demand, although this grace shall ever make me her servant." Thereupon, "now finding judgement and brave courtship, she longs for his so-

ciety, and these accompanied with seeing his excellently sweet and ever conquering loveliness, did join as to the conquest of her" (194). Upon next meeting
him, she teasingly accuses him of being ashamed of his name, to which, always
the gallant, he replies, "Although, excellent lady, it may be my name is not so
fortunate as to have come to your ears with any renown, yet am I not ashamed
of it, a vow only having made me conceal it" (195). When she then insists, he
after all breaks his potent "vow" and declares himself Amphilanthus, King of
the Romans.

When she next openly reveals her love for him, the narrator says that Amphilanthus was "rather sorry than glad" to hear of it, "but considering grate-
fulness is required as a chief virtue in every worthy man, he courteously replied
that, till that time, fortune had never so honoured him as to bring him to the
height of so much happiness as to be graced with such an affection" (196), and
she, "who loved and desired, took the least word he spoke for a blessed consent." Wishing to learn "the manner of ending the enchantment" in a quest
he is just then pursuing (i.e., allegorically some political purpose), he continues
to act as if he is responding in kind to Luceania's affection: "He kindly entertained her favours and courteously requited them, and one day, the more to
express his respect to her, he took this course, which in his own mind was
plotted rather to get more freedom and to make proof of his valour": he and
his friend don new armor and, as mentioned, he wears the lady's favor into the
day's jousting. Thus Wroth gives us a vivid portrait of Pembroke in political
action with the help of his womanizing powers.

To what extent the failure of the Pembroke faction in the first Jacobean
decade to pursue their objectives effectively may be attributable to Pembroke's
personal qualities admits of no clear answer. But we can suppose that his habits
would have led many, both men and women courtiers, to be less inclined to
trust him as time went on. Not that they became any the less ready to praise
him, even to like him, and to accept the benefits of his money and influence,
when these could be had.

As for Wroth's presentation of herself, through Book I she shows Pamphilia
exercising every possible skill and effort to keep secret her troubling affection
for Amphilanthus, whom she considers committed—or ought to be committed—to Antissia. In two very sharply realized episodes at the Morean court,
where Antissia is living as Pamphilia's guest and companion, the Romanian
princess is shown becoming suspicious that something is up between Pamphilia
and Amphilanthus. She painfully confronts Pamphilia, who in the first of these
scenes resorts to a series of ingenious equivocations worthy of any Jesuit, while
in the second she humorously triumphs and gets off the hook when the spying
Antissia, thinking that Pamphilia is secretly meeting Amphilanthus in the
woods, finally must see that it is not he but Pamphilia's brother Rosindy
(Robert Sidney the Younger), who just then needs her sympathy and help to

mitigate their father's anger about his own secret marriage of an unapproved lady—in her real life correlate Dorothy Percy, daughter of the Earl of Northumberland.[16]

Let us conclude this view of the *Urania*'s presentation of Pembroke and Wroth with a look at the equivocation scene just mentioned, showing her victory at verbal sparring with her jealous chief rival for his affection in these years. Pamphilia, thinking herself alone in a wood, has just been lamenting her secret love in morose declarations and in a sonnet that she carves in a tree, when the eavesdropping Antissia confronts her with the accusation that she loves Amphilanthus. " 'Alas!' cried Pamphilia, 'can so base an humour as suspicion creep into so brave a heart as Antissia's . . . Truly I am sorry for it, and would advise you quickly to banish that devil from you' " (114). Not so easily stumped, Antissia replies, "I know it is the worst of monsters. Yet this is no answer to my question."

Pamphilia next tries another evasive tack, a counterquestion: "But I pray you Antissia, what do you see in me that I should love Amphilanthus more than respectively?" and continues, "Hath my speech at any time betrayed me? Hath my fashion given you cause to suspect it? Did I ever enviously like a lover seek to hinder your enjoying him? Did I unmannerly press into your companies?" (115). But again Antissia will not take a digression for an answer: "cried she, 'so great a wit and matchless a spirit would govern themselves better than to offend in such fond parts.' " She declares that since Pamphilia is "the best of our sex" and he the "rarest object," they must be drawn to each other, and again poses her accusation.

Pamphilia next employs the subjunctive mode in "if" clauses, along with a claim (most dubious, as by then we know) that Amphilanthus's love for Antissia is fixed beyond question.

> If all these things were true, and that I loved Amphilanthus, what then? Were it any more than my extremest torment, when I should see his affections otherwise placed? The impossibility of winning him from a worthy love, the unblessed destiny of my poor unblessed life, to fall into such a misery, the continual afflictions of burning love, the fire of just rage against my own eyes— these were all. . . . What need should they have to molest you, since so perfectly you are assured of his love as you need fear no occasion?

Antissia, breaking down with emotion and losing track of the grammatical level of the comments, replies that if Pamphilia loved Amphilanthus, she would lose all her content, merely for knowing herself to be up against such a matchless rival. With the next move Pamphilia has her persuaded, at least for the moment:

"Well then, be satisfied," said the sweet but sad Pamphilia, "my love to him proceeds from his never enough praised merits, but not for love otherwise than I have already expressed." Antissia was with this answer thoroughly satisfied, taking the princess in her arms, protesting her life too little to pay for requital for this royal freedom she had found in her. (116)

But what is it that Pamphilia has "already expressed"? Nothing but questions, subjunctives, conditionals, and hypotheses, so posed. Wroth, looking back and writing in her time of early widowhood and now certainly consummated love for Pembroke (Miller and Waller 5), is portraying herself as she and the other courtier ladies of the parlor games seem indeed to have been—piercingly sharp of wit and tongue and skilled at creating impressions to suit their purposes. In writing her *Urania*, she would have the world believe that she and "Amphilanthus" did not consummate their love until some time after her years at court, indeed after her husband Wroth's death. We have no way to confirm that view. We do know that one month before her husband's death early in 1614, she bore a son, James, whom Robert Wroth believed to be his (as the terms of his will show—Roberts *Poems* 23). The surviving references to her two later illegitimate children by Pembroke, one in a Robert Sidney letter of 1615,[17] would support the view that she did not have children by Pembroke until after her husband's death, whatever may have been their earlier relations.

If Wroth's portrait of Pembroke as Amphilanthus in the *Urania* is credited—and other evidence about him accords with it—we can hypothesize that his character was one more reason among others why the Pembroke faction could no longer, after the first Jacobean decade, hold together as a functioning political agency with a recognizable ideological agenda. As noted above (chapter 5, n. 7), Overbury, their shrewdest political operative, had been so thoroughly discredited that his former friends had no sympathy for him even in his imprisonment and gruesome murder. In sum, we have here another angle on the major shakeup of powers and deterioration of governmental functioning that occurred with the death of Robert Cecil, Earl of Salisbury. To pursue these developments further would take us beyond this chapter's scope; I have considered the first decade of the reign and some of the contexts of women as writers within that period.

Donne's "Death Be Not Proud" and
the Countess of Bedford's Elegy for Mrs. Bulstrode

When Cecily Bulstrode died in mid-1609 at age twenty-five, the socializing of the "News" circle, as they had known it, came to an end. As Donne said in concluding his "Elegie on Mris. Boulstred," after noting that "immoderate grief" would be sinful, "Some teares, that knot of friends, her death must cost, / Because the chaine is broke, though no linke lost" (Shawcross ed. 254). If even the rancorous Jonson could offer a salute (*Ungathered Verse* no. 9), a number of her friends did more sincere poetic tributes, including this one by Donne (along with a second elegy he later wrote) and another by her patroness the Countess of Bedford. Donne spends the first half of his elegy in fanciful meditations on Death as the great feeder devouring all of life, even in the ocean, "Where harmelesse fish monastique silence keepe"; he ends that section with an assertion that Mrs. Bulstrode is among God's elect, imaged in macabre fashion from the realm of falconry as the few chosen from the leavings of ravaging Death, a trained bird that always brings its prey for the master's selection (read Election).

> . . . though thou beest, O mighty bird of prey,
>   So much reclaim'd by God that thou must lay
> All that thou kill'st at his feet, yet doth hee
>   Reserve but few, and leaves the most to thee.
> And of those few, now thou hast overthrowne
>   One whom thy blow makes, not ours, nor thine own [i.e. God's].

It seems that in Bulstrode's last months or weeks she turned to cleric friends for prayer and spiritual advising and must have died in a way moving to the bystanders: whatever exactly her "last Act" was—perhaps words of encouragement to her friends—the countess praises it as follows:

> Blinde were those eyes, saw not how bright did shine
> Through fleshes misty vaile the beames divine.
> Deaf were the eares, not charm'd with that sweet sound
> Which did i'th spirit-instructed voice abound.
> Of flint the conscience, did not yeeld and melt,
> At what in her last Act it saw, heard, felt.
>
> (Lewalski "Bedford" 76)

The elegy ends by urging her friends not to weep any longer, rather to

> Calme the rough seas, by which she sayles to rest,
> From sorrowes here, to a kingdome ever blest;
> And teach this hymne of her with joy, and sing,
> *The grave no conquest gets, Death hath no sting.*

While this last segment of the elegy is addressed to "that knot of friends," as Donne's elegy calls her circle, the greater part (about four-fifths) is addressed to Death, taking the form of a reply to Donne's holy sonnet number 10, "Death be not proud." When we look at the opening lines of his elegy ("Death I recant, and say, unsaid by mee / What ere hath slip'd, that might diminish thee"), it appears that he and the countess must have had the idea of writing their two elegies as responses to that earlier sonnet, and both with an opening section addressing death. This sounds, fittingly, like a game Cecily herself might have devised, a round of "Let's rebut the same poem in the same format." The countess begins

> Death be not proud, thy hand gave not this blow,
> Sinne was her captive, whence thy power doth flow;
> The executioner of wrath thou art,
> But to destroy the just is not thy part.
> Thy comming, terrour, anguish, griefe denounce;
> Her happy state, courage, ease, joy pronounce.
> From out the Christall palace of her breast,
> The clearer soule was call'd to endlesse rest.

And she ends this section by telling Death not to gloat over the survivors' sorrow:

> Glory not thou thy selfe in these hot teares
> Which our face, not for hers, but our harme weares,
> The mourning livery given by Grace, not thee,
> Which wils our soules in these streams washt should be.

Lewalski sees here an oblique reference to "the scandals about Bulstrode" ("Bedford" 75), from which presumably any sins that had been on her conscience would have been washed away by her own tears and those of her grieving friends, in a state of grace.

Donne in his elegy attempts a more overt recouping of Cecily's reputation, through the rhetorical strategy of insulting Death by claiming that he has made a mistake to take her so young, that her "beauty and wit, apt to doe harme" would have supplied many occasions, sometimes through no fault of hers, for people to fall to sin and thus death.

> Thou should'st have stay'd, and taken better hold,
>   Shortly ambitious; covetous, when old,
> She might have prov'd: . . .
>   Abundant virtue [might] have bred a proud delight.
> Had she perever'd just, there would have bin
>   Some that would sinne, mis-thinking she did sinne.
> Such as would call her friendship, love, and faine
>   To sociablenesse, a name profane,
> Or sinne, by tempting, or, not daring that,
>   By wishing, though they never told her what.
>
> (Shawcross ed. 254., ll. 54–66)

Donne is implying that this is what actually happened and caused the rumors about her. The countess's more oblique handling and affectionate general washing away of Cecily's sins, whatever they might have been, seems the more tactful and sensible way of treating the issue. Her poem movingly expresses affection for her kinswoman and companion, through smoothly flowing lines that show a practiced hand at versifying and a rhetorically sophisticated sense of address, to Death and then to the grieving circle of friends.

The "First Anniversary" and the Ideologeme

So far as we know, neither Donne, Jonson, nor the Countess of Bedford made any poetry about Mrs. Bulstrode's death that would win great fame, however strong their feelings might have been. Since this is the only known surviving poem by the countess (Donne mentions others), we cannot tell how representative it is of her verse. Of course the absence of ear- and mind-catching poetic merit does not call for explanation; rather its presence might. I hypothesize with Kristeva that those productions which prove especially rich for rereading, appealing to diverse readers, and generative of ongoing interpretive traditions must have been, in their original writing, energized by the writer's tapping into the patterns of some functioning unit of libidinally energized ideological meaning, whether an ideologeme as here identified or some other kind of unit or "desiring machine" not yet recognized.

I want next to explore how one of Donne's most famous works, written within two years after Jonson's *Epicoene* and the death of Cecily Bulstrode, makes one kind of revisionist or dialectical response to the ideologeme identified earlier. Donne himself was puzzled about why he proved able in 1611 to write one of his best poems in honor of a fifteen-year-old girl who had little personal importance for him: "The First Anniversarie. An Anatomy of the World." His poems to the Countess of Bedford, who was important to him as a friend and sounding board as well as for her influence and financial backing, turned out to be lesser efforts—competent and in many ways interesting, but not with the fire of "inspiration" in them. Hoping to justify himself, he began a verse letter to the countess on why he had written so honorifically of another woman, but could find no way to finish it ("To the Countesse of Bedford. Begun in France" Shawcross ed. 239). Jonson called the "First Anniversary" blasphemous and said it would have amounted to something if it had celebrated not Elizabeth Drury but the Virgin Mary—never mind the Countess of Bedford (*Conversations* 32-5).

Donne's intensely hyperbolical idealization of young Elizabeth was of course not meant to be taken as devotion to her particular image; rather her death had provided, as his subtitle says, an "occasion" for him to lament "the decay of this whole World" by contrast with a human figure of idealized virtue.

To mention a few of the instances of "decay" that were on his mind, the un-intelligent and insatiate Somerset now had the king entirely enthralled; Salis-bury's and the "undertakers' " "Great Contract," the only serious plan on the scene for a cooperation of king and Parliament that would fund and control the profligate royal spending, had failed; the upper ranks of the party Donne supported were scandal-ridden and ineffectual; some of the Scots at court (e.g., Lord James Hay), generally allies of the Howards, were displaying hitherto unimagined extravagance; Henri IV lay dead and the intolerant Catholic Guises now ruled France; and Donne himself had still found no livelihood (some of these points are allegorized in Lady Wroth's *Urania*—see Brennan *Victory* In-troduction). Furthermore, the seeming decay in James's realm and in its inter-national context paralleled another level of decay in the larger mind of Europe, as it mused on the collapse of its ancient geocentric cosmography: not only could the earth no longer be seen as center of the universe, but the orbits of heavenly bodies were being shown to have no necessary symmetry and whole stars to appear and disappear; the sense of a divinely mathematical and perma-nent universe was collapsing right along with the confidence in the divine right-ness of kings, and for Donne personally, right along with the Protestant career-ist self-concept he had struggled to build. He had tried for nearly a decade for a civil post at court, hoping to support his burgeoning family and to remain a private religious seeker—a former Catholic still not entirely sure of his bear-ings, but happy to pursue his interests and write poetry. He had failed. Political as well as personal and cosmic decay become explicit themes in the poem's con-clusion, where the lamenting voice expresses the feeble hopes that surely

> . . . some Princes have some temperance;
> Some Counsaylors some purpose to advance
> The common profite; and some people have
> Some stay, no more then Kings should give, to crave;
> Some women have some taciturnity;
> Some Nunneries, some graines of chastity.

Much of the reference here has been explained, and it would not serve my purposes to review the many studies of how Donne combines the personal, the political, and the metaphysical in these (for him) more than usually sonorous lamentings;[18] somehow he manages to load them all onto the figure of a young girl whose wealthy father, Sir Robert Drury, has come to the poet's rescue at this financially desperate moment.

I am interested in that "somehow"—how could he load so much onto the frail dead shoulders of Elizabeth Drury? And how could he in this highly mi-sogynist era—when as Donne here explicitly says, the virtues still ostensibly expected of a woman were "taciturnity" and "chastity"—how could he make so much of a woman, barely even a woman, fifteen years old? What follows will not be a full-fledged interpretive reading of "The First Anniversary" (though obviously it includes elements of interpretation) but an effort to indicate something: the particular ideologeme or sociolinguistic "desiring machine" of male self-image propagation as government, both at work and being resisted, even combated, in the writing process of the poem, through which resistance Donne flushes it out to the textual surface.

A possible suggestion is that his dealings with witty, intelligent women of strong religious sensibility, such as the Countess of Bedford and others in the "News" circle, had enabled him to imagine a poetic construct of ideal virtue embodied in a woman. At least, through these friendships he had become able to think of his own soul as something not just automatically in force but to be claimed—claimed through honoring the worthiness of other people one is privileged to know, even possibly including women who are not one's lovers. And if his women friends all had flaws, still he could conceive the thought of one who had none—or none beyond original sin itself—in the person of his patron's much-loved girl, spared by early death from any wifely wiles or Evish deeds (the "stayne of *Eue*" had remained "out of her thoughts"—ll. 180–81). Jonson's evocation of the Blessed Virgin is apropos: Donne concedes his subject to share the guilt of original sin but otherwise holds her sin-free—she is then, in the poem's early passages, like the Blessed Virgin without the Immaculate Conception, a sort of Protestant stand-in.

> When that rich soule which to her Heaven is gone,
> Whom all do celebrate, who know they'have one,
> (For who is sure he hath a soule, unlesse
> It see, and Judge, and follow worthinesse,
> And by Deedes praise it? He who doth not this,
> May lodge an In-mate soule, but tis not his)
> When that Queene ended here her progresse time, . . .
> This world, in that great earth-quake languished.
>
> (Shawcross ed. "First Anniversarie," 1–11)

As to how Donne could think such a poem, perhaps the answer does at least begin with the ladies we have been studying, "most hermaphroditical," as Jonson declared them to be. Certainly their vein of "newsy" aphorism shows its imprint in many of the poem's moralizings, such as that just cited on the soul's authentication, or others that could have turned up in some round of "News" or "Edicts": "The worlds proportion disfigur'd is, / That those two legges whereon it doth relie, / Reward and punishment are bent awrie" (ll. 302–304), or "For good, and well, must in our actions meete: / Wicked is not much worse than indiscreet" (ll. 337–39). There is even, perhaps surprisingly, one that sounds as if from a "News" round of "the men" against "the women": "One woman at one blow, then kill'd us all, / And singly, one by one, they kill us now" (ll. 106–107).

The fact is, before reading long we have to cancel out the idea that Elizabeth Drury as here lauded is female. She began female enough—in the poem-opening young "queen" passage cited above; but then, Donne's lamentor claims that the "world"—this all-that-matters-of-reality, which he rolls up into one ball and all at once laments—this world has now, without her, lost the power of speech and forgotten its own name; he likens that world to an unbaptized child, with Elizabeth Drury as its planned godfather. The point of her maleness, or at least nonfemaleness, will become more explicit later, but here it is introduced in the figure of a prince, a term with an acceptable usage in reference to female monarchs (e.g., to Queen Elizabeth):

> For as a child kept from the Font, untill
> A Prince, expected long, come to fulfill
> The Ceremonies, thou [World] unnam'd hadst laid,
> Had not her comming, thee her Palace made:
> Her name defin'd thee, gave thee forme and frame,
> And thou forgetst to celebrate thy name.
> Some moneths she hath beene dead . . .
>   long shee 'ath beene away, long, long, yet none
> Offers to tell us who it is that's gone.
>
> (ll. 33–43)

Who indeed, we wonder by this point in the poem, rather as the disciples asked after the storm, "Who is this, that the winds and waves obey him?"

Though "the world," a body, is dead because Elizabeth its godfather-soul is gone, we next hear that the poet will nevertheless dissect or "anatomize" something that remains of it, for

> there's a kind of world remaining still,
> Though shee which did inanimate and fill
> The world, be gone, yet in this last long night,
> Her Ghost doth walke; that is, a glimmering light,
> A faint weake love of vertue and of good
> Reflects from her, on them which understood
> Her worth; And though she have shut in all day,
> The twi-light of her memory doth stay;
> Which from the carcasse of the old world, free,
> Creates a new world; and new creatures be
> Produc'd: The matter and the stuffe of this,
> Her vertue, and the forme our practice is.
>
> (ll. 67–78)

Donne has now obliterated the real world, traced in his painful memories of events, and substituted for it a reconstituted one, generated on the paradigm of the ideologeme we have been discussing: the ideal male person, seen as a light, has "elemented" some new creatures who reproduce "her" virtue—dimly, since hers in itself was, after her departure to heaven, but a ghostly glimmering light. Now the elegiac lamentor can begin "anatomizing," instructing the reconstituted world about its own parts and frailty.

Analysts of the poem have long agreed that with line 90 its introductory framing segment ends, and the lamentor voice takes up his grievings on a new level, as it were, inside the frame just created. What a surprise, if we thought this was a poem idealizing a woman, when now we launch into stock misogynist diatribe, ending in the aphorism already noted.

> How witty's ruine? how importunate
> Upon mankinde? It labour'd to frustrate
> Even Gods purpose; and made woman, sent
> For mans reliefe, cause of his languishment.
> They were to good ends, and they are so still,
> But accessory, and principall in ill.
> For that first mariage was our funerall:
> One woman at one blow, then kill'd us all,
> And singly, one by one, they kill us now.
>
>   (ll. 98–108)

Where did this male "we-us" voice suddenly come from, declaiming against the "they-them" of womankind, not even omitting the point that each coitus with a woman shortens "our" life? He next laments the shrinkage of "man" since the golden age, who used to "strive" with the sun for glory and longevity, but now "We're scarse our Fathers shadowes cast at noone" (144). Again we note the image linking Donne's poem to the king's ideologeme through an emblematic formulation of it: by men's forefathers' standing to the light of the sun-father God, "man" should now be existing as a divine image-shape cast by that sunlight, having fallen upon the proper pattern of an earlier Father—but "man" is failing to do so. Where are women in this elaborated metaphoric scene? Where is Elizabeth Drury? It is as if woman, having committed the first sin, is now no longer at all present in the picture being painted inside the Elizabeth Drury frame-fiction—as if woman is not human in the sense in which the poem is interested. She cannot be a speaker of value-laden meanings who can resurrect the meaning-dead world that the lamentor is grieving for.

Suddenly remembering Elizabeth Drury again, he now declares that her soul is not female at all—only her dead body was.

> She in whom vertue was so much refin'd,
> That for Allay unto so pure a minde

Shee tooke the weaker Sex, she that could drive
The poysonous tincture, and the stayne of *Eue*,
Out of her thoughts, and deeds; and purifie
All, by a true religious Alchimy;
Shee, shee is dead; shee's dead; when thou knowest this,
Thou knowest how poore a trifling thing man is.
And learn'st thus much by our Anatomee,
The heart being perish'd, no part can be free.

(177–86)

So the soul of Elizabeth Drury is not female but "pure"; that spirit only took on femaleness as a precious metal takes in a base one, to be mingled with it in an alloy of necessary toughness, that can survive amidst the corruptive powers of this fallen world. Femaleness at best, then, can be useful, though base. (Unless the influence of Eve is rejected, it will be "poysonous.") With this identification of the soul of his titular "lady" as masculine or (what here functions as the same thing) ungendered, the lamentor has discovered the potent lyric refrain pattern that will recur four more times (roughly every 60–80 lines) through the rest of the poem, stitching together its vastly encompassing and prophetic lamentations:

She, she is dead, she's dead; when thou knowest this,
Thou knowest how. . . . . a . . . . is.
And learnst thus much by our anatomy,
That. . . . . y.

Donne further defines the ungendered nature of her soul with the same image Jonson had used of good women's souls in the *Masque of Beauty*. Drury is the "measure of all Symmetree," and if Anaxagoras had seen her,

. . . who thought soules made
Of Harmony, he would at next have said
That Harmony was shee, and thence infer,
That soules were but Resultances from her,
And did from her into our bodies go,
As to our eyes, the formes from objects flow

(ll. 310–16)

In parsing out this concept of the ungendered soul of Elizabeth Drury as a pattern that all the world is failing to follow, the four last segments of the poem will treat, respectively, the corruption of the sublunary world; that of the supralunary world, namely the solar system and stars; that of human knowledge and sense perception; and that of earthly life, even in its reproductive processes. For example, the following, starting with another bit that could serve as a "News" invention, epitomizes that fourth segment.

Tis now but wicked vanity to thinke,
To color vitious deeds with good pretence,
Or with bought colors to illude mens sense.
Nor in ought more this worlds decay appeares
Then that her [Drury's] influence the heav'n forbeares,
Or that the Elements doe not feele this,
The father, or the mother barren is.
The clouds conceive not raine, or doe not powre
In the due birth-time, downe the balmy showre.
Th'Ayre doth not motherly sit on the earth,
To hatch her seasons, and give all things birth.
What Artist now dares boast that he can bring
Heaven hither, or constellate any thing . . .
For heaven gives little, and the earth takes lesse"

(ll. 375–97).

With the ungendering or masculinizing of Elizabeth Drury, brought to clear expression in the lines about her pure mind before it took on the weaker sex (a kind of down-scale step parallel to God's taking on of human flesh), I submit that Donne was able to line his poem up within the force field of the ideologeme he needed both to work with and to challenge. For each of the poem's succeeding segments climaxes in a celebration of him/her as a pattern giver or image giver of some sort, to whom the decadent beings of this corrupted world must look for modeling, or for being stamped with an image. She is a magnet drawing ships back into their proper courses (ll. 221–26), a "first originall / Of all faire copies" (227–28), an *ur*-perfume that has given the spice islands all their sweet odors, and the pattern stamped on "single money, coyn'd from her" (234). Further, she is "measure of all Symmetree, / by whose lines proportion should bee / Examined" (308–309), and the "type" from whom the ideal proportionality of Noah's ark was imitated, eliminating discord among the animals (as it would do among humans, if only followed); further, from her colors of "white, and redde, and blue" and "verdure," the "liveliest stones" have taken their color (361–69). In sum, Drury is

She from whose influence all Impressions came,
But, by Receivers impotencies, lame
Who, though she could not transubstantiate
All states to gold, yet guilded every state. (ll. 414–17)

It is this last passage—on her gilding of the state or body politic to supply it with some small hope that the better people and policies will prevail—that brings us to the passage cited above about the existence of "some" good uncorrupted counselors and "some" taciturn and chaste women, who serve as a sign of hope in so dark a world.

In sum, Donne has taken up ground for his poetic voice here within the ideologeme of male self-image propagation, to produce an inversion of its usual metasyntactic pattern in Pembrokean usage: using an S_1 term of propagating selfhood that at first seemed nonfunctional because female, then through his prefatory segment redefining that self as male, he set up the possibility of a semio-narrative motion in the following pattern, whereby the S_2 term (the world) tracks from the passage where Drury's masculine "Ghost" or soul (actorializing the S_1) is said to create in its own image a new world of possible goodness, down to the end of the poem.

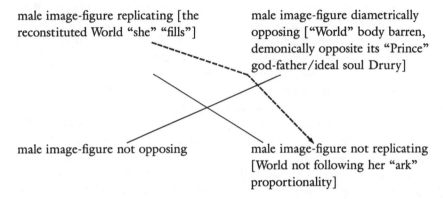

male image-figure replicating [the reconstituted World "she" "fills"]

male image-figure diametrically opposing ["World" body barren, demonically opposite its "Prince" god-father/ideal soul Drury]

male image-figure not opposing

male image-figure not replicating [World not following her "ark" proportionality]

In terms of the poem's base narrative program, this is a motion of loss rather than gain, of the S_2's failing to convey (i.e. keeping) governance of its cumulative valorized instances, here namely of that "World's" creatures, i.e., in the formula's terms of chapter 5, the "Object" invested with "v" (value) remains conjoined to S_2: "The art is lost, and correspondence too." Donne then appropriately ends the poem with an image of himself as lamenting prophetic singer: he has been chanting a Jeremiad of the party he identified with, the Pembrokeans, and by extension of the whole realm and Europe at large.

> But as in cutting up a man that's dead,
> The body will not last out to have read
> On every part, . . .
>   the worlds carcasse would not last, if I
> Were punctuall in this Anatomy.
> Nor smels it well to hearers, if one tell
> Them their disease, who faine would think they're well.
>
>   (ll. 439–43)

He likens himself to Moses, who delivered a hard message to God's people in the form of a

> song, because hee knew they would let fall
> The Law, the Prophets, and the History,
> But keepe the song still in their memory.

> Such an opinion (in due measure) made
> Me this great Office boldly to invade.

In modern criticism Donne has not been much remembered for exercising the office of a prophet, declaiming a moral word on the political scene. But I believe he did so here. Since he left the identity of his "diseased hearers" unspecified, not even alluded to in hints, his prophetic declamation presumably went unheard in many quarters. King James's opinion of him as ripe for the pulpit moulted no feather. But with the Countess of Bedford his standing fell—he had thought she meant to pay off his debts when he entered the church, as he now finally saw himself constrained to do; but for some reason she did not (cf. Donne's Letters). He was leaving behind his court life among the Pembrokeans with a grandly lugubrious denunciation of it all and entering a new alliance with Somerset and the king that would eventually bring him, as preacher at Whitehall, into a compromised position concerning the Overbury-Howard affair.[19] But that would be too long a story to take up here.

Why was it necessary for Donne to adopt this roundabout approach to his Jeremiad, namely of starting with a female figure and then ungendering her, rather than taking a male figure to start with? Perhaps something of a Catholic sensibility was still at work in his idealizing imagination, and he wanted a gentle, pure, sorrowing figure, grieving over the ruined world to be painted out as failing to reflect that idealized image—indeed the Blessed Virgin. But why could he not, as Milton later did, take Christ as such a presiding image? Or could he not have used someone's promising, youthfully dead son, instead of Elizabeth Drury? Jonson, for example, for his part in the grand entrance festivities for King James in 1604, had had no trouble—against all the long tradition of London as a lady in civic pageantry—making the City a male Genius instead, suitable to image the qualities of its new monarch (Bradbrook "Politics" 64). But I suspect that Donne needed a female figure not only because of past Marian (or even Petrarchan) habits of the idealizing male mind, but because he was, as it were, ironizing the very ideologeme he had to use, and thus needed a starting point from outside its terms. The idea of innocent femaleness—in the terms of King James's ideologeme an oxymoron—provided him with that starting point, which then had to be regendered within the initial intellectual action (i.e., the first "instrumental narrative program") of the poem. At this low point of Donne's personal and career life, "The First Anniversary" not only acts out a denunciation of all parties on the courtly scene, especially the one with which Donne had engaged himself, but it also offers a dark commentary on the view of women that Donne brought away from his time in the woman-dominated courtly circle of the Countess of Bedford.

7

Popery and Politics

Lady Falkland's Return to Writing

IN STUDYING THE milieu of Elizabeth Tanfield Cary, Lady Falkland, as an instance of intraconsensual conflict, I propose, as noted in chapter 2, that something of the same process of moving from consensus to conflict among the group surrounding Edward Dering and the "admonishers" of Parliament in the late 1560s and 1570s can be seen in the associates of Richard Neile, Bishop of Durham, among whom William Chillingworth was prominent in the early 1620s (see Trevor-Roper). Chillingworth had come into his own as an Anglican controversialist among these Arminian-inclined gentry and clerics socializing at Durham House, who included William Laud, Augustine Lindsell, Francis Burgoyne, Matthew Wren, and John Cosen, later himself Bishop of Durham. There Roman Catholics going to mass at the French ambassador's chapel crossed paths, from both the river and street sides, with Anglicans who considered themselves to be the true, doctrinal "catholics": faithful to the nature of the church as it had been in the time of St. Augustine but unable to submit to the corrupt rule of the Bishop of Rome. Their partial consensus with Roman Catholics was based on an idea earlier in James's reign, pursued by Hugo Grotius and based on James's own wish to be the internationalist leader to heal the breach of Christendom, that the English church would strike some agreement with Rome to be regarded as cocommunicating, as the Greek Orthodox church had done. Among the Durham House circle was Lady Falkland, who had long been attracted to Rome but had been persuaded that Anglicans were the truer catholics. Sometimes people would go over indeed to the Roman Catholic side, as Lady Falkland did in 1626. In Jürgen Habermas's terms (117, 209),[1] she shifted from consensual communicative action within the Arminian group to strategic action against her former fellow travelers, in what she considered the correct continuation of their cause, after the Arminian consensus collapsed when Neile and Laud joined forces with the Duke of Buckingham to become an anti-Romanist court faction.

As was studied in a little more detail in chapter 2, such situations sometimes supplied women with a new paratextual motive and chance to write, through certain processes of group dynamics. In other words, Habermas proposes that

Tudor and Stuart Women Writers

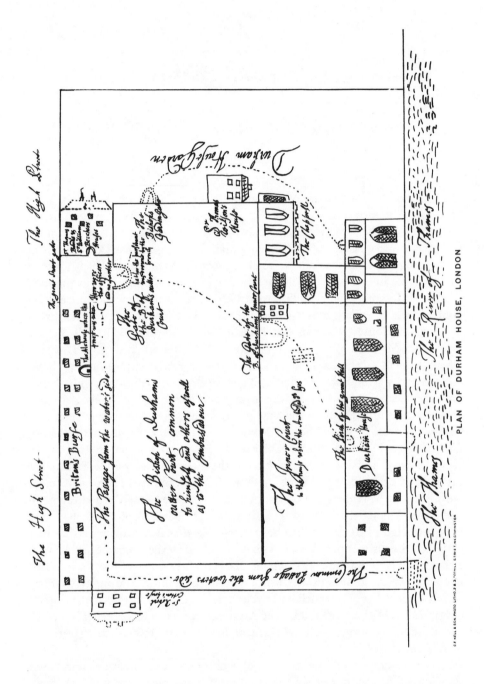

PLAN OF DURHAM HOUSE, LONDON

when consensual discourse, within a "we/you-and-I" identity and mode of address, has continued for a time, enabling some conflicts to be resolved, a point may come when consensus starts to break down. Then opposing subgroups move into what he calls "discourse" (proper), that is, oppositional but cooperative argumentation attempting to reach some new, mutually acceptable base definitions from which to rebuild consensus (3–4, 209). A flurry of back-and-forth argumentative documents (publicized or circulated) typically signals this stage of things—as with the debate between King James and the Cardinal du Perron, out of which came the Perron treatise Lady Falkland would soon translate. If such efforts fail to achieve consensus, the "we" identity eventually collapses, some of the people one formerly identified with become a "they"—the opponents—and the former group members, if able to do so, turn to confrontational strategic action against each other.

In the latter stretches of the time when that sequence is occurring, I suggest, a sense of urgency allows fissures to open in which the previously unnoted "system of domination" (Habermas xv) operative within the group becomes newly visible; at such a time, previously dominated or marginalized people within the group may find a new way to think of themselves vis-à-vis the group and thereby a new way to speak and write through contributing marginally to efforts in progress. And having found such a paratextual voice (i.e., in translations, prefaces, dedications, etc.), they may move on to saying more. This I think was the pathway Lady Falkland eventually found for returning to writing for publication after she had excluded herself from it for fourteen years, since the recall of her youthful play *Mariam Queen of Jewry*, published in 1613 (*Life* 9).

In 1621 King James's favorite, Buckingham, thought about converting to Catholicism, and soon Chillingworth himself actually did it. He went to France and began studies for the priesthood but eventually became disappointed and returned to England, ostensibly still a Roman Catholic, where he underwent a gradual return to Anglicanism, wavering back and forth most amazingly. That is, he still considered himself the great *convertisseur*, called and competent to persuade everyone to believe as he did; only he could not decide what he wanted to believe. Staying with Lady Falkland as a supposed Catholic helping to convert her daughters, he was behind her back persuading them to remain Anglicans. His actions illustrate the kind of volatile and overcharged religio-political situation of the 1620s, in which after Lady Falkland converted, the highest ranking people pleaded with and harangued her to return to Anglicanism— they knew that the mighty Buckingham's sister, Susan Feilding, Countess of Denbigh, had had a private friendship pact with Lady Falkland to convert also when the latter did. The countess refrained, or was pressured out of the idea, and even tried to prevent her friend from taking the leap; but the danger was felt to be intense. Lady Falkland's conversion of late 1626 gave her the chance once more to become a writer of public and semipublic texts.

"By Publike Language Grac't":[2] The Young Wife's Twin Plays

Before continuing with consideration of the mid-1620s and Lady Falkland's reentry into writing, let us briefly look back for contrast to her earlier years as a young wife, avid theater-goer, and reader of histories (*Life* 9) and to the pair of plays she then wrote. One of them—*Mariam Queen of Jewry*—was published in 1613 with a prefatory sonnet dedicating it to her close friend and sister-in-law Elizabeth Bland Cary (wife of Henry's brother Philip), imaged as the chaste Diana, while her "brother" Phoebus, the world-traveling sun (i.e., her brother-in-law, Cary's own husband, Sir Henry, away in continental wars the first three years of their marriage, 1602–1605), is there said to be the dedicatee of a twin play to this one, set in Sicily. Thus the twin deities of moon/chastity and sun/poetry are celebrated as images of the inspiring friend Elizabeth Bland Cary and her "brother," the idealized husband not yet known, Henry. During the years Elizabeth Tanfield Cary and her new same-name sister-in-law lived with their mother-in-law, Lady Katherine Cary, they seemingly enjoyed together the reading and theater-going that we recognize behind *Mariam*; and the presentation of Cary's two plays as twinned productions offers some suggestion of what the now lost Sicilian play may have treated, as we can consider shortly.

I will not here propose another extensive interpretation of *Mariam*; quite a few have appeared in recent years, and Barbara Lewalski usefully sums them up, adding one of her own (*Writing* 190–201). My reading sees Mariam less as a feminist heroine than as a kind of foil to Cary's own highly idealistic self-image as a widely read, self-possessed yet enormously dutiful young wife, who assumes that she will get intellectual respect from her new husband and will in turn pay him absolute wifely loyalty and duty. That is, Mariam fails where the youthful Cary herself plans to succeed, not expecting to have to face any such morale-breaking horrors as does the fictional heroine—little did she know what hardships her marriage would bring. I suggest that the Sicilian play was a kind of correlate exemplary tale for her husband, against tyranny, just as *Mariam* was the exemplary tale for herself and her sister-in-law, against inadequate dutifulness in wives. For while portraying Mariam's dilemma sympathetically, the play ultimately celebrates an ideal of submissive wifeliness whereby the queen, though innocent of the alleged adultery for which her husband kills her, is yet censured for not having cheerfully welcomed him home, even though he had murdered her father and brother![3] On this point of censure Cary is very directly following her source, Thomas Lodge's translation of Josephus's *Antiquities of the Jews* (Dunstan ed. xiv). She did indeed portray the tyrannically misused Mariam sympathetically, depicting her dilemma and feelings from the wife's viewpoint; and act 5 is indeed devoted to Herod's fury of remorse and grief when he has to confess that he has falsely accused and killed his chaste wife.

But these emphases mainly go to show that husbands must refrain from tyrannical cruelty, so that wives will be able to live in proper dutiful submissiveness. Mariam's soliloquy about herself and the chorus's succeeding reiteration of its point are clear, as a framing endorsement of traditional wifely humility:

[Mariam] Had I but with humilitie bene grac'te,
As well as faire I might haue prou'd me wise:
But I did thinke because I knew me chaste,
One vertue for a woman, might suffice.
That mind for glory of our sexe might stand,
Wherein humilitie and chastitie
Doth march with equall paces hand in hand . . .

(IV.viii., ls. 1833–40)

Likewise, the chorus says in conclusion to its ode on forgiveness, of which the opening stanzas are often cited:

Had *Mariam* scorn'd to leaue a due [of revenge] vnpaid,
Shee would to *Herod* then haue paid her loue:
And not haue bene by sullen passion swaide[.]
To fixe her thoughts all iniurie aboue
    Is vertuous pride. Had *Mariam* thus bene prou'd [*sic*],
    Long famous life to her had bene allowd.

(IV.viii., ls. 1934–39).

If we had only the chorus's word for this, we could think that their view ought to be weighed lightly, that Cary was simply "problematizing" the issues and showing a diversity of perspectives surrounding the events. But with Mariam herself rendering the verdict just quoted, it should be given the play's own weight of moral investment. Nor, I think, should the wicked Salome's attempt to claim for women the Jewish male right of divorce be read as a protofeminist brief for women's right to leave bad marriages: the point is rather that husbands should not have this right any more than wives do (as in Christian times, Cary would be glad to say, they do not).

The twin play of Sicily dedicated to Cary's husband Henry, I propose, would have been likely to draw its plot from material similar to the tale of Herod and Mariam, as Cary had found the latter in Lodge's Josephus. Lodge's history represents a standard kind of reading such as the group of women in Lady Katherine Cary's household would have done together, namely vernacular compendia or collected, translated summaries of ancient histories (see chapter 1 on reading groups—Cary's private reading as an only child in her lawyer father's library had evidently ranged farther afield, but I am here speaking of the years when she lived in her new mother-in-law's household). An idea of the character of such books may be gained sheerly from the title of one from 1603, a newly enlarged edition of Sir Thomas North's translation of Plutarch: *The Lives of the Noble Grecians and Romaines . . . Translated out of Greeke into French by Iames Amiot Abbot of Bellozand, Bishop of Auxerre . . . With the liues of Hannibal and of Scipio [by D. Acciajuoli]: translated . . . by Sir Thomas North, Knight. Hereunto are also added the lives of Epaminondas, of Philip of Macedon, of Dionysius the elder, tyrant of Sicilia . . . : with the liues of nine other excellent Chieftaines of warre: collected out of Aemylius Probus, by S. G. S. [Simon Goulari, Senlisien] and Englished by the aforesaid Translator.* The life of Dionysius I of Sicily, famous for wittily terrifying a flatterer in the "sword of Damocles" episode, provides a number of parallels in events and relationships to the tale of Herod and Mariam (see pp. 35–50 of this 1603 *Lives*), so that it could easily have been the basis of the lost play presented as a twin to *Mariam* but addressed to a husband rather than a wife. As the dedicatory sonnet "To Dianaes earthlie Deputesse" proposes a model of chastity and proper wifeliness in the goddess, it proposes sun-like generous warmth and creative power for Cary's husband, in the ideal of the god Apollo—to whom the cruel though strong and poetic Dionysius of Syracuse would be a foil, as Mariam was a foil for Cary's view of proper wifeliness: inadequate, though with certain celebrated virtues, and a situation that might seem to excuse the character's failings.

Like Herod, the lowborn Dionysius consolidated power by marrying the daughter of his city's highest ranking aristocrat, the general Hermocrates, and marrying his sister Tescha to Hermocrates' brother Polyxenes. As Herod ordered Mariam's father and brother killed, Dionysius ordered the mother of his second wife killed (allegedly for bewitching the daughter's fertility), and late in his reign of terror allowed his own brother to be killed for being a political threat, as well as his own mother. As Herod forced his brother Pheroras to marry his niece for policy, Dionysius approved the marriage of his brother Thearides to his niece Arete. Dionysius, when he first married, for a while supposedly "changed his first sournesse and cruelty of a tyrant into gentleness" and began to treat his subjects civilly instead of banishing and killing them. Once firmly in power, he "gloried more in his verses than he did in his warres" and brought in learned poets to discuss his poems and tragedies, though when his brother-in-law Philoxenus critiqued a piece too sharply, he was sent to the rock quarries; he won release when he wittily equivocated his critique, saying that the "verses to arouse pity were indeed pitiful" (46). After thirty-eight years of rule Dionysius died, either of poison or too much drinking. The translator offers commentary verses on his life as follows: "Base Tyranny is wrong, unhappy mother, / Witnesse this wretch, in shew both graue and wise / Yet he himself beguiling, and each other, / Shew'd that his heart was fierce and full of vice."

Another possible source of matter for Cary's Sicilian play would have been Plutarch's account of the noble Athenian Nicias and his wars against the Syracusans, a tale of campaigns in Sicily, battle strategems, and hardships in the field (*Lives* 1603, 548–59). This could have been suitable for a piece to impress her husband, away at the wars. Or there were other tyrants of Sicily to be studied and perhaps dramatized, concerning whom there was a considerable trade in witty apothegms—Gelon, Hiero, Dionysius the Younger, Dion.[4] But none of these would offer so much material as the Dionysius story, if the piece was to be particularly twinned with *Mariam*.

Since Cary's Sicilian play has not survived, we can of course not determine its exact source. My point here is only to suggest the kind of reading in compendious histories out of which the plots for her two early plays came, and something of her respectful though inventive and spirited moralistic handling of such materials, highly traditional as they were in their gender concepts. But for all that the young Elizabeth Tanfield Cary might celebrate dutiful wifeliness and in a companion play appeal to her husband for intellectual companionship and respect for her writing, she was to find when *Mariam* was published in 1613 (whatever exactly was her own degree of agency in the venture—see n. 10) that "publick language" was not permitted her, that she was expected to be content with producing babies (eleven—see n. 7) and with writing "things for her private recreation, on several subjects and occasions" (*Life* 9).

A Return to Writing

Two things that Elizabeth, by then Lady Falkland, began writing after her conversion to Catholicism in 1626 were a translation of Book I of a treatise of Jacques Davy, Cardinal du Perron (himself a converted Huguenot), namely *The Reply of the Most Illustrious Cardinall of Perron to the Answeare of the Most Excellent King of Great Britain* (Douay, 1630), and *The History of the Life, Reign, and Death of Edward II* (written probably in the spring of 1628, publ. 1680).[5] The latter is a prose narrative that she termed a "historical relation" not meant to be a history per se but something to serve "the Truth."[6] It works somewhat in the vein of ancient historians such as Thucidydes, Tacitus, or Diodorus Siculus (source of the Sicilian material noted above) and for us can perhaps best be read as a kind of forerunner of the historical novel: that is, it treats researched characters and events but through invented thoughts, motives, speeches, and conversations. (More will be said of it shortly.) In what order she wrote these two things we do not know; in the prefatory material to each stands the defensive claim that it was written in only one month and should not be much criticized.[7] Perhaps she did the bulk of both in the first rush of returning freedom to write. Her daughter's biography says that she began the Perron treatise in a Lenten time in a run-down house by the Thames after everything had been taken from her; and it mentions much else that she wrote in her last years, but so far as we know nothing else has survived except the two poems given below (in reading manuscripts, one should keep an eye out for an early verse "Life of Tamurlaine" and a poem on the annunciation to the virgin, especially in materials associated with the Buckingham ladies, or any family or connections of Elizabeth Howard Knollys, Lady Banbury).

First let us sample the Perron treatise, to see what she so delighted to write as a Catholic, wishing to persuade her formerly like-minded associates to take the same step she had. The work includes within itself a proposal, answer, counteranswer, and counter-counteranswer process, indicative of a time of intraconsensual conflict. For its preface presents a letter Davy wrote to King James via the refugee Protestant scholar Isaac Casaubon, which the king answered in detail, those answers being in turn answered at length by Davy.

Her sentence style is forceful, and one can sense her enjoyment of Davy's polemic strategies and skillful light irony. He epitomizes major points with entertaining mythological anecdotes taken as similes. Each chapter begins with a summary of the king's statement on the point to be considered, then proceeds with Davy's answer to that answer. Chapter 2, for example, begins by showing the king claiming that he belongs to the true catholic church:

> Now the king belieues simplie . . . that the Church of God is one only by name and effect Catholicke and vniuersall, Spread ouer all the world. out of which he affirmes himselfe, there can be noe hope of Saluation: he condemnes and detestes those which . . . haue departed from the faith of the Catholicke Church

"The Replie" then begins:

> Telesius a Stripling of Greece, hauing won the prize and victorie of the Combate in the Pythian games, when there was question of leadinge him in triumph, there arose such a dispute betweene the diuers nations there present, euery one being earnest to haue him for theire owne, as the one drawing him one waie, the other an other waie, instead of receiuing the honor which was prepared for him, he was torne and dismembred euen by those that stroue who should honor him most. Soe happenes it to the Church: . . . [when Christians] come to debate of the true bodie of this societie, then euery sect desirous to draw her to themselues, they rent and teare her in peeces . . . (*Replie of . . . Perron*, p. 18)

Davy argues then that sects basing their identity on newly devised creeds and separate national institutions yet claiming a hold on the true spiritual, worldwide church of all times and places are like the deadly crowd of the tale.

Or again, starting the chapter on predestination, which Davy says that King James has used as a digression to get the debate off the nature of the true church:

Heere the most excellent Kinge behaues himself like *Hippomanes*, who run-
ninge with *Atalanta* for masterie, cast out golden apples in her way, to delaie
her with takinge them vp: soe his Maiestie putts rubbes in this discourse, to
staie the course of my pen, and to stoppe me to examine them. But I hope
to remoue them so quickly, that I shall be time enough at the end of my
carrere. (p. 52)

He comments that St. Paul in speaking of Christians' assurance that they will
not be separated from the love of Christ is using a rhetorical figure that must
be recognized as such for the passage to be rightly interpreted:

> . . . he speakes there of all the predestinate in generall, into whose number
> he puts himselfe, and those to whom he writes, by a figure which the gram-
> marians call *syllepsis*; and accordinge to the rule, not of Faith, but of Charitie,
> which wills, that in all thinges concealed from vs, we should iudge in the
> better parte. . . . For betweene the certaintie of saluation, and despaire, there
> is a middle way, which is *hope*, that while it lastes, (as it ought alwaies to laste
> in a Christian man) is incompatible with despaire, and suffizeth to comforte
> vs. . . . (pp. 54–55)

As one would gather here, the central issue of the treatise is whether the
true church consists, as King James said, in an invisible spiritual unity of all the
people predestined to salvation and holding the essential Christian doctrines
(though with diverse institutions of governance), or consists in an institution
with continuity of physical and social existence reaching back to the time of
the apostles. In arguing the latter view, Davy adopted for one chapter a strategy
that Lady Falkland probably enjoyed as delicious irony. The king had proposed
that his English church was closer to the nature of the church in St. Augustine's
time than was the modern Roman Catholic church with all its corruptions.
Taking the Protestants' own doctrine of sacraments as "outward and visible
signs" of "inward and invisible" grace, Davy says in effect 'Well, let us consider
the outward signs of Augustine's church, and see whose church now exhibits
them.' He then rolls down a catalogue that becomes more and more persuasive
as it continues, from adoration of the Eucharist as the real body of Christ, to
the use of altars dedicated to the memory of martyrs, prayers for the dead, the
keeping of Lent, clerical celibacy, etc., all in quite concrete detail of "outward
signs," e.g.,

> [it was] A Church which in the Ceremonies of baptisme vsed oyle, salte, waxe
> lights, exorcismes, the signe of the Crose, the word *Epheta* . . . A Church that
> vsed *holy water*, consecrated by certaine wordes and ceremonies . . . A Church
> that held free will, for a doctrine of faith, & reuealed in the holy scripture . . . A
> Church wherein their seruice was said throughout the East in *Greeke*, and

through the west . . . in *Latine*, . . . a church . . . that accompanied the dead to their sepulcher with wax tapers in sign of ioy and future certainty of their resurrection. . . . And finally a Church which held, that the Catholicke Church had the infallible promise, that she should be *perpetually visible and eminent in her communion* . . . [Now] let his Maiestie see, whether by these features he can knowe the face of Caluines Church, or of ours. (pp. 72–73)

Such was the treatise of over four hundred pages that Lady Falkland delightedly rushed through, translating from French, and claimed that the copyist had spent four times as long on it as she had.

By early 1628, just over a year after her conversion, Lady Falkland had begun to write again, namely the two works here noted; during the intervening years since the publication and probably pressured recall of *Mariam*, she perhaps wrote occasion poems, but most of what her daughter lists from before her conversion is attributed to her early married years. As far as publication or any detectable coterie circulation went, she had spent fourteen years of silence since the publication of *Mariam*. As soon as Lady Falkland had made the break to Rome and thus permitted herself one little tiny exception to that lofty ideal of wifely duty—namely that only "for the sake of conscience" would she ever at all cross her husband—then she could find a written voice again. What she found was the voice she had conceived for herself as part of the Durham House process described above. And according to her daughter, none of the hardships she suffered while her husband and the court tried to reassert their authority—betrayal by close friends, house arrest, and loss of her children and all income—none of these could hold a candle to the pleasure she found, through a late winter in a tumbled-down house by the Thames with only fish and bread and one serving woman, writing and writing as much as she pleased.

The Cary *Life* says that after becoming a Catholic she spoke those prayers that the church most valued (perhaps the *gloria*, "our father," *ave Maria*, and Act of Contrition?) as if they were especially her own, for "she did more hope to be heard as a child of the church."[8] To see what this means we must look at a deliberately obscure and cautious passage early in this biography (16–17), concerning two times of severe depression, said to have occurred when Cary was pregnant with her second and fourth children; the passage then makes comments that must refer to the latter of these two episodes, since it says that in the years afterward, always but once she was able to control depression by excess sleeping (the one exception is not explained). The fourth pregnancy was in 1613 to early 1614.[9] At that time, says the biography, she ate or drank nothing for two weeks but once a little beer, until the child ceased to move, though later it was fine. It had been in 1613 that her play *Mariam* was published, and as the daughter elsewhere mentions, Lady Falkland had officially recalled a work of hers—surely the only work of that decade that she published, her play:[10] she declared, so the biography reports, that it had been stolen from a friend's rooms and published against her will. This stock claim goes so against the attitudes she everywhere else expressed toward her own writing that she must have been pressured to the recall, though apparently she did blame her sister-in-law and dear friend Elizabeth Bland Cary (the dedicatee of *Mariam*, who in 1610 had named her first daughter "Miriall" [Dunstan xviii]) for taking some part in putting her own desire to publish into effect: the biography tells of a breach between them, afterward healed. Apparently Cary suffered a time of painful self-contradiction, severe depression, and perhaps a debilitating effort to internalize the rightness of her silencing.

Then after fourteen years, most ironically, the saying of some ancient ritual prayers restored a written individual voice to (as she then was) Lady Falkland, not without one last time of severe depression (in 1627) while she learned what her conversion was costing her. That the leap into the freedom to say those prayers, which so many a Catholic schoolchild has considered the ultimate of bondage, should have restored a voice of her own must show that for her they meant the chance at long last to make an assertion—an assertion addressing the intragroup conflicts of the Anglo-Catholics who were or had been her friends, and one that threw off the constraints of the male authority of her husband and the court under Buckingham.

Buckingham's sister, as noted, tried to have her restrained by force from going to Lord Ormond's stable, where the "reconciliation" took place; once it had, Lady Denbigh immediately ran and told the event to her brother, and he to King Charles.[11] A surviving painful letter to her from Lady Falkland refers to this and related events and to the intense pressure that was immediately put on her to reconvert, including an all-day "bellowing" harangue by the cleric John Cosen. She asks Lady Denbigh what has become of "your friendship to mee," and ironically thanks "you and my lord your brother, for your care of mee though I wish it had been in another kinde," likewise declaring herself "Bound to mr. cosens, while I live, for the paines hee takes, though I wish any man else, had been imployde rather"; she adds that Secretary John Coke "was with me even now" trying to win her back to the Church of England.[12] I believe it was this betrayal and related subsequent actions by people she had trusted, along with her severe financial troubles and loss of her children, that sent her into the depression of late 1627: the "only one" more referred to in the daughter's *Life*, and in the preface to *Edward II*. She finally wrote her way out of it in the Lenten fast time of 1628:[13]

To out-run those weary hours of a deep and sad Passion, my melancholy Pen fell accidentally on this Historical Relation; which speaks a King, our own, though one of the most Vnfortunate; and shews the Pride and Fall of his Inglorious Minions. I have not herein followed the dull Character of our Historians, nor amplified more than they infer, by Circumstance. I strive to please the Truth, not Time; nor fear I Censure, since at the worst, 'twas but one Month mis-spended; which cannot promise ought in right Perfection. If so you hap to view it, tax not my Errours; I my self confess them. E. F.

Her *Edward II*

This *History of the Life, Reign, and Death of Edward II*[14] incorporates the techniques of prose "charactery" as they had been developed in conversational games of James's court (cf. chapter 5) in which women were major players,[15] especially by such writers as Sir Thomas Overbury (poisoning victim of the Countess of Somerset) and, a little later, by John Earle: the "characters" are verbal portrait pieces that vividly describe the looks and ways of some stereo-typical character (e.g., a "court parasite") by stringing out a few paragraphs of satirical witticisms on his or her behavior. With the characterist's mode of stereo-typical description Lady Falkland interweaves the ancient historians' practice of inventing suitable supposed speeches for serious or admired characters at moments of high emotion, very distinctly using the blank verse rhythms of Jacobean drama, but setting the speeches like the rest of the narrative as prose (marked off by italics in the 1680 text). Most notably, she treats Edward II and his favorites Gaveston and Spencer as analogous to King James and his favorites Somerset and Buckingham, evaluating homoerotic royal favoritism from a po-sition of long considered analysis and disapproval.[16] (We should recall that not only Buckingham's sister, but also Somerset's sister-in-law, Elizabeth Howard Knollys, Lady Banbury, was a close friend of Lady Falkland's; her perspective was an insider's.) Her most general moral in *Edward II* is that this, like any other harmful self-indulgence in royalty, if it is not to ruin the kingdom, must be kept private and politically inconsequential, rather than causing the favorites to acquire powers far beyond their competence: the epigraph under her title is a revision of King James's motto, "Qui nescit dissimulare nescit regnare" (He who does not know how to dissimulate does not know how to reign) to "Qui nescit Dissimulare, nequit vivere, perire melius" (He who does not know how to dissimulate cannot live, rather can lose).

An "Epitaph upon the death of the Duke of Buckingham" by Lady Falk-land expresses her attitude toward him with an ingenious ambiguity that cov-ered her tracks for the eyes of any reader sympathetic to Buckingham (he was assassinated in August, 1629):

Reader stand still and see, loe, here I am
Who was of late the mighty Buckingham;
God gave to me my being, and my breath;

Two kings their favours, and a slave my death
That for my Fame I challenge, and not crave
That thou beleeve two kinges, before one slave.[17]

A reader expecting the epitaph to be flattering to Buckingham would take the last two lines to mean "My claim to fame is that two kings favored me while it was only a low-ranking fellow who killed me; I do not ask you to prefer (do not care whether you prefer) the kings' opinion over that of the fellow." But quite another reading readily—perhaps more readily—suggests itself: "I wish my fame to be that two kings favored me while it was only a low-ranking fellow who killed me, rather than asking you to believe that two kings were subjected before one low-ranking fellow [i.e., Buckingham himself]." A clear denunciatory epitaph on Buckingham would not have been possible in her circumstances, dependent as she always remained on King Charles's toleration along with his queen's support. But the view that Kings James and Charles were both erotically or at least emotionally subject to a man of no innate rank or stature here finds a just barely safe expression, one that illustrates her wit and high verbal ability.

Her *Edward II* narrative in its latter half focuses on the dilemma of Queen Isabella, caught between the duty to remain a faithful wife and the need to do something about a husband who is ruining his kingdom—a wifely dilemma similar to that explored in *Mariam.* The queen's maneuverings and escape to France, her royal brother's betrayal of her, her bringing of an army from Flanders, successful capture of England, and fall to the temptations of an affair with Mortimer and even tearful consent to her husband's murder—all this is told with a combination of sympathy and disapproval, governed by the view that the queen was driven to her faults by her husband's extreme failures. It is as if the whole painful saga of the destructive effects of Somerset and Buckingham is being treated by fictional displacement: an assertive French queen of England, albeit a tainted one, of whom Queen Henrietta Maria is a potential superior analogue,[18] takes action. Isabella is tainted because she violates wifely duty, even conspiring her husband's death; yet she is irresistible as a role model, because she succeeds politically and militarily against the ruinous favorite. The keynote of Isabella's importance to the narrative as a whole is caught in a terse early sentence, concluding the account of Edward's marriage in France: "The Solemnity ended, and a Farewel taken, he hastens homewards, returning seised of a Jewel, which not being rightly valued, wrought his ruine" (*History* 5). What he had thought a mere possession, his queen, became a human agent and deposed him and his intolerable favorites.

All this is not to say that the queen's faults fail to meet with due judgment at Lady Falkland's hands. Especially her actions in publicly parading, demeaning, and torturing Spencer after her victory are roundly denounced. So far had she declined from her earlier virtue that her actions showed "a savage, tyrannical disposition"; she should have respected his station as a peer, though only "by creation" (one of many instances of marked aristocratic bias in the history). Just as it had been said of Mariam in the play that she should have forgiven her husband and not shown "sourness," the narrator declares that Queen Isabella ought to have shown "a kinde of Sweetness in the disposition" that would "pity his [Spencer's] Misfortune," if not the man himself. The queen's vindictiveness was "too great and deep a blemish to suit a Queen, a Woman, and a Victor" (129). Lady Falkland even gets so carried away with denouncing the queen's cruelty on this occasion as to have her narrator declare that "we may not properly expect Reason in Womens actions" (130). She also of course should not have consented to her husband's deposition and murder, but the treatment of that episode is oddly milder in its critique of the queen.

On the whole the treatment of her is sympathetic, according with the history's conclusion that even though it was Edward's own wife and son that brought him down, "had he not indeed been a Traytor to himself, they could not all have wronged him" (160). For "it is much in a king to be himself dissolute, licentious, and ill-affected; but when he falls into a second errour, making more delinquents Kings, where one is too much, he brings all into disorder, and makes his Kingdome rather a Stage of Oppression, than the Theater of Justice" (158).

Sensing the disastrous direction Charles's reign was taking in 1628, Lady Falkland harbored a wish to see Queen Henrietta Maria and the French crown follow in the steps of Queen Isabella, doubtless only so far as to take some decisive action to rid England of its canker the royal favorite, not to depose the king (which deed, as noted, she condemns in Isabella's party, even after having shown how hopelessly incompetent a ruler he was). At several points in this *Edward II*, and especially in the moralizing conclusion, the narrator relates the medieval story in terms that refer just as well or better to the contemporary case. For example, a mention of the king's first favorite as skilled at poisoning is more reminiscent of the Overbury murder than of anything in Gaveston's career. Similarly, the portrayal of a groom of the royal chamber flattering his way into power fits the Jacobean better than the Edwardian situation. Or again, a mention of another deposed king, Henry VI, notes that he "had a *Suffolk* and a *Somerset* that could teach the same way" to deposition (156).

Lady Falkland does not hesitate to speak directly of "Gaveston his [the king's] Ganymede" (4) and to speculate on the origins and nature of a homosexual disposition, as well as its functioning in a powerful man: her narrator wonders whether it might be hereditary but finds that improbable since neither Edward's parents nor son showed signs of it. She supposes too that once it becomes "confirmed by continuance of Practice, and made habituary by custom," even the will of the man himself cannot alter it (3ff.). As to its impact on the ruler's ability to govern: it is a particular instance of "the general Disease of Greatness, and a kinde of Royal Fever, when they fall upon an indulgent Dotage, to patronize and advance the corrupt ends of their Minions, though the whole Society of State and Body of the Kingdom run in a direct opposition" (16)—a particularly dangerous instance when the favorites are male, since they can get ruinous powers into their own hands. (The *History* was, incidentally, brought out in 1680 for the purpose of lobbying against the very great influence of one of Charles II's mistresses.)

As for Lady Falkland's personal situation under Buckingham's regime, just when Parliament was trying to impeach him and Sir Henry Yelverton was declaring that he should beware of becoming a latter-day Hugh de Spencer, Lady Falkland as a Catholic convert and, still in some measure, friend of Susan Denbigh, found herself in the enormously painful position of having to depend on Buckingham's relatives and subordinates because, aside from a few Catholic friends who helped in small ways, such as one James Clayton (see prefatory poems in the Perron translation, and *Life* 166), no one else would help her. On one level her *Edward II* is an attempt to cope with that situation. And after she wrote it, she seems to have found more favor with Queen Henrietta Maria, to whom she dedicated the Perron translation in 1630 (see n. 18 for her dedicatory sonnet to the queen, preserved in what would seem to have been her presentation copy).

As sample texts to indicate the feel of her writing, let us take excerpts from a passage describing Gaveston as flattering court parasite and favorite, and then from a later portion, the queen's prophetic denunciation speech to the shores of France after her cause has been slighted, foretelling revenge by her son. In the first passage, Edward has just arranged for the base-born Gaveston to marry a daughter of the Earl of Gloucester, who is much distressed:

> To take away that doubt, the new-married man is advanced to the Earldom of *Cornwal*, and hath in his Gift the goodly Castle and Lordship of *Wallingford*; so that now in Title he had no just exception; and for conditions, it must be thought enough his Master loved him. To shew himself thankful, and to seem worthy of such gracious favour, *Gaveston* applies himself wholly to the Kings humour, feeding it with the variety of his proper appetite, without so much as question or contradiction: Not a word fell from his Sovereign's tongue, but he applauds it as an Oracle, . . . If the King maintain'd the party, the servant was ever fortunate, his voice was ever concurrent, and sung the same Tune to a Crochet. The discourse being in the commendation of Arms, the eccho stiles it an Heroick Vertue; if Peace, it was an Heavenly Blessing; unlawful Pleasures, a noble Recreation; and Actions most unjust, a Royal

Goodness. These parasitical Gloses so betray'd the itching ear that heard them, that no Honour or Preferment is conceited great and good enough for the Relator. A short time invests in his person or disposure all the principal offices and Dignities of the Kingdom. . . . In the view of these strange passages, the King appear'd so little himself, that the Subjects thought him a Royal Shadow without a Real Substance. This Pageant, too weak a Jade for so weighty a burden, had not a brain in it self able enough to manage such great Actions; neither would he entertain those of ability to guide him, whose honest freedom might have made him go through-stitch with more reputation. He esteems it a gross oversight, and too deep a disparagement, to have any creature of his own thought wiser than himself. . . . This made him chuse his Servants as his Master chose him, of a smooth fawning temper, such as might cry ayme, and approve his actions, but not dispute them. Hence flew a world of wilde disorder . . . (pp. 19–21)

Here we see, among other features, Lady Falkland's delight in a profusion of metaphors tumbling over each other: in the same sentence Gaveston is a "pageant" (a mere Skinnerian repertoire of behaviors), a feeble horse, a fellow of little brain, and then a seamstress who might have gone "through-stitch" through his affairs if he had at least sought competent sewing advice. Notice the progressive diminution effected by this series, which makes him in the end a quasi-woman and an incompetent one at that.

As a sample of the dramatic, as it were arioso speeches in blank verse rhythm (but printed as prose), consider the queen's as she leaves France, having been cast off by a brother whose help she has begged but who fears to start a war over a mere "female passion":

Farewel (quoth she) farewel, thou glorious Climate, where I first saw the World, and first did hate it; thou gavest me Birth, and yet denyest me Being; and Royal Kinred, but no Friends were real. Would I had never sought thy Help or Succour, I might have still believ'd thee kinde, not cruel: but thou to me art like a graceless mother, that suckles not, but basely sells her children. Alas! what have I done, or how offended, thou shouldst deny my life her native harbour? Was't not enough for thee in my Distresses to yeeld no Comfort, but thou must Expel me, and, which was worse, Betray me to my Ruine? The poorest soul that claims in thee a dwelling, is far more happie than thy Royal Issue: but time will come thou wilt repent this Errour, if thou remember this my just Prediction; my Off-spring will revenge a Mothers Quarrel, a Mothers Quarrel just and fit for Vengeance. Then shalt thou seek and sue, yet finde more favour from him thy Foe, than I could win, a Sister. (*History* 108)

This could easily be printed as blank verse, and we recognize the dramatist of *Mariam* and the lost Sicilian play[19] (about twenty when she wrote those plays), now in her maturity with more potential as a writer, devising a generic format for something that she can only imagine existing in a few manuscripts, in a few friends' libraries: "If you hap to view it, tax not my Errours," says her preface to this indulgent reader. Perhaps she understood that it would not survive even there unless she left it among her husband's papers, unsigned except by initials, letting it be mistaken for a work of his. Thus it was published and thereby preserved in 1680.

EPILOGUE

Theoretical Perspectives

THE CHAPTERS OF this book are roughly in chronological order as to the writers treated, beginning with the 1560s and ending with Lady Falkland in 1630. They also move through a kind of ad hoc theoretical order, in pursuing the general question how various Tudor and Stuart women found motivation and positioning to write anything beyond the sheerly personal, when so much stood against their doing so. I have sought models adequate to this question in several spheres of textual and cultural study that appear commensurable. From certain of Catherine Stimpson's and Wendy Hollway's ideas about gendered writing and reading, integrated with Tony Bennett's concept of "reading formations" (applied in chapters 1 and 3), I moved on to Jürgen Habermas's analysis of ideological group dynamics joined with Gérard Genette's account of the paratextual (applied in chapters 2 and 7), to Julia Kristeva's concept of ideological loadings within the "social text" (chapter 4), and in chapters 5 and 6 to Fredric Jameson's concept of the ideologeme as a "desiring machine" of social production (in the sense of Gilles Deleuze and Felix Guattari), here articulated so as to enable focus on gender study. Let us briefly review these concepts, something of their placement in the current scene of literary and cultural theory, and how they relate to each other.

Bennett's proposals about reading formations come from practices of neo-Marxist analysis that study social class identities and how these function within processes of utterance and listening, writing and reading. Within a culture, people can be seen to have particular habits and modes of reading that are specific to their class identities and that savvy writers will attend to in composing and paratextually framing texts: i.e., writers address themselves to such a "reading formation" with the aim of garnering and shaping a desired pertinent audience or readership, for their own ideologically invested purposes. It struck me that the gender-specific reading habits of certain kinds of Renaissance women could well be explored under this model, if it were articulated so as to include gender categories. With the help of Catherine Stimpson's insights about what may happen when women are addressed as a readership and what new economic powers they may claim under certain conditions, and with the further help of Wendy Hollway's ideas about gendered subject and object positions offered by particular discourses about sex, I applied Bennett's idea to the widely pervasive Renaissance practice of women's reading aloud to each other, in household groups encompassing a great lady and her attendants and subservient male protégés. The first result was an account of how waiting women (whether of lower-gentry or merchant class) such as Whitney, Tyler, and Lanyer came to feel competent for claiming a female public voice, something hitherto almost unknown for women of their station. And further, in treating the Countess of Pembroke's development as translator and poet (Chapter 3), I argued that the supportiveness and particular structures of this, as it were, gynocritical reading formation were crucial to the aristocratic and politically specific voice she came to have by the late 1590s.

Like the Countess of Pembroke, certain other aristocratic women took part not only in household readings and conversation, but also in broader spheres of politicized discourse and activism. To study their writings on that level, I found Habermas helpful. His theory of "communicative action," which he says he has proposed as a start on a field of "formal pragmatics," is based on the speech-act theory of J. L. Austin and John Searle. In other words, he has devised a mode of sociology attuned to, and largely structured by, text linguistics and the pragmatics of communicative interaction. For he starts from the idea that people speaking or writing are not primarily communicating abstractable messages across a void from one mind to another, but instead are doing things to each other, having impacts on and modifying each other, thereby to "communicate." In analyzing, among many other topics, the internal, processual workings of ideologically homogeneous groups, Habermas notes that such a group's participants are likely, after a time of unity, to find that internal conflicts arise, leading to disputes and an ensuing effort of opposing subfactions to find new ground for reestablishing consensus (which effort may or may not succeed). During the stretch of time when these latter phases of the group's existence occur, fissures may open that allow something to become newly visible that was operative in the group all along, namely the structures of domination within it, whereby some members have had leading voices and others little or no voice. I have proposed that such a stage in an ideological group's life might provide women with opportunities for new voices, and that this is part of what happened when we see women moving from very marginalized paratextual spaces (e.g., translation), to textual spaces where they achieve a more particularized voice. Thus the four Cooke sisters (in the 1570s) and Lady Falkland (in the 1620s) moved from translation to dedicatory and patronage verse and finally to more original reshapings of genres that they claimed for themselves: mortuary elegies for Lady Russell, a fictionalized prose history in semidramatic mode for Lady Falkland. While I found Habermas's concepts especially useful, this analysis could also be seen in Pierre Bourdieu's terms of "symbolic capital," of which he says that some people within a system of domination have so much that they "effortlessly command attention," while others have little or none ("Economics" 650). Such was the socioideological context in which the Cooke sisters found themselves as marginalized female participants in the Protestant reformist activism of the 1570s.

The concepts of Kristeva, Jameson, and A.-J. Greimas that I used in chapters 5 and 6 will not, I believe, be found thus combined anywhere else, except in my forthcoming study *Cultural Semiotics, Spenser, and the Elizabethan Captive Woman*. Kristeva took up the term "ideologeme" from *The Formal Method in Literary Scholarship* (published as by P. N. Medvedev but now believed to be Mikhail Bakhtin's or at least to represent his thinking—cf. Morson and Emerson); she defined it as the unit of meaning through which the "social space" constructs the ideological values of its signs. Each text, she said, has as its composite ideologeme, stretching along its length, the sum of those ideological values. Jameson, taking up the "ideologeme" in his *Political Unconscious* and seeing it as more explicitly identifiable than Kristeva had, defines it as at once a sociosemiotic unit of meaning and a Deleuzean "desiring machine" of meaning-production, given instances of which can be named and some of their usages traced; these carry libidinalized political loadings that are read into and out of the ideologeme's internal patterns in particular ways by speakers and writers of particular class or factional identities. That is, each ideologeme functions as a "desiring machine" in the sense of Deleuze and Guattari, generating the pulses of ideologically energized meaning-making into which producers of cultural artifacts can channel and thereby intensify their own libidinal energies, through their ideological identifications and positioning. In thus construing the ideologeme, Jameson is drawing also on Jean-François Lyotard's *Libidinal Economy*, seeing the ideologeme as a sociolinguistic site for production of libidinal investment. In other words he sees Lyotard's "libidinal positions" as existing in a social matrix that is to some degree chartable, rather than in Lyotard's manner, as comprising a surging superheated flux of shifting positions for investments and disinvestments of ideologically charged energies (Lyotard 113). These positions become chartable through the identification of ideologemes as sociosemiotic quasi-units (an appropriation that Lyotard himself would perhaps disavow).

My own experiment with these last theoretical materials has been threefold: to posit an internal gender category—i.e., maleness-femaleness as a classematic, bipolar, culturally loaded opposition—that can be carried from term to term within the ideologeme construct; further, to hypothesize that a given ideologeme can be identified through a discourse analysis of a highly influential political text, and then to carry out that analysis (in this case of King James's *Basilicon Doron*, widely circulated and keenly read as he came to the English throne in 1603); and finally, to pursue the results for both male and female Jacobean writers. (The algorithm and results of the particular discourse analysis make up Appendix 1 below.) The arc of this experiment posits that Deleuze and Guattari's desiring machines, operative at both the personal and social levels, can be analyzed as to their internal functioning through Greimas's base narrative program formula, as follows. Deleuze and Guattari describe the desiring machines as "binary processes" in which desire is the outcome of a process of production: they are composed of "the flows-schizzes or the break-flows that break and flow at the same time on the body without organs . . . the myriad little connections, disjunctions, and conjunctions by which every machine produces a flow in relation to another that breaks it, and breaks a flow that another produces" (Adams and Searle 303). Carrying Jameson's integrations of Greimasian semiotics with Deleuzean thinking one step further than he did (he worked only with the semiotic square), I have assumed that those very "connections, disjunctions, and conjunctions" along the flow of desire within an ideologeme can be tracked and charted through Greimas's "base narrative program" formula, which itself is an aggressional binarism. I.e., the formula is that a subject takes control of a secondary subject from which it is disjoining or to which it is reconjoining (i.e., losing) an object invested with value (see chapter 5 and Appendix 1 for details).

The secondary outcome of my experiment was a proposal that there was in the opening Jacobean decade an ideologeme of "male self-image propagation as government": a desiring-production "machine" that writers both male and female encountered as operative within their available social text and which they often reproduced—and were produced by—but in differently gendered ways. As one might expect, the enunciative position for this ideologeme was male-tagged; male writers could thus often plug into it with unproblematic directness (though even they might choose to take surprising tacks against it—as I argue Donne did in "The First Anniversary"), while women, having no ideologeme with a female-tagged enunciative subject-position available to them, resorted to even more surprising maneuvers when relating to this one. Within this context I have studied the verbal parlor-game playing of women attending Queen Anne (especially Cecily Bulstrode and Lady Anne Southwell), the political-factional identities that interlaced their playing, the relation of these to Ben Jonson's play *Epicoene, or the Silent Woman* as well as his masques of *Blackness* and *Beauty*, and the importance of this context and ideologeme for Lady Mary Wroth's pastoral play *Love's Victory*.

In sum, I have pulled together a number of approaches from the spheres of discourse pragmatics, discourse psychology, Marxist and psychoanalytic theory, sociology, feminist textual study, and cultural semiotics, applying them to the uses of politically specific period study and reassessment of women's texts and writing processes. My theoretical proposals are obviously not constructs of high polish or thorough elaboration; rather they are explorations, which I hope will contribute to studies of textuality, gender, and culture. They are based on the assumption that gender study will not be able to offer an adequate account of the functioning of gender identities unless these are studied within the interplay of the several kinds of systems of domination, in their political and sociosemiotic manifestations, within a given society.

My project of pursuing these concepts through some of the vastly complex surfaces and depths of the surviving records of early modern England has not been any such excursus of cool, algorithmic application as the above account has probably made it seem. The work was a process of alternating trajectories. Moments of unabashedly self-investive interpretation by a localized twentieth-century mentality (obviously with its own urges, agenda, and limitations) have interspersed with moments of attention to certain upper-level theoretical abstractions, posited to have a kind of semiotic use-value, for taking an analysis through interpretation and into the conditions of meaning-making.

Identification of the Ideologeme Described in Chapter 5, from Discourse Data of the Basilicon Doron*

Section 1.
Algorithm or Description Procedures Used, for the Discourse Analysis of the *Basilicon Doron*, by James VI and I

(Terms are from Greimas and Courtés, *Semiotics and Language: An Analytical Dictionary*, 1982. The ordering of the procedures is mine.)

   I. *Objectification of the text as enunciation.* Goal: to retrace and bracket out the initial stage of discoursivization, the projection of a "not-I, not-here, not-now" by the enunciator.

      A. Transcribe the outer-level category of person: for pronouns or nouns referring to the whole-text speaker/addressee substitute the terms enunciator/enunciatee.

      B. Eliminate all time indications "relative to the now" of the whole enunciation (though keeping indicators of internal time systems).

      C. Eliminate all enunciation-level phatic elements (attention gestures to an implied reader).

  II. *Segmentation.* Goal: hypothetical analysis of the text into semio-narrative sequences (i.e., a set of utterances that presuppose each other, comprising, e.g., a "test," or argumentative point). These are "textual" not "discursive" units—i.e., they are segments of the textual surface. The boundary identifications can be corrected if necessary, with information gained in later stages.

      A. Search for demarcators such as "but" or other transition signals that indicate a "frontier between two sequences," and on the other hand for grammatical anaphora or other continuity signals, indicating sequence continuation.

      B. "Recognize categorical disjunctions," such as the spatial (here/elsewhere), temporal (before/after), thymic (euphoria/dysphoria), topical (same/other), actorial (I/he or she), logical (causing/caused, or other), referential (dialogue/narrative). [Note: "The degree of certitude of the operation rises with the number of concomitant disjunctions," though these will not always be

---

*Special thanks are due to my colleague Lynn Gordon for help with and corroborative application of the concepts for identifying focal elements of tone-information units (III. B. below).

located at precisely the same place; i.e., between two sequences there may be an area of proximate disjunctions, analogous to the proximate isoglosses defining the dialectal zone boundaries in a language.]

C. List the resulting hypothetical semio-narrative sequences (leave results temporarily aside).

III. *Extraction of terms for a corpus.* Goal: to identify a set of isotopically indicative lexemes, by scanning for the most frequently occurring open-class lexemes (words with other than grammatical semes, i.e., eliminating closed-class words such as articles, conjunctions, etc.), and recording the word counts, hypothesizing that the most frequently occurring of the discourse's focal words will, after proper processing, yield the "general semantic isotopy of the text." ["Focal" is here used in the sense of Quirk and Greenbaum (1985).]

A. Decide whether to use the whole text or selected sequences as the material for identifying the isotopically indicative lexemes. In the present case (of the *Basilicon Doron*) I chose to use four of the six identified sequences (comprising about 3/5 of the total text), omitting a stretch of text that began with distinct general-to-particular (abstraction-to-examples) shift signals.

B. Using the topic-focus distinction as defined by Quirk and Greenbaum (pp. 1355–1391 and other sections—i.e., explaining the nature and identification of end-focus in tone-information units in English), select the focal open-class lexemes from each tone-information unit, along with the page and line number of each one's occurrence.

C. Alphabetize this list, so that the occurrences of the same lexeme (including inflectionally varied instances of each) are thrown together. Scan this list looking for a frequency drop-off level such that, taking all the words of that frequency and up, one will have a list of several dozen (not above 100) words. With the *Basilicon Doron* sequences 1-3 and 6, this level proved to be four occurrences.

D. Eliminate from consideration (besides the closed-class or grammatical lexemes) three further categories:

1. euphoria/dysphoria tags (e.g., "good," "wicked," "delightful," "drearisome")
2. qualifiers/quantifiers (e.g., "specially," "often," "more," "part")
3. general purpose lexemes that in isolation carry too little semantic import to be useful, i.e., that rely for their semantic import on contextual combinatory partners (e.g., "cause," "take," "say," "set," "man," "tend")—except where these appear possibly to be thematized in relation to other lexemes of the list; another exception to this exclusion would be those occurring in combination with separable-verb components, e.g., "set forth"—keep those). [This third step is my proposal, not, so far as I know, suggested by Greimas/Courtés.]
4. Include classemes (e.g., "high"-"low," "life-death") in the initial inventory, in case they might be thematized in relation to the other lexemes; but eliminate them later if they do not prove to be so: the goal here is to recognize indicators of isotopic kernel semes.

E. List the lexemes thus produced, hypothesizing that they are substantially the suitable corpus for analysis, i.e., the surface indicators of the text's semantic isotopy.

IV. *Structuration*: the sememic description of the semantic isotopy. Goal: to recognize and formulate the recurrent sememes (combinations of semes, often hypotactic) in the isotopically indicative lexemes identified by the inventory process.

    A. Sort the list of isotopic indicators into batches of synonymous or partially synonymous (parasynonymous) lexemes, and formulate the shared seme/sememe grouping of each batch.

    B. Make a semic inventory for selected lexemes—the most frequently occurring few—of the hypothesized semantic isotopy, with both kernel seme indicators and contextual semes (including classemes or classematic opposition categories, e.g., verticality-horizontality, sound-silence, plant-animal, youth-age). A descriptive metalanguage for the semes and subordinate sememes must be devised.

    C. Carry out the dual operation of reduction/homologation.

        1. Reduction: "transforming an inventory of sememic occurrences, parasynonymous in nature, into a constructed class or 'constructed sememe' joining together many occurrences of a sememe dispersed throughout a discourse and belonging to different lexemes."

        2. Homologation: recognizing, with respect to the sememic category being constructed, whatever occurrent contradictory and contrary terms belong to the structure, the description of which is sought (i.e., projecting the constructed sememe onto the semiotic square).

    D. Eliminate any few "stray" lexemes from the corpus—those with no synonyms/parasynonyms nor any apparent relation to the emergent groupings. Often these are words, most or all occurrences of which came in a single passage that happened to be repetitious.

    E. Divide the constructed sememes into actants and predicates, the latter in turn into those of doing and those of state.

    F. Attribute substantive form (i.e., with -ing, -age, -tion, etc.) to all sememes; then transcribe and sort them into "semantic messages," using the following notation:

Function: F (for predicates)
Subject: S (for subject actants)
Object: O (for object actants)
conjunction: ^
disjunction: U
function of doing:$----\rightarrow$

[Note: Greimas no longer uses the concept of "qualification" to characterize the relation of terms in utterances of state. Thus he has abandoned his earlier F/Q notation.]

V. *Identification of the discourse's "base narrative program."* Goal: to make that identification and also to correlate/superpose the semantic/thematic isotopy with the actorial isotopy, and thereby to localize the "instrumental narrative programs."

    A. Using the constructed sememes as indicators, identify the discourse's prethematized value or values, which can be either descriptive or modal, and their thematizations (which will be middle-level abstractions, e.g., for a descriptive value such as "freedom," thematized to "spatial escape" and "temporal escape"—later to be figurativized as a trip to faraway seas and a return to childhood; or for a modal value such as competence, i.e., being-able-to-do, poetic skill figurativized as a laurel wreath).

B. Determine the figurative isotopy by tracing the two phases of figurativization from the above determined themes:
    1. "conversion of themes into figures."
    2. iconization ("endowing [these figures] with particularizing investments").

C. Again using the constructed sememes and sorted "semantic messages" as indicators,
    1. Identify the (thematized) "subject actant" behind the various actors carrying out the base NP.
    2. Apply the notation of the NP as "an utterance of doing governing an utterance of state":
        $NP = F: S_1 \dashrightarrow (S_2 \cup O_v)$ or $NP = F: S_1 \dashrightarrow (S_2 \wedge O_v)$.
    [Note: the notation "NP" may cause confusion since linguists commonly use it in English to mean "noun phrase"; keep in mind that here it means "narrative program."]

D. To the sequences hypothesized in II above, apply the thematic and figurative isotopies evident for the constructed sememes, so as to relate the "instrumental narrative programs" to the sequences, using the "np" equation notation.
    1. Once the base narrative program has been identified, use the "reference system" of the "utterative time" within the discourse to "localize" the instrumental NPs.
    2. Reconfirm the textual locations of the instrumental narrative programs within sequences, by beginning at a proposed sequence boundary and scanning until the formula, through actorializations of each element of the base NP, can once again be completely rewritten in positive (not contrary or contradictory) terms, with either disjunction or conjunction of S_2 and O_v. [This is my own proposal, not, so far as I know, suggested by Greimas/Courtés.]

E. List the formulas for the base narrative program (i.e., the derived version of it specific to this text) and the instrumental narrative programs, indicating their sequence boundaries.

Section 2.
Data of Application of the Preceding Algorithm to *Basilicon Doron*

I. Text Used: the Waldegrave edition of 1603, ed. James Craigie (Edinburgh: Blackwood, 1950); this 1603 edition sold thousands of copies in England as James was coming to the throne. In this step, references to James and his son Prince Henry as particular persons and as author and addressee were eliminated, i.e., replaced by enunciator-enunciatee positions.

II. Sequences identified by the anaphoric subtitles and other boundary markers (as defined above) were found to be
    1. Sonnet. The Argument (p. 5)
    2. The First Booke (pp. 25–51)

3. The Second Booke, portion comprising pp. 53–71, down to "And that ye may the readier . . . govern your subjects"
4. The Second Booke, portion comprising pp. 71–103, down to "But it is not ynough to a good King . . . well to gouerne, . . . if he joyne not therewith his vertuous life in his owne person."
5. The Second Booke, portion comprising pp. 103–161.
6. The Third Booke

(Of these, # 1–3 and 6 became the data base.)

III. The corpus of indicator lexemes that were focal in the tone-information units of Sequences 1–3 and 6 was compiled: a ten-page, three-column list of words with each occurrence location noted by page and line number.

IV. Words of 4 occurrences and up, with noun form attributed, after exclusions (words occurrent all in one passage, + other exclusions noted in the above algorithm), were sorted into parasynonym groups (with indicators of contrary or contradictory opposites bracketed, and parasynonymous words of 2 or 3 occurrences subjoined in boldface to their parasynonyms). The numbers are of pages and lines in Waldegrave.

figurativized ruler

God/God's33.13 3.34 49.31 69.29 173.27 201.21 25.13 25.23 27.24 27.29 29.11 29.17 29.19 31.11 31.13 31.17 31.29 33.24 35.15 35.35 37.28 37.31 39.21 39.6 43.33 49.21 49.24 49.29 5.4 63.18 67.11
King (God as)5.14 5.6
god (king as)5.1 25.25

ruler

king/king's203.30 31.28 39.15 169.11 189.11 191.12 27.31 39.14 39.28 53.9 69.26 kings181.24 29.15 35.26 kingly45.16; (king)me201.25 me191.10 my207.21
rule/ruler175.28 43.33 163.24 61.18 59.15 195.22 195.28
[tyrant167.9 55.13 55.31 61.28 197.30 him55.18]

second figurativization of ruler

parent/parents'67.32 65.32 67.24 67.30
father55.26 65.33 207.12

figurativized ruling

Law (divine)29.19 33.17 33.24 35.9 5.7
religion201.14 31.15 31.30 37.27 41.30
scripture31.22 31.31 31.33 37.11 37.22 47.32 49.19

ruling

reign/*regentis*5.5 57.20 53.21
calling185.15 27.15 51.18 37.23 51.9 55.23 53.7
censor/censure185.26 45.22 185.17 69.19
judge/judgment185.26 45.21 181.26 183.20 43.17 69.29
justice5.9 33.18 47.17 53.10 63.13 69.34 205.18
law/lawful173.21 53.13 181.24 187.22 187.24 65.34 177.25 201.5 5.7 53.13 55.11 59.28 59.31 61.15 61.17 61.25 [unlawful193.16 193.25 41.12 57.31]

office163.12 183.21 183.25 191.23 201.29 205.21 31.28 51.10
   reward59.15 65.16 163.25 [punish63.29 65.24 35.20]
   execution59.21 59.25 203.23
   effect51.14 63.18
[vanity/vain177.18 39.23 51.9 49.10]

figurativized ruler image (ruled subject/citizen)

Christ171.25 51.20 29.10 33.18 3.32 35.27 37.30 me(quoted Christ)29.10
heaven163.25 51.19 57.23 5.6 163.25

ruler image (ruled subject/citizen)

posterity185.20 57.28 207.20 67.18
prince(as)ye165.31 ye191.24 you205.21 you191.10 you27.14 you27.15 you29.13 you67.10
   you69.13 yours27.13; prince187.26 67.15 princes[rulers]185.13
son165.11 189.24 201.28 205.11 207.11 25.22 43.23 59.14 67.26 69.13

second figurativization of ruler image

servant/service181.27 53.14 167.12 175.27 43.33 43.34
court177.23 199.30 59.31 courtesies181.20 courtier173.14 courtisan173.12

figurativized object (to be conjoined with ruled subject/citizen)

Christian171.27 171.29 199.17 25.12 45.16 53.9
godliness27.26 51.23 193.13 43.13 5.12
   faith37.26 39.33 41.14
   prayer39.5 41.16 39.7
[sin27.17 27.20 27.21 41.15 43.11]

object (to be conjoined with ruled subject/citizen)

other197.15 201.11 201.17 207.18 25.26 29.14 39.18 47.30 205.27 25.10 27.11 27.12 67.13
   another27.13 27.14 27.15
outwardness163.13 163.14 165.12 179.13 179.15 201.30 51.22
   body191.28 203.16

figurativization of object

country177.23 181.20 201.16 63.22
man/man's/men's69.26 165.15 183.23 25.25 29.34 41.32 49.19 47.31 61.13 193.13 25.26
   47.19 51.9 59.18
kingdom201.4 31.21 61.31
people163.12 201.23 201.7 205.23 25.12 27.25 27.27 55.15 55.25 57.12 71.13 57.16
person/s195.11 199.29 53.14 65.23 67.16 197.23
subjectis/subjects207.29 187.22 55.29 57.21 57.25 57.32 59.20 69.28
world31.12 33.15 35.17 49.23 51.26

value: "wanting-to-be [ruled]"

commitment45.24 63.25 63.26 65.26
civility71.14 173.23 71.17 71.25
conscience31.33 41.30 43.23 43.28 45.23 45.25 51.12
   obedience5.3 65.14
   patience/patient41.23 203.18 183.22 41.17
[trouble41.24 41.27 71.30 195.20]

FURTHER, LOWER ORDER FIGURATIVIZATIONS

Of the ruler

heart203.21 37.12 51.14 179.11 55.28

inwardness163.16 165.13 201.30 63.19 51.21

mind181.10 183.14 185.20 191.28

    thought69.14 177.11 183.17

own(adj.)181.27 187.17 187.21 199.29 203.16 205.10 205.29 207.19 25.10 31.28 45.20 47.30
    49.12 49.14 53.14 65.23 67.27 69.21

secret171.17 177.29 51.20 171.19

    obscurity183.16 193.18 193.21

    private57.14 167.10 183.23

self35.25 37.17 45.20 65.24 67.8

Of ruling

*artes/artifex/*artifice207.27 199.9 179.26 167.31

craft185.18 189.17 199.14 207.19

[natural177.18 55.25 167.26 177.16]

clothes/clothe175.11 175.27 177.12 177.14 177.19] (contains sememes of both revealing
    and concealing)

    raiment171.30 171.32

fashion169.16 175.13 179.17 181.19

gesture165.17 179.21 179.25 181.16 163.11

playing195.21 195.23 195.24 195.26 195.30 193.29 195.29

reasoning/reason183.22 183.24 199.20 183.19

revelation/reveal47.23 31.30 37.21 49.14

    mirror27.32 35.25

truth163.17 193.21 47.21 69.13

publicness/publish165.30 199.26 165.26 167.11 185.27

writer/writing185.29 191.10 183.31 185.25

    example/exemplary205.26 39.19 53.15 53.20 27.21

    precepts35.15 205.25

    language179.21 181.32 187.17 201.14 187.19

poem/poet187.16 207.21 53.18 187.14 35.17

prose185.13 185.24 187.13 187.16

word29.8 33.14 43.34 49.18 49.28 49.31 187.12 51.16

sentence183.26 203.20 179.29

speech179.21 183.16 185.10

Of the ruled subject/citizen

neighbor31.14 31.26 57.21 57.33

eye27.13 177.32 179.24 203.16 67.28

    looking43.19 181.16 203.17

hearing/hear41.19 203.11 203.18 29.2

knowledge/know37.20 29.7 41.31 47.34 49.13

    [uncouth57.17 181.18 185.26]

V. Two Sample Seme/Sememe Structurations of the Above Groupings

kernel semes/sememes:	*classemes attached to them:*

A. for "*ruler*"

dominator of [=sender of narrative Program to]	humanness (not animality) maleness (not femaleness) euphoria (not dysphoria)

humans
  individual
  familial
  factional
	maleness (not femaleness)

possessor of	maleness (not femaleness)

legitimacy [=sending of narr. Program of
              "wanting-to-be [ruled]"
  enforcement [=sending of narr. P. of
            "having to do"]	

B. for "**ruling**"

putting into effect [="realizing" modality] of domination of	

humans
  individual
  familial
  factional
	maleness (not femaleness)

possession of
  legitimacy
  enforcement	

VI. Identification of Base Narrative Program, with two Figurativizations: U = disjoined from

God	begets [RULES]	Christ	U	Christian having/wanting- to-be [ruled]
RULER	EFFECTS DOMINATION OF	RULER IMAGE	U	CITIZEN HAVING/ WANTING, ETC.
S_1 --------------------------------→		S_2	U	O ᵥ
king	writes/stages	prince	U	people (valorized by alethic/ bulestic modalities)
self/private	writes/stages	self/public	U	other

APPENDIX 2

Further Poems by Women Discussed Above

1. By the Cooke Sisters

A. By Elizabeth Cooke, Lady Hoby/Lady Russell: Verse on the Hoby Tombs at Bisham (from Ashmole, II)

Two worthy Knights, and HOBY'S both by Name
Inclosed within this Marble Stone doth rest;
PHILIP, the first, in Caesars Court hath Fame,
Such as, tofore few Legatts like possessed.
A deepe discovering Head, a noble Brest,
A Courtier passing, and a courteous Knight,
Zealous to God, whose Gospell he profest,
When greatest Stormes gan dym the sacred Light.
A happy Man, whome Death hath now redeem'd
From Care to Joy, that cannot be esteem'd.
THOMAS in France possessed the Legats Place,
And with such Wisdom grew to guide the same;
As had encreas'd great Honour to his Race,
If suddaine Fate had not envied his Fame,
Firme in Gods Truth, gentle and faithfull Friend,
Well learned and languaged, Nature beside,
Gave comely Shape, which made rufull his end,
Since in his Flower in Paris Towne he died,
Leaving with Child behind his wofull Wife,
In Forraine Land opprest with heapes of Grief,
From parte of which, when she discharged was
By fall of Teares, that faithfull Wives do shed;
The Corps, with Honour, brought she to this Place,
Performing here all due unto the dead,
That done, this noble Tombe she caused to make,

And both these Brethren closed within the same;
A Memory left here for Vertues sake,
In spight of Death to honour them with Fame.
Thus live they dead, and we learn well thereby,
That yee, and wee, and all the World must dye.

ELIZABETHA HOBAEA conjux, ad THOMAM HOBAEUM,
Equitem Maritum

O dulcis conjux, animae pars maxima nostrae,
   Cujus erat vitae, vita medulla meae.
Cur ita conjunctos divellunt invida fata?
   Cur ego sum viduo sola relicta thoro?
Anglia faelices, faelices *Gallia* vidit,
   Per mare, per terras noster abivit amor,
Par fortunatum fuimus dum viximus una,
   Corpus erat duplex, spiritus unus erat.
Sed nihil in terris durat charissime conjux,
   Tu mihi, tu testis flebilis esse potes.
Dum patriae servis, dum publica commoda tractas,
   Occidis, ignota triste cadaver humo.
Et miseri nati flammis febrilibus ardent.
   Quid facerem tantis, heu mihi mersa malis!
Infaelix conjux, infaelix mater oberro,
   Te vir adempte fleo, vos mea membra fleo.
Exeo funestis terris, hic rapta cadaver
   Conjugis, hinc prolis languida membra traho.
Sic uterum gestans, redeo terraque Marique
   In patriam luctu perdita, mortis amans.
Chare mihi conjux, et praestantissime *Thoma*,
   Cujus erat rectum, et nobile quicquid erat.
Elizabetha, tibi quondam gratissima sponsa,
   Haec lacrymis refert verba referta piis.
Non potui prohibere mori, sed mortua membra,
   Quo potero, faciam semper honore coli.
Te Deus, aut similem Thomae mihi redde maritum,
   Aut reddant Thomae me mea fata viro.

   [Elizabeth Hoby, wife, to Thomas Hoby Knight, her husband
   Sweet husband, greatest part of our one soul,
      The life of whom was the marrow of my life,
   Why do envious fates divide those once united?
      Why am I left alone to a widow's bed?

England saw us happy, *France* saw us happy,
    Through sea and lands our love has passed,
Equally blessed we were as we lived together,
    The body was twofold, the spirit one.
But dearest husband, nothing on earth endures,
    As you can be sad witness, you for me.
While you serve your country, public affairs in hand,
    You have died, a sad corpse in an unknown land.
And the piteous children burn with feverish flames.
    What shall I do, ay me, immersed in such misfortune!
I wander about a hapless wife, a hapless mother,
    I weep for you, my own body, husband seized from me.
Plundered as here I've been, I leave these funereal lands,
    I take my husband's corpse and children's feeble limbs.
And so with filling womb I return by land and sea
    To our homeland, lost in sorrow, loving death.
Husband dear to me, most excellent THOMAS,
    In whom was right and noble all that was:
ELIZABETH, a wife most pleasing once to you,
    Declaims these words replete with pious tears.
I could not keep off death, but this body of death
    So well as I can, I'll always hold in honor.
O Lord, grant me a husband much like THOMAS
    Or let my fates return me to my THOMAS.]

ELIZABETHA HOBAEA, soror ad PHILIPPUM HOBAEUM,
Equitem fratrem.

Tuque tuae stirpis non gloria parva *Philippe*,
    Cujus erat virtus maxima nota soris.
Itala quem tellus norat, *Germania* norat,
    Qui patriae tuleras commoda magna tuae,
Tuque meo *Thoma* frater dignissime fratre,
    Mens quibus una fuit, sensus et unus erat.
Tu michi, tu *Thomam* voluisti jungere fratrem,
    Judicioque tuo sum tibi facta soror.
Sic ego conjugium, sic omnem debea prolem,
    Cuncta mihi dederas, haec tribuendo duo.
Reddere quid possum, suspiria vana recusas,
    Praeteritoque malo sera querela venit.
Faelices animae caeli vos regia caepit,
    Mortua nunc capiet corpora funus idem.

Et soror et conjux vobis commune sepulchrum,
　　Et michi composui, cum mea fata ferent.
Quod licuit feci, vellem michi plura licere,
　　Sed tamen officiis quaeso faveto piis.
Jamque vale conjunx, semper mea maxima cura;
　　Tuque *Philippe*, michi cura secunda, vale.
Non ero vobiscum, donec mea fata vocabunt,
　　Tunc cineres vestros consociabo meis.
Sic, o sic junctos melius nos busta tenebunt,
　　Quem mea me solum tristia tecta tenent.

[ELIZABETH HOBY, sister, to PHILIP HOBY Knight, brother

No little glory have you and your family, PHILIP,
　　Whose virtue was especially known abroad.
Whom the land of ITALY and GERMANY both knew,
　　Who for your homeland did important service,
You, brother to my THOMAS, most worthy brother,
　　Between whom there was one mind, one understanding.
It was you, you wanted your brother THOMAS to marry me,
　　Through your judgment I have been to you a sister.
Thus to you I owe my husband, thus I owe each child,
　　You had given me all of these in tribute.
The thanks that I can speak you brush off as empty breath
　　And now that ill luck has happened, complaint comes late.
The kingdom of heaven has received you both, happy of soul,
　　And now the same burial will receive your bodies.
Both sister and wife, I have planned one tomb for you
　　In common—and for me, when my fates strike.
I have done what was allowed, I wish more were allowed me,
　　But still in holy rites I pray that it be blessed.
And husband, now goodbye, always my greatest care;
　　And you, PHILIP, for me a second care, goodbye.
I shall not be with you until my fates call,
　　Then I'll join your ashes with my own.
Thus, O better thus the tomb will hold us joined
　　Than my sad house will hold me now alone.]

μὴ δάκρυσιν κοσμεῖ, μὴ κλαυμασιν* ἔνθα*
　　βιασμὸν* ποιεῖ εἶμι ἐαρίζουσα* δι' ἄστρα θεῷ

---

*[Translator's note: This text, from Ashmole's *Antiquities of Berkshire*, contains four
nonexistent words: I have read κλαυθμασιν as κλαύμασιν; ἔντα as ἔνθα; φιασμον as
βιασμὸν; and ἐάρζω as ἐαρίζω.]

[Do not adorn [this] with tears, do not perform violence there
with weeping. I go like spring, through the stars to God.]

Nemo me lacrimis decoret, neque funera fletu faxit cur? vado per astra Deo.

[Let no one honor me with tears, nor should a funeral be held
with mourning—why? I go through the stars to God.]

ELIZABETHAE HOBEAE, Matris, in obitum duarum filiarum
ELIZABETHAE, et ANNAE, Epicedium.

ELIZABETHA jacet, (eheu mea viscera) fato
  Vix dum maturo, vigo tenella jaces.
Chara michi quondam vixisti filia matri,
  Chara Deo posthac filia vive patri,
Mors tua crudelis, multo crudelius illud,
  Quod cecidit tecum junior ANNA soror.
ANNA patris matrisque decus, post fata sororis,
  Post matris luctus, aurea virgo jaces!
Una parens, pater unus erat, mors una duabus,
  Et lapis hic unus corpora bina tegit.
Sic volui mater tumulo sociarier uno,
  Una quas utero laeta genensque tuli.
                    Istae duae generosae, optimaeque spei
                           sorores, eodem Anno viz. 1570.
                    Eodemque Mense, viz. Februario,
                           paucorum dierum spatio
                           interjecto, in Domino
                                  obdormiverunt.

[An Epicedion by Elizabeth Hoby, mother, on the death of her two
daughters ELIZABETH and ANNE

        ELIZABETH lies here (oh my visceral pangs), by fate
          You lie here, delicate maiden, scarcely grown.
        Dear to me you lived once, a daughter of your mother,
          Now live dear to God, a daughter of your father.
        Your death was cruel, a crueler one
          Because your younger sister ANNE died with you.
        ANNE, glory of your father and mother, after your sister's fate,
          After your mother's tears, golden maiden, here you lie.
        There was one mother, one father, one death for two,
          And here a single stone conceals two bodies.
        Together in one tomb, thus I your mother wanted you,
          Whom I, with joy and crying, carried in one womb.

> These two noble sisters,
> the best of hope, having died
> in the same year, 1570,
> and the same month, February,
> in the space of a few days,
> have fallen asleep in the Lord.]

B. On the tomb of Katherine Killegrew (Ballard 204–205), by Elizabeth, Lady Hoby/Lady Russell

Elizabethae in Obitum Katharinae Sororis Epicaedia

Εὐσεβίης διδαχῆς κομψείας σεμνὸν ἄγαλμα
    Μειλιχιοῦ τε τρόπου νήλει πίπτε μορῷ
Ἧς Καθαρίνα γλυχεία διχοτμηθεῖσα ἀδελφῆς
    Ἀρμονιὴν αὐλῇ νῦν ποθέουσα πόλου.

Chara valeto Soror, in Coelo morte triumphas,
Mors tua vita tibi, mors tamen illa tuis.
Mens tua labe carens, pietas, doctrina, modesta
Vita, lepos suavis digna fuere Deo.
Ut junxit Sanguis, nos jungat in aethere Christus:
Interea taceo mortua morte tua.

> [Epicedia of Elizabeth on the death of her sister Katherine
>
> The holy image of piety, learning, elegance,
>   And a gracious manner, she falls to pitiless fate,
> Sweet Katherine, cut off from her sister, now in the court
>   Of the heavens ardently desires harmony.
>
> Goodbye, beloved Sister, in death you reign in heaven,
> Your death is life for you, though death to your loved ones.
> Your unstained mind, your pious, learned, modest
> Life and sweet grace have made you worthy of God.
> As kinship has joined us, in heaven may Christ unite us:
> Meanwhile I am silent, dead in your death.]

C. From the tomb of Thomas Noke, Esq., d. 1567 (Ballard 491), by Elizabeth, Lady Hoby

> O multum dilecte senex, pater atque vocatus,
>   Vel quia grandevus, vel quia probus eras.

Annos vixisti novies decem, atque satelles
   Fidus eras Regum, fidus erasque tuis.
Iam fatis functus valeas, sed tu Deus alme
   Sic mihi concedas vivere, sicque mori.

   [O greatly honored elder, called father too
      Because you were aged or because you were upright,
   You lived for ninety years and were an attendant
      Faithful to the King, and faithful to yourself.
   Now the fates having acted, farewell; but kindly God,
      Allow me thus to live, and thus may I die.]

D. From the tomb of Sir Anthony Cooke at Rumford, probably by one of the Cooke sisters: (from John Strype, *Annals of the Reformation*)

An epitaph upon the death of the right worshipful sir Anthony Cook, knt. who dyed the 11th day of June, 1576

You learned men, and such as learning love,
Vouchsafe to read this rude unlearned verse.
For stones are doombe, and yet for man's behove
God lends them tongues sometimes for to reherse
Such words of worth as worthiest wights may pierce.
Yea, stones sometimes, when bloud and bones be rot,
Do blaze the bruit, which else might be forgot.
And in that heap of carved stones do ly
A worthy knight, whose life in learning led,
Did make his name to mount above the sky.
With sacred skill unto a king he read;
Whose toward youth his famous praises spred.
And he therefore to courtly life was call'd,
Who more desir'd in study to be stall'd.
Philosophy had taught his learned mind
To stand content with country quiet life:
Wherein he dwelt as one that was assign'd
To guard the same from sundry stormes of strife.
And, but when persecuting rage was rife,
His helping hand did never fail to stay
His countries staff, but held it up alway.
Nor high avaunce, nor office of availe,
Could tempt his thoughts to row beyond his reach.

By broont of books he only did assaile
The fort of fame, whereto he made his breach,
With fire of truth which God's good word doth teach.
The wealth he won was due for his degree,
He neither rose by rich reward nor fee.
And yet although he bare his sail so high,
The gale of grace did spred his course so fast,
That in his life he did right well bestow
His children all before their prime was past.
And like them so that they be like to last.
What should I say but only this in sum,
Beatus sic qui timet Dominum.
Their only skill to learning bears the bell,
And of that skill I taught poor stones to treat;
That such as would to use their learning well,
Might read these lines, and therewith oft repeat,
How here on earth his gift from God is great,
Which can employ his learning to the best.

2. By Elizabeth Weston, from *Parthenicon* (1607)

Aesopic Fables

De pulice & Milite

Pulicis interdum est audacia magna pusilli:
  Aevo si veteri sit tribuenda fides.
Fama refert, illum pulsa formidine, quondam
  Saltibus intrepidis insilluisse pedi
Militis eximii, multorum caede cruenti;
  Quem voluit stimulis exagitare suis.
Vnde etiam hic tremulo gemibundus pectore, Numen
  Herculeum vota flebiliore vocat:
Suppetias misero ut veniat; viresve ministret,
  Aut acres morsus, saevitiemque domit.
Negliget Alcides nequicquam vota ferentem,
  Ridiculis renuens edere rebus opem.
Jamque adeo observans nullam restare salutem
  Haesitat, ambiguus mentis, opisque carens.
Dum tandem adductus pulex maercre precantis
  Aufugit, atque alium quaerit in aede locum.
Haec ubi facta: imo suspiria pectore ducens
  Miles iners, tremula talia voce refert:

Tu qui pugnaci virtute domare rebelles,
　　Imbellesque soles fuste juvare viros:
Si contra exiguum non fortius iveris hostem,
　　Quid sperem, si me nunc graviora gravent?

(II, B7ᵥ)

[Of the flea and the Soldier.

A tiny flea's audacity is sometimes great,
　　If faith be granted to an ancient time:
Rumor reports that once a flea, all fear forgot,
　　With intrepid leaps sprang upon the foot
Of a worthy soldier, bloodied from the slaughter of many,
　　Whom the flea wished to torture with its stings.
Wherefore the soldier, groaning from trembling breast,
　　In quite tearful prayer calls to the god Hercules:
"O that he might come with aid for the wretched; or give
　　Strength; or subdue the stinging bites and cruelty."
Hercules ignores the soldier offering prayers in vain,
　　Declining to give aid for silly matters.
And seeing now indeed no safety can be found,
　　He pauses, ambiguous in mind, and lacking help.
Then finally the flea, stirred by the suppliant's cries,
　　Fled and sought another place in the house.
When this was done, drawing sighs from deep in his breast,
　　The simple soldier says with trembling voice:
"You who are used to taming rebels with fighting virtue,
　　And helping peaceful people with your club:
If you would not fight a tiny foe more stoutly,
　　What can I now hope if something graver threatens?"]

Leo ac Rana

Vox Ranae fuerat delapsa Leonis ad aures,
　　Ranae, quae in pigro garrit inepta lacu.
Ille diu attonitus, nescit quae bestia rauco
　　Quodve animal tantos evomat ore sonos.
Exserit at tandem faucem ambitiosa loquacem;
　　Saltat, & in sicco voce coaxat agro.
Quam Leo cum voltu spectarat forte superbo,
　　Advolat & querulam protoenus ungue terit.

(II, B6)

[The Lion and the Frog

> The voice of a frog had fallen upon a Lion's ears,
>> A frog absurdly chattering in a dull lake.
> A while amazed, the lion did not know what beast,
>> What animal from raucous mouth spewed out such sounds.
> Ambitiously the frog now swells its prattling throat;
>> It leaps onto dry land and sounds its croaks.
> The lion, when by chance he saw the haughty creature,
>> Pounces, and with one claw its querulous noise he ends.]

Occasion Poems

Ad Eundem [i.e. Nicolaum Majum, Sac. Caes. Mtis in Regia Appellationum Curia, Consiliarium ac tum Supr. vallis Ioachimicae Praefectum; amicum sibi patris instar colendum] Cum periculoso Pragae affligeretur morbo.

> Non equidem immerito miraris candide Maje,
>> Et mea jure tuo Musa vocatur iners,
> Quod raro calamos tractet quod tempore tanto
>> Torpeat; & scribat carmina nulla tibi.
> Non torpore tamen, sed moestis anxia, curis
>> Illa latet; gemitu semisepulta suo.
> Aspice cum lumen Phoebi sit nube subactum,
>> Quam tristem tellus exhibeat faciem?
> Quum Regni Rector satis agitatur iniquis,
>> Quam torquet populos anxia cura leves!
> Quando tremiscentem sors desperata senatum
>> Angit, quae cives solicitudo premit?
> Quis vetet Aonias Phoebo lugento sorores
>> Suspenses Cytharis squallidiora sequi?
> Cum mihi sis Phoebus, dic cum te dira fatiget
>> Febris, & hac Stygiae torreat umbra Deae;
> Num tua suaviloquas spirabunt pectora Musas?
>> Num poteris numeris applicuisse fides?
> Magnum opus, & labor est; nec curant maesta Camena:
>> Nec luctu raptos dia poesis amat.
> Carmina tranquillo scribentem pectore quaerunt:
>> At vere lyricum neglegit ager opus.
> Hac mihi causa fuit, Musis haec causa regoris:
>> Hac vivam amota, vivet & ipsa chelys.
> Tum demum calamos teretes, plectrumque reposcam:
>> Gaudiaque erepto laeta dolore canam.

Salve, vive, vale, plures viridissime in annos
  Maje; petas sero CANDIDUS astra senex.

(I, B4)

[For the same man (i.e. Nicolaus May, named to the Sacred Emperor's Majesty's royal court, Counselor, and Chief Prefect of Joachimsthal; noble friend to her as to her father) when he was afflicted with a dangerous illness in Prague.

Not without cause indeed you wonder, eminent May,
  And call my Muse with right inert
Because she rarely uses her quill, when at such a time
  She should be working and should write poems for you.
Nonetheless, she is languid not from torpor but from gloomy
  Anxious cares; she is half buried in her grief.
Do you see when Phoebus' light is blocked by clouds
  How sad a face the earth displays?
Or when the Ruler of the Realm is quite engaged with foes,
  How anxious fear torments the unsteady people?
When desperate chance affrights the trembling senate,
  What extra care afflicts the citizens?
With Phoebus mourning, who forbids the Aonian sisters
  With their lyres to follow gloomier matters languidly?
Since you are Phoebus to me, speak, although dire fever
  Wearies, and shade of the Stygian goddess parches you;
Will not your breast inspire sweet-speaking Muses?
  Can you not apply the meters to the lyre?
Great is the work and labor; nor does a sad Muse care for,
  Nor poetry long love, one seized with sorrow.
Poems seek out a writer with tranquil heart:
  And surely those depressed neglect the lyric task.
This was the cause for me, this the reason for numbness in my Muses.
  But when this has been removed, both I and my lyre will live.
Then I'll take up the polished quill and plectrum
  And with sadness left behind I'll happily sing of joy.
Hail, live, be strong for many years, most vigorous May;
  May you as a SEASONED elder late seek the stars.]

Virgini Nobili, Margarethae Baldhoveniae, B. Martin a Baldhoven &c: Senioris. filiae svaviss. novae nuptae.

Margari, quae monitu Fratris tibi carmina promam?
  In thalamumque tuum vota precesque feram?

Non alia, ac ipsi mihi quondam Sponsa rogarem;
    A Phoebo & Musis, vota precesque dabo.
Auspiciis ineas igitur sacra foedera laetis:
    Et sponsum vere, quo redameris, ames.
Omnibus officiis illum lenire memento;
    Si vitare velis jurgia crebratori.
Est mandare viri, nostrum esse parere: maritus
    Est caput, ac ipsi mutua membra sumus.
Vt caput est Christus sancti (sancta UNIO!) coetus,
    Sic sponsum sponsae fas caput esse suae.
Tu sis gemma viro preciosa: quod omine nomen
    Ipsum MARGARIDOS prosperiore natat.
Sit pietas rectrix morum vitaeque: sine illa
    Vix formosa suo est sponsa futura viro.
Margaris artificis digitis quae includitur auro,
    Gestanti semper gratior esse solet.
Sic ubi virgineos moros, vitamque gubernant
    Et pudor & pietas, gratia major inest.
Est species fallax, ac ornamenta caduci
    Corporis: hei! subito, ceu levis umbra, cadunt.
Sola manet nobis virtutis fama superstes:
    Haec sponsos ornet dos pretiosa satis.
Sed quid opus monitis: ignosce, PUELLA, puellae,
    Quae restant thalamo, caetera dicet amor!
Vive-vale: sponsoque tuo sis gemma: vicissim
    Iste tibi firmam praestet amore fidem.
Sint procul a vobis rixae: concordia lectum
    Servet: & amborum sint rata vota, precor.

                                    (I, C7)

[For a noble maiden Margaret Baldhoven, gentle daughter of Bernhard
Martin von Baldhoven the Elder, a new bride.

    What poems shall I sing you, MARGARET, as fraternal counsel?
        Shall I bring votive prayers to your wedding chamber?
    None but the very ones for me, if ever I were a bride:
        From Apollo and the Muses I'll give votive prayers.
    With happy auspices, then, may you enter holy bonds:
        May you truly love your husband and he love you.
    Remember in every duty to accommodate him
        If in the marriage bed you want no strife.
    It is for the man to order, for us to obey: he
        Is the head, and we his conjoint members;

As Christ is head of the blessed oneness (holy UNION!)
　　So is by right a husband head of his wife.
To your husband may you be that precious gem
　　That your name, MARGARET, propitiously denotes.
Let piety be mistress of your character and life;
　　Without her, scarcely can you be a lovely bride.
As a pearl surrounded by gold, set in a ring,
　　Is always more pleasing to the wearer,
So when reserve and piety frame a woman's character
　　And life, it also is more pleasing.
There is deceit in looks and outer beauties of a frail
　　Body; alas, suddenly as empty shadows they fade.
Only the lasting name of virtue will survive for us:
　　This precious dowry will adorn your spouse.
But do you need such admonition: GIRL, forgive a girl,
　　To your marriage love will speak more words that last.
Live and be strong: be a gem for your husband; in turn
　　May he give strong faith in love to you.
May strife be far away; may concord rule the marriage,
　　And may you both find answers to your prayers, I pray.]

Ad eundem (i.e., Ioanni Leoni pro carminum Natalitiorum editione).

　　Quid tibi pro donis, LEO concelebrande, refundam?
　　　Vincula quove mihi sunt soluenda modo?
　　Nil superesse reor, digne quo munera pensem;
　　　Nexibus & dicar jure soluta tuis
　　Sed restat, quod spero, dies; qua Numine dextro
　　　Pro meritis potero par retulisse tuis.
　　Temporis interea quidni tibi vincta manerem?
　　　Sic tamen ut doctos, Jane, revincit amor.

　　　　　　　　　　　　　　(I, C4ᵥ)

[To the same man (i.e., Johann Leo, for the editing of her Christmas poems).

　　What gift shall I give you, celebrated LEO,
　　　Or how must I dissolve these obligations?
　　I think no gift can worthily repay you.
　　　By law indeed I'm said to owe no debt to you,
　　And yet I hope for the day, God willing, when
　　　I can indeed compensate your merits.
　　Meanwhile, how long shall I stay bound to you?
　　　So it is, Johann, that love rebinds the learned.]

Patronage Poems

Illustrissimo Principi, & Dno, Dno Petro Wock a Rosenberg &c. Dno ac
Mecaenati suo gratiosissimo.

Inter minora sidera
Qualis refulget Cynthia,
Quum nox lacessit horridum
Morphei redux insomnium:
> Talis Dynastas emicas
> Inter, jubar late explicas
> Virtute, PRINCEPS inclute,
> O PETRE flos virens Rosae!

Sacri efficace Numinis
Ardes amore; literis
Clemens faves: patronus eo
Egentium inter divites.
> Te liberalem in hospites
> Cum fratre jure dicerem:
> Meo Parenti indulseras
> Possessiones liberas;

Quas LIVOR immerentibus
Rabidis refrendens dentibus,
(o fata) tollens, pauperes
Coegit esse flebiles.
> In rebus his est innocens
> CAESAR: malus nocet, docens
> Nostri fame aeris. Numinis
> Vindicta summi noveris!

Sed cum modo, Illustrissime
Princeps, referri commodae
Pro liberali pectore
Sat vix queant tibi gratiae:
> Cum matre id unicum precor,
> Vt exigas nostri memor
> Annos tuos; sed suaviter,
> Vivas DEO, prece gnaviter.

Ut hoc solutus corpore,
Pertaesus hujus seculi,
Durante laudis adorea,
Petas beatus sidera.

(I, A3ᵥ)

[To the most illustrious Prince and Lord, Lord Peter Wock von Rosenberg, etc. Most gracious Lord and Maecenas

> Just as Cynthia shines
> Among the lesser stars
> When night returned provokes
> The horrid dreams of Morpheus,
>> So among unfriendly rulers far
>> And wide you give radiance
>> With glorious virtue, Prince,
>> Peter, thriving bloom of the Rose.
> Consumed with powerful love
> Of the Holy Spirit, you generously
> Favor letters: among the rich you are
> A patron of the needy.
>> As to a brother I'd say you
>> Are liberal to strangers;
>> To my father you grant
>> Generous possessions,
> Which ENVY unjustly taking,
> Gnashing with rabid
> Teeth (O fates), it leaves behind
> Lamenting paupers.
>> The emperor is innocent in these things:
>> Misfortune harms, teaching
>> By the dearth of our estate. See the
>> Blows of the high gods!
> But recently, most illustrious
> Prince, when for your generous
> Heart I could scarcely
> Give you thanks,
>> One thing my mother and I
>> Have prayed: That mindful of us
>> You pleasantly live out your years
>> With God, in faithful prayer;
> That freed of this body
> Wearied with this age,
> In the glory of lasting praise
> Blessed, you may seek the stars.]

Nobili & clarissimo Viro G. Martin a Baldhoven, Silesio &c. amico suo
singulari.

Ecquis ad officium Musas revocabit inertes,
    Compositaeque melos addet Apollo lyrae?
Ut tibi promeritas dicam modulamine grates;
    Et tribuam Musis praemia digna tuis.
Ausus es altisono me vatem dicere cantu:
    Et Parnassiacis associare choris!
Me celebras equidem, propria sed laude coruscas
    Ipse magis, fidibus dignior ipse cani.
Nam, qui sis, produnt tua te mihi carmina: legi,
    Et flexere animum, ceu volvere, meum.
Res & verba fluunt leni tibi tramite; possis
    Nasonem numeris ut superare tuis.
At mihi, vix primis quae libo puella labellis
    Aonidum fontes, non ea vena salit.
Nec fortuna favet, nec restant ocia Musis,
    Quae fuerant quondam liberiora, meis.
Ergo quod in versu vel pecco, vel ordine currunt
    Singula confuso, dic age; Virgo dedit.
Tempus erit, quo me speculabitur aethere Phoebus,
    Et curas perimet: tunc meliora dabo.
Interea tibi fata precor felicia: teque
    WESTONIAE ut pergas usque favere, rogo.

                                              (I, C5)

[To a noble and most eminent man, G. Martin von Baldhoven, Silesian &c.,
her singular friend.

Will someone recall to duty inert Muses,
    Will Apollo add a tune to the well-made lyre?
That I may sing you measures of thanks deserved,
    And pay your Muses as tribute a worthy prize.
You dared to call me prophet of high-resounding song
    And join me with the chorus of Parnassus.
You honor me indeed, but lift me up with due acclaim;
    You yourself are worthier to be sung with the lyre.
For who you are your poems make known to me: I've read,
    And they flexed, or rather turned my soul.
Things and words in easy motion flow for you,
    You could conquer Naso with your measures.
But for me, a girl who scarce with untried lips tastes
    Aonian springs, such power does not flow.

And fortune shows no favor, nor are the swifter,
 Freer things still there for my Muses.
Thus if I in verse somehow offend, or if all runs
 In garbled order, then say: a maiden has offered it.
A time will be when Phoebus from above will watch me,
 And take away my cares: then better things I'll offer.
Meanwhile for you I pray a happy fate,
 And ask you always still to favor WESTON.]

Epigrams

Amor insipiens.

 Et sapere, et stolidi sensisse pericula amoris,
  Vix est concessum, qui parit illa, DEO.

[Befuddling Love

  To have known the risks of foolish love and to be wise
  Is scarcely granted even to God, who begets them.]

Idem.

 Et malesana Venus, rerum et sapientia victrix
  Vix in divino pectore conveniunt.
 Est in amore furor, qui lumina mentis obumbrat;
  Qui facit et summos desipuisse viros.

[On the Same

  Love-crazed Venus and Wisdom, conqueress of all things,
   Can scarcely coinhabit the divine breast.
  In love is a madness that clouds the mind's lights,
   Which has made the greatest men be fondly foolish.]

Idem.

 Novit amans amens cupidis quid mens sua votis
  Optet: quid sapiat, non videt ullus amans.

[On the Same

  A mindless lover knows what his mind would seek
   With passionate pleas; what is wise no lover sees.]

Amor faemineus.

 Faemina quando palam nullo vel amine peccat,
  Apta magis socio dicitur esse viro.

Vitare aut poterit deprendere aperta maritus:
  Certaque praevisi damna cavere mali.

[Feminine Love

  When a woman sins without concealment, openly,
    She's said to be just right for a sociable man.
  The husband can ignore the act or catch her at it,
    Can guard against the sure loss of a known misfortune.]

Aliud.

  Aut amat, aut odit mulier; non tertia vis est
    Ulla: sed haec magni criminis auda putes.

[Another

  A woman either loves or hates; there's no third action:
    But you would think these ventures were great crimes.]

Amor suspicax.

  Plurima laesus amor falso sibi nomine fingit:
    Nam cui caecus amor, Dux quoque caecus orit.

[Suspicious Love

  Many things can cheated love pretend to itself through false names:
    For a guide whose love is blind will also be blind.]

Idem.

  Stertenti ut subolet, vigilans quoque somniat idem;
    Mollia cui blandus pectora mulcet amor.

[On the same

  As she listens to the snorer, the wakeful one will also dream;
    For her a flattering love soothes her gentle breast.]

Amoris offensi redintegratio.

  Gratia in ingratas si quando dissilit iras;
    Cura has obsequiis debilitare tuis.
  Adde preces; precium, ni sufficit, adde vel imas
    Immitem quae animum mitificent lacrymas.

[Love with Repeated Offense

  If pleasantness should dissolve in unpleasant rages,
    Take care to stop their force with your submission.

Add prayers, gifts, if that does not suffice then
　　Deep-drawn tears, which soften the unsoft mind.]

Vel.

　Si cupis iratum compescere rursus amantem,
　　Iracunda tuis corda riga lacrymis.

[Or again

　If you want to restrain an angry lover,
　　Sprinkle his heart with your anger-drawn tears.]

Sola diuturnitas amoris victrix.

　Non potis est Cyprias abolere potentia flammas;
　　Longa tamen poterit quas hebetare dies.

[Time the only Conqueress of Love

　No power will have the power to abolish Cyprian flames,
　　Which a long day, however, will have power to destroy.]

Idem.

　Spernit flamma minas: sed caedere cogitur aevo:
　　Major et est magna vi revoluta dies.

[On the same

　Passion disdains threats, but by time is made to die down:
　　Greater, and of great force, is the passing day.]

Remedium amoris.

　Qui rapidos animis flagrantibus incutit ignes;
　　Dum modo vult, idem hos extenuare potest.

[A Remedy for love

　Whoever stokes the rapid flames with fiery spirit,
　　If only he wishes can likewise dampen them.]

Sacred Poems

DOMINICA LAZARI jacentis ante fores divitis.

　O aeterne DEUS mirandi rector Olympi,
　　Qui subjecta cupis nos tua membra cruci;
　Ah turbae miserere tuae, quae spretae Potentum,
　　Te patiente, Ducum nunc jacet ante fores.

Tu Samaritanus mihi sis; mea vulnera succis
  Vnge; saluti feram ferque misertus opem.
Et quia principium vitae caelestis in ista
  Firmare innocuos per mala mille jubes;
Da benefactores, qui saucia vulnera lingant;
  Qui nos officiis, qui pietate juvent.
Durima flecte etiam variorum corda Midarum,
  Queis sunt Divitiae spesque, fidesque, suae.
Vt loca, quae torquent animos, meditentur: ibidem
  Ne cum damnato Divite sorte luant.
Da revocati ineant aevi melioris ut annos;
  Et verbi capiant jussa verenda tui.

(II, A5)

[THE LADY LAZARUS lying at the gates of wealthy Dives.

  O God eternal, ruler of marvellous Olympus,
      Who want us to pity your body shown on the cross,
  Ah, pity your people, who now lie scorned
      At the doors of mighty rulers, while you are patient.
  Be for me a Samaritan, anoint my wounds
      With salve; pitying, bring me saving help.
  And since therein is the start of heavenly life,
      You bid the innocent stand firm through countless evils;
  Grant us benefactors who lick the open wounds,
      Who in their duties, in their piety help us.
  Bend the hardest hearts of even those Midases
      For whom their riches are their hope and faith,
  That they recall the places that torture souls; further,
      That they not suffer pains for harmful wealth.
  Let those, reformed, enter the years of a better age
      And heed the honored bidding of your word.]

Mortem non gustabunt

  Non fratres inter tantus fuit ardor amantes,
      Quos decepta tulit Laeda furore Jovis:
  Quanto hominum mitis flagrabat amore Redemptor,
      Qui DEUS, & puro corpore purus homo est.
  Mutat enim Pollux charo cum Castore vitam
      Fratre suam; certa conditione tamen.
  Alter ut alterius moriatur origine vitae:
      Dumque hic surgite quis, ille feratur aquis.

At vitam, alterius Christus sine morte perennem
    Obtinet, Electis & dat habere suis.
Vivus ovat; non te mors illius ergo fefellit:
    Ne pereas, sed eas per supera, ille perit.
Omnia qui te eum victurus secula, solus
    Expertem stygiae te facit esse plagae.

                     (II, A6)

["They shall not taste death"

    No such ardor was between the loving brothers
        Whom Leda bore, deceived by Jove's great passion,
    As that of the kind Redeemer, afire with love of mankind,
        Who is pure God and fully man in a pure body.
    For Pollux exchanged his life for Castor,
        His dear brother, but with a fixed condition:
    That one would die when the other's life began,
        That while one rose from the waters, the other would fall.
    But Christ obtained for others endless life without
        Death, to give this life to his Elect.
    Let the living rejoice. His death has not destroyed you;
        He died that you not die, but go to heaven.
    He alone, who will with you the ages overcome,
        Saves you from the Stygian pit.]

Dissolvi cupio.

    Quid mea mendosae laceratis pectora curae?
        Praevaleat stimulis nil caro blanda suis.
    Nil sapiat, stupidi quod amat dementia vulgi,
        Et falso summum quod putat esse bonum.
    Dissolvi cupio vitae melioris amore:
        Nam bene velle sat est, & potuisse mori.

                     (II, A6)

[I long to be dissolved.

    Deceitful cares, why batter so my breast?
        Weak flesh may not resist its own tormentings.
    Let it not know what the vile crowd's madness loves,
        And what it falsely thinks the highest good.
    I long to be dissolved in love of a better life:
        For it is enough to wish and be able to die.]

De Nomine Jesu

Verte stylum, mea Musa; procul mundana recedant:
    Cedant a calamis nunc leviora tuis.
Iam neque pro laetis modulis gratabere Amicis;
    Nec dictura frequens versibus ibis, Ave.
Carmine lugubri non fata sinistra dolebis:
    Ad Proceres nec jam ducet arundo preces.
Non supplex mea vota feres ad Caesaris aulam;
    Nec mihi difficilem sollicitabis opem:
Legibus haud metricis sapientum dicta virorum
    Involves: nusquam buccina laudis eris:
Non hilari accipies nascentum festa sonore:
    Nec lacrymas dabimus, quas ciet aeger amor:
Sed veteri graviora modo meditabimur: aether
    Materiam auspiciis praebuit ecce novis!
Namque dies micuit, quo guttula prima cruoris,
    Pro nobis nostra proque salute cadit.
Quis fundat, quaeris? teneris ex artibus infans,
    Infans matre miser Virgine, patre DEUS.
Cesso heic: tanta meam superant mysteria mentem:
    Mater homo est, nullo sed temerata viro.
Hic ubi vix, quam sors humana humanitus offert,
    Octo dies alma luce potitus erat,
Se circumcidi patitur, pro more vetusto,
    Et JESUM aligeri, Patre volente, vocant.
Dic igitur JESU carmen de nomine Musa:
    Quid distet reliquis illud, & unde gerat.
Sunt quibus hoc nomen fuit olim; JOSUA, Mosis
    Successor, simili nomine dictus erat.
Tuque Sacerdotem tali de nomine magnum
    Zacharia, scriptis ante fuisse doces.
Non tamen aeternam populo hi struxere salutem:
    Sed peritura fuit, si fuit illa salus.
Josua deduxit Cananaea per arva fideles.
    Exigua illa salus, si meditaris, erat.
Post hos, SYRACIDES dictus cognomine JESUS,
    Contulit e multis ethica multa libris.
Sint haec magna quidem & magni pendenda: sed illa
    Non Christi summis aequiparanda bonis.
Virginis ac Divum soboles, cui sidera rorant,
    Sola mihi JESUS, sola Redemptor erit.

Non hominum ratio, sed Patris diva voluntas
   Nomen id ante dedit, quam vagus orbis erat.
Angelus hoc nobis sacrata voce revelat;
   Et certa dici de ratione monet.
Una salus miseris datur hoc; ut crimine liber
   Vivat homo, & verae gaudia lucis agat.
Nam licet a cuncto sanentur corpora morbo;
   Non tamen est nobis vera putanda salus.
Pectora peccato quod si releventur ab omni,
   Ista salus demum crede perennis erit.
Nam quicunque fuit maledicto a crimine liber,
   Nil huic vel morbus, pauperiesve nocet.
Hunc neque tot gradibus mors impetuosa movebit:
   Solo etenim JESU nomine salvus agit.
Qui non salvus erit solius nomine JESU,
   Nil hunc fluxa salus divitiaeque beant.
Nulla profanorum meveat me cura bonorum,
   Caelestis deceat sed diadema domus.
Sic ego salvabor; sic mens & vita valebunt:
   Sic mors, sic furiae nil nocuisse queunt.
Adde & Calliope, quibus hic sit missus in orbem:
   Mortifero quosnam liberet ille jugo.
Non aliena quidem Messias agmina curat:
   Sed sibi devote membra caduca fovet.
Grex alienus is est, qui nescit credere dictis:
   Quique redemptorem nescit amare suum.
Sed vera quicunque fide complectitur ipsum,
   Ille, DEI populus cur reputetur, habet.
Crede modo Christi verbis, sacra jussa capesse:
   Si ratio pugnat, sufficit; αντος εφα
Qua ratione suos divina propago tuetur?
   Fallor? an EX MERITO, crimine liber agis?
Non ita; sed Christi merito Patris ira recessit:
   Salvifica Christi morte repensus homo est.
Hoc verae fidei qui nixus robore perstat,
   Vivet, & in media morte beatus erit.
Namque bonis nomen JESU bona plurima confert:
   De caelesti homines nempe salute docet.
Non aliud nomen sub Caelo restat in orbe,
   In quo nos salvos jusserit esse DEUS.
Nominibus reliquis merito praeponitur unum.
   Quo semel audito flectitur omne genu.

Angelus e caelo veram conferre salutem
    Nescit; at a JESU vera petenda salus.
Quisquis in hoc dulci, spe firma, nomine credit,
    Salvus hic, inferno liber ab hoste, manet.
Nil EXTERNA tamen genuum SUBJECTIO prodest:
    Ni mens se flectat, flexio nulla juvat,
Ergo Salvator JESU suavissime salve;
    Mente tibi pura carmina fusa cape.
Sis clemens famulae; peccata remitte; guberna
    Affectus, Sensus, ora manusque tibi.
Ut tibi semper agam, JESU, pro munere grates,
    Inque meo officio jussa fidelis agam.
Sic mihi Salvator vere, dulcissime JESU:
    Fac, quod in orbe cano, sic super axe canam.

[On the Name of Jesus

Now change your pen, my Muse; let mundane things recede:
    Let lighter things now leave your quill.
No longer will you honor friends in cheerful measure;
    Nor will you speak in verse your frequent greetings.
You'll not lament my unkind fates in mournful song;
    Nor any more lead prayers to Princes with your pipe.
Nor will you, suppliant, take my pleas to Caesar's court;
    Nor beg on my behalf for hard won help:
You will not put the wise men's sayings into meter;
    No longer will you serve to trumpet praise.
You will not honor birthday feasts with merry sound:
    Nor will we weep the tears that anxious love brings on.
But we in ancient form will treat more solemn things:
    Look, heaven has set a new auspicious theme.
For the day has dawned on which the first small drops
    Of blood for us and our salvation fell.
Who sheds this blood, you ask? A child from his tiny member,
    By his Virgin mother a piteous child, by his father God.
Here I pause: such mysteries surpass my mind.
    The mother is human, but not at all defiled by man.
He, when he'd enjoyed for scarce eight days the kindly
    Light that human fate bestows on us,
Lets himself be circumcised, by ancient custom,
    And the angels call him JESUS, the father willing.

Proclaim then Muse, a song about the name of JESUS:
    Why it differs from the rest, and whence he bears it.
Others had this name before; Joshua, who followed
    Moses, was called by a similar name.
And in the scripture, Zechariah, you teach that there was
    Once a great high priest of such a name.
But these did not win the people eternal safety:
    Rather, if there was salvation, it could not last.
Joshua led the faithful through the fields of Canaan.
    But brief was this salvation, if you think it over.
Besides these men, Syracides, called Jesus by forename,
    Compiled philosophies from many books.
Such wisdom may be great and greatly honored; but it
    Does not compare with the highest good in Christ.
Child of a virgin and of God, for whom the stars drop dew,
    JESUS alone for me, my savior he alone will be.
Not human reason, but the father's will divine
    Decreed that name from before the world had lapsed.
An angel to us with sacred voice reveals this,
    And says it is decreed with firm intent.
The sufferers thus are given one salvation; that free of fault
    Mankind may live, and seek the pleasures of true light.
For though our bodies be saved from every ill,
    Yet truly saving health cannot be counted on
Unless our hearts are freed from every sin,
    Then trust that such salvation lasts forever.
For whoever has been freed from cursed crime, nothing,
    Not disease nor poverty will hurt him.
Nor will impetuous death in any measure move him.
    For only by the name of JESUS will a redeemed man live.
The one unwilling to be saved by JESUS' name alone
    Will not be blessed by either health or flowing riches.
May care of worldly goods not move me. But may
    A crown of the heavenly home well suit me.
Thus am I to be saved; my mind and life will flourish;
    Thus death, thus passion cannot do me harm. And add,
Caliope, that the one by whom this Son was sent
    Into the world, will free us from death's yoke.
Indeed the Savior does not tend an alien flock,
    But cherishes our mortal bodies faithfully himself.
There is a foreign flock, not knowing how to trust his words,

Not knowing how to love its redeemer.
But he holds whoever in true faith embraces
    Him—thereby God's people are defined.
Only believe the words of Christ; take up his holy commands:
    If reason oppose, it is enough that he has spoken.
On what account can the holy Son maintain his own?
    Am I mistaken? Do you live free from guilt BY MERIT?
Not so; but by Christ's merit does the Father's ire diminish.
    By Christ's redeeming death mankind has been restored.
Whoever, having taken his strength, persists in true
    Belief will live and in the midst of death be blessed.
To someone good, the name of Jesus offers many goods:
    Undoubtedly it teaches men divine salvation.
No other name there is on earth, or under heaven
    By which God will have bade us to be saved.
One name is placed above the rest by merit,
    Whenever it is heard each knee is bent.
No angel of heaven knows how to give salvation;
    But from JESUS true salvation must be sought.
Whoever with firm hope in this sweet name believes,
    Untouched by the infernal host, he will be saved.
Yet outward bending of the knees gains nothing;
    Unless the mind will genuflect, no bending helps.
Therefore Savior, sweetest JESUS, I greet you.
    Receive my songs poured out for you with pure intent.
Be merciful to me your handmaid; forgive her sins, direct
    My affections, senses, mouth, and hands for you.
That I may always thank you, JESUS, for your gifts,
    And in my calling faithfully perform your will.
Sweetest JESUS, to me be truly savior: see to it
    That what I sing here, beyond the poles I'll sing again.]

In SYMBOLAM Westoniae Auctoris.
SPES MEA CHRISTUS.

In te, CHRISTE, mihi spes derivata recumbit;
    Sed ne confundant me mala tot, fer opem:
Non ego imaginibus confido, ne arte; salutis,
    Quam spero, certae nil mihi praestat homo.
Tu spes, tu mea res, Meus es, per saxa per ignes:
    Si vis esse, sequar per freta: si esse jubes
Per freta; freta tuo munimine vinco: petitis
    Certa, vel hic, summi vel patris aede tui.

[On the MOTTO of the Author Weston,
CHRIST MY HOPE

> In you, Christ, lies the hope that comes to me;
>> Grant help, that all these ills may not confound me:
> I do not trust in images nor art; the saving help
>> For which I hope, mankind does not provide.
> You are mine, my hope, my focus, through rocky ways and fire:
>> If you so will, I'll go through stormy seas—if you command,
> Through stormy seas; I conquer them in your protection. You call
>> For trust, both here and in your father's highest home.]

3. Excerpt in Modernized Text from the Title Poem of Aemilia Lanyer's *Salve Deus Rex Judaeorum* (1611)

(Dedicated in margin to "The Lady Margaret Countess Dowager of Cumberland")

> Sith *Cynthia* is ascended to that rest
> Of endless joy and true Eternity,
> That glorious place that cannot be expressed
> By any wight clad in mortality,
> In her almighty love so highly blessed,
> And crowned with everlasting Sovereignty,
>> Where Saints and Angels do attend her Throne,
>> And she gives glory unto God alone,
>
> To thee great Countess now I will apply
> My Pen, to write thy never dying fame;
> That when to Heaven thy blessed Soul shall fly,
> These lines on earth record thy reverend name:
> And to this task I mean my Muse to tie,
> Though wanting skill I shall but purchase blame:
>> Pardon, dear Lady, want of woman's wit
>> To pen thy praise, when few can equal it.
>
> And pardon, Madam, though I do not write
> Those praiseful lines of that delightful place [Cookham],
> As you commanded me in that fair night
> When shining *Phoebe* gave so great a grace,
> Presenting *Paradise* to your sweet sight,
> Unfolding all the beauty of her face
>> With pleasant groves, hills, walks, and stately trees,
>> Which pleasures with retired minds agrees. . . .

Thy Mind so perfect by thy Maker framed,
No vain delights can harbor in thy heart,
With his sweet love thou art so much inflamed
As of the world thou seem'st to have no part;
So love him still, thou need'st not be ashamed,
Tis He that made thee what thou wert and art:
  Tis He that dries all tears from Orphans' eyes,
  And hears from heaven the woeful widow's cries. . . .

The Heavens shall perish as a garment old,
Or as a vesture by the maker changed,
And shall depart, as when a scroll is rolled;
Yet thou from him shalt never be estranged,
When He shall come in glory that was sold
For all our sins, we happily are changed,
  Who for our faults put on his righteousness,
  Although full oft his Laws we do transgress. . . .

With Majesty and Honor is He clad,
And decked with light, as with a garment fair;
He joys the Meek and makes the Mighty sad,
Pulls down the Proud and doth the Humble rear:
Who sees this Bridegroom never can be sad;
None lives that can his wondrous works declare:
  Yea, look how far the East is from the West,
  So far he sets our sins, that have transgressed.

He rides upon the wings of all the winds,
And spreads the heavens with all powerful hand;
Oh who can loose when the Almighty binds?
Or in his angry presence dares to stand?
He searcheth out the secrets of all minds;
And those that fear him shall possess the Land.
  He is exceeding glorious to behold,
  Ancient of Times, so fair, and yet so old. . . .

That great *Jehova* King of heaven and earth,
Will rain down fire and brimstone from above
Upon the wicked monsters in their berth
That storm and rage at those whom he doth love:
Snares, storms, and tempests he will rain, and dearth,
Because he will himself almighty prove:

And this shall be the portion they shall drink,
That thinks the Lord is blind when he doth wink.

Pardon, good Madam, though I have digressed
From what I do intend to write of thee,
To set his glory forth whom thou lov'st best,
Whose wondrous works no mortal eye can see;
His special care on those whom he hath blessed,
From wicked worldlings how he sets them free:
    And how such people he doth overthrow
    In all their ways, that they his power may know.

The meditation of this Monarch's love
Draws thee from caring what this world can yield;
Of joys and griefs both equal thou dost prove,
They have no force to force thee from the field:
Thy constant faith like to the Turtle Dove
Continues combat, and will never yield
    To base affliction, or proud pomp's desire,
    That sets the weakest minds so much on fire.

Thou from the Court to the Country art retired,
Leaving the world before the world leaves thee:
That great Enchantress of weak minds admired,
Whose all-bewitching charms so pleasing be
To worldly wantons, and too much desired
Of those that care not for Eternity,
    But yield themselves as prey to Lust and Sin,
    Losing their hopes of Heaven, Hell-pains to win. . . .

That outward Beauty which the world commends
Is not the subject I will write upon,
Whose date expired, that tyrant Time soon ends;
Those gaudy colors soon are spent and gone:
But those fair Virtues which on thee attends
Are always fresh, they never are but one:
    They make thy Beauty fairer to behold
    Than was that Queen's for whom proud *Troy* was sold. . . .

Twas Beauty bred in *Troy* the ten years strife,
And carried *Helen* from her lawful Lord;
Twas Beauty made chaste *Lucrece* lose her life,
For which proud *Tarquin's* fact was so abhorred:

Beauty the cause *Antonius* wronged his wife,
Which could not be decided but by sword:
　　Great *Cleopatra's* Beauty and defects
　　Did work *Octavia's* wrongs and his neglects. . . .

Holy *Matilda* in a hapless hour
Was born to sorrow and to discontent,
Beauty the cause that turned her Sweet to Sour,
While Chastity fought Folly to prevent.
Lustful King *John* refused, did use his power
By Fire and Sword to compass his content:
　　But Friends' disgrace, nor Father's banishment,
　　Nor Death itself could purchase her consent. . . .

This Grace, great Lady, doth possess thy Soul,
And makes thee pleasing in thy Maker's sight;
This Grace doth all imperfect Thoughts controll,
Directing thee to serve thy God aright,
Still reckoning him the Husband of thy Soul,
Which is most precious in his glorious sight:
　　Because the World's delights she doth deny
　　For him who for her sake vouchsafed to die. . . .

These high deserts invites my lowly Muse
To write of Him and pardon crave of thee;
For Time so spent I need make no excuse,
Knowing it doth with thy fair Mind agree
So well as thou no Labor wilt refuse
That to thy holy Love may pleasing be:
　　His Death and Passion I desire to write,
　　And thee to read, the blessed Soul's delight.

But my dear Muse, now whither wouldst thou fly
Above the pitch of thy appointed strain?
With *Icarus* thou seekest now to try,
Not waxen wings but thy poor barren Brain,
Which far too weak, these seely lines descry;
Yet cannot this thy forward Mind restrain,
　　But thy poor Infant Verse must soar aloft,
　　Not fearing threatening dangers, happening oft.

Think when the eye of Wisdom shall discover
Thy weakling Muse to fly that scarce could creep,
And in the Air above the Clouds to hover,

When better 'twere mewed up and fast asleep,
They'll think with *Phaeton* thou canst n'er recover,
But helpless with that poor young Lad to weep,
   The little World of thy weak Wit on fire,
   Where thou wilt perish in thine own desire.

But yet the Weaker thou dost seem to be
In Sex or Sense, the more his Glory shines,
That doth infuse such powerful Grace in thee
To show thy Love in these few humble Lines;
The Widow's Mite with this may well agree,
Her little All more worth than golden mines,
   Being more dearer to our loving Lord
   Than all the wealth that Kingdoms could afford.

Therefore I humbly for his Grace will pray,
That he will give me Power and Strength to Write,
That what I have begun, so end I may,
As his great Glory may appear more bright;
Yea in these Lines I may no further stray
Than his most holy Spirit shall give me Light. . . .
   Then will I tell of that sad black fac't Night
   Whose mourning Mantle covered Heavenly Light.

That very Night our Savior was betrayed,
Oh night! exceeding all the nights of sorrow,
When our most blessed Lord, although dismayed,
Yet would not he one Minute's respite borrow,
But to *Mount Olives* went, though sore afraid,
To welcome Night, and entertain the Morrow;
   And as he oft unto that place did go,
   So did he now, to meet his long nursed woe. . . .

None were admitted with their Lord to go,
But *Peter* and the sons of Zebed'us
To them good *Jesus* opened all his woe,
He gave them leave his sorrows to discuss,
His deepest griefs he did not scorn to show
These three dear friends, so much he did entrust:
   Being sorrowful and overcharged with grief,
   He told it them, yet looked for no relief. . . .

But now thy friends whom thou didst call to go,
Heavy Spectators of thy hapless case,

See thy Betrayer, whom too well they know,
One of the twelve, now object of disgrace,
A trothless traitor and a mortal foe,
With feigned kindness seeks thee to embrace
   And gives a kiss, whereby he may deceive thee,
   That in the hands of Sinners he might leave thee.

Now muster forth with Swords, with Staves, with Bills
High Priests and Scribes and Elders of the Land,
Seeking by force to have their wicked Wills,
Which thou didst never purpose to withstand;
Now thou mak'st haste unto the worst of Ills,
And who they seek thou gently dost demand.
   This didst thou Lord t'amaze these Fools the more,
   T'inquire of that thou knew'st so well before. . . .

Those dear Disciples that he most did love
And were attendant at his beck and call
When trial of affliction came to prove,
They first left him, who now must leave them all;
For they were earth and he came from above,
Which made them apt to fly and fit to fall:
   Though they protest they never will forsake him,
   They do like men, when dangers overtake them. . . .

Now *Pontius Pilate* is to judge the Cause
Of faultless *Jesus*, who before him stands,
Who neither hath offended Prince nor Laws,
Although he now be brought in woeful bands.
Oh noble Governor, make thou yet a pause,
Do not in innocent blood embrue thy hands;
   But hear the words of thy most worthy wife,
   Who sends to thee to beg her Savior's life.

Let barbarous cruelty far depart from thee,
And in true Justice take affliction's part;
Open thine eyes that thou the truth mayst see,
Do not the thing that goes against thy heart,
Condemn not him that must thy Savior be,
But view his holy Life, his good desert.
   Let not us Women glory in Men's fall
   Who had power given to overrule us all.

Till now your indiscretion sets us free
And makes our former fault much less appear;
Our Mother *Eve*, who tasted of the Tree,
Giving to *Adam* what she held most dear,
Was simply good and had no power to see;
The after-coming harm did not appear:
   The subtle Serpent that our Sex betrayed
   Before our fall so sure a plot had laid.

That undiscerning Ignorance perceived
No guile or craft that was by him intended;
For had she known of what we were bereaved,
To his request she had not condescended.
But she, poor soul, by cunning was deceived,
No hurt therein her harmless Heart intended:
   For she alleged God's word, which he denies,
   That they should die, but even as Gods be wise.

But surely *Adam* cannot be excused;
Her fault was great, yet he was most to blame.
What Weakness offered, Strength might have refused;
Being Lord of all, the greater was his shame;
Although the Serpent's craft had her abused,
God's holy word ought all his actions frame,
   For he was Lord and King of all the earth
   Before poor *Eve* had either life or breath.

Who being framed by God's eternal hand,
The perfectest man that ever breathed on earth,
And from God's mouth received that strait command,
The breach whereof he knew was present death,
Yea, having power to rule both Sea and Land,
yet with one Apple won to lose that breath
   Which God had breathed in his beauteous face,
   Bringing us all in danger and disgrace.

And then to lay the fault on Patience back,
That we poor women must endure it all—
We know right well he did discretion lack,
Being not persuaded thereunto at all;
If *Eve* did err, it was for knowledge's sake;
The fruit, being fair, persuaded him to fall:

No subtle Serpent's falsehood did betray him,
If he would eat it, who had power to stay him?

Not *Eve*, whose fault was only too much love,
Which made her give this present to her Dear,
That what she tasted he likewise might prove,
Whereby his knowledge might become more cleare;
He never sought her weakness to reprove
With those sharp words which he of God did hear:
   Yet Men will boast of Knowledge, which he took
   From *Eve's* fair hand, as from a learned book.

If any Evil did in her remain,
Being made of him, he was the ground of all;
If one of many Worlds could lay a stain
Upon our Sex and work so great a fall
To wretched Man by Satan's subtle train,
What will so foul a fault amongst you all?
   Her weakness did the Serpent's words obey,
   But you in malice God's dear Son betray.

Whom, if unjustly you condemn to die,
Her sin was small to what you do commit;
All mortal sins that do for vengeance cry
Are not to be compared unto it.
If many worlds would all together try
By all their sins the wrath of God to get,
   This sin of yours surmounts them all as far
   As doth the Sun another little star.

Then let us have our Liberty again,
And challenge to yourselves no sovereignty;
You came not into the world without our pain,
Make that a bar against your cruelty;
Your fault being greater, why should you disdain
Our being your equals, free from tyranny?
   If one weak woman simply did offend,
   This sin of yours hath no excuse, nor end.

To which, poor souls, we never gave consent,
Witness thy wife, O *Pilate*, speaks for all,
Who did but dream, and yet a message sent
That thou should'st have no thing to do at all
With that just man, which if thy heart relent,

Why wilt thou be a reprobate with *Saul?*
  To seek the death of him that is so good,
  For thy soul's health to shed his dearest blood. . . .

First went the Crier with open mouth proclaiming
The heavy sentence of Iniquity,
The Hangman next, by his base office claiming
His right in Hell, where sinners never die,
Carrying the nails, the people still blaspheming
Their maker, using all impiety,
  The Thieves attending him on either side,
  The Sergeants watching, while the women cried.

Thrice happy women that obtained such grace
From him whose worth the world could not contain,
Immediately to turn about his face,
As not remembering his great grief and pain,
To comfort you, whose tears poured forth apace
On *Flora's* banks, like showers of April rain:
  Your cries enforced mercy, grace, and love
  From him, whom greatest Princes could not move

To speak one word, nor once to lift his eyes
Unto proud *Pilate*, no nor *Herod* king,
By all the Questions that they could devise
Could make him answer to no manner of thing;
Yet these poor women by their piteous cries
Bid move their Lord, their Lover, and their King
  To take compassion, turn about, and speak
  To them whose hearts were ready now to break.

Most blessed daughters of Jerusalem,
Who found such favor in your Savior's sight,
To turn his face when you did pity him,
Your tearful eyes beheld his eyes more bright;
Your Faith and Love unto such grace did climb
To have reflection from this Heavenly Light:
  Your Eagles' eyes did gaze against this Sun,
  Your hearts did think, he dead, the world were done.

When spiteful men with torments did oppress
The afflicted body of this innocent Dove,
Poor women, seeing how much they did transgress,
By tears, by sighs, by cries entreat, nay prove

What may be done among the thickest press;
They labor still these tyrants' hearts to move,
   In pity and compassion to forbear
    Their whipping, spurning, tearing of his hair. . . .

Most blessed Virgin, in whose faultless fruit
All Nations of the earth must needs rejoice,
No Creature having sense though ne'er so brute
But joys and trembles when they hear his voice,
His wisdom strikes the wisest persons mute,
Fair chosen vessel, happy in his choice,
   Dear Mother of our Lord, whose reverend name
    All people Blessed call, and spread thy fame, . . .

[The angel said] "Hail Mary, full of grace,
Thou freely art beloved of the Lord,
He is with thee, behold thy happy case."
What endless comfort did these words afford
To thee that saw'st an Angel in the place
Proclaim thy Virtues' worth, and to record
   Thee blessed among women, that thy praise
    Should last so many worlds beyond thy days. . . .

How canst thou choose, fair Virgin, then but mourn
When this sweet offspring of thy body dies,
When thy fair eyes beholds his body torn,
The people's fury, hears the women's cries,
His holy name prophaned, He made a scorn,
Abused with all their hateful slanderous lies:
   Bleeding and fainting in such wondrous sort
    As scarce his feeble limbs can him support. . . .

His joints disjointed, and his legs hung down,
His alabaster breast, his bloody side, ·
His members torn and on his head a Crown
Of sharpest Thorns to satisfy for pride,
Anguish and Pain do all his Senses drown,
While they his holy garments do divide:
   His bowels dry, his heart full fraught with grief,
    Crying to him that yields him no relief.

This with the eye of faith thou mayst behold,   TO MY LADY
Dear Spouse of Christ, and more than I can write,   OF CUMBERLAND
And here both Grief and Joy thou mayst unfold,

To view thy Love in this most heavy plight,
Bowing his head, his bloodless body cold;
Those eyes wax dim that gave us all our light,
   His countenance pale yet still continues sweet,
   His blessed blood watering his pierced feet. . . .

This is the Bridegroom that appears so fair,
So sweet, so lovely in his Spouse's sight,
That unto Snow we may his face compare,
His cheeks like scarlet and his eyes so bright
As purest Doves that in the rivers are
Washed with milk, to give the more delight;
   His head is likened to the finest gold,
   His curled locks so beauteous to behold,

Black as a Raven in her blackest hue,
His lips like scarlet threads, yet much more sweet
Than is the sweetest honey dropping dew,
Or honeycombs where all the Bees do meet;
Yea, he is constant and his words are true,
His cheeks are beds of spices, flowers sweet,
   His lips like Lillies, dropping down pure myrrh,
   Whose love before all worlds we do prefer.

Ah! give me leave, good Lady, now to leave   TO MY LADY
This task of Beauty which I took in hand;   OF CUMBERLAND
I cannot wade so deep, I may deceive
Myself before I can attain the land;
Therefore, good Madam, in your heart I leave
His perfect picture, where it still shall stand,
   Deeply engraved in that holy shrine,
   Environed with Love and Thoughts divine. . . .

Ofttimes he hath made trial of your love,
And in your Faith hath took no small delight
By Crosses and Afflictions he doth prove,
Yet still your heart remaineth firm and right,
Your love so strong as nothing can remove,
Your thoughts being placed on him both day and night,
   Your constant soul doth lodge between her breasts
   This Sweet of sweets, in which all glory rests.

Sometimes he appears to thee in Shepherd's weed
And so presents himself before thine eyes,

A good old man that goes his flock to feed;
Thy color changes, and thy heart doth rise,
Thou call'st, he comes, thou find'st tis he indeed,
Thy Soul conceives that he is truly wise,
   Nay more, desires that he may be the Book
   Whereon thine eyes continually may look.

Some time imprisoned, naked, poor, and bare,
Full of diseases, impotent, and lame,
Blind, deaf, and dumb he comes unto his fair,
To see if yet she will remain the same;
Nay sick and wounded now thou dost prepare
To cherish him in thy dear Lover's name:
   Yea thou bestow'st all pains, all cost, all care
   That may relieve him and his health repair. . . .

Thy beauty shining brighter than the Sun,
Thine honor more than ever Monarch gained,
Thy wealth exceeding his that Kingdoms won,
Thy Love unto his Spouse, thy Faith unfeigned,
Thy Constancy in what thou hast begun,
Till thou his heavenly Kingdom have obtained,
   Respecting worldly wealth to be but dross,
   Which, if abused, doth prove the owner's loss. . . .

Good Madam, though your modesty be such
Not to acknowledge what we know and find,
And that you think these praises overmuch
Which do express the beauty of your mind,
Yet pardon me although I give a touch
Unto their eyes, that else would be so blind
   As not to see thy store and their own wants,
   From whose fair seeds of Virtue spring these plants.

And know, when first into this world I came,
This charge was given me by th'Eternal powers
The everlasting Trophy of thy fame
To build and deck it with the sweetest flowers
That virtue yields; then Madam, do not blame
Me when I show the World but what is yours,
   And deck you with that crown which is your due,
   That of Heaven's beauty Earth may take a view.

Though famous women elder times have known,
Whose glorious actions did appear so bright
That powerful men by them were overthrown,
And all their armies overcome in fight—
The Scythian women by their power alone
Put King Darius unto shameful flight,
   All Asia yielded to their conquering hand,
   Great *Alexander* could not their power withstand—

[Their] worth, though writ in lines of blood and fire,
Is not to be compared unto thine;
Their power was small to overcome Desire,
Or to direct their ways by Virtue's line;
Were they alive, they would thy Life admire,
And unto thee their honors would resign:
   For thou a greater conquest dost obtain
   Than they who have so many thousands slain. . . .

Whose excellence hath rais'd my spirits to write
Of what my thoughts could hardly apprehend;
Your rarest Virtues did my soul delight,
Great Lady of my heart: I must commend
You, that appear so fair in all men's sight;
On your Deserts my Muses do attend:
   You are the Arctic Star that guides my hand,
   All what I am, I rest at your command.

FINIS

4. Selections from Lady Anne Southwell's Verse: from Folger MS V.b.198, "The workes of the Lady Ann Sothwell. 1626"

Fol. 9

Dialoge Sonnet

Anger what art thow? Hast thow treuth to tell:
               A flame of hell.
Where is thy Dwelling? or thy tutring schooles?
               The Hart of fooles.
What is thy hopes in all thy fierce intrusion?
               Confusion:

Who did begett the? or who gaue the place.
                    The want of Grace.
Where woldst thow place the Tropheyes of thy Euills?
                    With the Diuills.
What dost thow gayne (think'st thow) in thy vexation?
                    Damnation
What might I call so monstrous an Elfe?
                    Madnes it selfe
Who are thy fellowes in the Earth or Ayre?
                    Hell & despaire
What wold'st thow leaue behynd the in thy moode?
                    Teares woundes or blood.
When will the fury of thy Source be turned?
                    When all is burned.
        Mapp of confusion and the worlds disturber
        Being plac'd in hell, who wold pursue the further?

Sonnet
Beauty, Honor, yeouth, and fortune
                    I importune
None of yow to be my freind
                    Theise Gambols end.
And I haue gaynd a Rosy bed
                    vppon your head
Trod out of thornes and cruell Cares
                    And now yor wares
Semes noysome trumpery to my thoughts
                    Things good for noughts
O happy state that dying liues
                    And reason giues
A iust accompt of her disdayning
                    By her loss gayning.

Fol. II
    Nature, Mistris off affection
    gaue my loue to thy protection
    Wher it hath receiued infection
                    and is dying.

    Fame the daughter great of wonder
    Brekeing from thy mouth like thunder
    rending truth and me assunder
                    all with lyinge

Loue that looked through mine eyes
neuer borrowed beam from lyes
or Sofft passions of disguise
>> or estranged

But all this serves not thy turne
thy hate like hell fiare doth burne
and at all my best acts spurne
>> and near changed

Eue to Adam, was his Croune
and can baldness be renowne
thus thou pullst thy owne state downe
>> O meere maddness

Much like to Pandoras purss
turne heauens blessing to a Curse
which I fear will still wax worss
>> To my saddness

Thou hast turnd my daye to night
putst my aged plumes to flight
that am hatefull in thy sight
>> as all men see

Can loue and hate together rest
Doues and serpents in one nest
Truth and falsehood in one brest
>> It cannot be

I see that loue and deere affection
is the nurss of my affliction
The eye of truth gives this direction
>> to my sick brest

Am I a yoakffellow, or slaue
What is my due I looke to haue
or else Ile digg my selff a graue
>> and ly at rest.

Fol. 19v

An Elegie written by the Lady A. S. to the Countesse of London Derrye
supposyenge hir to be dead by hir longe silence

Since thou fayre soule, art warblinge to a spheare
from whose resultances these quicknd were

Since thou hast layd that downy Couch aside
of Lillyes, Violletts, and roseall pride
And lockt in marble chests, that Tapestrye
that did adorne the worlds Epitome,
soe safe, that Doubt it selfe can neuer thinke,
fortune or fate hath power, to make a chinke,
Since, thou for state, hath raisd thy state, soe farr,
To a large heauen, from a vaute circular,
because, the thronginge virtues, in thy breste
could not haue roome enough, in such a chest,
what need hast thou these blotted lines should tell,
soules must againe take rise, from whence they fell,
From paradice, and that this earths Darke wombe?
is but a wardrobe till the day of Dome?
To keepe those wormes, that on hir bosome bredd,
till tyme, and death, bee both extermined,
Yet in thy passage, fayre soule, let me know
what things thou saws't in riseinge from below?
Whether that Cynthia regent of the flood
wthin hir Orbe admitt of mortall brood?
Whether the 12 Signes serue the Sun for state?
Or elce confine him to the Zodiaque!
And force him retrograde to bee the nurse
(whoe circularly glides his oblique course)
Of ALMA MATER, or vnfreeze the wombe
of madam Tellus? wch elce proues a tombe,
whether the starrs be Knobbs uppon the spheres?
Or shredds compos'd of Phoebus goulden hayres?
Or whether th'Ayre be as a cloudy siue?
the starrs be holes through wch the good soules driue?
whether that Saturne that the 6 out topps
sitt euer eatinge of the bratts of Opps?
Whose iealousye is like a sea of Gall
vnto his owne proues periodicall?
But as a glideinge star whoe falls to earth
Or louers thoughts, soe soules ascend theyr birth,
wch makes mee thinke, that thyne had noe one notion,
of those true elements, by whose true motion,
All things haue life, and death, but if thyne eyne,
should fix a while uppon the Christalline,
Thy hungrye eye, that neuer could before,
see, but by fayth, and faythfully adore,

should stay, to marke the threefould Hierarchye,
differinge in state, not in foelicitye
How they in Order, 'bout Jehoua moue,
In seuerall offices, but wth one loue,
And from his hand, doe hand in hand come downe,
till the last hand, doe heads of mortalls crowne.
Fayne would I know from some that haue beene there?
what state or shape coelestiall bodyes beare?
For man, to heauen, hath throwne a waxen ball,
In wch hee thinks h'hath gott, true formes of all,
And, from the forge howse, of his fantasie,
hee creates new, and spins out destinye.
And thus theise prowd wormes, wrapt in lothsome rags,
shutt heauens Idea upp, in letherne baggs.
Now since in heauen are many Ladyes more,
that blinde deuotion busyely implore,
Good Lady, freind, or rather louely Dame,
if yow, be gone from out this clayie frame,
tell what yow know, whether th'saynts adoration?
will stoope, to thinke on dusty procreation,
And if they will not, they are fooles (perdye)
that pray to them, and robb the Trinitye,
The Angells ioy in o^r good conuersation,
Yet see vs not, but by reuerberation,
And if they could, yo^w s^{ts} as cleere eies haue,
if downe yow looke to earth, then to the graue,
Tis but a Landkipp, more, to looke to Hell
in viewinge it, what strange thinges may yow tell!
From out that sulphrous, and bitumnous lake,
where Pluto doth his Tilt, and Tournay make,
where the Elizium, and theyr purgatorye
stande, like two suburbs, by a promontarye,
poets, and popleings, are aequippollent,
both makers are, of Gods, of like descent,
poets makes blinde Gods, whoe with willowes beates them,
popelings makes Hoasts of Gods, & euer eates them.
But let them both, poets, & popleings, passe
whoe deales too much wth eyther, is an Asse,
Charon conduct them, as they haue deuised.
the Fall of Angells, must not bee disguised,
As 'tis not tirrany, but louinge pittye,
that Kings, build prisons, in a populous cittye,

Soe, the next way, to fright vs back to good,
is to discusse the paynes, of Stigian flood.
In Eue's distained nature, wee are base,
And whipps perswade vs more, then loue, or grace,
Soe, that if heauen, should take a way this rodd,
God would hate vs, and wee should not loue God,
For as afliction, in a full fedd state,
like vinegar, in sawces, doe awake
dull Appetites, and makes men feed the better,
soe when a Lythargye, or longnes doth fetter,
the onely way, to rouse againe o^r witts,
is, when the surgions cheifest toole is whips.
Brasse hath a couseninge face and lookes like gould
but where the touchstone comes it cannot hold.
That Sonne of ours, doth best deserue our rent,
that doth wth patience beare, o^r chastisement,
each Titmouse, can salute the lusty springe,
and weare it out, wth ioyllye reuellinge,
but yor pure white, and vestall clothed swan,
sings at hir death, and neuer sings but than,
O noble minded bird, I envy thee,
for thou hast stolne, this high borne note from mee.
But as the prophett, at his M^{rs} feete,
when hee ascended, up the Welkin fleete
Watcht, for his cloake, soe euery bird, & beast,
When princely Adam, tumbled from the nest,
catcht, from his knoweinge soule, some qualitie,
and humbly kept it, to reedifye,
theyr quondam Kinge, and now, man goes to schoole,
to euery pismire, that proclaymes him foole,
But stay my wanderinge thoughts, alas where made I?
In speakeinge to a dead, a sencelesse Lady.
Yow Incke, and paper, be hir passeinge bell,
The Sexton to hir knell, be Anne Southwell.

Fol. 21

An Epitaph, vppon Cassandra MacWillms wife to Sr Thomas Ridgway Earle of London Derry by ye Lady A. S.

Now let my pen bee choakt wth gall.
since I haue writt propheticall
I wondred, that the world did looke,

of late, like an vnbayted hooke
Or as a well, whose springe was dead
I knew not, y^t her soule was fledd
Till that the mourneinge of hir Earle
did vindicate, this deare lost pearle.
You, starr gasears that view the skyes?
saw yow of late a new star rise?
Or can yow by yor Art discouer
hir seate neere the coelestiall mouer?
She is gone that way, if I could find her,
and hath not left, hir match behind hir,
I'le prayse noe more, hir blest condicion,
but follow hir, wth expedition.

A. S.

Fol. 25

The more my soule doth shrinke from loue, ye more loue doth inflame her
   and when I seeke to finde the cause, t'is *Cos: amoris amor*
I sett my reason Centenall, that passions may not shame her
   who tells me they like shadowes pass, for *omnia vincit amor*
If with Angellick winges from hence, shee fly can mortalls blame her
   since from heauens lampe comes all her light, for *Cos: amoris amor*
Then let her mount, with faith, hope, loue, where sine nor death can lame her
   where all afflictions end theire rage, for *omnia vincit amor*.

My loue from Cherubs soueraintye, was in a manger laid
   the second of the Trinitye did soiorne with a maide
Went from the Cratch, vnto the Cross, from Cross, to graue and hell
   only to free my guiltye soule that there was Judgd to dwell
Now is the hand writt cancelled, the debt it trulye paid
   the Judge is fullye satisfyed; My soule be not dismaide
Now death, and hell haue lost theire stinge, the graue's ye bed of rest
   or gate to let the Faithfull in, to Christ for euer blest.

Behold the purchase, true loue doth Inherit,
Christ Iesus is the price of o^r saluation,
and for a pledge he leaues his holye spiritt
him selff a full rewarde (Oh) hy donation
Then let no other loues my soules Loue waite,
but to thee, in thee, and for thy deere sake.

Notes

Introduction

1. An interesting effort in this line is Lynette McGrath's comparison of Emilia Lanyer's "vision of woman's movement toward self-discovery and unity with the divine" with "Irigaray's celebration of the '*mysterique*,' the me-hysteric of the escaped, abandoned, ecstatic woman" (110).

2. She usually ends the chapters with a deconstructionist turn to irony, mystification, slipperiness, and self-questioning of the perspective and argument until then prevailing in the chapter. My own hunch is that one can trust readers to supply adequate mystification and slippage, and thus need not trouble to build it in.

3. Roughly the same question is taken up at the beginning of Krontiris's *Oppositional Voices*, and she treats several of the same writers discussed here. But I have worked from different theoretical perspectives from those of Krontiris, and generally to different effect.

4. Jana Sawicky in *Disciplining Foucault* revises Foucauldian concepts for feminist purposes. Analogously, if I may make so bold, my chapter on women and the Jacobean ideologeme of "male self-image propagation as governance" might be called "Disciplining Jameson."

1. Women's Household Circles as a Gendered Reading Formation

1. Alison Jaggar has referred to such contexts as "womanspace."

2. Jones (2) quotes the film critic Christine Gledhill to say that "meaning . . . arises out of a struggle or negotiation between competing frames of reference, motivation and experience. This [process] can be analyzed at three different levels: institutions, texts and audiences." Jones's application of this perspective in treating two English women and several continental ones as love poets is highly stimulating and useful (I cite her at certain points in this study), but I would expand the above theoretical model by noting that there are more possible nodes or focal points for studying individual writers' interactions with social forces than just the three named above—for example, sociolinguistic usages such as ideologemes (see chapter 5) and social practices such as reading formations, which cut across the spheres of institutions, texts, and audiences. Thus I work with somewhat different concepts from those of Jones and try to keep particular English political factions recurrently in view.

3. It would help if commentators on women writers of the early modern era would agree on a name format. Current practices may cause confusion: for example, referring to both the Countess of Pembroke and her niece Lady Wroth as "Mary Sidney" may result in generations of anthology readers who think they were the same woman. For the first mention of a particular woman in each chapter, I give her full set of names and titles, thus: Mary (Sidney) Herbert, Countess of Pembroke. (This format also has the merit of tracking important kinship connections.) Subsequent references will then as consistently as possible use whichever brief form of her name was generally used in her own lifetime: i.e., the Countess of Pembroke, or Lady Russell. Exception will be made for reference to times before someone's marriage, but the full name can still be given for the first mention, as "Anne Cooke, later

Lady Bacon." Or again, first reference will be to Elizabeth Jane (Weston) Leo or Löwe—who oddly for the time had a middle name—while later references will be to Elizabeth Weston (Elizabetha Westonia), as she was called by readers of her published poems, even when they knew that she was "uxor Ioannis Leonis." Furthermore, it would help if reference works would follow the usual practice of library catalogs, which for titled persons order the entry under the title (Pembroke for the countess) and for other married women under the first marriage name, while including all possible cross-references.

4. Lamb (*Gender* "Introduction") offers insights about how gender concepts of the time impacted upon writing and emphasizes the explicit sexualizing of women's public or semipublic speech and writing, effected by male denunciation of it as harlotry, a point further illustrated by the example of women's penitential rituals in my Introduction.

5. See B. L. Add. 15232, known as the Bright MS. Lamb's case for a woman as writer of the unsigned lyrics (of which she gives her transcriptions and a modern-spelling text) is mainly paleographic, and her analysis of the writer's handling of male poetic conventions also well supports this view. Possibly the lyricist was Wroth's younger sister Catherine (Sidney) Mansell, Lamb suggests (198), or the Countess of Pembroke's daughter Lady Anne Herbert, who died at age twenty-one. One would think of Philip Sidney's daughter Elizabeth Manners, Countess of Rutland—praised as a poet by Ben Jonson—but samples of her handwriting survive and, according to Lamb, that of the poems does not match it. The other two poems are "A most careless content of favor or disgrace" and "Love by the beams of beauty sets on fire."

6. The condition of the few surviving copies demonstrates this point—cf. W. Schleiner "feu caché" 294.

7. Or let me say, something that modern historians would characterize as lesbian. I leave aside here the whole much-discussed issue whether "homosexuality" in the modern sense existed at all in earlier eras. But to risk a pancultural, ahistorical hypothesis, perhaps a social-class power differential in a warm personal relationship, whether homosexual or heterosexual, typically carries a potential for erotic loading—a possibility Gallop mentions.

8. On this issue in the *Amadis de Gaul* see W. Schleiner "feu caché."

9. Jones (38) has also noted Whitney's intimations that "slander" of some sort cost her her post; Jones goes on to discuss her uses of Ovidianism.

10. I have modernized spelling and punctuation.

11. After another prefatory epistle by her friend Thomas Berry, which says that her book will "declare / To Cuntreywarde her love and friendly care" (Bii$_v$, i.e., the intended lady of service must live somewhere in the country near London), the first seven "flowers" are as follows:

I.   Such friends as have been absent long
          more joyful be at meeting
    Than those which ever present are
          and daily have their greeting.   [A reunion would bring joy.]

II. When perils they are present, then
          doth absence keep thee free,
    Whereas, if that thou present wert
          might dangers light on thee.   [It's good she has been away
                                 for this troubled time.]

III. The presence of the mind must be
          preferred, if we do well,

> Above the body's presence, for
>   it far doth it excell. [She has been there in spirit.]

IV. Yet absence sometimes bringeth harm,
>   when friends but fickle are,
> For new acquaintance purchase place
>   and old do lose their share. [But longer absence may make her forgotten.]

V. What profit things that we possess
>   do by their presence bring
> We cannot know till by their lack
>   we feel what harms do spring. [She now knows how to value her post.]

VI. For to abound in every thing
>   and not their use to know,
> It is a pinching penury,
>   Wherefore thy goods bestow. [The lady should be generous.]

VII. A saying old—once out of sight
>   and also out of mind—
> These contraries: that absent friends
>   much joy at meeting find. [Again, reunion would bring joy.]

12. As noted in No. 11, the Nosegay sends its message "to countryward" (Bii$_v$).

13. See Fehrenbach "Whitney," and also on the *Nosegay*, Travitsky's " 'Wyll and Testament.' "

14. Fehrenbach ("Letter") notes that a pamphlet of 1567 (just Whitney's time in London) called *A Letter sent by the Maydens of London* paints a vivid picture of their way of life.

15. Excerpts from it appear in Travitsky's *Paradise of Women*.

16. Beilin (100–101) has generally well characterized the poem as "unconventionally feminine in assuming many tones, from comic to pious, ironic, acerbic and apocalyptic" (though I do not find the last one here).

17. Quilligan's proposal about the *Urania* ("Wroth" 273–74) seems related to this category: Pamphilia "complains of [Amphilanthus's] infidelity and insists . . . on her own constancy. . . . She fills the social emptiness with poems. Wroth has reformulated a potentially transgressive active female desire but dressed it up in a former female virtue, patient constancy. Out of this maneuver, she creates Pamphilia's authority" as a writer.

18. Another discussion related to this point is Lamb's subsection "Reading like a Woman" (*Gender* 84–89).

19. The importance of music for international circulation of material among such reading groups could easily make the subject for a whole essay. Lady Anne Clifford, like the Countess of Pembroke, is portrayed playing the lute and singing. The countess clearly tried out many of her Psalm renditions as song—a MS with settings of two of them survives (B. L. Add MS 15117, ff. 4$_v$–5$_v$—see Joiner). I thank Margaret Hannay for sending me Joiner's article.

20. Ben Jonson in *Eastward Ho!* also refers to the practice of waiting women reading out continental romances to their ladies (see chapter 5).

21. Mrs. Tyler's preface declares that since men dedicate works to women and thus expect women to read them, women must also be competent to write stories. She leads up to that claim—which shows she was quite able to imagine writing an original romance herself and probably would have liked to—by passing some of the stations of women's possible pathways into writing in that age: she hopes no one would force her to write about religion, she says, as she would not be competent to deal with its controversies; and no one should feel that she has overstepped her female prerogatives in writing this work, since translation is "a

matter of more heede then of deepe invention or exquisite learning." She has not after all
gone so far as to write an original piece. She contrasts two possible metaphors—one alarming
and one reassuring—for her act of translating a martial, knightly piece: perhaps she has imagi-
natively "intermeddled in arms" like the Amazons and Claridiana in the story; but no, she
has rather simply "entertained a stranger" in taking in this Spaniard and naturalizing him.
Thus she imposes a proper female image, a metaphor of hospitality, on her activity of writing.

22. Again, see my article "Margaret Tyler."

23. Ballard (37) cites the tomb of Elizabeth Lucar (1510–1537), daughter of the merchant
Paul Withypoll, as saying that "Latine and Spanish, and also Italian / She spake, writ, read,
with perfect utterance," as well as doing arithmetic for bookkeeping.

24. Lamb ("Agency" 354) goes so far as to assert that Clifford "conveys no sense of
herself as a 'woman reader'," a point I would want to qualify through the discussion here.

25. *Diary of Lady Anne Clifford*, Spring 1617: "Coz Maria" reads from the *Metamorphoses*,
Moll Neville from *The Faerie Queene*; Aug. 1617, Moll Neville from the *Arcadia*. Spring 1617,
Mr. Rivers reads from "Montaigne's Plays"; Jan. 1619, Wat Conniston from [Augustine's]
City of God.

26. See Williamson *Lady Anne Clifford* 65n.

27. A. L. Rowse published Lanyer's poems (from her book, printed 1611), with an introduction intermingling well-documented information about her with speculation (presented
as fact) that she was Shakespeare's dark lady. Who knows but that she was; but Rowse has
made only a minimal circumstantial case for the claim. If anyone comes across further evidence about her, the hypothesis would obviously be intriguing to pursue.

28. Lewalski also concludes ("Re-writing" 106) that this time shortly after the Countess
of Cumberland was widowed is the likely period for Lanyer's brief service with her.

29. An interesting example of a waiting-lady's being inspired to a combination of writing and needlework is the lyric from Richard Johnson's *Crowne Garland of goulden Roses*
(1612) entitled "A short and sweet sonnet made by one of the maides of honor vpon the death
of Queene Elizabeth, which she sowed vppon a sampler in red silke." It is to be sung "To a
new tune or to Phillida flouts me":

Gone is Elizabeth,
   whom we haue lou'd so deare:
She our kind Mistris was,
   full foure and forty yeare,
England she gouernd well
   not to be blamed:
Flanders she succord still,
   and Ireland tamed.
France she befrended,
   Spaine she hath foiled:
Papists reiected,
   and the Pope spoyled.
To Princes powerfull,
   to the world vertuous:
To her foes mercifull,
   to subiects gracious.
Her soule is in heauen,
   the world keepes her glory:
Subiects her good deeds,
   and so ends my story.

       Sig. C$_4$-C$_{4v}$

30. In Kristevan terms I think that they (the male 'objects') would represent the denotative position, in the provided utterance structure.

2. Activist Entries into Writing

1. The term "discourse" here has its common text-linguistic meaning of a mode of discourse, i.e., a brand of language use, written and/or spoken, characterized by certain features specific to the mentality and ways of a particular group, context, or sociopolitical framework. (Habermas also uses "discourse" in a second sense, to be defined shortly.) I believe that "mode of discourse" in this sense also correlates with Foucault's concept of a "discursive formation," though Foucault (*Archaeology of Knowledge* 124–25) is describing his concept in a carefully nonpositivist fashion (or so as to defend his "positivities").

2. Donald Guss's recent view (1167) that in Habermas "strategic action" means violence is inaccurate although the relation it is based on could include violence.

3. This is my own proposition, not that of Habermas.

4. Certain textual issues need to be cleared up concerning this book. First, as her title states, Elizabeth Cooke (probably Lady Hoby at the time of translation) rendered this treatise from its original Latin, not from the French version, though her preface mentions the latter. Second, the preface shows that she had done the translation many years earlier than its publication, since she says that "the dead"—i.e., either the author Ponet or the editor-publisher her father—approved her translation himself: Ponet died in late 1556, Cooke in 1576. It is not immediately clear from this preface who was the work's author; since she says the "book" was "made" fifty years ago in Germany by a good and learned man, McIntosh argues that she thought her father the author, especially as his name appeared on the French translation and, McIntosh states, on the original Latin one. In fact, however, it does not appear in the 1557 first edition of the Latin, published by Cooke in Strasbourg (at least not in the C. U. L. copy I consulted). She could have meant that her father made the book in that he took the treatise from among Ponet's papers, edited it, and saw it through the press—indeed he made the *book* as such. It seems highly unlikely that she would have been so ill-informed as to think her father the author. And if she had, why would she not have ascribed the treatise to him on her title page, proud of him as she was? As for Ponet, there was ample reason not to name him as author of a book one was publishing in England, even as late as 1605. He was best remembered for his Marian exile treatise advocating deposition, even assassination, of religiously unsuitable monarchs (*A Shorte Treatise of Politike Power*, 1556). Had he lived to return home at Queen Elizabeth's accession, he would have received no welcome from her. Nor would King James have approved of such a writer, after what had happened to his mother. In short, Lady Russell must have known exactly who the author was but was judiciously avoiding mentioning him, while still claiming her part in the Marian exile milieu. The *Diallacticon* itself was not radical, representing Zwingli's and Cranmer's moderate position on the Eucharist (between the poles of Catholic "real presence" and Calvinist "outward sign"), which had become central to the Elizabethan consensus. Lady Russell saw herself as doing something analogous to her sister Lady Bacon's earlier publishing of an English rendering of Bishop John Jewel's *Apology*, a definitive text for the English church.

5. Selecting from the Anne Cooke/Ochino sermons requires care. The printer John Day put out various print runs of them with different numbers of sermons, none of these dated. It appears that first he took six Ochino sermon translations by a certain R. Argentine that had been published in Ipswich (1548) and combined them with fourteen more sermons translated by Anne Cooke, thus printing twenty sermons with a preface (presumably still

Argentine's) stating that the translator has done six sermons and hopes to do more. Next, Day printed a batch with the full set of twenty-five sermons (nineteen of them by Anne Cooke), yet still with the old preface announcing "vi" sermons, and still setting Argentine's six sermons first (not all later editions do): such is the copy (C.U.L. Syn 8.55.23) from which I have cited here. Finally, Day published the set of twenty-five with Anne Cooke's dedication of the book to her mother (not found in the C.U.L. copy) replacing the earlier preface by R. Argentine. All these undated versions have the long title beginning *Certayne Sermons of the ryghte famous and excellente Clerk Master Barnardine Ochine* and are dated by catalogers c. 1550. Some years later (c. 1570), Day republished the sermons with the title *Sermons of Barnardine Ochyne (to the number of 25) concerning the predestination and election of God . . . Translated out of Italian by A. C.* (still with Argentine's six included) and with a preface by one "G. B.," defending the work as "honest" and the fruit of time well spent, even though a woman wrote it. Finally, it seems that someone later did a still fuller compilation, adding sermons rendered by yet a third translator and reverting to something like Day's 1550 title: *Certain Sermons of the right famous and excellent clerk, Master Bernardino Ochino . . . Twenty-five Sermons, translated into English . . . by a gentleman and the last twenty-five . . . by a young lady* (i.e., nineteen of the last twenty-five being Anne Cooke's). I have not seen a copy of this last work, so am surmising about it. In short, when checking Ochino sermons for Anne Cooke's translations, one must take care to get the right ones.

6. Six are by another translator—see n. 5.

7. See Habermas (108) on this kind of identity and the nature of its mode of address as a speech act.

8. Instances such as this would make valuable material for exploring the sociocultural dimensions of what Foucault calls the Renaissance episteme—see *The Order of Things*.

9. If someone would read B. L. MS Add. 48096, the minutes of the Italian foreigners' church, and B. L. MS Landsdowne 10, fol. 177 (listing its members), we might learn more about Sylva. His preface says that he served in the Netherlands as a surgeon with the forces of Don Lope d'Acugna and there began writing on cosmography. (See also n. 13 below.) He does not recount a religious conversion; possibly he was already inclined to Protestantism before leaving Turin, a bastion of the movement. Since the point of the book's presentation was to take the queen's mind off of religious controversy and portray Dering and his party as learned and cosmopolitan, the absence of partisan religious material is what one would expect.

10. Dering's contribution is really two linked poems, on the author, then on himself; both play on Sylva's name as "woods."

Ῥωμαῖοι Silvam σὲ καλοῦσι Γραίκοι ὕλην
  τοὔνομα κ' ἀναφέρεις ἔνθα καὶ ἔνθα τέον
ὕλην μὲν γὰρ ὁμῶς ἔργῳ καὶ ῥήματι ἔσσι
  Σημαίνει ταὐτὸν τοὔνομα νοῦς τε σέθεν
Silvam κεῖνον ἔχει νοῦς καὶ πνευκάλιμον
  τὸ πίστον βίβλος κ' ἀμφοτερώθεν ἔδω
Silva γὰρ βίβλος ὧν γε γέμει λογίοιο νόοιο
  νοῦν ἄρα καὶ φώνην εὔπορος ἔσσο δάρον.

        τοῦ αὐτοῦ
Ὃς ταυτὴν σκοτοδασυπυκνόκλαδον ἡμῖν ἄνοιγεν
  λόχμην λοχμαῖον οὐκ ἀνέωξε χάριν

τὴν γῆν τὴν αὖραν τὴν αἰθέρα τὴν τε θάλασσαν
ἢ νοῦν πιπνύμενος ἢ πόδας ὤκυς ἴδεν.

[On Bartolo Silva, excellent doctor,
An epigram by Edward Dering

> The Romans call you Silva, Greeks the 'woods,'
>   And you take the name as yours, this way and that;
> So with deed and word equally you clothed the woods;
>   The name and your mind signify this fact,
> Thus in both ways here: your mind comprises that 'Silva,'
>   and the fair-breathing 'woods' your pledge, a book;
> For Silva, when being a book, is full of logical thought,
>   And alone it easily clothed the mind and voice.

On himself

> He who has opened for us the shaded, bushy, dense, leafy
> And wooded thicket has not opened up favoring grace,
> Albeit as one either sharp in mind or swift of foot he saw
>   The earth, the air, the ether, and the sea.]

11. Her brief poem in the Sylva MS is rather striking:

> Anna Dering in Barth: Sylvam Medicum Taurinensem
> Ut iuuat umbriferum liuibus nemus omne susuris
> Luminaque in viridi cuncta colorem tenet
> Sic exculta tuis tua mens iuuat artibus omnes
> O SYLVA, omnigenis SYLVA repleta bonis.

> [Anne Dering on Bartholo Sylva, Doctor of Turin
> As a shady grove delights all with gentle murmuring,
> And holds all lights in the color green,
> So your mind renewed delights all with your arts,
> SYLVA, O SYLVA filled with all-bearing gifts.]

In 1560 Anne Vaughan Locke (later Dering, later Prowse) had published translations of *Sermons of John Calvin, upon the Songe that Ezechias made*. Susanne Woods believes (Women Writers Workshop, Clark Library, Los Angeles, November 1990) that the sonnets of penitence appended to these sermons, sonnets which Locke says "a friend" has given her, were by Locke herself; Hannay ('Unlock my lipps') also argues that Locke wrote them, asserting that they are stylistically linked to the book's preface, signed "A. L." Church historians have taken them to be by her much-admired friend John Knox, who could not publish under his own name in England (Collinson "Role of Women").

12. Burghley, for his part, claimed in a letter to Sandys, Bishop of London, that he liked Dering's forthrightness and that it was others who were suppressing him (Collinson *Mirror* 22). Lady Burghley's poem in the Sylva MS. was the following.

By Mildred Lady Burghley, from Bartholo Sylva, *Il Giardino Cosmografico*

Ὡς πρώτιστα ἔναιον ἐπὶ χθόνι πολυβοτείρῃ
  νήπιοι ἄνδρες ὅλος κόσμος ἄκοσμος ἔην
ὡς φρονιμοὶ ἐγένοντ' ἄνδρες πολυδένδρεος ὕλη
  ὕλην τοῖς κήποις ἀνθεμέοισι πόρεν

νῦν κ᾽ ἐφύτευσε κάλον σόφος ὡς ἐκ νηρίτου ὕλης
ὕλη ἐφαρμόσσων ὃν πότε κῆπον ὁρᾷς.

[When foolish men first dwelt on the much-nourishing
     earth, the whole world-order was unordered:
When sensible men arose, the much-branching forest
     gave a woodland for the blossoming garden;
Now a wise man has made from vast forest a lovely garden,
     In the woods arranging a garden that you see.]

13. Reference works on sixteenth-century Italian doctors and Italian Protestants do not show any information about Dr. Bartholo Sylva of Turin, presumably an obscure young man when he left home to serve as a surgeon in the Low Countries (see n. 7). A possible connection is to a "Silva" family of publishers of medical books in Turin: i.e., early in the sixteenth century a Francisco Silva published books by Pietro Bairo, and in 1532 a Bernardino Silva published *De morbo gallico* by Jacopo Lagomarsini.

14. I also thank my husband Winfried Schleiner for much help with rough translations of the Latin as we worked in England.

15. Bernardo Ochino had in his last years been denounced for heresy and exiled from Switzerland (d. 1564 in Bohemia) for advocating something like a Socinian or unitarian view of the nature of God (i.e., questioning the doctrine of the trinity) and for guardedly advocating polygamy. His writings and fate would certainly have been known in England by 1570, through members of the Italian foreigners' church. For a stirring account of his last years see McNair. On Lady Bacon's activism as an elderly widow see Collinson ("Elizabethan Puritans" 257, 439–40).

16. See Collinson (*Mirror*) on Dering's published and unpublished letters.

17. Dering's letters to her of the early 1570s close with greetings to her little Nan, Bess, and Mary. Of these girls only Anne seems to have been still living in 1576 when Sir Anthony Cooke's will listed bequests for all his grandchildren (for Cooke's will see Emmison).

18. Killigrew gave money for the founding of the Puritan-inclined Emmanuel College (Collinson *Elizabethan Puritan Movement* 125) and was a friend of Pierre Loiseleur de Villiers, minister of the French church in 1574 (*Elizabethan Puritan* 536). See also A. Miller. Hoby, for example, signed a petition for reinstatement of a nonconformist minister (C. U. L. MS Mm. 1.42, f. 62).

19. The terminus is set by the fact that W. Kytton, recording these verses, says they are to "My Lady Cycyll"; after Jan. 1571 he would have said "My Lady of Burghley."

20. He has, for example, a format for prophesying meetings in Buckinghamshire, fols. 85–87.

21. Ballard (204) cites this, from her monument in St. Thomas the Apostle Church, Vintry Ward, London:

In mortem suam haec Carmina dum vixerat scripsit D. Katharina Killigreia

Dormio nunc Domino, Domini virtute resurgam;
     Et σωτῆρα meum carne videbo mea.
Mortua ne dicar, fruitur pars altera Christo:
     Et surgam capiti, tempore, tota, meo.

[While she lived Lady Katherine Killegrew wrote this poem on her death

Now I sleep in the Lord, in His virtue shall I rise again;
     And I shall see my Savior in the flesh.

Speak not of me as dead, my other self delights in Christ:
And I shall rise up, by the head, the face, the whole of me.]

22. See V. Wilson (14–91, 224–37) for extensive extracts from her letters.

23. The paraphrastic eighteenth-century translation printed by Travitsky derives, as she says, from Paul Hentzner's travel book in Latin (1598); it renders the two sets of verses, in Latin and Greek, beginning "Mens mea crudeli laniatur saucia morsu."

24. We do not know who wrote the verses honoring Sir Anthony and his wife; possibly the other sisters contributed something there. The verses are in Strype, Pt. 2, 604–607 (see Appendix 2).

25. They are in Crull and Hentzner.

26. The stone-carver seems to have misplaced this tag. We have moved it to where it makes sense, between the two poems (respectively in Greek and in Latin) by the mother, on the theme of the grieving Russell daughters: thus the second is "by the same, on the same, in Latin."

27. Geoffrey Fenton dedicated to her his *Monophylo . . . a philosophical discourse and division of love* (1572), on Platonic love.

3. Authorial Identity for a Second-Generation Protestant Aristocrat

1. Fraunce, Breton, and Daniel portray themselves as having stayed at Wilton or nearby Ivychurch and found intellectual support, while Watson in his *Amintae Gaudia* (1592) shows himself hoping for that status; and the composer Thomas Morley looked for artistic as well as financial support from her, even if at a distance, in asking her to promote his songs through her singing. Her letters of later years show that she also exchanged MSS by post with literary friends. Thus it cannot be amiss to study the mutual influences between her and such people, considered as inner and outer circles of writers and musicians, even if those in close touch with her at Wilton and in London were, as Brennan says, "only a handful" (*Patronage* 78), and the older view of Wilton as a "college" with literati constantly dancing attendance was overstated. Lamb also makes this latter point ("Countess of Pembroke's Patronage"). A handful was enough for her purposes.

2. That the queen in the 1580s considered the earl's and countess's residences, particularly Wilton and in London Baynard's Castle, as places of intrigue and likely opposition to her generally cautious international policies is evidenced in Brennan (*Patronage* 43), the most famous incidents being the Sidney/Dudley group's planning at Baynard's Castle of Sidney's notorious letter criticizing the queen's planned d'Alencon marriage, and Sidney's subsequent stay at Wilton. Freer ("Mary Sidney" 483) states that the countess, though residing in the West country, "remained a favorite of the queen," but he does not give any evidence for this assertion. The queen is likely to have regarded her as a highly placed possible critic, to be honored but also kept under scrutiny.

3. My analysis of her poem to Queen Elizabeth "Even now that care which on thy crown attends" appears in chapter 6 of my forthcoming study *Cultural Semiotics, Spenser, and the Captive Woman*.

4. Spriet (90–91) argues that the Delia sonnets, portraying a most respectful and diffident stance of poet to lady whereby he never hopes for more than to kiss her hand, were written for her. But they could have been, like Thomas Watson's "Passions," initially written to an imaginary lady, "Delia" being an anagram for "Ideal."

5. Daniel is clearly honoring her in dedicating to her the first full edition of his *Delia* sonnets (1592), and Marlowe also does so, at the recently dead Watson's behest he says, in addressing her as "Delia" in the dedication of the *Amintae Gaudia* (likewise 1592).

6. By tradition Daniel had earlier served the Herberts as a tutor and accompanied one of their young relatives to Italy; the point cannot be traced to a primary source, but see Daniel (*Works* 1:xvii); and Esdaile ed., xxi–xxiv. As for his being at Wilton, Daniel in the dedication to his later *Defense of Rhyme* credits the countess with having given him "the first notion for the formal ordering of these compositions [the Delia sonnets] at Wilton, which I must euer acknowledge to haue been my best school" (*Works* 1:xvi).

7. We have Nicholas Breton's record of a time when he lost the countess's favor for a while (*Works* 2:19) and Watson's portrayal of a quarrel between "Corydon"—probably Fraunce (cf. Moore Smith xxxvii)—and another poet he names "Faustulus" (*Amintae Gaudia*, Epistola Tertia)—perhaps Daniel, given Daniel's later debunking of Fraunce's quantitative metrics.

8. Cf. Brennan "Date of Death."

9. See chapter 1 of my *Living Lyre in English Verse*.

10. Brennan (*Patronage* 57), speaks highly of Sanford's abilities.

11. Indeed, it is highly likely that Fraunce's two-page Latin poem "Amintas Phillidi consecrauit mortuae moriturus" ("Amintas dying consecrates his death to Phillis"—*Ivychurch* 3:148) is meant to be spoken as in the voice of Watson, recently dead at that point.

12. Fraunce's *Lawyers Logicke* (1588) served, for the countess and others, as a handbook of poetic passages (many from Spenser's *Shepheardes Calender*, for example) illustrating rhetorical devices.

13. See Hannay (*Phoenix* 63–64) on her letter of 1594 to Sir Edward Wotton asking him to return his copy of a poem of grief she had sent to him earlier, because she has lost it and needs it again—perhaps a draft of the "Doleful Lay," Hannay argues.

14. For the broader context of Genette's study of paratextuality see *Palimpsestes* (1–16) and n. 15.

15. In *Palimpsestes* Genette proposes the term "transtextuality" as an umbrella rubric for all forms of possible relations between texts, then subdivides it into five kinds. Besides "paratextuality" (see above, and the whole of *Seuils*), he characterizes "intertextuality" by narrowing down Kristeva's original sense of that term (she coined it) to something exemplified by Riffaterre's micro-unit intertextual stylistics, and further proposes the term "hypertextuality" for the relation of two texts whereby the earlier seems to have served as a whole-scale progenitor to the later one—e.g., the *Iliad* and the *Aeneid* or, we could add, the *Orlando Furioso* and *The Faerie Queene*.

16. It may be worth noting, about the other end of the chart, that computer-programmed translation seems possible only up to level 4, since the levels beyond that require nonsystematizable interpretive choices based on so broad a range of such diversely representable physical and social recollections that it is very hard to imagine they could be programmed into a computer.

17. For an account of the minor ways in which the countess's translation departs from the original, see Luce 42. The dialogue portions, although in blank verse, are fairly close to a level 4 translation, while the rhymed act-ending choral odes represent level 5 in the shifted range markedly constrained by prosody.

18. There may be a tendency among scholars working on women writers to be rather too laudatory, in their eagerness to bring neglected writers to recognition. On the other hand, there is a ring of prematureness to Brennan's statement (*Patronage* 69) that scholars should "avoid failing into the trap of attempting to elevate [the countess's] literary talents to complement her exalted social position" and importance as a patron. First let us study her productions in their context, in some detail; only then will we have a reasonably concrete impression of what her literary talents produced. On technical matters of versification and uses of rhetorical figures of sound, certainly, women's work can be analyzed pretty much as

one does that of their male contemporaries; but on issues of metaphorics, voice, stance, politics, and sociolinguistic usage and patterning, issues of gender difference will have to come into play, for the sake of accurate description of what women writers had to work and cope with. Beyond these matters, the issue of quality or "elevation" is neither more nor less subjective for judgment of women's writings than for those of men, being probably best left to the slow quantitative vote of critical practice, as it finds texts rewarding or not rewarding for repeated analysis.

19. I refer to my forthcoming study *Cultural Semiotics, Spenser, and the Captive Woman.*

20. In his prefatory epistle to Greene's *Menaphon* Nashe praises Fraunce for his "excellent translation of Maister Thomas Watsons sugred *Amintas,*" which influenced other poets by animating "their dulled spirits to such high witted indeuours." For a collection of such praises, even from Spenser and Lodge, see Moore Smith (*Victoria* "Introduction" xxi).

21. Perhaps Breton was trying to help Watson gain favor with the countess, and Fraunce was opposing him.

22. On the grammatical and rhetorical traits of song mode as distinguished from declamatory and conversational modes in Elizabethan and Jacobean verse, see my *Living Lyre* (8ff).

23. *Living Lyre* 36–45.

24. According to Moore Smith ("Introduction" to Fraunce's neo-Latin play *Victoria*, xxxvii), Spenser in "Colin Clout's Come Home Again" (1591, publ. 1595) was referring to Fraunce, a lawyer at Ludlow, in the lines on Corydon the "hablest wit of most I know this day . . . though meanly waged," Fraunce getting the name from his translation of Virgil's 2d eclogue, one of the pieces dedicated to the countess in Part II of *The Countesse of Pembrokes Yuychurch* (1591).

25. See Brennan "Date of Psalms."

26. Noting this difference, Svensson (45) argues that the countess's version was written first, Daniel's sonnet then, as a tribute to her, juxtaposing the already linked metaphors without needing to include the link. The conclusion does not seem inevitable: Daniel could have written his sonnet version first, then the countess could have spun out the sequence of ideas at more length, supplying a suitable linkage.

27. For a convenient summary of them see Snare's "Introduction" to his edition of *The Third part of the . . . Yuychurch, entitled Amintas Dale* (xiv–xv), and for a fuller account, Ringler's edition of Sidney's poetry, under "Master Drant's Rules."

28. The countess, like other women of the time in their verse and narratives, frequently uses colloquial language features (as one would expect, given their lack of formal training in writing). An especially common one in Emilia Lanyer is the dialectal plural verb with 's,' e.g., "Which pleasures with retired minds agrees," ("Salve Deus," l. 24). The features we must note here are ellipses of two kinds, apparently common in oral narrative: omission of forms of the verb "to be" and omission of relative pronouns introducing restrictive clauses. The former appears several places, as in "So rare [was] thy fairest mind," the latter in such lines as "This finished now [that] thy matchless Muse begun." That such are not simply blunders resulting from the pressure of a metered syllable count, but instances of colloquial locution, which left her syntax still comprehensible to the countess and her readers though hard for us, is clear if we recall how common they are in her niece Lady Wroth's *Urania* romance, which is not in verse but prose—i.e., under no syllable constraint. Let me give randomly spotted examples. "But then [as it was] growing almost night, Urania went home" (32); "Antissius in the same ship [that] had thither brought them, took again to the sea" (Salzman ed., *Anthology* 73); "he did not suffer me to enter the town as myself (by reason of a great hate [that] had been between our parents)" (96); "when time is past you shall know the means [that] might have prevented it" (168); "the good man, hearing that these were two of them [who] relieved and won Rumania, . . . came to welcome him" (196)—etc.

29. I am not sure if the "Lay of Clorinda" is hers, or entirely hers, though Spenser's poem explicitly says it is; she could have recast an earlier drafted poem to make it fit his frame stanza pattern—or he could have adopted that pattern because an already existing poem of hers was to be incorporated. Perhaps he heavily edited it. Much of "The Lay" seems of a piece with Spenser's introductory poem preceding it, and not in tone much like her other known poems (though perhaps generic difference would account for this fact). See Waller's (*Critical Study*) and Brennan's (*Patronage*) opposing arguments about this issue.

4. Catholic Squirearchy and Women's Writing

1. On the economic and sociosemiotic dimensions of my usage of this term, see my forthcoming study *Cultural Semiotics, Spenser, and the Captive Woman*.

2. See Kristeva "Semiotics: A Critical Science," 75, 87.

3. See especially Montrose "Elizabethan Subject."

4. These points were noted by Joanne Knowles.

5. See my forthcoming *Cultural Semiotics, Spenser, and the Captive Woman*.

6. I believe it was a serious attempt—a socially suitable husband of French royalty, whose personality and relative youth made him seem controllable, could be genuinely tempting to her. But even if she was only playing her usual marriage game, my perspective on her motives in this case for doing so remains the same.

7. On these and related matters see Marie Rowlands's well-documented study.

8. See, e.g., that to Elizabeth of Easter 1569 (from Wingfield), Nov. 10, 1569 (from Tutbury)—both in Labanoff 2—and of Nov. 27, 1571 (from Sheffield)—in Labanoff 3.

9. Spenser, as I read *The Shepheardes Calender*'s "February" fable (where the chopped-down Oak Tree has always been agreed to evoke Norfolk getting decapitated), portrayed Oxford (in the Briar) treacherously betraying his older cousin and mentor Norfolk into Burghley's hands, for the advantage just then of marrying into Burghley's family; Protestants other than the highest-ranking court insiders had sympathized with Norfolk and considered him a victimized Protestant hero, as he had boldly presented himself on the scaffold. But later knowledge of State Papers does not lend credit to this view of his innocence.

10. Ellen Moody's comments (158) accord with this account, though without including supporting evidence.

11. For a lively account of Oxford's quarrel with Sidney over that issue, the famous "tennis court" encounter, see Quilligan "Sidney."

12. May proposes that his argument holds also for the single sonnet on the Princess of Espinoy that Southern prints and attributes to Queen Elizabeth. I have not tried to argue that question here, but think that the queen could easily have indulged in such a Euphuist writing exercise if she wanted to. As has been suggested since the eighteenth century, her likely displeasure at seeing such a thing in print would explain why only two copies of *Pandora* survive.

13. On Watson as sonneteer see my *Living Lyre* 17–27.

14. We have no information about Southern's life nor how he came by his English name—perhaps either by Anglicizing a French one or by having an English father and French mother.

15. For these rules determining what syllables to consider "short" or "long," see the section on "Master Drant's Rules" in William Ringler's edition of *The Poems of Sir Philip Sidney*.

16. Ovid in translation was enormously popular among Elizabethan women, and men too, for pleasure reading—particularly the *Heroides* (poems mostly in the voices of legendary women) in George Turberville's translation and the *Metamorphoses* in Arthur Golding's, both

available since the 1560s. The sexually explicit *Amores* did not appear in printed translation, so far as is known, until Marlowe's of 1600 (though his versions probably circulated in MS somewhat earlier). The elegy to Tibullus itself, however, has nothing offensive and could well have been rendered at times as a private translation by ladies' secretaries. In any case, Anne Cecil de Vere, daughter of the classically trained Mildred Cooke Cecil, may have been taught enough Latin to read it herself.

17. Queen Elizabeth is here flattered as Cynthia/Diana or the moon, a very common mode of courtly address to her.

18. The text reads "hath take"—if not a misprint, this could be one of Southern's edits. The countess correctly uses "hath ta'en" (spelled "tanne") for this form in sonnet #2, so I think this one should be emended.

19. As Ronsard occasionally does (e.g., *Oeuvres: Texte de 1587* II pp. 88, 313), the Countess of Oxford sometimes puts in quotation marks a passage that she is directly translating from another poet. A quick scan of Petrarch's *Rime*, Watson's *Hekatompathia*, and the love poems of Ronsard's 1587 *Oeuvres* has not turned up a source of these lines; perhaps someone will come across it.

20. Queen Elizabeth officially continued the d'Alencon marriage negotiations into 1581, but by then Oxford publicly recanted his Catholicism and betrayed three of his fellow crypto-Catholic courtiers (see Read *Burghley* 275).

21. Bethune (19–20) attributes another poem to Anne Dacre Howard: repeating a proposal of Edmund Lodge, the eighteenth-century collector of aristocratic family papers, he states that "In sad and ashy weeds I sigh" appears on the cover of a letter in the Countess of Arundel's handwriting and evidently refers to her husband's death in 1598. But Donald Foster tells me that he has found other occurrences of this poem, presenting it as an elegy on the death of Prince Henry (in 1612); thus he does not credit the Lodge attribution of it to the countess. Of course she could have written it, and someone else later finding it could have taken it for (or used it as) one of the many laments called for by the shocking death of the eighteen-year-old prince. The (then dowager) Countess of Arundel herself was still alive until well after 1612 (*DNB* 28:73). Perhaps the matter deserves further study, but there may be no way to determine a definite attribution.

22. For the letter see Labanoff ed. VI:190–94.

23. Hans Walther, *Initia Carminum ac Versum Medii Aevi posterioris Latinorum* (Göttingen: Vandenhoeck u. Ruprecht, 1969), 352, shows a similar twelfth-century hymn in the same meter, "Gabrielis nuntium/novum tulit gaudium," surviving in MS at Leipzig: 224, fol. 178v.

24. The two lines just preceding these have been lost from the MS by bookbinder cutting of the page.

25. The Catholic identity of Elizabeth is clearly attested in her poems, that of her brother John Francis by his years of attendance at the Jesuit Clementine school in Prague starting in 1585 (as reported in *Enchiridion* 5: 471) and his later studies at Ingolstadt, a Catholic haven. Originally baptized John and Elizabeth, the two later had double names, possibly indicating that they were rechristened in Bohemia. We do not know whether the family was Catholic before Kelley's alchemical ambitions took them abroad.

26. In her poem on her mother's death ca. 1606 (*In obitum nobilis et generosae faeminae, dominae Ioannae p. m. magnifici et generosi domini Edovardi Kellei de Imany, equitis aurati sacraeque Caesareae Maiestatis consiliarii, derelictae viduae, matris suae honorandissimae charissimaeque, lachrymabunda effudit filia*), as summarized by Bassnett ("Revising" 3), Weston says that her father died when she was six months old, that later she lost her two grandmothers, and then lived with her kind stepfather; in her poem on Ovid's *Tristia*, she says that the same month which "saw you out to the Sarmatian shore" saw her likewise out to exile; this

would probably have been, as events fall into place, December of 1584, just after Kelly had become established in Prague (see *Tristia* 1.11.4, on Ovid's crossing the Adriatic from Italy in a December). In Dee's detailed diaries of his household with children and servants from 1583–88, including Edward and Joan Kelley, no mention is made of the Weston children (unless the new, more complete edition of these by Julian Roberts, now in progress, will have something).

27.   According to information from Susan Bassnett, kindly sent on to me by Donald Cheney, an eighteenth-century copy of the now lost parish register of Chipping Norton near Oxford shows the marriage of John Wessone and Joan Cowper on June 27, 1579, their son's baptism, and an undated entry for their daughter Elizabeth's baptism, falling between March 4 and October 31, 1581. Elizabeth's tomb in Prague, stating that she was born in London 30 years earlier (i.e., 1582), seems to be wrong about the year and the place—for its text see Gottfried J. Dlabacz, *Allgemeinsches historisches Künstler-lexikon für Boehmen*, 1815).

28.   If this claim of noble lineage (so much stressed in Weston's poems) had any basis at all, perhaps John Weston the clerk was somehow part of one of the two Weston lineages in *The History and Antiquities of . . . Surrey*, I: 135–36 and III: 41), both deriving from a twelfth-century knight. As a possibility from these, the wealthy land-owner judge Sir Richard Weston of Skreens, Essex (d. 1572—whose grandson would later be Earl of Portland), had an uncle in Henry VIII's time, William Weston "of New College Oxford," to whom an Oxford "clark" such as Elizabeth's father could have been a son or grandson. (On the Westons of Skreens see Sr. Mary Catherine Brentwood, "Papist Tombs in Essex Churches II, Writtle," *Essex Recusant* 3 [1961]: 31–37; and on the uncles of Sir Richard Weston of Skreens, R. E. Chester Waters, 93ff.)

29.   The Elizabeth Weston entry in the *Allgemeine deutsche Biographie* (Leipzig, 1892; 42: 193–96) states that some personal papers, presumably in Bohemia but no further identified, contain embarrassing revelations contradicting statements in her published writings, but does not recount these. I do not know just what papers were used for the several twentieth-century Czech articles on Weston cited in the *Enchiridion* entry on her of 1982, or by Vaclav Kaplicky in his 1980 biography of Kelley in Czech. While this popular-style socialist publication does not have footnotes, it seems to be based on some scholarship in primary records about the Kelleys' and Westons' Bohemian years because he supplies some otherwise unnoted names and places (even though on their English backgrounds he is following erroneous traditions). I thank Valerie Tumins for translating the *Enchiridion* entry and extensive passages of the Kaplicky biography from Czech.

30.   Kaplicky states (102ff.) that Kelley and "Lady Weston" married in Bohemia, with two imperial ministers, Trautsohn and Rumpf, serving as witnesses.

31.   Kaplicky (68) relates that the two imperial agents who witnessed the wedding, Rumpf and Trautsohn, had already been monitoring Kelley and Dee since 1585, when they first arrived in Prague, because the emperor had feared they were spies.

32.   Evans (218–28) carefully documents the registration of Kelley's title in the Bohemian parliamentary record (1589), the time of his first imprisonment in May 1591, and a number of other facts of the 1590s, all of which accord with Kaplicky's account of events; but Evans is unaware of Kelley's Weston connection, though he also has a section on "Westonia," the noted poet.

33.   The account here supersedes my *CaudaP* article, which was based on the German and Bohemian accounts perpetuating the claim of a "noble" Weston father, and on Kaplicky's report of the Bohemian Kelley-Weston marriage.

34.   Fell Smith (197 and 201) reports Dee's diary entry that Joan Kelley set out for England from Trebon October 17, 1588, and notes that she was back with Kelley in Prague by early 1591.

35. The official reason was that Kelley had killed a court official named Jiri Hunkler in a duel (*Enchiridion* 5: 471).

36. Kaplicky (207) supports their view, referring to "Hammon" as "an immigrant." Ludwig Fränkel (*Allgemeine deutsche Biographie* 1892, 42: 194) says she attended Hammond's humanistic school in Brüx, and perhaps with more nationalist pride than exact information calls it the "nach bewährtem sächsischen Muster eingerichteten Brüxer Schule des Johann Hammon" [the Brüx school of Johann Hammon, established according to the well-tried Saxon pattern].

37. Kaplicky calls him Jan Lva z Eisenach [Johann Löwe aus Eisenach]; since all the early contexts where his name appears are in Latin, he is otherwise referred to as "Leo."

38. She comments on the editing of her *Parthenicon* book (which as Donald Cheney informs me has a poem to a child who died in 1607) in handwritten verses in a copy of it now at the British Library, B. L. Cat.C.61.d.2., two leaves before the frontispiece. Her complaint here about the intermingling of other people's poems with hers is well founded: e.g., a whole section of poems by Georg Carl von Carlsberg is confusingly labeled with no more than his name above the first one and several pages later a rubric, *hactenus Georg Carl von Carlsberg* (thus far von Carlsberg). And indeed, later commentators have cited some of those poems as hers. I thank my husband, Winfried Schleiner, for transcribing and helping me translate these handwritten verses:

> . . . Lector, quaecunque libello
>   Nomine sub nostro publica facta vides:
> Non me diffiteor scripsisse, sed . . .
> Nimirum quod sint congesta sine ordine cuncta,
>   Junctaque Parthenicis quae nova nupta dedi.
> Atque typographicis scateant hinc indeque mendis.
>   E quas vereor tribuat ne mihi livor iners
> Prolibituque meas opplet sine iure pagellas
>   Nescio cui fidens, alter amicitiae. . . .
> Hinc omissa scias mea plurima, multa videbis
>   Hinc modulis passim mixta aliena meis.
> Hunccine Westoniae dici vis, quaeso, libellum
>   Tu, qui Westoniae vix sinis esse locum?
> At melius proprias integro Codice laudes
>   Condere, quo digne concelegrere, fuit.
> Quam tua foemineis iunxisse poemata opellis,
>   Grandia sic parvis q- minuisse modis. . . .
> Tempus erit sine te (faveat modo Parca.) pagellas
>   Impleat ut numeris Westonis ipsa suis

>   Elizabetha Joanna, Uxor Ionnis Leonis . . . Pragae 16. Augusti Ao 1610

> [. . . reader, all that in a little book
>   You see made public under our name:
> I do not deny having written it, but . . .
> Certainly all the things are randomly jumbled and joined,
> These Parthenicon poems, which I newly married gave out.
>   Thus they also abound in typographic errors,
>   And I fear that pure malice does not allow me these;
>   The other one [von Baldhoven?], to be pleasing, fills up my little pages wrongfully,
>   Out of friendship trusting I don't know whom. . . .

Here you must know many of my pieces are omitted, many
   Others mixed here and there with my rhymes.
I ask, do you want the little book to be called Weston's,
   You who scarcely allow Weston any room?
Better to form these brief praises into a separate
   Book, in which to honor them worthily.
How can your poems be mixed with little female works,
   Grand things thus being reduced to the scale of small ones? . . .
One section was quite without you [i.e., herself] (Fate somehow allowed);
   The man fills the little pages with his as well as Weston's measures.

Elizabeth Jane, Wife of Johann Leo . . . Prague, August 16,

1610

39. See her letter to Stephen Lesieur, a secretary of James for international affairs whom she had met in Prague, and his reply denying what she had been told (*Parthenicon*, Bk. III, Sig. A4v-H7). She writes that a Captain William Turner visited her and, among insulting remarks, revealed that her verses had been casually received at James's court, saying that the messenger had presented them as ghost-written for her. This William Turner was perhaps the shady-sounding espionage agent of that name, a letter from whom survives in the Hatfield House MSS (Calendar, Part XVII, 544–45) ("Versatur in hac Urbe Pragensi quidam conterraneus noster [si tamen ita dicendus] nomine, quo se venditat, Guilhelmus Turnes [*sic*]; qui ante duas, nisi fallor, hebdomadas huc ex Patria redens, conclave nostrum, ubi cum matre eram, ingressus, post ostentatas iterum atque iterum literas, quas a Regne nostro Potentissimo, Reginaque serenissima, nec non a te ipso, aliusque Regni Anglicani Proceribus ad Caesar. Mtem. & Consiliarios ejusdem mitti falso [quod tandem eventus probavit] affirmabat, multa, eaque ignominiosissima minacissimaque verba non in nos solummodo, sed etiam in Consiliarios S. C. Mtis. audacter satis impudenterque effundebat."—etc.).

40. See the letter from John Francis Weston in *Parthenicon*.

41. This whole epistle is to his former pupil Perilla, whom some classicists take to have been Ovid's stepdaughter, and several of its details must have seemed to Weston entirely a propos for herself: he tells his letter to go look for its young addressee sitting beside her sweet mother, or else among her books and her own writings; he urges her to continue writing learned poems and recalls that he was a fatherly guide to her when they read their poems aloud to each other.

42. Schede, incidentally, had years before exchanged verses with Queen Elizabeth (see Bradner ed. of the queen's verse). On Weston's poetic reputation see Evans, Binns (110–14), Schkelenko, and Patzak.

5. Parlor Games and Male Self-Imaging as Government

1. Savage (xl) suggested that the two "Newes" pieces attributed to "A. S." might have been by Anne Clifford Sackville, Countess of Dorset, the diarist. But besides the fact that she would have signed "A. C." or "A.D.," Jean Klene's identification of Anne Harris Southwell, wife of Sir Thomas of Spixworth and Poulnalong, as the "A. S." of the "Newes" items is far more cogent. Her commonplace book (Folger V.b. 198) from her Irish years shows verbal and thematic echoes of the "A. S." "Newes" pieces (Klene 12) and a strain of vigorous wit distinctly redolent of them. Savage had further suggested that the "Lady Southwell" of the "Edicts" was the lady-in-waiting to Queen Anne (as she had been to Queen Elizabeth), Lady "Frances" Howard Southwell, daughter of Charles Howard, Earl of Nottingham, and widow of Sir Robert Southwell. Donald Foster has written (letter of July 21, 1993, in answer to my

inquiries) that Savage and the *DNB* are wrong about this lady's first name, that it was Elizabeth, and he again raises the possibility that she, not Anne Southwell, wrote the "Edicts from Eutopia" in the *Wife* (see Savage), ascribed there to "Lady Southwell," though he believes Anne Southwell to have written one at least of the "Newes" items; Foster further states that the Mrs. Southwell (cf. State Papers Domestic) who in 1603 met Queen Anne at Berwick in quest of patronage (Klene 3) was the wife of a different Thomas Southwell, namely of Woodrising and knighted 1603, while Thomas Southwell of Spixworth and Poulnalong became Sir Thomas only in 1615. While this is not the place for a full elaboration, putting Foster's valuable new information together with my own studies of thematic similarities, verbal echoes, and other internal matters in the Folger MS and in the three pieces from the *Wife*, I believe the latter are all Anne Harris Southwell's. When the two "answers to the Newes" pieces first appeared in the second impression of the *Wife* (1614), both subscribed "A. S.," that was the accurate way to refer to her; the "Edicts" first appeared in the 6th impression, of 1615, the year Sir Thomas was knighted, and thus she could be called "Lady Southwell." Since the other "Newes" pieces are likewise attributed only by initials, it is not surprising that "A. S." was in subsequent impressions of the *Wife* kept for them, and indeed as the subscript after only the second "Answer" piece (which ends a kind of unit consisting of the first five, thematically interconnected inventions, including the two "Answer"s by "A. S."). If there should prove to be some particularly convincing reason for thinking the high-ranking Lady Elizabeth Southwell was the writer of the "Edicts" and willing to have her name attached to them, one would have to suppose that she played very closely similar games and referred to the same affairs as did the members of the "Newes" circle.

2. The MS is Newberry Library Case Msfy 1565.W95; Josephine Roberts is preparing an edition of it. For the Pamphilia sonnets and other poems of Wroth, see Roberts's edition of the *Poems*.

3. She is not named in the poem, but Jonson later identified her as its subject in his *Conversations* with Drummond of Hawthornden (Herford et al. 1:76–77).

4. Lewalski (*Writing* 402, n. 20) accepts Jonson's published list of the *Beauty* masquers (Herford et al. 7:178, 191); but Brennan shows, from Antimo Galli's account of *Beauty's* performance, that Wroth did take part in it, as in *Blackness* (*Victory* "Introduction" 11). It is telling, then, that her name was omitted from the sixteen Jonson listed for *Beauty*. Presumably, at the time of its publication the queen no longer wanted to be publicly associated with her. The omission of her name is, I believe, a strong clue that her disgrace dated from c. 1610. The point is also supported by her whereabouts from summer 1610 through spring 1611, recorded in Sidney correspondence, which shows her circling among Loughton and Durance (Wroth's Essex residences), Pembroke's London residence Baynard's Castle, and the Sidneys' Penshurst (Waller "Romance" 42).

5. See Wroth (*Poems* 30; *Victory* "Introduction").

6. So says Cavanaugh, and she adds that Lady Southwell was the sister of Sir Edward Harris, a judge in Ireland. (However, Cavanaugh's further statement that she had been lady-in-waiting to Queen Elizabeth must represent a confusion of her with Lady Elizabeth Southwell—see n. 1). For the text of the letter cited from Anne Southwell's MS below, see Cavanaugh.

7. This she had in common with Donne, Jonson, and Lady Wroth. Jonson wrote in his *Conversations with Drummond* that Overbury had first been his friend, then his mortal enemy; Donne, for his part, seems to have made a veiled plea to the king to pardon Carr, after the murder conviction (see W. Schleiner "Coterie"). Wroth allegorized Frances Howard's situation sympathetically in a late episode of the *Urania* (*Urania* I. iv. 478; also see chap. 6, below). Thus Overbury had apparently alienated almost the whole "News" circle, who had been his friends and allies, though in the *Conceited Newes* William Strachey does have an elegy among others lamenting his murder.

8. See especially his letters to Henry Goodyere—he would probably have succeeded, had not the king himself, as is often noted, determined that Donne should get no post but in the church.

9. It uses concepts of A.-J. Greimas's *Semiotics and Language, an Analytical Dictionary*, along with the topic-focus distinction as elaborated in the Quirk and Greenbaum standard linguistic grammar of English.

10. Lewalski's *Writing Women in the Jacobean Era*, available after the present study was drafted, also makes this assumption and treats some of the same materials discussed in my chapters 5–7, as well as the lives of other court women who left letters and diaries. As will be evident, my approach focuses less on description of lives per se than on women's circulated writings that can be read as belletristic, studied within the framework of feminist and sociosemiotic perspectives. Another book appearing after this one was finished and also treating Mary Wroth is Krontiris's *Oppositional Voices*.

11. My treatment on this point accords with those of Riggs (154–63) and Lewalski (*Writing* 108–10) but supplements them in treating the significance of the Overbury-Jonson-Rutland details and the allusions to "Penthesilea" and "Mavis."

12. The countess addressed her simply as "Wallingford," by titled name, as the collegiate ladies in *Epicoene* do with each other; Jonson obviously found this presumptuous, as if they had taken over their husbands' identities—indeed the Countess of Bedford had done so, her country-dwelling husband being incompetent for a courtier life, first because of his disgrace in the Essex rebellion, then through his incapacitating injury in a riding accident.

13. Unlike the other plays of this peak time of his popularity, no quarto of it is known to have been published, not until 1620, after it had first appeared in his folio of 1616. Jonson himself told Drummond: "When his play of a Silent Woman was first acted, there was found verses after on the stage against him, concluding that that play was well named The Silent Woman: there was never one man to say plaudite to it" (*Conversations*, Herford et al. 1:617–19). For the queen's masque of *Tethys Festival* in June 1610 she turned to Samuel Daniel instead of Jonson. Roy Strong supports this view of the queen's turning away from Jonson at this point, though without noticing that *Epicoene* could have been to blame: Jonson had become, Strong says, "first and foremost the King's poet. . . . The fact that Anne turned to Samuel Daniel [in mid-1610] probably indicates a quest for a masque writer other than Jonson. *Tethys Festival* was clearly unsuccessful and Daniel was not used again, which must account for the reversion to Jonson for the Queen's masque in 1611" (Strong 160).

14. See Savage for the identifications of them.

15. Literally speaking, they may have had little trouble getting slept with. While Jonson scorned Mrs. Bulstrode's love affairs, we might be more sympathetic. Ladies-in-waiting of medium rank were often poor relations of the better-heeled women they served; they were in such service because their fathers could not come up with a dowry to get them a husband suitable to their status, and thus they could not marry. (Anne Clifford's diary shows her waiting women to have been also unmarried daughters of lesser gentry.) Those at court, finding themselves regularly flattered by men out to gain notice from their powerful employers, must have found secret affairs a natural way of life. *Epicoene* also denounces them for using contraceptives and abortifacients.

16. The MS (Folger V.b.198) has many other pages of verse, mostly of Lady Anne's own composition, including a mock elegy on her friend the Countess of Londonderry (see above and Appendix 2), and then a shorter sincere one written when she learned that the lady indeed had died. Klene further mentions two prose meditations in a different MS, on the third and fourth commandments (B. L. Lansdowne 740, ff. 142–67b.).

17. The same usage of the term ideologeme for my purposes has already been elaborated in my forthcoming study of Elizabeth's reign, *Cultural Semiotics, Spenser, and the Captive Woman*.

18. The kind of opposition functioning as a classeme, often culturally conditioned, derives from the mechanisms of human sensory and/or social perception (i.e., high-low, hot-cold, male-female), being based on a sense of two oppositional poles with gradations possible in between. Thus it is not logically rigorous, as are the oppositions "contradiction" and "contrariety," and cannot be articulated (as the term at issue) on the semiotic square. But it can be carried (as initial term or classemic opposite) from position to position on the semiotic square, in conjunction with other semes or sememes.

19. There may be other units of ideologically constituted meaning than that identified here as an ideologeme, units or subunits not yet recognized. I do not suppose that the ideologeme as here conceptualized will explain everything about ideology and meaning-generation, only that it may contribute to explaining something.

20. Goldberg's influential study of James's self-representation habit and its influence on major writers (including Shakespeare in *Measure for Measure*) is quite in accord with my analysis here, though I am taking a theoretically different approach to the issues involved, raising different kinds of questions, and focusing on gender.

21. See the succeeding chapter, on Donne's "First Anniversary," for political characterization of that "moment."

22. To what extent it continued in use beyond that period I am not investigating here; that would require another study.

23. Beyond these, there can of course be limitless ranges of diversely triggered readings.

24. I am not arguing that the king as the sun was a newly invented metaphor (of course the trope of ruler as sun is ancient), but rather that it was taken up and oriented in a particular way under James within the ideologeme pattern I am describing. Stella Revard discussed the Emperor Augustus and later figures as rising suns in an address, "The Nativity Ode: Apollo and the Flight of the Pagan Gods," Milton Society Meeting, New York, Dec. 28, 1992.

25. A related song is Sir Jack Daw's madrigal in *Epicoene* (II.iii.123ff.), "Silence in woman is like speech in man."

26. On related issues of female agency in *Blackness* see Hall.

27. On this point my discussion has profited from conversations with J. M. Massi.

28. Their father, Edward Vere, 17th Earl of Oxford, was a first cousin of Thomas Howard, Duke of Norfolk, who had been executed in 1572 for plotting to marry Mary Stuart, King James's mother: Norfolk was the father of the Jacobean Suffolk (who could not inherit his stripped title), grandfather of Arundel, and brother of Northampton.

29. On the Italian backgrounds of English pastoral drama as Wroth would have known it, specifically in connection with the Sidney protégé Samuel Daniel and his *Queene's Arcadia*, see Donno ed. *Three Renaissance Pastorals* and Lewalski "Pastoral."

30. Rustic as the villainous would-be husband Sir Robert Rich in this improved version of real life marries, as he should have, an emotional and intellectual light-weight, Dalina.

31. Gossip reported these latter two secretly married at Spa—or not married, as the gossiper preferred.

32. I thank my husband, Winfried Schleiner, for this suggestion.

33. Musella laments her situation:

O Eyes, that day can see, and cannott mend
What my joys poyson, must my wreched end
Proceed from love? And yett my true love crost,
Neglected for bace gaine, and all worthe lost
For riches? Then 'tis time for good to dy,
When wealth must wed us to all misery.

(V. 1–6)

34. As Roberts pointed out (Wroth *Poems* 38), the character constellation here, including Arcas, Rustic, Dalina and the three serious couples, is the same as that used in an episode from Part II, Book 2 of the *Urania* (Part II never having been published, a MS of it is now in the Newberry Library—see n.2 above and chapter 6). Wroth could have written the play first and then adopted its character set for an episode in her continuation of the *Urania*, or vice versa.

35. The 18th earl had traveled much abroad, and like the Pembroke faction was opposed to James's Spanish flirtations. The rumor of this possible marriage floated as Lady Wroth marched in Queen Anne's funeral (see *DNB* "Mary Wroth").

36. Naomi Miller's suggestions about the female speaker's perspective on love in the *Pamphilia* sonnets seem akin to my analysis here, e.g., "The evolving dynamic among the central characters soon differentiates Wroth's perspective from that of her male predecessors in the genre. In particular, the speaker's relation to Cupid shifts when the sonneteer is a lady" (298).

37. It found one prototype in Socrates' mythologizing in the *Symposium*, where Love is portrayed as the son of Poverty and Invention.

38. Here I am taking up Kristeva's interlocking concepts of the "enunciative" position and "denotative" position, which together define the trajectory of a given discourse. The first is the sememically defined position, the semantic "place," as it were, from which the discourse is enunciated, while the second position is that toward which the trajectory of this enunciation moves, that which it addresses. These I believe correlate with Greimas's S_1 and S_2 positions in the base narrative program formula, rather than with what he calls the enunciator-enunciatee pair (roughly equivalent to the older concept of "implied writer-implied actual reader"); that is, her dyad is internal to the text in its derivation—as are Greimas's "actants of narration" (here the S_1 and S_2). In other words, Kristeva has gone farther than Greimas in combating essentialism (or substantification) in her terminology, though he also does this by speaking of functions and roles rather than entities: she speaks in terms of positionality, doing without the substantification and even personification involved in the "actant" concept—for which one can substitute actantial role, within Greimas's system. (On these Kristevan concepts see her book *Revolution in Poetic Language* and "D'une Identité l'autre" in *Desire in Language*.)

39. Waller does not explain what he means by "discursive positions"; perhaps my text-linguistic materials here are in accord with his view.

6. Factional Identities and Writers' Energies

1. In the *Basilicon Doron* he advised Prince Henry to judge supporters by how faithful they had been to his parents and affirmed the loyalty of those who had supported his mother—i.e., the squirearchist party, then also centering in the Howards—who had tried to liberate Mary Stuart by arranging for her a marriage that Queen Elizabeth would tolerate.

2. Riggs's portrayal of two main factions (the Pembrokeans rallying to Prince Henry) supports my account here: "Whereas James, the ungainly and effeminate King, was peaceable, Henry, the athletic and virile Prince, was warlike. The father sought to prevent religious wars in Europe by promoting dynastic intermarriages; the son was eager to invade the Continent. . . . The King leaned toward the Spanish faction; the Prince naturally inclined to the interests of France. James's government was dominated by the Howards and by Salisbury, whom Henry disliked intensely; Henry's favorite companions included the young Earl of Essex and Lady Bedford's brother, Sir John Harington" (164–65).

3. Burton coauthored an academic play called *Alba*, performed for James's 1605 visit

to Oxford, and afterward wrote and revised his *Philosophaster* in the hope that the king would return, or later, that it could be performed at Cambridge or Royston, as were such Cambridge plays as the *Ignoramus* and *Susanbrotus* (Burton, McQuillen ed. "Introduction").

4. This was the year of Salisbury's failed "Great Contract" attempt, a desperation measure to put the king on a supportable income. Parliament was to promise a yearly subsidy of £200,000, and he was to make over to them his feudal perquisites (customs duties, etc.). But neither Parliament nor the king would agree to this. For a brief account of the ensuing events concerning Overbury and Somerset, see Prestwich (104–10).

5. Since he told Drummond that she was "unworthily married on a jealous husband" (*Conversations* 299–300), we may conclude that he sympathized with her position enough, in his own valuations, to excuse her adultery (with Cecily he was not so charitable).

6. Henry Brooke, Lord Cobham, and his brother George Brooke. The planned execution of those two and their associate Lord Grey of Wilton, which King James theatrically halted with a last-minute pardon arriving at the gallows, is most probably alluded to in the penchant of Duke Vincentio for theatrical mercy in *Measure for Measure* (see my "Providential Improvisation").

7. For a useful brief account of the workings of the two factions from 1610–1613 see Lee (242–45).

8. As for Jonson's religious loyalty, he had been a Catholic for twelve years but was just at this time returning to the Anglican church.

9. This fundamental concept of her whole fiction suggests, by the way, that she began writing it only after the death of Elizabeth Manners, Countess of Rutland, Sidney's daughter, who according to Jonson was a good poet, "nothing inferior to her father."

10. Roberts ("Knott" 122–23) shows in detail from family correspondence that Pembroke's former tutor and editor of the *Arcadia* Hugh Sanford (depicted in the romance as "Forsandrus") in late 1604 had "played a prominent role in arranging both of the marriages," i.e., of Pembroke with Mary Talbot and of his cousin Mary with Robert Wroth; Forsandrus confesses on his deathbed that he acted cruelly in separating the two cousins and that he was bribed by Amphilanthus's future mother-in-law (read the Countess of Shrewsbury) to set up that marriage.

11. Of treatments of its topical references see Salzman "References," Miller and Waller, Hannay "Vertuous," Roberts "Knott," Roberts ed. *Poems*, and Brennan ed. "Introduction."

12. As Hannay notes ("Mentor" [see "Vertuous" 29]), this state of affairs when Pembroke and Wroth had not yet acknowledged their love to each other is also represented in the Laurimello episode of I, Book II, where the Pembroke figure, "not imagining my end, married another Lady," and the speaker spent "some two years" in "an ill and froward life" with the husband forced upon her. This "two years" is autobiographical, for Wroth left her husband in late 1606 to come to court, there to remain some four years until scandal sent her home to Robert Wroth (as I argue from Jonson's omitting her name in the published text of the *Masque of Beauty*—see chapter 5).

13. Through later stretches of the romance the association of Antissia with the two cousins is shown as long-term and recurrent. If she depicts Pembroke's wife Mary Talbot, whom he wooed for himself as Amphilanthus does Antissia, and who like Antissia in *Urania* Part II was supposedly "mad" in later years, then Wroth has in this case split the image of Pembroke's wife into two personae (in the story Amphilanthus marries someone else, as Antissia does also), probably out of a need not to be too offensively transparent in her allegorizing so close to home. As Salzman points out (*Prose* 144), Antissia is shown in *Urania* Part II as an eccentric writer of "fustian poetry" (II. i. fol. 30), dressing very oddly and possessed with "poetical raptures and fixions." I.e., if she does portray Talbot, Wroth has made a pru-

dential exception to her usual habit of more forthright allegorizing and has clouded the equivalency. Pamphilia is in her youth on close terms with Antissia, who suffers great jealousy when she suspects that Amphilanthus loves Pamphilia. In the *Urania* Part II (Newberry Case Msfy 1565.W95, I. i. fol. 14$_v$), there is a scene of an early *de praesenti* marriage (a present-tense betrothal before witnesses) between Pamphilia and Amphilanthus, which Roberts thinks might refer to an actual event, or might be wish fulfillment on Wroth's part. Either way, this would represent the pact of early affection between Pembroke and Wroth that was disrupted by the two cousins' separate marriages, and would in Wroth's mind justify many refractions in the depictions of Pembroke's marriage and her own.

14. Page references are to the Salzman *Anthology*.

15. This Luceania resembles Lucy Harington Russell, Countess of Bedford, on several counts; besides the sound of "Lucy" in the name, she is noted for "exquisite wit and rare spirit, so perfect as . . . her perfections were styled masculine" (Salzman ed. 193—see chapter 5 on Jonson's epigram to the countess); her husband is "a great lord" yet "unable to flatter himself with conceit of worth sufficient to end" a joust—Edward, Earl of Bedford had suffered a riding injury and did not take part in court affairs much less jousts; and she "before had known love rather by name than subjection" (194).

16. As Roberts notes ("Knott" 124), Rosindy's betrothal to "Meriana, Queen of Macedon" in all probability refers to the younger Robert Sidney's secretly arranged marriage in 1616 with Dorothy Percy, daughter of Henry, 9th Earl of Northumberland. Since this "wizard earl" was a noted collector of scientific treatises, even commissioning translations of some, it may be that another episode—of Rosindy's friendship with "Sophia" or wisdom, a lady portrayed in a scientific library (I. fol. 61$_v$)—is showing under another name the same Dorothy Percy.

17. Roberts (*Poems* 24–26) quotes these references, of which an undated poem to Mary Wroth from Edward, Lord Herbert of Cherbury (entitled "On the birth of my Lord of Pembroke's child in the spring"), seems to refer to the daughter Catherine's birth ("My muse therefore no farther goes / But for *her* [emphasis mine] feet craves shoes and hose.") Robert Sidney's letter of 1615 approves of his wife's decision to "put away Wil" (i.e., send him somewhere else to be raised), as it would be "too great shame" to keep him in their house. A likely reading of these documents would be that Wroth's illegitimate son William Herbert was born in 1615, then the daughter Catherine in a springtime between 1616 and 1618 (i.e., probably before the rumored negotiations for Wroth's possible marriage to Henry Vere, Earl of Oxford, in 1619, when I suggest she wrote *Love's Victory* to present herself as the chaste Sylvesta, now free of the Pembroke affair—see chapter 5 on *Love's Victory*).

18. See the new Donne *Variorum* volume on the "Anniversaries" and the "Epicedes and Obsequies," vol. 6, but the first to appear of a planned ten.

19. On Donne's apparent effort to plead for a pardon for Somerset before King James, see W. Schleiner "Coterie."

7. Popery and Politics

1. As noted in Ch. 2, Habermas distinguishes strategic from communicative action as follows: "In communicative action a basis of mutually recognized validity claims is presupposed; this is not the case in strategic action. In the communicative attitude it is possible to reach a direct understanding oriented to validity claims; in the strategic attitude, by contrast, only an indirect understanding via determinative indicators is possible" (209).

2. The phrase is from Cary's play *Mariam, Queen of Jewry* (1613), l. 1226.

3. As Lewalski concedes while still finding her a stirring female rebel, Mariam in the end "admits that the conjunction of chastity and humility is the feminine ideal" (*Writing* 200).

4. See *Plutarch, Morals*, 405–408.

5. Lewalski (*Writing* 317–20) gives the full case for Lady Falkland's authorship.

6. She says she has "not followed the dull character of our historians herein."

7. In the *History*, this is in her own "Preface to the Reader," in the Perron treatise in the Latin verses and sonnet by her friend James Clayton, as well as the verses by Father Leander [John Jones] of Douay.

8. Cary *Life* 117.

9. See *Scots Peerage* III: 609–12, Lewalski (*Writing* 384, n. 19), and Jesse Swan (Diss: Arizona State, forthcoming). In 1609 Cary's first child, Catherine, was born, then in 1610 the second, Lucius (later second Lord Falkland), followed by Lawrence, 1613; there followed Anne, 1614; Edward (b. and d.), 1616; Elizabeth, 1617; Lucy, 1619; Victoria, 1620; Mary, 1622; Patrick, 1624; and Henry, 1625. The fourth pregnancy, which resulted in Anne (later Dame Clementina of Cambray), was from 1613 to 1614. Anne, in youth a maid of honor to Queen Henrietta Maria and leading light of the daughters who converted, may well have written the biography; this story of the depression during that pregnancy would have been told to her as of providential significance. The perspective in the *Life* and its reported conversations between Anne and Elizabeth (the younger) indicates that one of them must be the writer. Lewalski (*Writing* 180) also suggests Anne Cary as author.

10. One could contend that it was only the dedicatory sonnet, to her sister-in-law and dear friend Elizabeth Bland Cary (cf. above), that is referred to as having been recalled, since that appears in some copies but not others. But this seems unlikely, since a brief poem to this person of no public importance would scarcely be matter of great interest or offense, needing to be "stolen out of her chambers" and then recalled.

11. This close friendship of Ladies Falkland and Denbigh, the latter being Buckingham's sister and having considerable influence on him, explains why the highest ranking people in the court and church, from Secretary John Coke to Cosen and Archbishop Laud, personally tried to pressure Lady Falkland back to Anglicanism and later to prevent further conversions in her family (see the *Life*, Laud's letter in its appendix, and the letter of Lady Falkland to Lady Denbigh cited here, n. 12).

12. Shapiro accepts the *State Papers* dating of this letter as c. 1625 (114), but its references to Cosen's, Coke's, and Lady Denbigh's actions clearly reflect the days of October and November 1626, immediately after Lady Falkland's conversion (see the *Life* 29ff.), when exactly the events mentioned in the letter occurred: Coke and Cosen coming personally to her house to try to proselytize).

13. The preface of the *History* is dated Feb. 20, 1627, which translated to Gregorian dating is 1628. The case for Lady Falkland's authorship of the *Edward II* has been accepted by Bradbrook and Krontiris, and convincingly restated by Beilen (316n, 159) and Lewalski (*Writing*, appendix 1). The spring of 1628 is the time referred to by official court correspondence (a letter from the king himself) informing Lord Falkland that money would be withheld from his salary if he continued refusing his wife an income; upon his proposing in January, 1628, to pay her £300/year and stipulating that she live at least ten miles from London (see the Cary *Life*, appendix), she evidently went to live in the run-down house by the Thames of which her daughter tells, "in a little town ten miles from London" (*Life* 37; also see Shapiro 69–70).

14. The eighteenth-century reprint by the Harleian Society is of the condensed quarto version (also 1680), probably done at the behest of the printer John Playford, possibly by Sir

James Harrington, to whom its preface is attributed (see *Dictionary of National Biography* 3: 1150).

15. See *The Conceited Newes of Sir Thomas Overbury and his Friends*, 1616, xxiiiff.

16. Bradbrook ("Review" 93) notes that "the work was surely meant as mirror for the subjection of the reigning king to his favorite Buckingham." Lewalski (*Writing* 179–211) also discusses this point and notes that Lady Falkland's emphasis on the agency of Isabella through the history's second half is unique among treatments of Edward II's reign up to that time.

17. I take the text from Shapiro 75, who cites BL, Egerton MS 2725, f. 60. Lewalski (*Writing* 383, n. 5) cites the same source but gives a slightly different text (perhaps Shapiro's is emended?).

18. Both the published prose dedication of the Perron translation, to Queen Henrietta Maria, and the handwritten sonnet (below) in the copy of it at the Beinecke Library, Yale University, express Lady Falkland's reliance on the queen, in whose chapel she would be buried (text from Shapiro, p. 81).

To the Queens most Excellent Majestie

'Tis not your faire out-side (though famous GREECE
  Whose beauties ruin'd kingdomes never sawe
A face that could like yours affections drawe)
  Fittes you for the protection of this peice
It is your heart (your pious zealous heart)
  That by attractive force, brings great PERROONE
To leave his SEYNE, his LOYRE, and his GARROONE;
  And to your handmaide THAMES his guiftes impart:
But staie: you have a brother, his kinge borne,
  (Whose worth drawes men from the remotest partes,
To offer up themselves to his desartes.)
  To whom he hath his due allegiance sworne
    Yet for your sake he proves ubiquitarie
    And comes to England, though in France he tarrie.

19. Stauffer's essay first suggesting Elizabeth Cary as author of this *Edward II*, by reprinting selections of the characters' speeches in a blank verse format—which are indeed written in blank verse rhythm—apparently created the false impression still abroad (see Krontiris ["Style"], opening paragraph, and Haselkorn and Travitsky's "Introduction") that it is a play, or draft of a would-be play. It is not a play at all but a prose narrative throughout, and much too long to have been conceived as a draft of a play.

Works Cited or Consulted

Select Bibliography of Primary Works

Manuscripts

B.L. Add. 15232 (the Bright MS, containing three poems by an associate of the Sidneys).

B.L. Add. 15117 (a song collection containing settings of certain psalms of the Countess of Pembroke).

B.L. MS Royal 17B. XVIII (translation of a St. Basil sermon from Greek by Mildred Cooke Cecil, Lady Burghley.

Cambridgeshire County Record Office, Consistory Will WR C20: 290 (1595—will of Margaret Tyler of Castle Camps).

C.U.L. Ii.5.37 (*Il giardino cosmografico* of Bartholo Sylva [in Italian], with prefatory poems by the Cooke sisters and others).

C.U.L. MS Ff.5.14 (Commonplace book of W. Kytton).

Folger MS V.b. 198, "The workes of the Lady Ann Sothwell, Decemb 2 1626."

Huntington MS HM 600 (*Love's Victory*, by Lady Mary Wroth—Act 5 missing).

Early Printed Books

Cary, Elizabeth [later Lady Falkland]. *Mariam Queen of Jewry*. London, 1613.

——. *The Reply of the Most Illustrious Cardinall of Perron to the Answeare of the Most Excellent King of Great Britain* [translation of treatise by Jacques Davy—copy at the Beinecke Library, Yale U, with sonnet by Lady Falkland]. Douay, 1630.

——. *The History of the Life, Reign, and Death of Edward II . . . Written by E. F. in the year 1627. And Printed verbatim from the Original.* London, 1680 (the folio, not the quarto).

Cooke, Anne (later Lady Bacon), trans. *Certayne Sermons of the ryghte famous and excellente Clerk Master Barnardine Ochine* [the copy C.U.L. Syn 8.55.23]. London, c. 1550.

Cooke, Elizabeth, Lady Russell, trans. *A Way of Reconciliation . . . touching . . . the body and blood of Christ in the Sacrament* [Latin original by Bishop John Ponet]. London, 1605.

Fraunce, Abraham. *Amyntas pastorall, the first part of the countesse of Pembrokes Yvychurch.* London, 1591.

Harington, John. *Orlando Furioso in English Heroical Verse.* London, 1591.

Hentzner, Paul. *Itinerarium Germaniae; Galliae; Angliae; Italiae.* Nuremburg, 1612.

Johnson, Richard. *A Crowne-Garland of goulden Roses.* London, 1612.

Josephus, Flavius. *The Famous and Memorable Workes of Josephus.* Trans. Thomas Lodge. London, 1602.

Overbury, Sir Thomas. *A Wife Now the Widdow of Sir Tho. Overburye . . . Whereunto are Added Many witty Characters, and conceited Newes.* 3d ed., London, 1614; 9th ed., London, 1616.

Plutarch. *The Philosophie Commonlie called the Morals.* Trans. Philemon Holland. London, 1603.

——. *The Lives of the Noble Grecians and Romans . . . with the lives of . . . other exellent Chieftaines of warre.* Trans. Sir Thomas North. London, 1603.

Reges, Reginae, Nobiles, Et alij in Ecclesia Collegiata B. Petri Westmonasterij sepulti. London, 1606.

Soowthern, John. *Pandora, The Musyque of the beautie of his Mistresse Diana.* London, 1584.

Tyler, Margaret, trans. *The Mirrour of Princely Deeds and Knighthood*, Bk. I. [Spanish original by Diego Ortuñez de Calahorra]. London, 1578.

Watson, Thomas. *Amintae gaudia.* London, 1592.

Weston, Elizabeth Jane. *Poemata . . . Studio ac opera Elisab. Ioan. Westoniae . . .* 1st ed, Frankfurt/Oder, 1602.

——. *Parthenicon Elisabethae Ioannae Westoniae, Virginis nobilissimae, poetriae florentissimae, linguarum plurimarum peritissimae* [B.L. Cat.C.61.d.2, with verses in Weston's hand]. Prague, n.d. [1607].

Whitney, Isabella. *A Sweet Nosegay or Pleasant posye. Contayning a hundred and ten Phylosophicall flowers.* London, 1573.

——. *The Copy of a Letter, lately written in meeter, by a yonge Gentilwoman: to her vnconstant Louer.* London, 1567 [?].

Wroth, Lady Mary. *The Countess of Montgomery's Urania*, Part I. London, 1621.

Secondary Works

Adams, Hazard, and Leroy Searle, eds. *Critical Theory since 1965.* Tallahassee: Florida State UP, 1986.

Adamson, J. W. "The Extent of Literacy in England in the Fifteenth and Sixteenth Centuries." *The Library* 10 (1930): 163–93.

Anderson, James. *Ladies of the Reformation.* London, 1855.

Ashdown, Dulcie M. *Ladies-in-Waiting.* London: Arthur Barker, 1976.

Ashmole, Elias. *The Antiquities of Berkshire.* 2 vols. London, 1719.

Axton, Marie. *The Queen's Two Bodies: Drama and the Elizabethan Succession.* London: Royal Historical Society, 1977.

Bakhtin, Mikhail. *See* Medvedev.

Bald, R. C. *John Donne. A Life.* Oxford: Oxford UP, 1970.

Ballard, George. *Memoirs of Several Ladies of Great Britain.* Oxford: W. Jackson, 1752.

Barns, Stephen J. "The Cookes of Gidea Hall." *The Essex Review* 21 (1912): 1–9.

Bassnett, Susan E. "Revising a Biography: A New Interpretation of the Life of Elizabeth Jane Weston (Westonia), Based on Her Autobiographical Poem on the Occasion of the Death of Her Mother." *Cahiers Elisabethains* 37 (1990): 1–8.

Beilin, Elaine. *Redeeming Eve: Women Writers of the English Renaissance.* Princeton: Princeton UP, 1987.

——. "Current Bibliography of English Women Writers, 1500–1640." *The Renaissance Englishwoman in Print: Counterbalancing the Canon.* Ed. Anne M. Haselkorn and Betty S. Travitsky. Amherst: U of Massachusetts P, 1990. 347–60.

Belsey, Catherine. *The Subject of Tragedy: Identity and Difference in Renaissance Drama.* London: Methuen, 1985.

Bennett, Tony. *Formalism and Marxism*. London: Methuen, 1980.

———. "Texts in History: The Determinations of Readings and Their Texts," *MMLA* 18 (1985): 1–17.

Benson, Pamela Joseph. *The Invention of the Renaissance Woman: The Challenge of Female Independence in the Literature and Thought of Italy and England*. University Park: Penn. State UP, 1992.

Bethune, George W., ed. *The British Female Poets: With Biographical and Critical Notices*. Freeport, NY: Essay Index Reprint Series, 1848; rpt. 1972.

Binns, J. W. *Intellectual Culture in Elizabethan and Jacobean England: The Latin Writings of the Age*. Leeds: Cairn, 1990.

Bornstein, Diane. "The Style of the Countess of Pembroke's Translation of Philippe de Mornay's *Discours de la vie et de la mort*." *Silent but for the Word: Tudor Women as Patrons, Translators, and Writers of Religious Works*. Ed. Margaret P. Hannay. Kent, OH: Kent State UP, 1985. 126–48.

Bourdieu, Pierre. "The Economics of Linguistic Exchange." *Social Science Information* 16 (1977): 645–68.

———. *Language and Symbolic Power*. Trans. Gino Raymond and Matthew Adamson. Cambridge: Polity, 1991.

Bradbrook, Muriel C. "The Politics of Pageantry: Social Implications in Jacobean London." *Poetry and Drama 1500–1700: Essays in Honour of Harold F. Brooks*. Ed. Antony Coleman and Antony Hammond. London: Methuen, 1981. 60–75.

———. Review of Betty Travitsky, ed., *The Paradise of Women. TSWL* 1 (1982): 93.

Brennan, Michael G. "The Date of the Countess of Pembroke's Translation of the Psalms." *RES* 33 (1982): 434–36.

———. "The Date of the Death of Abraham Fraunce." *The Library*, 6 ser. 5 (1983): 391–92.

———. "Nicholas Breton's *Passions of the Spirit*." *RES* 38 (1987): 221–27.

———. *Literary Patronage in the English Renaissance: The Pembroke Family*. London: Routledge, 1988.

———. *See also* Wroth.

Breton, Nicholas. *The Works in Verse and Prose*. Ed. Alexander B. Grosart. 2 vols. 1879; rpt. New York: AMS, 1966.

Brezan, Vaclav. *Posledni Rozmberkove*. Ed. J. Dostal. Prague, 1941.

Burton, Robert. *Philosophaster*. Ed. Connie McQuillen. Binghamton, NY: MRTS, 1993.

Cary, Elizabeth Tanfield (later Lady Falkland). *The Tragedy of Mariam*. Ed. A. C. Dunstan. Oxford: Malone Society, 1914.

Cary, Sister of Cambray [either Anne or Elizabeth the younger]. *The Lady Falkland: Her Life*. Ed. Richard Simpson. London: Catholic Publishing Soc., 1861.

Cavanaugh, Jean C. "Lady Southwell's Defense of Poetry." *ELR* 14 (1984): insert following 284.

Church, Frederic C. *The Italian Reformers 1534–64*. New York: Columbia UP, 1932.

Clifford, Lady Anne. *See* Sackville.

Collinson, Patrick. "The Elizabethan Puritans and the Foreign Reformed Churches in London." *Proc. Huguenot Soc.* 20 (1958–64): 525–55.

———. *A Mirror of Elizabethan Puritanism. The Life and Letters of Godly Master Dering*. London: Williams Trust, 1964.

———. "The Role of Women in the English Reformation Illustrated by the Life and

Friendships of Anne Locke." *Studies in Church History.* 2 vols. Ed. G. J. Cuming. London: Nelson, 1965.

———. *The Elizabethan Puritan Movement.* London: Methuen, 1967.

Cressy, David. *Literacy and the Social Order: Reading and Writing in Tudor and Stuart England.* Cambridge: Cambridge UP, 1980.

Crull, Jodocus. *The Antiquities of St. Peter's, or, the Abbey-Church of Westminster.* 2d ed. 2 vols. London, 1722.

Daniel, Samuel. *Complete Works in Verse and Prose.* Ed. Alexander B. Grosart. 5 vols. 1885; rpt. New York: Russell, 1963.

Deacon, Richard. *John Dee: Scientist, Geographer, Astrologer and Secret Agent to Elizabeth I.* London: Muller, 1968.

De Lauretis, Teresa. *Technologies of Gender. Essays on Theory, Film, and Fiction.* Bloomington: Indiana UP, 1987.

Deleuze, Gilles, and Felix Guattari. *Anti-Oedipus: Capitalism and Psychoanalysis.* Trans. Helen R. Lane et al. New York: Penguin, 1977.

Dering, Edward. *M. Derings workes. More at large then euer.* 1597; rpt. New York: Dacapo, 1972.

Donne, John. *Letters to Severall Persons of Honour.* Ed. Charles E. Merrill, Jr. New York: Sturgis and Walton, 1910.

———. *The Complete Poetry of John Donne.* Ed. John T. Shawcross. New York: Doubleday-Anchor, 1967.

———. *The Variorum Edition of the Poetry of John Donne: The Anniversaries and the Epicedes and Obsequies.* Vol. 6. Ed. Donald R. Dickson et al. Columbia: U of Missouri P, 1992.

Donno, Elizabeth Story, ed. *Three Renaissance Pastorals: Tasso, Guarini, Daniel.* Binghamton, NY: SUNY P, 1993.

Eccles, Mark. *Christopher Marlowe in London.* Cambridge, MA: Harvard UP, 1934.

Emmison, F. G. *Elizabethan Life: Wills of Essex Gentry and Merchants.* Chelmsford: Essex Co. Council, 1978.

Enchiridion renatae poesis Latinae in Bohemia et Moravia cultae. Ed. Antonin Truhlar and Karel Hrdina. 5 vols. Prague: Sumptibus Academiae Scientiarum, 1982.

Enterline, Lynn E. "Gender and Prohibition in Milton's Italian Sonnets." *Milton and the Idea of Woman.* Ed. Julia M. Walker. Urbana: U of Illinois P, 1988. 32–51.

Esdaile, Arundell, ed. Introduction. *Daniel's Delia and Drayton's Idea.* London: Chatto and Windus, 1906.

Evans, R. J. W. *Rudolf II and His World.* Oxford: Oxford UP, 1973.

Ezell, Margaret J. M. *Writing Women's Literary History.* Johns Hopkins UP, 1992.

Fehrenbach, Robert J. "Isabella Whitney and the Popular Miscellanies of Richard Jones." *Cahiers Elisabethains* 19 (1981): 85–87.

———. "A Letter sent by the Maydens of London (1567)." *ELR* 14 (1984): 285.

Fell Smith, Charlotte. *John Dee 1527–1608.* London: Constable, 1909.

Fellowes, Edmund H., ed. *English Madrigal Verse 1588–1632.* 3d ed. rev. Sternfeld and Greer. Oxford: Oxford UP, 1967.

The Feminist Companion to Literature in English: Women Writers from the Middle Ages to the Present. Ed. Virginia Blain, Isobel Grundy, Patricia Clements. New Haven: Yale UP, 1990.

Ferguson, Margaret W. "Renaissance Women as Readers and Writers." *The Comparative*

Perspective on Literature: Approaches to Theory and Practice. Ed. Clayton Koelb and Susan Noakes. Ithaca: Cornell UP, 1988.

Ferguson, Moira. *First Feminists: British Women Writers 1578–1799.* Bloomington: Indiana UP, 1985.

Firpo, Luigi. "John Dee, scienziato, negromante e avventuriero." *Rinascimento* 3 (1952): 60–62.

Fischer, Sandra K. "Elizabeth Cary and Tyranny, Domestic and Religious." *Silent but for the Word: Tudor Women as Patrons, Translators, and Writers of Religious Works.* Ed. Margaret P. Hannay. Kent, OH: Kent State UP, 1985.

Flynn, Dennis. "Donne and a Female Coterie." *LIT* 1 (1989): 127–36.

Foster, Donald W. " 'Against the perjured falsehood of your tongues': Frances Howard [Countess of Hertford] on the Course of Love." *ELR*, forthcoming.

Foucault, Michel. *The Order of Things.* Ed. R. D. Laing. New York: Pantheon, 1971.

———. *The Archaeology of Knowledge and the Discourse on Language.* Trans. A. M. Sheridan Smith and Rupert Swyer. New York: Pantheon, 1972.

Fraunce, Abraham. *Complete Works.* Ed. Alexander B. Grosart. St. George's, Lancashire, 1871.

———. *Victoria: A Latin Comedy.* Ed. G. C. Moore Smith. Louvain: Uystpruyst, 1906.

———. *The Third Part of the Countesse of Pembrokes Yvychurch, entitled Amintas Dale.* Ed. Gerald Snare. Northridge: California State UP, 1975.

Freer, W. Coburn. *Music for a King: George Herbert's Style and the Metrical Psalms.* Baltimore: Johns Hopkins UP, 1972.

———. "Mary Sidney Countess of Pembroke." *Women Writers of the Renaissance and Reformation.* Ed. Katharina M. Wilson. Athens: U of Georgia P, 1987. 481–90.

Gallop, Jane. *Thinking through the Body.* New York: Columbia UP, 1988.

Genette, Gérard. *Palimpsestes. La littérature au second degré.* Paris: Seuil, 1982.

———. *Seuils.* Paris: Seuil, 1989.

Goldberg, Jonathan. *James I and the Politics of Literature.* Baltimore: Johns Hopkins UP, 1983.

Gordon, D. J. *The Renaissance Imagination: Essays and Studies by D. J. Gordon.* Ed. Stephen Orgel. Los Angeles: U of California P, 1975.

Gossett, Suzanne. " 'Man-maid, begone!': Women in Masques." *ELR* 18 (1988): 96–106.

Greer, Germaine, et al., eds. *Kissing the Rod: An Anthology of Seventeenth-Century Women's Verse.* New York: Farrar Straus Giroux, 1989.

Greimas, A.-J., and J. Courtés. *Semiotics and Language: An Analytical Dictionary.* Trans. Larry Crist, Daniel Patte, et al. Bloomington: Indiana UP, 1982.

Guss, Donald L. "Enlightenment as Process: Milton and Habermas." *PMLA* 106 (1991): 1156–69.

Habermas, Jürgen. *Communication and the Evolution of Society.* Trans. Thomas McCarthy. London: Heinemann, 1979.

Hacket, John. *Scrinia Reserata, A Memorial of John Williams.* 2 vols. London, 1692.

Hall, Kim. "Sexual Politics and Cultural Identity in *The Masque of Blackness.*" *The Performance of Power: Theatrical Discourses and Politics.* Ed. Sue-Ellen Case and Janelle Reinelt. Iowa City: U of Iowa P, 1991: 3–18.

Hannay, Margaret P. " 'Doo What Men May Sing': Mary Sidney and the Tradition of Admonitory Dedication." *Silent but for the Word. Tudor Women as Patrons, Translators, and Writers of Religious Works.* Ed. Margaret P. Hannay. Kent, OH: Kent State UP, 1985: 149–65.

——. "Mary Sidney, Lady Wroth." *Women Writers of the Renaissance and Reformation*. Ed. Katharina M. Wilson. Athens: U of Georgia P, 1987: 548–54.

——. " 'Princes you as men must dy': Genevan Advice to Monarchs in the *Psalmes* of Mary Sidney." *ELR* 19 (1989): 22–41.

——. *Philip's Phoenix. Mary Sidney, Countess of Pembroke*. Oxford: Oxford UP, 1990.

——. " 'Your vertuous and learned Aunt': The Countess of Pembroke as a Mentor to Mary Wroth." *Reading Mary Wroth: Representing Alternatives in Early Modern England*. Ed. Naomi J. Miller and Gary Waller. Knoxville: U of Tennessee P, 1991.

——. " 'Unlock my lipps': the Miserere mei Deus of Anne Vaughan Lok and Mary Sidney Herbert, Countess of Pembroke." *Privileging Gender in Early Modern England*. Ed. Jean R. Brink. Tempe, AZ: Sixteenth-Century Studies Conference, 1992.

Haselkorn, Anne M., and Betty S. Travitsky, ed. Introduction. *The Renaissance Englishwoman in Print: Counterbalancing the Canon*. Amherst: U of Massachusetts P, 1990.

Hentzner, Paul. *A Journey into England. By P. Hentzner, in the Year MDXCVIII*. Trans. Richard Bentley, ed. Horace Walpole. Strawberry Hill, 1757.

Herbert, Mary Sidney, Countess of Pembroke. *The Countess of Pembroke's Antonie*. Ed. Alice Luce. Weimar: Emil Felber, 1897.

——. *The Psalms of Sir Philip Sidney and the Countess of Pembroke*. Ed. J. C. A. Rathmell. New York: New York UP, 1963.

——. *The Triumph of Death and Other Unpublished and Uncollected Poems*. Ed. Gary F. Waller. Salzburg: Institut für Englische Sprache, 1977.

Herford, C. H., et al. *See* Jonson.

Hollway, Wendy, Julian Henriques, et al. *Changing the Subject: Psychology, Social Regulation, and Subjectivity*. London: Methuen, 1984.

Hull, Suzanne. *Chaste, Silent, and Obedient: English Books for Women, 1475–1640*. San Marino: Huntington Library, 1982.

Jacobus, Mary. *Reading Woman. Essays in Feminist Criticism*. New York: Columbia UP, 1986.

Jaggar, Alison M. *Feminist Politics and Human Nature*. Totowa, NJ: Rowman and Held, 1983.

Jameson, Fredric. *The Political Unconscious: Narrative as a Socially Symbolic Act*. Ithaca: Cornell UP, 1981.

Jenkins, Elizabeth. *Elizabeth the Great*. London: Victor Gollancz, 1958.

Joiner, Mary. "British Museum Add MS 15117: A Commentary, Index, and Bibliography." *RMA Research Chronicle* 7 (1967): 51–109.

Jones, Ann Rosalind. *The Currency of Eros. Women's Love Lyric in Europe, 1540–1620*. Bloomington: Indiana UP, 1990.

Jonson, Benjamin. *Works*. Ed. C. H. Herford, Percy Simpson, and Evelyn Simpson. 11 vols. Oxford: Clarendon Press, 1925–52.

Jordan, Constance. "Representing Political Androgyny: More on the Sienna Portrait of Queen Elizabeth I." *The Renaissance Englishwoman in Print. Counterbalancing the Canon*. Ed. Anne M. Haselkorn and Betty S. Travitsky. Amherst: U of Massachusetts P, 1990: 157–76.

Kaplicky, Vaclav. *Zivot Alchymistuv* [The Life of an Alchemist]. Prague: Ceskoslovensky spisovatel, 1980.

Klene, Jean. "Recreating the Voice of Lady Anne Southwell." *Voices of Silence: Editing the Letters of Renaissance Women*. New York: MLA, Renaissance English Text Society Panel, 1990: Paper 2, 1–21.

Knowles, Joanne. "Intertextuality in Elizabethan England: Mary Stuart's Writings and Embroidery." Pacific Northwest Renaissance Conference, Tacoma, Washington, April 10, 1992.

Kristeva, Julia. "D'une identité l'autre." *Desire in Language: a Semiotic Approach to Literature and Art*. Trans. Thomas Gora et al. New York: Columbia UP, 1980.

——. *Revolution in Poetic Language*. Trans. Margaret Waller. New York: Columbia UP, 1984.

——. *The Kristeva Reader*. Ed. Toril Moi. New York: Columbia UP, 1986.

Krontiris, Tina. "Breaking Barriers of Genre and Gender: Margaret Tyler's Translation of *The Mirrour of Knighthood*." *ELR* 18 (1988): 19–39.

——. "Style and Gender in Elizabeth Cary's *Edward II*." *The Renaissance Englishwoman in Print: Counterbalancing the Canon*. Ed. Anne M. Haselkorn and Betty S. Travitsky. Amherst: U of Massachusetts P, 1990: 137–56.

——. *Oppositional Voices: Women as Writers and Translators of Literature in the English Renaissance*. London: Routledge, 1992.

Labanoff, Prince Alexandre. *See* Mary Stuart.

Lamb, Mary Ellen. "The Myth of the Countess of Pembroke: the Dramatic Circle." *YES* 11 (1981): 194–202.

——. "The Countess of Pembroke's Patronage." *ELR* 12 (1982): 162–79.

——. "The Cooke Sisters: Attitudes toward Learned Women in the Renaissance." *Silent but for the Word: Tudor Women as Patrons, Translators, and Writers of Religious Works*. Ed. Margaret P. Hannay. Kent, OH: Kent State UP, 1985: 107–25.

——. *Gender and Authorship in the Sidney Circle*. Madison: U of Wisconsin P, 1990.

——. "Women Readers in Mary Wroth's *Urania*." *Reading Mary Wroth: Representing Alternatives in Early Modern England*. Ed. Naomi J. Miller and Gary Waller. Knoxville: U of Tennessee P, 1991: 210–27.

——. "The Agency of the Split Subject: Lady Anne Clifford and the Uses of Reading." *ELR* 22 (1992): 347–68.

Lanyer, Aemilia. *Salve Deus Rex Judaeorum*. Ed. Susanne Woods. 1611; Oxford: Oxford UP, 1993.

——. Emilia Lanier, *The Poems of Shakespeare's Dark Lady*. Ed. A. L. Rowse. New York: Clarkson Potter, 1979.

Leclerc, Annie. "La Lettre d'Amour." *La venue a l'écriture*. Ed. H. Cixous, M. Gagnon, and A. Leclerc. Paris: Union Generale d'Editions, 1977.

Lee, Maurice, Jr. *Great Britain's Solomon: James VI and I in His Three Kingdoms*. Urbana: U of Illinois P, 1990.

Lewalski, Barbara K. "Lucy, Countess of Bedford: Images of a Jacobean Courtier and Patroness." *The Politics of Discourse: The Literature and History of Seventeenth-Century England*. Ed. Keven Sharpe and Steven N. Zwicker. Berkeley: U of California P, 1987.

——. "Mary Wroth's *Love's Victory* and Pastoral Tragicomedy." *Reading Mary Wroth: Representing Alternatives in Early Modern England*. Ed. Naomi J. Miller and Gary Waller. Knoxville: U of Tennessee P, 1991: 88–108.

——. "Re-writing Patriarchy and Patronage: Margaret Clifford, Anne Clifford, and Aemilia Lanyer." *YES* 21 (1991): 87–106.

——. *Writing Women in the Jacobean Era*. Cambridge: Harvard UP, 1993.

Luce, Alice, ed. *See* Herbert.

Lunn, David. *Elizabeth Cary Lady Falkland—1586–7—1639*. Ilford, Essex: Royal Stuart Society, 1977.

Lyotard, Jean-François. *Libidinal Economy*. Trans. Iain Hamilton Grant. 1974; Bloomington: Indiana UP, 1993.

Manning, Owen, and William Bray. *The History and Antiquities of the County of Surrey*. 3 vols. Rpt. 1974; London: John Nichols, 1804–1814.

Masello, Steven J. "Thomas Hoby, a Protestant Traveler to Circe's Court." *Cahiers Elisabethains* 27 (1985): 67–81.

May, Steven. "The Countess of Oxford's Sonnets: A Caveat." *ELN* 29 (1992): 9–19.

McGrath, Lynette. "Metaphoric Subversions: Feasts and Mirrors in Amelia Lanier's *Salve Deus Rex Judaeorum*." *LIT* 3 (1991): 101–13.

McIntosh, Marjorie K. "Sir Anthony Cooke: Tudor Humanist Educator and Religious Reformer." *Proc. American Philosophical Society* 119 (1975): 233–50.

McLaren, Margaret Anne. "An Unknown Continent: Lady Mary Wroth's Forgotten Pastoral Drama, 'Loves Victorie.' " *The Renaissance Englishwoman in Print: Counterbalancing the Canon*. Ed. Anne M. Haselkorn and Betty S. Travitsky. Amherst: U of Massachusetts P, 1990: 276–94.

McNair, Philip. "Ochino's Apology: Three Gods or Three Wives." *History* 60 (1975): 353–73.

McQuillen, Connie, ed. *Robert Burton's 'Philosophaster.'* Binghamton: SUNY UP, 1992.

Medvedev, P. N. [and Mikhail Bakhtin]. *The Formal Method in Literary Scholarship*. Trans. A. J. Wehrle. 1928; Baltimore: Johns Hopkins UP, 1978.

Michie, Helena. *Sororophobia: Differences among Women in Literature and Culture*. New York: Oxford UP, 1992.

Miller, Amos C. *Sir Henry Killigrew: Elizabethan Soldier and Diplomat*. Amsterdam: Leicester UP, 1972.

Miller, Naomi J. " 'Not much to be marked': Narrative of the Woman's Part in Lady Mary Wroth's *Urania*." *SEL* 29 (1989): 121–37.

———. "Rewriting Lyric Fictions: The Role of the Lady in Lady Mary Wroth's *Pamphilia to Amphilanthus*." *The Renaissance Englishwoman in Print: Counterbalancing the Canon*. Ed. Anne M. Haselkorn and Betty S. Travitsky. Amherst: U of Massachusetts P, 1990: 295–310.

Miller, Naomi J., and Gary Waller, ed. Introduction. *Reading Mary Wroth: Representing Alternatives in Early Modern England*. Knoxville: U of Tennessee P, 1991.

Miscellanea I and *Miscellanea XII*. vols. 1 (1905) and 22 (1921) of *Publications of the Catholic Record Society*. 46 vols. London: Catholic Record Society, 1905-1950.

Montrose, Louis Adrian. "The Elizabethan Subject and the Spenserian Text." *Literary Theory/Renaissance Texts*. Ed. Patricia Parker and David Quint. Baltimore: Johns Hopkins UP, 1986: 303–40.

Moody, Ellen. "Six Elegiac Poems, Possibly by Anne Cecil De Vere, Countess of Oxford," *ELR* 19 (1989): 153–69.

Morson, Gary Saul, and Caryl Emerson. *Mikhail Bakhtin: Creation of a Prosaics*. Palo Alto: Stanford UP, 1990.

The Muster Returns for Divers Hundreds in the County of Norfolk 1569, 1572, 1574, 1577. Transcribed by M. A. Farrow. Norwich: PRS, 1935.

O'Leary, John G. "Essex and Parliament during the Reformation." *Essex Recusant* 1 (1959): 4–14.

Overbury, Thomas. *See* Savage.

Panofsky, Richard J., ed. Facsimile of Hugh Plat, *The Floures of Philosophy*, and Isabella Whitney, *A Sweet Nosegay*. New York: Delmar, 1982.

Patzak, Irmgard. "Eine Prager Dichterin im Zeitalter Rudolfs II." *Praguer Jahrbuch.* Prague: Volk u. Reichverlag, 1941–1943.

Pearse, Nancy C. "Elizabeth Cary, Renaissance Playwright." *TSLL* 18 (1977): 601–608.

Peck, Linda Levy. *Northampton, Patronage and Policy at the Court of James I.* London: Allen and Unwin, 1982.

———. " 'For a King not to be bountiful were a fault': Perspectives on Court Patronage in Early Stuart England," *Journal of British Studies* 25 (1986), 41–51.

———. *Court Patronage and Corruption in Early Stuart England.* Boston: Unwin, 1990.

Plat, Hugh. *See* Panofsky.

Prestwich, Menna. *Cranfield, Politics and Profits under the Early Stuarts.* London: Oxford UP, 1966.

Publications of the Catholic Record Society. See Miscellanea I and Miscellanea XII.

Quilligan, Maureen. "The Comedy of Female Authority in *The Faerie Queene*." *ELR* 17 (1987), 156–71.

———. "Sidney and His Queen." *The Historical Renaissance: New Essays on Tudor and Stuart Literature and Culture.* Ed. Heather Dubrow and Richard Strier. Chicago: U of Chicago P, 1988: 171–96.

———. "Lady Mary Wroth: Female Authority and the Family Romance." *Unfolded Tales: Essays on Renaissance Romance.* Ed. George M. Logan and Gordon Teskey. Ithaca: Cornell UP, 1989. 257–80.

Quirk, Randolph, Sidney Greenbaum et al. *A Comprehensive Grammar of the English Language.* New York: Longman, 1985.

Rabine, Leslie W. "Romance in the Age of Electronics: Harlequin Enterprises." *Feminist Studies* 11 (1985): 39–60. Rpt. *Feminisms: An Anthology of Literary Theory and Criticism.* Ed. Robyn R. Warhol and Diane P. Herndl. New Brunswick: Rutgers UP, 1991: 878–93.

Radway, Janice. "The Readers and Their Romances," from *Reading the Romance: Women, Patriarchy, and Popular Literature.* Chapel Hill: U of North Carolina, 1984. Rpt. *Feminisms: An Anthology of Literary Theory and Criticism.* Ed. Robyn R. Warhol and Diane P. Herndl. New Brunswick: Rutgers UP, 1991: 551–85.

Read, Conyers. *Lord Burghley and Queen Elizabeth.* London: J. Cape, 1960.

The Register of St. Olave, Hart Street, London 1563–1700. Ed. W. B. Bannerman. London: Harleian Soc., 1916.

Riggs, David. *Ben Jonson. A Life.* Cambridge: Harvard UP, 1989.

Ringler, William, ed. *See* Sidney.

Roberts, Josephine A. "The Huntington Manuscript of Lady Mary Wroth's Play, *Loves Victorie*." *HLQ* 46 (1983): 156–74.

———. "Radigund Revisited: Perspectives on Women Rulers in Lady Mary Wroth's *Urania*." *The Renaissance Englishwoman in Print: Counterbalancing the Canon.* Ed. Anne M. Haselkorn and Betty S. Travitsky. Amherst: U. of Massachusetts P, 1990. 187–207.

———. " 'The Knott Never to Bee Untide': The Controversy Regarding Marriage in Mary Wroth's *Urania*." *Reading Mary Wroth: Representing Alternatives in Early*

Modern England. Ed. Naomi J. Miller and Gary Waller. Knoxville: U of Tennessee P, 1991: 109–32.

Rowlands, Marie B. "Recusant Women 1560–1640." *Women in English Society 1500–1800*. London: Methuen, 1985.

Rowse, A. L. "Bisham and the Hobys," *Times, Persons, Places. Essays in Literature*. London: Macmillan, 1965.

Sackville, Lady Anne Clifford, Countess of Dorset/Countess of Pembroke and Montgomery. *The Diaries of Lady Anne Clifford*. Ed. D. J. H. Clifford. London: Sutton, 1990.

Salzman, Paul. "Contemporary References in Mary Wroth's *Urania*," *RES* 29 (1978): 178–81.

——. *English Prose Fiction 1558–1700*. Oxford: Clarendon P, 1985.

——, ed. Introduction. *An Anthology of Elizabethan Prose Fiction*. Oxford: Oxford UP, 1987.

Savage, James E., ed. *The "Conceited Newes" of Sir Thomas Overbury and His Friends: A Facsimile Reproduction of . . . Sir Thomas Overbury His Wife* (1616 ed.). Gainesville, FL: Scholars' Facsimiles, 1968.

Schkelenko, Raissa. "Die neulateinische Dichtung am Hofe Rudolfs II." *Praguer Jahrbuch*. Prague: Volk u. Reichverlag, 1941–1943.

Schleiner, Louise. "Providential Improvisation in *Measure for Measure*." *PMLA* 97 (1982): 227–36.

——. *The Living Lyre in English Verse, from Elizabeth through the Restoration*. Columbia: U of Missouri P, 1984.

——. "Margaret Tyler, Translator and Waiting Woman," *ELN* (1992): 1–8.

——. *Cultural Semiotics, Spenser, and the Captive Woman*. Bethlehem, PA: Lehigh UP, forthcoming.

Schleiner, Winfried. "Donne's 'Coterie Sermon,'" *John Donne Journal* 8 (1988): 1–8.

——. "Male Cross-Dressing and Transvestism in Renaissance Romances," *Sixteenth Century Journal* 19 (1988): 605–19.

——. "*Le feu caché*: Homosocial Bonds between Women in a Renaissance Romance," *RenQ* 45 (1992): 293–311.

The Scots Peerage. Ed. James Balfour. Edinburgh, 1906.

Shapiro, Arlene I. "Elizabeth Cary: Her Life, Letters, and Art." Diss.: SUNY Stony Brook, 1984.

Showalter, Elaine. "Towards a Feminist Poetics," in *Women Writing and Writing about Women*. Ed. Mary Jacobus. London: Croom Helm, 1979: 22–41.

——. "The Female Tradition." *A Literature of Their Own: British Women Novelists from Brontë to Lessing*. Princeton: Princeton UP, 1977. Rpt. in *Feminisms: An Anthology of Literary Theory and Criticism*. Ed. Robyn R. Warhol and Diane P. Herndl. New Brunswick: Rutgers UP, 1991: 269–88.

Sidney, Sir Philip. *The Poems of Sir Philip Sidney*. Ed. William A. Ringler. Oxford: Clarendon, 1962.

Sinfield, Alan. *Literature in Protestant England 1560–1660*. London: Croom Helm, 1983.

Smith, A. Hassell et al., eds. *The Papers of Nathaniel Bacon of Stiffkey*. 2 vols. Norwich: PRS, 1979–1983.

Smith, Bruce R. *Homosexual Desire in Shakespeare's England: A Cultural Poetics*. Chicago: U of Chicago P, 1991.

Smith, G. C. Moore, ed. *See* Fraunce.

Snare, Gerald, ed. *See* Fraunce.

Southern [Soowthern], John. *Pandora, The Musyque of the beautie, of his Mistresse Diana* (London, 1584). Facs. Ed. George B. Parks. New York: Columbia UP, 1938.

Spriet, Pierre. *Samuel Daniel, 1563–1619, sa vie, son oeuvre.* Paris: Didier, 1968.

Spufford, Margaret. *Small Books and Pleasant Histories: Popular Fiction and Its Readership in Seventeenth-Century England.* London: Methuen, 1981.

Stauffer, Donald A. "A Deep and Sad Passion." *Essays in Dramatic Literature: The Parrott Presentation Volume.* Ed. Hardin Craig. 1935; rpt. New York: Russell, 1967.

Stimpson, Catharine. *Where the Meanings Are: Feminism and Cultural Spaces.* London: Methuen, 1988.

Stone, Lawrence. *The Family, Sex, and Marriage in England, 1500–1800.* New York: Harper and Row, 1977.

Strachan, Michael. *Sir Thomas Roe 1581–1644: A Life.* Wilton: Michael Russell, 1989.

Strong, Roy. *Henry Prince of Wales and England's Lost Renaissance.* London: Thames and Hudson, 1986.

Strype, John. *Annals of the Reformation.* Oxford, 1824.

Stuart, James, James VI and I. *Basilicon Doron.* Ed. James Craigie. 2 vols. Edinburgh: Blackwood, 1950.

Stuart, Mary, Queen of Scotland. *Letters of Mary Queen of Scots.* Ed. and trans. Agnes Strickland. 2 vols. London: Henry Colburn, 1844.

——. *Lettres, Instructions et Mémoires de Marie Stuart, Reine d'Ecosse.* Ed. Alexandre Labanoff. 7 vols. London: Dolman, 1844.

——. *Queen Mary's Book. A Collection of Poems and Essays by Mary Queen of Scots.* Ed. Mrs. P. Stewart-Mackenzie Arbuthnot. London: Bell, 1907.

Svensson, Lars-Hakan. *Silent Art. Rhetorical and Thematic Patterns in Samuel Daniel's "Delia."* Lund: Gleerup, 1980.

Swift, Carolyn Ruth. "Feminine Self-Definition in Lady Mary Wroth's *Love's Victorie* (c. 1621)." *ELR* 14 (1984): 171–88.

Tedeschi, John A. *Literature of the Italian Reformation.* Chicago: Newberry Library, 1971.

Travitsky, Betty. "The 'Wyll and Testament' of Isabella Whitney," *ELR* 10 (1980): 76–94.

——. "The Feme Covert in Elizabeth Cary's *Miriam." Ambiguous Realities: Women in the Middle Ages and Renaissance.* Ed. Carole Levin and Jeannie Watson. Detroit: Wayne State UP, 1987.

——, ed. *The Paradise of Women: Writings by Englishwomen of the Renaissance.* Westport, CT: Greenwood, 1981.

Trevor-Roper, Hugh. *Catholics, Anglicans and Puritans.* London: Secker and Warburg, 1987.

Tudor, Elizabeth (Elizabeth I). *The Poems of Queen Elizabeth.* Ed. Leicester Bradner. Providence, RI: Brown UP, 1964.

Waller, Gary F. *Mary Sidney, Countess of Pembroke. A Critical Study of Her Writings and Literary Milieu.* Salzburg: Institut für Anglistik, 1979.

——. "Mary Wroth and the Sidney Family Romance: Gender Construction in Early Modern England." *Reading Mary Wroth: Representing Alternatives in Early Modern England.* Ed. Naomi J. Miller and Gary Waller. Knoxville: U of Tennessee P, 1991: 35–63.

Warnicke, Retha M. *Women of the English Renaissance and Reformation.* Westport, CT: Greenwood, 1983.

Waters, Robert E. Chester. *Genealogical Memoirs of the Extinct Family of Chester of Chicheley.* 2 vols. London: Robson and Sons, 1878.

Watson, Thomas, and Abraham Fraunce. *Thomas Watson's Latin "Amyntas" (1585) and Abraham Fraunce's Translation "The Lamentations of Amyntas."* Ed. Walter F. Staton, Jr., and Franklin M. Dickey. Chicago: U of Chicago P, 1967.

Wayne, Don E. *Penshurst. The Semiotics of Place and the Poetics of History.* Madison: U of Wisconsin P, 1984.

Weidemann, Heather L. "Theatricality and Female Identity in Mary Wroth's *Urania.*" *Reading Mary Wroth: Representing Alternatives in Early Modern England.* Ed. Naomi J. Miller and Gary Waller. Knoxville: U of Tennessee P, 1991: 191–209.

Whitney, Isabella. *A Sweet Nosegay. For facsimile, see* Panofsky.

Williams, Ethel Carleton. *Anne of Denmark: Wife of James VI of Scotland, James I of England.* Harlow: Longmans, 1970.

Williams, Neville. *Thomas Howard Fourth Duke of Norfolk.* London: Barrie and Rockliff, 1964.

Williamson, George C. *Lady Anne Clifford, Countess of Dorset, Pembroke and Montgomery. 1590–1676.* 1922; rpt. East Ardsley, Yorkshire: Titus Wilson, 1967.

Wilson, Violet A. *Society Women of Shakespeare's Time.* London: Bodley Head, 1924.

Witherspoon, Alexander M., and Frank J. Warnke, ed. *Seventeenth-Century Prose and Poetry.* 2d ed. San Diego: Harcourt Brace, 1982.

Woodbridge, Linda. *Women and the English Renaissance: Literature and the Nature of Womankind.* Urbana: U of Illinois P, 1984.

Wroth, Mary Sidney. *The Poems of Lady Mary Wroth.* Ed. Josephine Roberts. Baton Rouge: U of Louisiana P, 1983.

———. *Lady Mary Wroth's Love's Victory. The Penshurst Manuscript.* Ed. Michael G. Brennan. London: Roxburghe Club, 1988.

———. *The Countess of Montgomery's Urania. The First Book.* Ed. Paul Salzman. *An Anthology of Seventeenth-Century Fiction.* Oxford: Oxford UP, 1991.

Index

Louise Schleiner is Associate Professor of English at Washington State University and author of *The Living Lyre in English Verse, from Elizabeth through the Restoration* and the forthcoming *Cultural Semiotics, Spenser, and the Captive Woman.*